3rd Edition

A SEARCH FOR THE ORIGINS OF LAW
Drugs, Death and Madness

John F. Galliher
University of Missouri, Columbia

Learning Solutions

New York   Boston   San Francisco
London   Toronto   Sydney   Tokyo   Singapore   Madrid
Mexico City   Munich   Paris   Cape Town   Hong Kong   Montreal

Cover Art: Courtesy of Stephanie Carter

Pearson Learning Solutions, 501 Boylston Street, Suite 900, Boston, MA 02116
A Pearson Education Company
www.pearsoned.com

Printed in the United States of America

1 2 3 4 5 6 7 8 9 10 XXXX 14 13 12 11 10 09

000200010270569421

CY/CA

ISBN 10: 0-558-57845-4
ISBN 13: 978-0-558-57845-9

CONTENTS

To Alfred Lindesmith

INTRODUCTION

The essays in this collection were published during a period of nearly 30 years, primarily appearing in professional journals. These papers were written by John Galliher, with the assistance of students, former students, colleagues and his brother James. The articles all ask the question of why a nation has the types of criminal law that it does. An answer to this question is found not only in the expressed motivations of individuals, here referred to as *triggering events,* but also in the cultural conditions existing in a given place at a given time, called *structural foundations.*

Most of the essays deal with marihuana laws and capital punishment. These are worthy of special attention as arguably two of the most irrational criminal controls in the modern world. The first article deals with the unsuccessful campaign of the late Alfred Lindesmith against government authority to bring rationality and decency into American drug control policy. Irony and contradiction helped motivate the study of "liberal" marihuana laws in conservative states such as Nebraska and Utah. These liberal reforms were especially interesting when compared to repressive marihuana controls in Nevada, a state known for flexible legal standards in dealing with gambling and prostitution. The special irrationality of substance prohibitions is not solely an American phenomenon as seen in the experience in Iceland, a nation long recognized for its democratic traditions. The studies of capital punishment legislation in Kansas, New York and Hong Kong show the important role that legal symbolism, as opposed to actual executions, plays in such law making.

In addition to the essays on the death penalty and drugs, one paper deals with the origins of sexual psychopath laws. This psychopath legislation is now recognized being wholly without merit or scientific grounding. The final paper offers a review of what was then known from the published research on the historical origins of criminal law. The shortcomings of some of the work of two of the 20th century's most distinguished sociologists, Howard Becker and Edwin Sutherland, are included in this collection. Finally, knowing the specific origins of criminal laws may sensitize us to the requirements for legal reform in a democratic society.

Readers will likely note in the third essay that marijuana is spelled with a "j" as opposed to all other articles where marihuana is spelled with an "h." I remember well that the spelling of this word in this article was insisted on by the editors of the journal where it originally appeared. Later I have always demanded the use of an "h" because of what can be called the politics of spelling that contains a political commentary that is all the more powerful because it is subliminal. While both spellings are technically correct, use of the soft Spanish "j," as opposed the hard anglo "h" implies that cannabis is a foreign substance forced on Americans by wicked people in other nations. This is false. Cannabis plants, in fact, are native to the United States and were once grown legally throughout the nation. The first essay describes the original prohibition of this drug in America. In any case, historian David Musto has found that drugs defined as having foreign origins have been subject to much more severe punishments than other drugs with a similar potential for harm but not associated with outsiders. Although the correlation is far from perfect, as a general rule sources that use the "h" describe the drug in much less threatening terms than those that use a "j." Thus the policy implications of the spelling of this drug are of considerable significance.

LINDESMITH V. ANSLINGER: AN EARLY GOVERNMENT VICT
IN THE FAILED WAR ON DRUGS*

JOHN F. GALLIHER,** DAVID P. KEYS,***
and MICHAEL ELSNER****

I. INTRODUCTION

The late Alfred Lindesmith was an Indiana University sociology professor who was a long-time advocate of medical treatment of addiction. We demonstrate below how the Federal Bureau of Narcotics (FBN) attempted to intimidate Lindesmith, stifle his research, and interfere with his publication of articles counter to FBN policies. In addition, we argue that the American banning of the 1946 Canadian film on drug addiction, *Drug Addict,* may have been a pivotal event in a pattern of censorship and disinformation carried on by the Federal Bureau of Narcotics (FBN) under the leadership of its long-time Director, Harry Anslinger. The FBN's campaign to suppress information played a significant role in the emerging public ideology and mythology regarding drug addicts and drug addiction in the United States. Lindesmith's unsuccessful efforts against the ban, as illustrated by his personal papers, his FBN file recently released to the National Archives, Anslinger's papers in the National Archives, and those recently released under the Freedom of Information Act, demonstrate the nearly absolute control of the information exercised by the FBN.

We attempt to put in historical context the FBN campaign to develop a prohibitive national drug control policy. As Howard Becker, who began an unhindered public criticism of FBN-inspired drug policies as early as 1963 with his famous monograph, *Outsiders,*[1] recently observed: "I never actually understood why Anslinger bothered with Lindesmith, who could have published whatever he wanted without having the slightest effect on policy. You can see that now when everyone under the sun is publishing whatever they want . . . and it doesn't change a thing."[2]

We will attempt to answer Becker's question by demonstrating how the political and cultural context from the 1930s through the early 1950's presented a vastly different

*Thanks are due to Howard Becker, the late Anselm Strauss, Ronald Farrell, Gideon Sjoberg, James McCartney, Joseph Gusfield, James Orcutt, William Chambliss, and anonymous reviewers for their suggestions for revision of earlier drafts of the manuscript. We also thank Robert and Karen Lindesmith for their help in locating Alfred Lindesmith's research files. The authors also thank Missouri University for financial support of the research.

**Professor of Sociology and Director of Peace Studies, University of Missouri-Columbia. Ph.D., Indiana University, 1967; M.A., Indiana University, 1964; B.A., University of Missouri, Kansas City, 1961.
***Ph.D., University of Missouri, 1998; M.A., University of Missouri, 1994; B.A., University of Missouri, Columbia, 1990.
****Assistant Professor of Sociology and Criminology, Gallaudet University-Washington, D.C. Ph.D. 1994 and M.S. 1980, American University, Washington, D.C.; B.A., University of Arizona, 1977
[1]Howard Becker, Outsiders: Studies in the Sociology of Deviance (1963).
[2]E-mail message from Howard Becker to John F. Galliher (Aug. 28, 1995) (on file with John F. Galliher).

Reprinted by special permission of Northwestern University School of Law, *Journal of Criminal Law and Criminology.*

uation for critics of American drug control policies compared to later periods after
a national drug policy was institutionalized.

II. LINDESMITH, THE SELF AND THE ADDICT

Lindesmith was a University of Chicago trained social psychologist who received
a Ph.D. in 1937. His training provided him with a grounding in interactionist theory
and concepts, a method of analysis, a specific orientation toward data collection, and
a key contact to begin collection of dissertation data. Lindesmith's five years at
Chicago brought him into contact with Herbert Blumer, whose research emphasized
the role of the self concept in human interaction.[3] Lindesmith also took courses from
Chicago sociologists Ernest Burgess and Louis Wirth, whose research emphasized
the critical role of fieldwork and the indepth treatment of qualitative data.[4] During
the early and mid-1930s, the reputation of *The Polish Peasant In Europe and America* by W.I. Thomas and Florian Znaniecki[5] was at its zenith at the University of
Chicago.[6] The book's emphasis on life history and Znaniecki's subsequent development of inductive methods[7] made an indelible mark on Lindesmith's career. Lindesmith was also close to criminologist Edwin Sutherland during Sutherland's brief
stay at Chicago (1932–35).[8] As a result of this association, Lindesmith became
acquainted with drug addicts and addiction through Broadway Jones, the subject for
Sutherland's *The Professional Thief*.[9] Consequently, at Chicago, Lindesmith mas-
tered a theoretical orientation, was prevailed upon to collect qualitative data in the
field, became dedicated to inductive methods, and was accorded valuable personal
contacts which set his career on a long-term path.

Lindesmith drew on the individual's self concept in his dissertation and later in his
Social Psychology textbook.[10] This concept in turn made possible Lindesmith's distinction between physical and psychological addiction. For physical addiction to
develop into psychological addiction, "the person's interpretation of his own withdrawal distress is a crucial event . . . made possible by the existence of language
behavior and conceptual thought."[11] In other words, a defining characteristic of all
human beings is that they have the capacity to see themselves as objects.[12] When the

---

[3] *See* Herbert Blumer, Symbolic Interaction 79 (1969).
[4] *See* Louis Wirth, The Ghetto (1928); Robert E. Park & Ernest Burgess, The City (1925).
[5] W.I. Thomas & Florian Znaniecki, The Polish Peasant in Europe and America (1919). Inductive methods
involve reasoning from patterns in empirical observations rather than an initial theoretical position.
[6] Herbert Blumer, An Appraisal of Thomas and Znaniecki's: The Polish Peasant in Europe and America
(1949).
[7] *See generally* Florian Znaniecki, The Method of Sociology (1934).
[8] Mark Gaylord & John F. Galliher, The Criminology of Edwin Sutherland 104–20 (1966).
[9] Edwin H. Sutherland, The Professional Thief (1937). Broadway Jones was both a career thief and a long-
time drug addict.
[10] Alfred R. Lindesmith & Anselm Strauss, Social Psychology (rev. ed. 1966). The concept of self is the
image or picture individuals have of themselves. *See generally id.*
[11] *Id.* at 355.
[12] *Id.* at 423–28.

intellectual connection between discontinuing drug use and withdrawal occu. initial euphoria from drug use "vanishes and is replaced by the negative effee relieving withdrawal distress."[13] Therefore, "the theory that only abnormal perso become drug addicts is untenable."[14] The proposition that addicts are in all ways nor mal human beings made punitive drug prohibitions seem less reasonable.[15] These ideas propelled Lindesmith's intense, lifelong, and narrowly focused intellectual and political position.

A. *Enter Harry Anslinger*

Lindesmith's views of human addiction and drug addicts were diametrically opposed by those of Harry Anslinger and the FBN.[16] Around the same time that Lindesmith began his graduate training, a new American drug control policy began to take shape through Anslinger's efforts. As a young man during World War I and the 1920s, Anslinger worked in the foreign service and served for several years in the ill-fated Prohibition division of the Department of the Treasury.[17] After scandal rocked the narcotics sector of the Prohibition division in the late 1920s, Anslinger was appointed head of the newly-created Federal Bureau of Narcotics in 1930.[18] The FBN was a division of the Treasury Department designated to enforce drug control statutes drafted as tax measures. Anslinger remained at this post until his apparently forced retirement in 1962.[19] For decades writers have marveled at the irrational direction of American drug policy after the creation of the FBN and the success of Anslinger in using law enforcement to control public opinion regarding drug use and addiction.[20]

The great migration of African-Americans to urban centers in the North, coupled with the emergence of an illicit narcotics market after the enactment of the Harrison Act of 1914, changed the face of addiction in cities like Chicago, Detroit, and New York.[21] Beginning after World War I and through the 1940s, there were wholesale demographic changes in the United States which created public anxiety and suspicion directed at African-Americans, immigrants, and Communists.[22] During the Great Depression of the 1930s, the expanding role of the federal government created an opportunity for Harry Anslinger to successfully exploit these fears by linking

[13]*Id.* at 352–53.
[14]*Id.* at 356.
[15]Alfred R. Lindesmith, The Addict and the Law (1965).
[16]*Id.*
[17]John McWilliams, The Protectors: Harry J. Anslinger and the Federal Bureau of Narcotics (1938–1962), 32 (1990).
[18]*Id.* at 42.
[19]*Id.* at 180. There is some evidence to suggest that President Kennedy forced Anslinger to retire in 1962.
[20]*See, e.g.,* David F. Musto, The American Disease: Origins of Narcotic Control (1973); Rufus King, The Drug Hang-Up: America's Fifty-Year Folly (1972); *see also* Michael Starks, Cocaine Fiends and Reefer Madness: an Illustrated History of Drugs in the Movies 61–62 (1982) (observing that Anslinger controlled the film industry's depiction of addiction).
[21]Harold Finestone, Epidemiology of Adult Addiction 142–45 (1962) (proceedings of the White House Conference on Narcotics and Drug Abuse).
[22]Nicholas Lemann, The Promised Land: The Great Black Migration and How it Changed America 323, 343–53 (1991).

gs to minorities. Anslinger had great political power because he maintained the
pport of both Democrats and Republicans, the Women's Christian Temperance
nion (WCTU), and many churches. Because the FBN controlled the licenses for the
mportation of opiates, Anslinger also received the support of drug companies.[23]
While exploiting these fears and cultivating special interest groups, Anslinger also
utilized the demographic changes in the addict population, from rural whites to urban
dwellers, including a growing number of minorities.[24]

Activities such as Anslinger's have been characterized as a moral crusade.[25]
Anslinger was also a savvy bureaucrat during the Great Depression of the 1930s who
excelled at protecting his organization from budget cuts by locating new legislative
mandates.[26] Above all Anslinger was a government operative, with experience in the
intelligence community, who through political harassment, adeptly controlled the
flow of information on drug addiction. According to Sloman, "[t]he thing that
Anslinger concerned himself with a lot was the dissemination of information. He
completely disagreed with the free exchange of ideas on the subject."[27] Allen Ginsberg recalled that, even as late as the 1950s, it was difficult to publish books which
referred to drugs or drug use:

> There was at the time [an] assumption: that if you talked about [drugs] on the bus or the
> subway, you might be arrested—even if you were only discussing a change in the
> law. . . . A decade later you still couldn't get away with a national public TV discussion
> of the laws without the Narcotics Bureau and the FCC intruding. . . . [T]he fear and ter-
> ror . . . was so real that it had been internalized in the . . . publishing industry, and so,
> before the book could be published, all sorts of disclaimers had to be interleaved with
> the text—lest the publisher be implicated criminally with the author.[28]

Foucault has described activities such as Anslinger's as "regimes of truth."[29] In
such instances, truth becomes a function of power rather than factual accuracy.
Accordingly, we will demonstrate that Anslinger and the FBN not only attempted to use
their legal authority to censor scientific inquiry they considered antithetical to their
interests, but sponsored "research" projects that had preordained results more to their
liking. Controlling the drug discourse in this way allowed Anslinger and the Bureau
to be taken seriously—even while trading in patent untruths—and in Foucault's
terms "marginalized, derided, excluded and even prohibited" any competing ideas.[30]
Thus "[t]ruth is not separated from power, rather it is one of the important vehicles

[23]*See generally* McWilliams, *supra* note 17, at 106.

[24]*Id.* at 48–49, 52–53.

[25]*See* Becker, *supra* note 1, at 145.

[26]*See* Donald T. Dickson, *Bureaucracy and Morality: An Organizational Perspective on a Moral Crusade,*
16 Soc. Probs. 143 (1968).

[27]Larry Sloman, Reefer Madness: History of Marijuana in the United States 199–200 (1983).

[28]William Burroughs, Junky vii–viii (1977) (quoting introduction by Allen Ginsberg).

[29]Alan Hunt & Gary Wickham, Foucault and the Law: Towards a Sociology of Law and Governance 11
(1994) (quoting Foucault).

[30]*Id.* at 8–9.

and expressions of power; power is exercised through the production and dissemination of truth."[31]

In the final analysis, Anslinger was not only a "moral entrepreneur" or a "rule creator," but a "moral enforcer" as well.[32] This allowed Anslinger to play a significant and unique role in creating an American "drug crisis." And in response to this drug crisis, Anslinger was ideally placed to provide a law enforcement response. In this fashion, he was able to guarantee himself, and the FBN, an enormous amount of political influence and legal power. Thus, Anslinger used his position in the FBN to define and legitimize his interpretation of the drug problem, to mobilize legislative initiatives, and to implement an official law enforcement plan of action, all of which Blumer argues is essential in the creation of social problems.[33]

B. Anslinger's Attempted Censorship and Neutralization of Lindesmith's Early Research

From the late 1930s to the early 1950s, the FBN concentrated on the intimidation of Lindesmith. The targeting of Lindesmith was possible because Lindesmith acted virtually alone in standing up against federal drug control policies. Anslinger took his first action against Lindesmith in 1939, not long after Lindesmith had completed his Ph.D. dissertation. Anslinger asked the FBN Chicago District Supervisor to inform Indiana University, Lindesmith's employer, that a drug addict and a "collection of racketeers" were among the sponsors of a drug research organization (the World Narcotics Research Foundation), an organization which Lindesmith publicly supported.[34] Thus, in response, the FBN began a campaign of intimidation and guilt-by-association against Lindesmith that would eventually span four decades.

The FBN's campaign against Lindesmith gained momentum in 1940 after Lindesmith published the *Dope Fiend Mythology* in *The Journal of Criminal Law and Criminology*. In this article, Lindesmith criticized "stereotyped misinformation about drug addicts" such as news stories "of the 'dope-crazed killer' or the dope fiend rapist."[35] This article so angered Harry Anslinger that he arranged to have San Francisco Circuit Judge Twain Michelson write an attack in response,[36] later published in this same journal.[37]

Recently released FBN records, made public under the Freedom of Information Act (FOIA), reveal that Anslinger consulted with the Assistant Secretary of the Treasury, Herbert E. Gaston:

---

[31]*Id.* at 11.
[32]Becker, *supra* note 1, at 147–62.
[33]*See* Herbert Blumer, *Social Problems as Collective Behavior*, 18 Soc. Probs. 298 (1971).
[34]Letter from Harry J. Anslinger to James J. Biggins (Oct. 9, 1939) (on file with John F. Galliher). Anslinger chose to attack Lindesmith for the first time at this point because the World Narcotics Research Foundation publicly supported medical treatment of addicts.
[35]Alfred R. Lindesmith, *Dope Fiend Mythology*, 31 J. Crim. L. & Criminology 199, 199 (1940).
[36]Letter from Harry J. Anslinger to Judge Twain Michelson (Sept. 7, 1940) (on file with John F. Galliher).
[37]Twain Michelson, *Lindesmith Mythology*, 31 J. Crim. L. & Criminology 375 (1940).

it is unfortunate that an article containing such misinformation and half-truths should be carried in a magazine devoted to the education of law enforcement officers, [but] I do not wish to place the bureau on the level of having to answer Lindesmith, and would like to have your suggestions as to counteracting this vicious propaganda.[38]

Mr. Gaston replied that Lindesmith's piece was nothing more than an "apology for addiction written from the standpoint of an addict. We might look for a college professor, a district attorney or other lawyer, or a law professor to answer him."[39] Accordingly, Anslinger recruited Judge Twain Michelson. Michelson's essay associated the spread of addiction with Japanese imperialism as well as a variety of crimes including "burglary, robbery, forgery, rape and murder."[40] As if all this were not enough to attempt to discredit medical treatment of addicts, even nudism was associated with drug addiction. Judge Michelson concluded that Lindesmith was a "pseudo-scientist."[41]

In 1948, Lindesmith published an article in *Federal Probation*[42] describing a case where the FBN allowed two affluent addicts to receive opiates for over twenty years, in contravention of the Bureau's avowed organizational mandate. This so outraged the FBN that they demanded a "correction" by that journal.[43]

It was also believed by Lindesmith and others that the FBN intended to plant narcotics in Lindesmith's house or automobile to set him up for arrest.[44] In addition, an internal FBN memo suggests that a secret tap may have been placed on Lindesmith's phone by the Bureau.[45] However, efforts to compromise Lindesmith were probably made more difficult because there is no record that he ever advocated, possessed, or used illegal drugs.

Lindesmith did not have wide support in the academic community for his antagonistic approach to the federal government's drug policy. For over two decades most prominent academicians either ignored Lindesmith's work or criticized it methodologically or substantively.[46] For example, Lindesmith's theory of addiction was crit-

---

[38]Memorandum from Harry Anslinger, Director, Federal Bureau of Narcotics, to Herbert Gaston, Assistant Secretary, U.S. Treasury Dep't (Sept. 17, 1940) (on file with John F. Galliher). Anslinger also noted that the journal editor, Robert Gault, Professor of Psychology at Northwestern University, "collaborate[d]" with Lindesmith, as reflected in the fact that Lindesmith served as an advisory editor of the journal. *Id.*

[39]Memorandum from Henry Gaston, Assistant Secretary, U.S. Treasury Dep't, to Harry Anslinger, Director, Federal Bureau of Narcotics (no date) (on file with John F. Galliher).

[40]Michelson, *supra* note 37, at 383.

[41]*Id.* at 400.

[42]Alfred R. Lindesmith, *Handling the Opiate Problem,* Fed. Probation, Dec. 1948, at 23.

[43]Letter from M.L. Harney to Harry J. Anslinger (Apr. 19, 1949) (on file with John F. Galliher).

[44]Letter from Alfred R. Lindesmith to John W. Ashton, Arts and Science Dean, Indiana University (Feb. 24, 1949) (on file with John F. Galliher); *see also* Anselm Strauss, *Obituary for Alfred R. Lindesmith,* ASA Footnotes 13 (May 1991); Charles Winick, *Social Behavior, Public Policy, and Nonharmful Drug Use,* 69 Milbank Q. 437 (1991).

[45]Memorandum from George H. White to Harry J. Anslinger (Nov. 22, 1954) (on file with John F. Galliher).

[46]*See* William E. McAuliffe and Robert A. Gordon, *A Test of Lindesmith's Theory of Addiction: The Frequency of Euphoria Among Long-Term Addicts,* 79 Am. J. Soc. 795 (1974); Ralph Turner, *The Quest for Universals in Sociological Research,* 18 Am. Soc. Rev. 604 (1953); W.S. Robinson, *The Logical Structure of Analytic Induction,* 16 Am. Soc. Rev. 812 (1951).

icized for ignoring statistical information and thereby failing to recognize that "addict criminality does not result primarily from a desperate need to relieve withdrawal sickness . . . but rather from the desire for euphoria."[47] But the fact that others in the academic community did not join Lindesmith during the 1940s and 1950s is also attributable to the political caution of his colleagues. Even more than his sociological research, Lindesmith's challenge to government policy may have served to isolate him from the mainstream of the profession. Lindesmith's writing however, was not the only target of censorship by Anslinger and the FBN, nor the only instance for conflict between these two men.

III. ANSLINGER'S BANNING OF *DRUG ADDICT*

In addition to FBN efforts to censor Lindesmith himself, the Bureau targeted a film that embraced his theories.[48] The film, *Drug Addict,* is a 1946 documentary made by the Canadian Film Board, with the assistance of the narcotics specialists in the Royal Canadian Mounted Police.[49] The film was intended to assist in the training of law enforcement and medical professionals. The film deals with the nature of drug addicts, addictive drugs, and drug trafficking. It also advocates modest reform and reconciliation of drug policy commensurate with the facts surrounding addiction.

Drug Addict won a Canadian Film Award and was cited as a "bold, honest record of the drug traffic and its toll in human misery. It is as honest as it is stark. The film treats drug addiction as an illness and thus has run afoul of some who would condemn as criminals all who use drugs."[50] As a documentary, "the film objects to the use of the term 'dope fiend' in describing addicts, most of whom are presented as sick and bewildered people."[51] According to McWilliams, Anslinger banned *Drug Addict* because the scenes of drug use and sales were "totally unacceptable" to him.[52]

A. Major Themes of The Film

This section provides an overview of the major themes and claims of *The Drug Addict:* (1) that addicts and traffickers are recruited from all races and classes; (2) that high-level drug traffickers are white; (3) that law enforcement only targets low-level dealers; (4) that addiction is a sickness; (5) that addiction to legal and illegal drugs are essentially the same; (6) that cocaine is not necessarily addictive; and (7) that law enforcement control of drugs is in the final analysis impossible.

---

[47]McAuliffe & Gordon, *supra* note 46, at 820.
[48]Note that the FBN was not predisposed to censor all films about drug use and drug trafficking. For example, after checking the scripts of *To the Ends of the Earth* (1948), and *Johnny Stool Pigeon* (1949), the agency gave them its approval. Starks, *supra* note 20, at 61–62.
[49]Drug Addict (Canadian Film Board 1946).
[50]Canadian Ministry of Information, Canadian Film Awards (Apr. 22, 1949).
[51]*U.S. Protest on Dope Film Stirs Canada,* Chi. Trib., *circa* Feb. 10, 1949 (on file with John F. Galliher). A typed copy of this article was found in Lindesmith's files.
[52]McWilliams, *supra* note 17, at 102.

1. Addicts are Recruited From All Races and Classes

"Contrary to popular belief, the traffic in drugs and the use of drugs is fostered by no one race. Drugs affect all races and classes of people."[53] Possibly to emphasize this perspective, *Drug Addict* depicts affluent whites injecting drugs, appearing in police lineups, and congregating on the street. The narrator says: "Addiction is by no means confined to the criminal class who are best known because of the exposed lives they lead. But there are many who do not need to buy from peddlers, who have found a means of diverting legal drugs to their own use."[54] At this point, a well-groomed man in a darkened room is shown holding a hypodermic needle.

Given Lindesmith's charges of bureau accommodation to affluent addicts in the *Federal Probation* article,[55] this scene undoubtedly made the FBN uncomfortable, and encouraged and contributed to the censoring.

2. High-Level Drug Traffickers are White

"The source of each city's supply of drugs is the man with the connection. His position is remote from the sale of drugs to the addict. He is in business and he is concerned with profits."[56] This is illustrated by a rotund white man, puffing on a cigar. This image of a high level drug trafficker contradicted Anslinger's efforts to associate drug trafficking with minorities.[57]

3. Law Enforcement Only Attempts to Control Low-Level Street Dealers

The peddler is the chief target of enforcement officers. He operates more or less in the open trusting his wits to keep him from being caught with drugs on his person. At the other end of such a remote network behind him are the men who supply the entire country with drugs.[58]

Even the street dealers shown are white. Since the major drug traffickers are the source of the drug problem, Anslinger would have taken exception to the claim that the FBN ignored their activities.

4. Drug Addiction is a Sickness

Drugs will bring the addict little pleasure, but he will need them just to feel normal. . . . But a cure by oneself is seldom if ever possible. . . . An addict must have his drug several times a day or he becomes very sick. It is a habit he must satisfy. He has no choice [and] an average habit with drugs bought from peddlers cost an addict as much as ten thousand dollars a year [in 1946]. Not many jobs can support an addiction. Those who buy illegal drugs steal to get the money . . . [while] very seldom does an addict commit

[53]Drug Addict, *supra* note 49.
[54]*Id.*
[55]*See* Lindesmith, *supra* note 42.
[56]Drug Addict, *supra* note 49.
[57]*See* Harry J. Anslinger & William F. Tompkins, The Traffic in Narcotics (1953); Musto, *supra* note 20, at 221; McWilliams, *supra* note 17, at 52.
[58]Drug Addict, *supra* note 49.

a crime of violence. To the man addicted to opiates the term dope fiend just doe, apply.[59]

Dope Fiend Mythology was the title of Lindesmith's 1940 article that so infuriated Anslinger.[60]

5. Illegal Drugs Cannot be Distinguished from the Problem of Addiction to Other Drugs

"Drugs are just one form of addiction," like "[i]ntemperate use of alcohol, [and] barbiturates."[61] Anslinger likely despised any linkage of drug laws to the failed alcohol prohibition. Anslinger had worked in the much maligned Prohibition division of the Treasury Department during the 1920s.[62]

6. Cocaine is Not Necessarily Addictive

"[C]ocaine [is] also a forbidden drug differing greatly from opium. Lack of it does not cause sickness and in that sense it is not habit-forming. Addicts who sometimes use it say it is just like ice cream. Nice if you can have it, but you can do without it."[63] Although Lindesmith argued that cocaine is not as addictive as opiates,[64] Anslinger never acknowledged the varying qualities of illegal narcotics—relying instead on the simple message that all illegal drugs were equally dangerous and equally addictive.[65]

7. Law Enforcement Control is Impossible

"Complete control of the traffic in drugs is impossible . . . [and] despite strict surveillance of customs officers and the closest international cooperation of enforcement agencies, the illicit traffic is heavier than that for legal use."[66] Anslinger clearly rejected the notion that stopping the flow of illegal drugs was impossible.[67] If Anslinger accepted the impossibility of completely stopping the flow of drugs into the United States, he would have admitted a weakness of his Bureau.

Anslinger knew of the potential political hazards which *Drug Addict* could engender if the public was presented with such a rebuttal—particularly one produced with the assistance of a government as credible as Canada and its national police force. Indeed, Anslinger wrote that he would "strongly urge" the Canadian government not

---

[59]*Id.*
[60]*See* Lindesmith, *supra* note 35.
[61]Drug Addict, *supra* note 49.
[62]McWilliams, *supra* note 17; *see also supra* text accompanying notes 17–18.
[63]Drug Addict, *supra* note 49.
[64]Alfred R. Lindesmith, Opiate Addiction 74 (1947).
[65]Drug Addict, *supra* note 49.
[66]*Id.*
[67]Anslinger & Tompkins, *supra* note 57.

allow the film to be sent to the United States.[68] Showing this film, Anslinger claimed, "would do incalculable damage in the way of spreading drug addiction."[69] Furthermore, he specifically refused to consider the possibility that any modifications in the film might make it more acceptable.[70] One of Anslinger's assistants complained that the film minimized the significance of law enforcement and left the impression that a "hospital cure" was the only effective response to addiction.[71] Another FBN agent complained that the person who has

> no medical need for narcotics and who secure[s] their drugs from underworld sources or in an illegal manner, is presented as a person muchly wronged by society and unjustly denied free and easy access to such unlimited supply of dangerous drugs as his own carnal craving demands. . . . The addicts shown in the picture are so presented as to excite the sympathy of the uninformed public.[72]

For Anslinger the ultimate proof that the film was "on the wrong side" was Lindesmith's support for it.[73]

In February of 1949, a Canadian government representative indicated to Lindesmith that Harry Anslinger had requested that the Canadian government not distribute *Drug Addict* in the United States.[74] Furthermore, Anslinger had the temerity to request that the Canadian government censor its film even within its own borders. The Canadian government rejected his request.[75] Short of a total ban, Anslinger demanded that Lindesmith be prohibited from viewing the film in Canada.[76] The Canadian government rejected this request as well, noting that: "we [can]not bind ourselves to any agreement that no United States citizen should ever see the film in Canada."[77]

IV. LINDESMITH'S RESPONSE

Lindesmith recognized the importance of the film not only for its intended purpose and audience, but also for its specific and damning rebuttal of the misinformation campaign carried out by Anslinger and the FBN. This was particularly appealing to Lindesmith, since he was nearly the sole opposition to Anslinger at that time and correctly identified the potential vulnerability of the FBN position on narcotics control if *Drug Addict* were to be distributed in the United States. Indeed, Lindesmith took a sabbatical leave in order to view the film in Ottawa and to orchestrate opposi-

---

[68]FBN Memorandum from Harry J. Anslinger (Oct. 19, 1948) (on file with National Archives).
[69]Letter from Harry J. Anslinger to Eric Johnston, President, Motion Picture Ass'n of America, Inc. (Feb. 28, 1950) (on file with National Archives).
[70]Letter from Harry J. Anslinger to Dr. Victor H. Vogel (Mar. 21, 1950) (on file with National Archives).
[71]Letter from M.L. Harney to Harry J. Anslinger (Oct. 18, 1948) (on file with National Archives).
[72]Letter from Garland H. Williams to Harry J. Anslinger (Oct. 18, 1948) (on file with National Archives).
[73]FBN Memorandum from Harry J. Anslinger (May 11, 1949) (on file with National Archives).
[74]Letter from K.C. Hossick to Alfred R. Lindesmith (Feb. 22, 1949) (on file with John F. Galliher).
[75]Letter from Hume Wrong, Canadian Ambassador, to Harry J. Anslinger (Mar. 27, 1950) (on file with National Archives).
[76]Letter from Harry J. Anslinger to Col. C.H.L. Sharman (Jan. 18, 1951) (on file with National Archives).
[77]Letter from G.D.M. Cameron, Deputy Minister of National Health, to Harry J. Anslinger (Jan. 12, 1951) (on file with National Archives).

tion to the ban,[78] with the support of Raymond Spottiswoode, the film editor of the *Saturday Review of Literature.*[79]

Lindesmith attempted to alert others to the impending censorship, but he failed to secure wide support. Many of the people Lindesmith contacted were either intimidated or complacent. For example, Victor H. Evjen, the managing editor of *Federal Probation,* expressed little interest in providing a public forum for discussion of the censorship or the banning of the film. He stated, "I have been told that the Canadian Government is not satisfied with certain phases of the film and at present is making some changes."[80]

However, Lindesmith was able to garner the support of the American Civil Liberties Union (ACLU) in this dispute. The ACLU demanded that Anslinger explain his actions.[81] Similarly, Lindesmith's congressional representative, Andrew Jacobs, was also supportive, but had no power to reverse the ban. Nonetheless, in a 1949 letter to Anslinger, Congressman Jacobs questioned the FBN's authority to censor film:

> The truth of the matter is there is no idea that is dangerous. . . . There has been entirely too much spoken and written in recent years about dangerous ideas . . . you cannot progress by trying to put ideas in jail. . . . One of the greatest dangers of government is that the hierarchy of government shall determine that certain questions are no longer debatable . . . and employ an illegal power which is expressly denied them.[82]

In his reply to Representative Jacobs, Anslinger falsely claimed that the film had been banned under the code of the motion picture producers and directors.[83] The Motion Picture Association of America denied taking such action on the film.[84] Lindesmith further incurred the wrath of the FBN by publishing a rebuttal in the *New York Times,* which revealed that Anslinger had lied when he said that the *Drug Addict* could not be shown in the United States because it violated the Code of the Motion Picture Industry.[85]

Additionally, noting that, contrary to the FBN's claim, the Motion Picture Association had not banned the film, Lindesmith wrote to the Secretary of State Dean Acheson, and implored him to lift the ban single-handedly imposed by Anslinger.[86] The Department of State replied through Otis Mulliken, the Acting Division Chief to the United Nations for Economic and Social Affairs, who said:

---

[78]Letter from Alfred R. Lindesmith to Paul Martin (May 17, 1949) (on file with John F. Galliher).

[79]Letter from Raymond Spottiswoode to Alfred R. Lindesmith (Feb. 16, 1949) (on file with John F. Galliher); Raymond Spottiswoode, *The Film Forum,* Sat. Rev. Literature, Mar. 26, 1949, at 41.

[80]Letter from Victor Evjen to Alfred R. Lindesmith (Mar. 8, 1949) (on file with John F. Galliher).

[81]Letter from Herbert M. Levy, ACLU Staff Counsel, to G.W. Cunningham, FBN Acting Director (Mar. 27, 1950) (on file with National Archives).

[82]Letter from Rep. Andrew Jacobs to Harry J. Anslinger (June 27, 1949) (on file with John F. Galliher).

[83]Letter from Harry J. Anslinger to Rep. Andrew Jacobs (Mar. 3, 1949) (on file with John F. Galliher).

[84]Letter from Joseph I. Breen, Vice President and Director, Motion Picture Ass'n of America, to Alfred R. Lindesmith (Aug. 9, 1949) (on file with John F. Galliher).

[85]Alfred R. Lindesmith, *Letter to the Editor,* N.Y. Times, Jan. 22, 1950, at 12.

[86]Letter from Alfred R. Lindesmith to Secretary of State Dean Acheson (June 2, 1949) (on file with John F. Galliher).

At Mr. Anslinger's request, the Department informed the Canadian Department of External Affairs that the Commissioner of Narcotics objected strongly to the showing of the film anywhere in the United States because the position it takes concerning the handling of the problem of drug addiction is contrary to the long-established policy of the United States. . . . The Public Health Service concurred in the attitude of the Commissioner of Narcotics.[87]

Lindesmith, however, wanted to know who was specifically responsible for imposing the ban,[88] but the State Department refused to identify the person at the Public Health Service who had agreed with Anslinger.[89]

Another government official, John L. Thurston, Acting Administrator of the Federal Security Agency of the Public Health Service, unintentionally revealed the source of the effort to stifle the film's distribution, when he advised Lindesmith that "as far as we are able to discover the [Public Health] Service took no part in arriving at the decision to ban the film."[90] This exchange of letters convinced Lindesmith that the FBN was solely responsible for the ban of the *Drug Addict*. It also affirmed the inability or unwillingness of other government officials to intervene.

The resistance that Lindesmith encountered during his campaign to air *Drug Addict* reveals that his perception of the addicted person, and his theory of addiction were under fire. The President of the Women's Christian Temperance Union (in Indiana), an organization which had a long association with Anslinger, personally cautioned Lindesmith:

Information has come to me that you are advocating the use of the Canadian film *The Drug Addict* in this country. While I am not familiar with the whole text of the film, it is my understanding that the drug addict is depicted as a sick person rather than a criminal. Surely, we would want nothing which would break down the legislation bearing on this subject. . . . We trust you will discontinue your effort to have this film shown in the United States.[91]

This letter, perhaps inadvertently, outlined exactly the course that Anslinger had charted for national drug policy from the beginning of his appointment in 1930. Anslinger deemed the addict a criminal and viewed opposition, such as the film, as a threat to the FBN policy of encouraging legislative efforts to stiffen drug penalties. At the time, the suppression of *Drug Addict* was considered by Anslinger and Lindesmith to be a key act in the drama surrounding the national drug control strategy. It was potentially a public relations obstacle for Anslinger's legislative agenda, while a rare opportunity for Lindesmith to halt the advancement of prohibitionist policies.

Such an important threat merited every possible precaution by Anslinger. It was predictable that his future attacks on Lindesmith were neither superficial nor timid.

---

[87]Letter from Otis E. Mulliken to Alfred R. Lindesmith (June 30, 1949) (on file with John F. Galliher).
[88]Letter from Alfred R. Lindesmith to Otis E. Mulliken (July 7, 1949) (on file with John F. Galliher).
[89]Letter from Otis E. Mulliken to Alfred R. Lindesmith (Aug. 3, 1949) (on file with John F. Galliher).
[90]Letter from John L. Thurston to Alfred R. Lindesmith (Aug. 22, 1949) (on file with John F. Galliher).
[91]Letter from Mrs. Herman Stanley to Alfred R. Lindesmith (July 1, 1949) (on file with John F. Galliher).

For example, in official co. "crackpot."[92] Similarly, in a com, ton Wright, the wife of a long-time, Anslinger referred to Lindesmith husband as a narcotics representative Indiana Board of Regents, Mrs. Han smith's January 22, 1950, letter to the New nt narcotics official who replaced he *Times,* Lindesmith focused on the hypocrisy c ional missions, condemned Linde film: es.[93] In his letter to the *New York* N's policy in suppressing the

> This incident suggests that the public is informed and misin.
> of the control exercised over the mass media of communica in this field because
> bureaucrats of the Federal Bureau of Narcotics. The same men who the policemen-
> to professional people in the United States the right to see a sober, unse matically deny
> honest educational film on drug addiction promote cheap radio thrillers and sens tional, and
> and inaccurate Hollywood productions on the same subject.[94]

Another woman wrote to the Indiana University President and to the Chair of the Indiana House and Senate Appropriations Committees:

> It is quite likely that this professor, who so flagrantly and vehemently attacks the United
> States Government for its narcotic law enforcement in the public prints, would also take
> the opportunity to spread his dangerous views in the classroom—thus corrupting future
> generations and hiding behind the cloak of academic freedom.[95]

Lindesmith was obviously energized by this issue for he, like Anslinger, concluded that the film presented an opportunity to rebut the claims of the American government with information endorsed and supported by an organization with an impeccable and irreproachable reputation—the Royal Canadian Mounted Police. In response, Anslinger was so alarmed that he formally requested information from J. Edgar Hoover regarding the possibility that Lindesmith was a "member of any Communist-Front organizations," since two members of the Canadian Film Board, which had produce the film, had been identified as Soviet spies.[96] The answer, if slow in coming, was positive. After Lindesmith arranged a visit by controversial poet Allen Ginsberg to the Indiana University campus, an FBN agent officially identified Lindesmith

---

[92]Letter from Harry J. Anslinger to Hume Wrong, Canadian Ambassador (Jan. 24, 1950) (on file with National Archives). Even prior to the conflicts over the film, Anslinger had called Lindesmith's work "trash," based as it was on "[t]he self-serving statements of the addicts—including a good proportion of 'leg pulling'" *See* Letter from Harry J. Anslinger to Pablo Wolff (Aug. 28, 1941) (on file with National Archives); Letter from Harry J. Anslinger to Major William Coles, Home Office, London (Nov. 23, 1948) (on file with National Archives).
[93]Letter from Mrs. Hamilton Wright to Indiana University Board of Regents (Jan. 31, 1950) (on file with John F. Galliher). *See supra* note 85 and accompanying text.
[94]Lindesmith, *supra* note 85, at 12.
[95]Letter from Mrs. L.E. Goetzke to Herman Wells, Indiana University President (Feb. 25, 1950) (on file with National Archives).
[96]Letter from Harry J. Anslinger to J. Edgar Hoover, FBI Director (Feb. 28, 1950) (on file with National Archives).

a member of the "W.E.B. DuBois [...n] has been declared a Communist organization."[97]

By the mid-to-late 1950s, due [...]g-time harassment of medical professionals, many physicians and lawy[...] [...]ed behind Lindesmith and helped him form a commission to investigate [...] problem. This effort produced a joint report authored by a committee [...]sed of representatives of both the American Bar Association (ABA) and[...] [...]merican Medical Association (AMA), which Lindesmith edited and arra[...] [...]o have published by the Indiana University Press.[98] The Committee's findin[...] [...]re critical of the FBN policies and concurred with much of what Lindesmith [...] been saying about addiction since 1937.[99] Anslinger attempted to suppress the [...]blication of the report by the Indiana University Press. Apparently, FBN agents [...]ade inquiries into the reasons for publication, whether public monies were being used, the number of copies to be printed, and how the distribution was to be financed.[100] These were the type of tactics which had been previously used to intimidate the Russell Sage Foundation and dissuade that organization from its original plan to publish the ABA-AMA report.[101] There is even evidence that Anslinger threatened to annul the Sage Foundation's tax-free status if they published the account of the joint committee's findings.[102]

In response to the publication of the ABA-AMA report, the FBN produced a rebuttal report.[103] The FBN used the same name, format, and layout as the ABA-AMA report to create confusion and minimize the impact of the joint report on the public.[104] Indeed, the genuine ABA-AMA report ultimately had little impact on the public or lawmakers. By the late 1950s, even the highly prestigious joint committee could not garner any significant political support for rethinking the criminal prohibition of addictive drugs, both because by this time the American public was angry and frightened by the specter of addicts and traffickers, and because Congress had already set its future course by dramatically augmenting the penalties for narcotic offenses in 1951, and again in 1956 following the suppression of the *Drug Addict*.

V. SUMMARY AND CONCLUSIONS

The potential impact of the film *Drug Addict,* which is still technically banned, is now only a matter of conjecture. All that is clear is that Anslinger and Lindesmith felt

---

[97]Letter from F.M. Rankin, Jr. to Charles G. Ward, FBN District Supervisor (Mar. 7, 1966) (on file with National Archives). The W.E.B. DuBois Club was named for a black sociologist accused of being a member of the Communist Party during the McCarthy era. Ginsberg's visit to Indiana University was in 1966.
[98]*See* Drug Addiction: Crime or Disease? (Alfred R. Lindesmith ed., 1961).
[99]*Id.* at 163, 170.
[100]Lindesmith, *supra* note 15, at 246; McWilliams, *supra* note 17, at 118.
[101]Lindesmith, *supra* note 15, at 246; King, *supra* note 20, at 173–74; McWilliams, *supra* note 17, at 118.
[102]*See* Arts and Science: Indiana University College of Arts and Science-Graduate School Alumni Association Newsletter 3 (1980); Letter from William Chambliss to John F. Galliher (Dec. 3, 1994) (on file with John F. Galliher).
[103]Comments on Narcotic Drugs: Interim Report of the Joint Committee of the ABA and the AMA on Narcotic Drugs (1959).
[104]Sloman, *supra* note 27.

that the film could be a significant influence on American perceptions of drug use and drug addiction. As a documentary film, almost naive in tone and unsophisticated in its articulation of narcotics addiction, it is a relic. Yet striking themes continue to emanate from the film, particularly its challenge to the racial bias that bolstered FBN rhetoric and to that organization's assertion of the criminal status of the addict. *Drug Addict* depicts all the addicts as white, well-dressed urbanites. At no time do any of the addicts commit violent crimes or otherwise behave viciously. Instead, the addicts are portrayed as desperate, pathetic, and sick individuals, suffering from guilt and withdrawal distress. Furthermore, the film questions enforcement of tough drug laws. The *Drug Addict* jeopardized the very existence of the FBN, the control of the public discourse, and the flow of ideas that were essential to government victories in the American war on drugs.

For his perspective on drugs, Lindesmith endured three decades of harassment by Anslinger and the FBN, while he was largely ignored in reputable academic circles. By the 1960s, the academic community had finally caught up with Lindesmith's ideas. Unfortunately, by this time draconian drug control policies had become institutionalized. Since the 1960s, few criminologists or criminal law professors have supported government drug policies. To this day, those setting American drug policy continue to ignore expert legal, academic, and medical advice.[105] In the academic community there is now a clear recognition of long-standing patterns of both the ineffectiveness of, and racism inherent in, American drug law enforcement.[106] Indeed, opposition to contemporary American drug control policy has become normative in the academic community. For example, Zimring and Hawkins demonstrate that while drug policy researchers may disagree on the best method of dealing with drug abuse, they nearly all agree that the current policy is an abject failure.[107]

In 1946 film, *Drug Addict,* in hindsight, appeared to be the last and best chance to create a rational and humane policy on narcotics. Following the banning of the film, Anslinger and the FBN were twice able to convince Congress to stiffen drug penalties and thus set the nation on a course that has led to its current failed drug policy. Only Lindesmith initially recognized the urgency of the situation and was willing to distinguish the possible policy alternatives that were available and necessary. Had Lindesmith been more successful in opposing the ban, it is conceivable that punitive drug policies would not have become firmly entrenched in our nation's laws.

---

[105]*See* Marc Mauer & Tracy Huling, Young Black Americans and the Criminal Justice System: Five Years Later (1995); Christina J. Johns, Power, Ideology, and the War on Drugs: Nothing Succeeds Like Failure (1992); Franklin E. Zimring & Gordon Hawkins, The Search for Rational Drug Control (1992). All these scholars agree that American prison populations are growing rapidly, primarily as to black offenders, and in disproportion to involvement with illegal drugs by blacks.

[106]*See, e.g.,* Mauer & Huling, *supra* note 105; Johns, *supra* note 105; Zimring & Hawkins, *supra* note 105.

[107]Zimring & Hawkins, *supra* note 104.

THE PUZZLE OF THE SOCIAL ORIGINS OF THE MARIHUANA TAX ACT OF 1937*

JOHN F. GALLIHER
University of Missouri, Columbia

and

ALLYNN WALKER
University of Wisconsin, Madison

Several recent studies of the origins of the Marihuana Tax Act of 1937, when analyzing the same data sources, have surprisingly come to differing conclusions. Contrary to the results of most of these studies, there is insufficient evidence to conclude that there was a major effort by the Federal Bureau of Narcotics to generate a public marihuana crisis to create pressure for this legislation. Indeed a review of newspapers as well as the Congressional Record does not demonstrate a nationwide marihuana crisis. Moreover, this legislation is not the important legislative change implied by these studies, but merely a symbolic gesture involving a Bureau promise of no increased funding required by this law's passage.

During the past few years a number of researchers have studied the origins of the first federal attempt to control marihuana in the United States, the Marihuana Tax Act of 1937. Superficially this legislation seems unnecessary; at the time of its passage all states already had laws prohibiting the sale and possession of marihuana. This law, which imposed a prohibitively high tax on the drug, was modeled after federal control of addictive drugs, and perhaps much of the interest in examining the origins of this law stems from researchers' beliefs in the irrationality of applying the same type of controls to marihuana. The implication of considerable scholarly attention is that this law represents an important legal change. Curiously, while these studies have used largely the same data, they have come to different and often contradictory conclusions. The purpose of this study is to re-examine these data as well as additional information in an attempt to integrate disparate findings.

The first of these studies is by Becker (1963), who sees drug prohibition in general, and marihuana control in particular, as coinciding with three traditional American values: (1) disapproval of behavior that could cause loss of self-control; (2) disapproval of action taken solely to produce states of ecstasy; and (3) a view that concern for human welfare or humanitarianism requires the suppression of drugs.

However, Becker claims that in the early 1930's neither the public nor law enforcement officials considered the use of marihuana a serious problem. Indeed he

---

*Thanks are due Alfred R. Lindesmith, Edward Hunvald, and James McCartney for their helpful comments on an earlier draft of this paper.

shows that in 1930 only 1u *juana Tax Act*
yet by 1937 all states had pas... *d laws prohibiting the use of marihuana,*
Becker's explanation is that the m... *tion. Why this sudden turn of events?*
Department's Bureau of Narcotics. ... *d the law's passage was the Treasury*

The Bureau's efforts took two forms: coop... *development of state legisla-*
tion affecting the use of marihuana, and prov... *and figures for journalistic*
accounts of the problem (Becker, 1963:138).

Becker (1963:141) shows that in the *Reader's Gui...* *riodical Literature no*
articles on marihuana appeared from January 1925–Jun... *but four appeared*
from July 1935–June 1937, and 17 from July 1937–June 19... *a rapid decline*
thereafter. He claims that during the bulge period, five of the seve... *en articles show*
explicit influence of the Bureau.

Regarding the motives of the Bureau, Becker (1963:138) says:

While it is, of course, difficult to know what the motives of Bureau officials w... we
need assume no more than that they perceived an area of wrongdoing that proper...
belonged in their jurisdiction and moved to put it there. The personal interest they satisfied in pressing for marihuana legislation was one common to many officials: the interest in successfully accomplishing the task one has been assigned and in acquiring the
best tools with which to accomplish it.

Dickson (1968) shows that Becker's data on publication are misleading given the
time intervals used. Indeed by looking at exact publication dates rather than broad
time intervals, it becomes clear that only one article appeared in the seven months
before the bill was signed into law. Dickson (1968:155) claims that, "The great bulk
of Bureau-inspired publicity came after the passage of the act, not before" and that
therefore the public was apathetic prior to and during the bill's passage. This post-
legislative propaganda, he asserts, shows that the Bureau director, H. J. Anslinger,
was not motivated by moral issues but only attempted to increase the Bureau's power
and scope of operations after the bill was passed.

After considerable discussion of Anslinger's motives, Dickson (1968:156) concludes, "It would be either naive or presumptuous to deny that some combination of
both moral and bureaucratic factors exist in any given crusade." It has, in fact,
become accepted practice to blame the Act on a publicity campaign waged by the
Narcotics Bureau under Mr. Anslinger's leadership rather than assessing relevant
social structural conditions at the time which might have influenced the bill's passage:

This Act was the result of a publicity campaign staged by the Federal Bureau of Narcotics under Mr. Anslinger's direction and leadership (Lindesmith, 1965:228).

In its report covering 1936, the bureau *first* (emphasis added) begins its continuous presentation of the "violent addict" myth. . . . brutal murders and other violent attacks are
lucidly presented which purportedly illustrate the homicidal tendencies and the general
debasing effects arising from marihuana use (Reasons, 1974:146).

...ced by the Bureau of Narcotics, the
⅃ a prohibitively high tax on marihuana
(Reasons, 1974:146).

Largely because of public concer[n]
Marihuana Tax Act was passed
and creating a whole new clas..ic concern and outrage could be instantly cre-

Reasons seems to sugge... Treasury Department played down the serious-
ated. Becker shows that ... hat newspaper articles had exaggerated the problem
ness of the problem, su...sts that in 1932 the Federal Bureau of Narcotics again
of marihuana use,
Musto (1973:22...ce of marihuana. The Bureau claimed that abuse of mari-
minimized the im..y in settlements of Latin Americans.
huana occurred

A great deal of ...lic interest has been aroused by newspaper articles appearing from time to time or ...e evils of the abuse of marijuana or Indian hemp, and more attention has been focus...upon specific cases reported of the abuse of the drug than would otherwise have be...ne case. This publicity tends to magnify the extent of the evil and lends color to an inference that there is an alarming spread of the improper use of the drug, whereas the actual increase in such use may not have been inordinately large (Musto, 1973:221).

Indeed as late as January 1937, Anslinger was quoted as saying that marihuana control was a state problem (Musto, 1973:221–222).

Unlike Becker, Lindesmith, and Reasons, Musto (1973:229) suggests that "the FBN does not appear to have created the marihuana scare of the early 1930s." Musto claims that the fear of marihuana was concentrated mainly in the southwestern states where there were the greatest concentrations of Mexican immigrants, who brought with them traditions of marihuana use. While Mexicans were tolerated during the economic boom of the 1920's as a source of cheap labor, during the 1930's the hatred toward this group escalated from the competition they created for scarce jobs and their willingness to work for low wages. Predictably, as this group became economically threatening, their habits also became more threatening.

Musto recently interviewed Anslinger to explore his motives in pressing for this legislation. Anslinger states that it was political pressure generated from these states and not the ambition of those in the Federal Bureau of Narcotics that was the crucial factor in the passage of the new law.

Southwestern police and prosecuting attorneys likewise protested constantly to the federal government about the Mexicans' use of the weed (Musto, 1973:220).

The pressure for a federal antimarihuana law was political, Anslinger states, from local police forces in affected states to the governors; from the governors to Secretary of the Treasury Henry Morgenthau, Jr.; from Morgenthau to the Treasury's General Counsel; and finally to the Commissioner of Narcotics (Musto, 1973:223).

In the summer of 1936 it therefore became obvious that there would be no law to placate the Southwest unless some federal legislation under traditional legal powers was enacted (Musto, 1973:225).

Bonnie and Whitebread (1974), unlike Becker, Reasons, Lindesmith, and Musto, claim that there was no intense concern with marihuana in the United States at the time the marihuana bill passed Congress and that this legislation went largely unnoticed.

All in all, neither narcotic drugs in general nor marihuana in particular were major public issues during the thirties (Bonnie and Whitebread, 1974:115).

Interest in marihuana was still regional, although transient interest had now been aroused elsewhere. Viewed nationally, apathy was the norm (1974:117).

Yet Bonnie and Whitebread acknowledge that Anslinger exerted considerable energy prior to 1937 to convince Americans of the dangers of marihuana. Until just prior to the Marihuana Tax Act's passage, however, Anslinger's suggested remedy for this problem was uniform state laws to handle the problem, for he doubted the constitutionality of federal attempts to control a drug where no importation from foreign countries was alleged.

Although there is some agreement among these writers, this small group of studies provides all possible combinations of results. Becker, Lindesmith, and Reasons see a national marihuana panic created by FBN propaganda which propelled the legislation through Congress. Dickson finds this panic to be a result of a FBN propaganda effort designed to increase the scope and power of the Bureau after the bill's passage. Musto finds a marihuana crisis prior to the bill's passage but one localized in the Southwest and not a result of Bureau propaganda. Bonnie and Whitebread see evidence of FBN propaganda but no national marihuana crisis.

There are three distinct issues raised by comparing the findings of these studies. One is, what in fact has been documented regarding the Federal Bureau of Narcotics activities involving the Marihuana Tax Act of 1937? After this has been determined, the next question to be raised involves the demonstrated effects of these activities. And finally, what conclusions can be drawn about the possible explanation of these Bureau activities?

METHOD AND DATA

This study is based on three types of information. One is a review of the information found in the previous studies which have been used to document the Bureau's lobbying efforts on behalf of the Act. This study also reassesses the Congressional Records involving the Marihuana Tax Act of 1937, including House and Senate floor debate and public hearings. This was done in part to document Bureau activities but also to reflect the existing sentiment at the time in the Congress. No claim is made that the use of this data source is innovative, since all the works cited above show a first-hand familiarity with these records. Yet, while they show an explicit reference to these records, they do not completely agree on their meaning and significance. A review of three metropolitan newspapers in the Southwest (*Dallas Morning News, Denver Post,* and *Los Angeles Times*) and New York City (*New York Times*) and Washington, D.C. (*Washington Post*) was made to assess the cultural milieu and public attitude toward marihuana in the year prior to the bill's passage (May 31, 1936–June 1, 1937). Reasons, Musto, and Becker claim that year to be of great

importance in changing public opinion. These newspaper data can be used to determine if indeed there was a crisis.

RESULTS

Cited Evidence of Bureau Propaganda

Becker (1963:142) cites an article in the July 1937 *American Magazine,* "Marihuana: assassin of youth," by H. J. Anslinger with Courtney Ryley Cooper. Becker
indicates that of the 17 articles on marihuana indexed in the *Reader's Guide* between
July 1937 and June 1939 five referred to this Bureau-inspired article. Lindesmith
(1965:228) cites no evidence for his claim that:

> This Act was the result of a publicity campaign staged by the Federal Bureau of Nar-
> cotics under Mr. Anslinger's direction and leadership.

Dickson (1968:152) also offers no specific support for the observation that:

> It seems clear from examining periodicals, newspapers, and the Congressional Record
> that the Bureau was primarily responsible for the passage of the act.

Reasons (1974:146) cites Dickson's unsupported assertion and the following unsupported claim:

> Many articles appeared in professional and policy [sic] journals which can be traced
> back to the Federal Bureau of Narcotics.

Reasons (1974:146) does cite some specific sources, however:

> Anslinger personally provided information for two articles that appeared in *Hygeia,*
> published by the American Medical Association.

Bonnie and Whitebread (1974:98) base their claims of propaganda just prior to the 1937
Act on the *American Magazine* article and on a 1936 speech by Anslinger on NBC.

In conclusion, Lindesmith and Dickson offer no support for their claims of FBN
propaganda. Bonnie and Whitebread cite one article and one radio speech. Becker
cites the same article and observes that five indexed articles also cited this article.
Reasons' claims are without support except for reference to Dickson's unsupported
claim and to two articles published by the AMA. This yields a total of three articles
and one radio speech, clearly a product of the FBN. Yet only Musto (1973:229) finds
insufficient evidence to prove a major propaganda role for the FBN. In fairness it
must be noted that it may still be that the FBN played a major role in propagandizing
on behalf of the law, but perhaps the contacts were largely informal and by word of
mouth, and therefore not a part of the documents available from this period.

Bonnie and Whitebread (1974:95) provide convincing evidence, however, that the
Bureau instigated an "educational campaign" on the evils of marihuana in the early
1930's as part of an effort to secure uniform state prohibitions of all drugs. This
campaign, however, was largely unsuccessful, although it undoubtedly contributed
to the general definition of marihuana as evil and its widespread prohibition in the states.

There was no floor debate on the ... ~~blic Hearings~~
discussion occurred during the hearings ~~House or the Senate. Indeed the on[ly]~~
that the bill was not a topic of dissent or di~~[Ho]use and Senate. This is a clear sign~~

Public hearings were held first by the Hou~~[se and Senate.] opinion within the Congress.~~
the bill originated, then in the Senate Finance C~~ and Means Committee where~~
testified at these hearings: (1) witnesses represent~~[ing]e. Three types of witnesses~~
tries who urged alteration of the bill as originally d~~hemp and birdseed indus-~~
from legal controls under the Act; (2) witnesses repres~~to exempt these groups~~
who spoke on behalf of the bill (Primary witnesses ~~government agencies~~
Anslinger, Commissioner, Bureau of Narcotics, and the Treas~~ group were H. J.~~
tant general counsel, Clinton M. Hester.); and (3) Dr. William C. ~~[De]partment's assis-~~
tive counsel of the American Medical Association, who spoke again~~ward, legisla-~~ the ~~[b]ill.~~

The government witnesses used two main techniques during the public hearings: unverified case histories of the tragedy caused by marihuana use and newspaper editorials cited as fact. Commissioner Anslinger provided lurid case histories from a variety of regions, all outside the southwestern states, during the House and Senate hearings. The theme emerges from his testimony that the country was not only faced with a crisis but a *widespread and national* crisis recently grown to major proportions.

> It is only in the last 2 years that we had a report of seizures anywhere but in the Southwest. Last year New York State reported 195 tons seized, whereas before that I do not believe that New York could have reported 1 ton seized (U.S. Cong., House, 1937b: 20–21, April 27).

> Last year the State of Pennsylvania destroyed 200,000 pounds (U.S. Cong., House, 1937b:25, April 27).

Mr. Anslinger (U.S. Cong., Senate, 1937:14) also offered opinion as fact to liven up his long list of cases:

> I believe in some cases one cigarette might develop a homicidal mania, probably to kill his brother [sic].

This opinion, as well as all of his other testimony, went unquestioned by Congress.

Newspaper articles were demonstrably effective as was newspaper editorial opinion, which was used as factual evidence, by Bureau representatives as well as members of Congress. In a House report to accompany the bill (U.S. Cong., House, 1937a:2), the sponsor, Rep. Doughton, expresses the following view:

> The seriousness of the problem is also emphasized by the fact that newspapers in over 100 cities in the country have reported the illicit use of marihuana within the communities which they serve.

And Mr. Hester during the House hearings (U.S. Cong., House, 1937b:6, April 27) quoted from an editorial of the *Washington Times* which also reflects national rather than regional concern:

ost insidious of all forms of dope, largely
rstand its fatal qualities.

The marihuana cigaret [sic] is
because of the failure of the pub inst it, having no Federal laws to cope with it
The Nation is almost defe or combatting it.
and virtually no organized c
The result is tragic. of peddlers who infest school neighborhoods.
School children are this buy the destructive weed without knowledge of its
High-school boys scienceless dealers sell it with impunity.
capacity for harm, a blem, and it must have national attention.
This is a nation garette must be recognized as a deadly drug and American
The fatal marij ana ed against it.
children must b rot

Similar editorials are then quoted by Mr. Hester from the *Washington Post* and the *Washington Herald*.

Near the end of the House hearings, expert medical testimony was heard on the issue of the necessity and desirability of this bill. The witness was Dr. William C. Woodward, legislative counsel of the American Medical Association, who was both a physician and lawyer. He was a well-known and prestigious figure, long a familiar personality in Congress representing the powerful AMA. He and his organization opposed the bill (U.S. Cong., House, 1937b:92, May 4):

> That there is a certain amount of narcotic addiction of an objectionable character no one will deny. The *newspapers* (emphasis added) have called attention to it so prominently that there must be some grounds for their statements. It has surprised me, however, that the facts on which these statements have been based have not been brought before this committee by *competent primary evidence. We are referred to newspaper publications concerning the prevalence of marihuana addiction. We are told that the use of marihuana causes crime* (emphasis added).

Dr. Woodward suggested a number of federal agencies which could have been called as possible sources of direct information regarding the effects of marihuana including the Bureau or Prisons, the Children's Bureau, the Office of Education, and the Public Health Service.

> The Bureau of Public Health Service has also a division of pharmacology. If you desire evidence as to the *pharmacology of Cannabis* (emphasis added), that obviously is the place where you can get direct and primary evidence, rather than the indirect hearsay evidence (U.S. Cong., House, 1937b:92, May 4).

Dr. Woodward objected to the bill's imposition of a tax on physicians prescribing marihuana because it would not address the problem of the clandestine distribution as described by the government. Instead of new federal legislation, he recommended reliance on existing state laws. He also questioned why the medical profession had not been consulted in the drafting of the bill (U.S. Cong., House, 1937b:116, May 4).

No medical man would identify this *na Tax Act*
marihuana is not a drug (emphasis adc. *edicine until he read it through, because
Yet on the basis of other information Co...ng., House, 1937b:117, May 4).
of the pharmacological properties of marihu. *eared to believe that his opinion

Mr. Dingell, *We know that it is a habit that is spread*...rong.
We learn that from the pages of the newspapers. . . . T...*cularly among youngsters.*
ing each year (emphasis added). *r of victims is increas-

Dr. Woodward. There is no evidence of that (U.S. Cong., House, ...b:117, May 4).

Mr. McCormack. There is no question but that the drug habit ha. bee. ...creasing rapidly in recent years.

Dr. Woodward. There is no evidence to show whether or not it has been (U.S. Cong., House, 1937b:118, May 4).

Mr. McCormack. It is used, we were told, by 200,000,000 people throughout the world. *All I know is what I have read about it* (emphasis added) (U.S. Cong., House, 1937b:118, May 4).

Against Dr. Woodward's testimony, the Chairman of the House Ways and Means Committee, Rep. Doughton, sponsor of the bill, presented two newspaper editorials from the *Washington Times* and *Washington Post* which, as indicated above, were earlier introduced into the hearings by Mr. Hester, the Treasury Department's legal counsel (U.S. Cong., House, 1937b:120, May 4).

Finally Mr. Anslinger and Mr. Hester helped sell the bill by arguing, both in the House and Senate hearings, that no new appropriations would be required by its enactment (U.S. Cong., House, 1937b:27, April 27; U.S. Cong., Senate, 1937:21). Dickson (1968:156) has shown that after the bill's passage, Mr. Anslinger continued to claim, during appropriations hearings, that no new funds were necessary to enforce the law; perhaps he did this because of parsimoniousness in the use of tax dollars. Indeed after the Act's passage in 1937 (perhaps to stay within budget constraints), Anslinger instructed his agents in a confidential memorandum to leave the massive number of small marihuana possession cases in state courts and act only in the much rarer cases of suppliers (Bonnie and Whitebread, 1974:180–181).

We are then left with two sources of information about the activities of the Federal Bureau of Narcotics: evidence from existing studies and the Congressional Record. Existing studies provide little evidence of a Bureau lobby on behalf of the Marihuana Tax Act of 1937 but some evidence of efforts to secure passage of uniform drug laws in all states. Included was an attempt to inform the public of the dangers associated with marihuana. The other sources of information regarding Bureau activities, the Congressional Record, shows several days of partisan testimony before House and Senate committees by Bureau employees.

Newspapers

The next question involves the consequences of the effort to inform the public about marihuana. A review of newspapers in southwestern cities and one each in New York and Washington suggests that the concern about marihuana was more diffuse than Musto's, but less intense than suggested by Reasons. These newspapers reported on domestic economic depression, massive union strikes, the Nazi takeover of Europe, the Spanish Civil War, and the threat of Russian communism. In the *Los Angeles Times,* for example, between May 31, 1936 and June 1, 1937, the twelve month period preceding the bill's passage, only seven articles concerning marihuana appeared; in the *Dallas Morning News* eleven such articles appeared, and in the *Denver Post,* eighteen. During the same time period, in the more nationally oriented *New York Times* and *Washington Post* there were nineteen and six articles respectively. This makes an overall average in all newspapers of approximately one article per month. Aside from the limited number of articles on marihuana, their location in the newspapers is instructive. Only two appeared on the front page. Prominence was usually reserved for news involving other drugs, especially heroin or opium. The infrequency and inconspicuousness of marihuana articles is surprising, given the frequent reference to newspaper articles about marihuana in Congress. Despite little evidence of a marihuana panic as reflected in these articles, marihuana was always characterized as a dangerous narcotic. That is how it is described by Congressmen; and there is evidence that concern with marihuana had increased from earlier in the decade.[1]

SUMMARY AND CONCLUSION

The cause of the activities of Anslinger and the Bureau is difficult to assess with the information available. Yet some analysis of the causes of Anslinger's behavior and that of his subordinates is possible. Anslinger argued publicly for uniform state drug laws. It is common for federal police officials to see merit in a uniform legal structure which simplifies federal relations with state police agencies. Also, Anslinger and Hester testified before Congress on behalf of the proposed legislation. Once an administration sets its policy, (Musto, 1973:223), it is common for federal bureau chiefs to testify in support of the policy. Anslinger's documented behavior is usual enough, and not that of a zealous, moral crusader or a power-hungry bureaucrat. Assigning major responsibility for legal change to a specific individual, as has

---

[1]A review of the *New York Times Index* reveals the following annual tally of articles on marihuana:

Year	N
1937	13
1936	9
1935	3
1934	4
1933	1
1932	1
1931	1
1930	0

been done in the case of the Marihuana Tax Act, leads to diverse psychological explanations, which are difficult to verify. Blaming a government official for what many, including liberals, see as a ridiculous law is not unexpected, except in sociologists trained to analyze structural conditions rather than individual characteristics.

It is probable that the Bureau campaign to secure uniform state drug laws had some influence on later definitions of marihuana. However, the evidence used by Becker, Lindesmith, Reasons, Dickson, and Bonnie and Whitebread does not support their claim of an FBN propaganda effort to secure passage of the Marihuana Tax Act of 1937. A total of three articles and one radio speech hardly constitutes a national propaganda effort. It appears that this role of the FBN has become an article of faith for many studying federal marihuana legislation.

The average of one article per month represents something less than the results of a zealous, national propaganda campaign and does not reflect a national crisis, even if it is an increase from previous years. A crisis of the time was the Nazi takeover of Europe, which accounted for at least one article a day. An energetic propaganda campaign would produce at least one news story a day, as in a national political campaign for President. Without a national crisis, assigning the responsibility for a widespread and effective propaganda campaign becomes a moot point; and there does not appear to have been a national crisis.

Becker, Dickson, and Reasons agree that prior to the Anslinger-orchestrated Bureau propaganda campaign, there was generally citizen apathy toward marihuana and that Anslinger and the Bureau were responsible for the public arousal. But this seems to give them too much credit. Long before the campaign got underway, many states had laws prohibiting sale and possession of marihuana, and prior to the first federal hearings, all states had such laws (Dickson, 1968:154).

Not only is there no evidence of a propaganda campaign, but contrary to Anslinger's and Hester's interpretation of the newspaper editorials which they presented at the Congressional hearings, there is insufficient evidence to demonstrate a national or local marihuana crisis just prior to the bill's passage. Any concern about marihuana use was not isolated in the Southwest, as Musto claims. Certainly the review of southwestern newspapers indicates something less than a public panic; they were filled with stories of international aggression and domestic economic depression. Marihuana stories offered slight competition at such a time. Indeed Alfred Lindesmith (1975) recently recalled:

> I was engaged in studying drugs when the marihuana law was passed but I didn't even know it nor did I notice any national furor.

Throughout the hearings no one challenged or questioned Mr. Hestor's or Mr. Anslinger's unsupported testimony except, of course, Dr. Woodward. This may indicate that the members of Congress were already convinced. Editorials were given more credence than medical testimony by the members of Congress, and the seeming lack of interest of most Congressmen, including their casual dismissal of Dr. Woodward's testimony, indicate that Congress was convinced of the danger in marihuana. The fact that some Congressmen relied heavily on the few and relatively inconspicuous newspaper articles indicates that these stories fit the common sense opinion of the period and were quoted for this reason. There is no evidence that this was a new view, or that Congress was startled by Anslinger's testimony. As Bonnie and Whitebread (1974:117) indicate, "Viewed nationally, apathy was the norm." The strong words used in the Congressional hearings by Anslinger and Hester do not prove a major propaganda effort by the FBN, contrary to Dickson, nor, of course, do these words necessarily reflect a national crisis. Anslinger could make such statements without fear of contradiction because his claims were supported by widespread but apparently low-level citizen approbation about the evil nature of marihuana, and no scientific evidence apparently existed at the time to contradict him as shown by Dr. Woodward's helplessness. It would seem that if such scientific evidence had existed, Dr. Woodward would have known of its existence and would have used it.

Finally, the symbolic properties of the Marihuana Tax Act are of great importance. Without new funding, this law clearly could not be fully implemented. It was largely a technical adjustment in federal law, duplicating existing state laws—not the important level change implied by Becker, Dickson, Reasons, Lindesmith, and Bonnie and Whitebread. These researchers seem to have been confused by the same symbolism as Edelman remarks in other observers of legislative action. Anslinger promised no budget increases to enforce the new law and indicated an unwillingness to allow his agents to spend great amounts of time on marihuana cases. Edelman (1964) suggests that the political behavior of people is determined by whether a piece of legislation symbolically reassures them. Similarly, Gusfield (1963, 1967) has argued that national prohibition of alcohol was largely unenforced, which permitted a public affirmation of the values of prohibitionists without great inconvenience to drinkers. As in the case of the 1937 Marihuana Tax Act, necessary funds to insure the implementation of prohibition were not appropriated (Gusfield, 1963:120).

It may be the case that pressure from law enforcement officials in the Southwest was an initial precipitating agent in the bill's passage. However, two points must be made in this regard: (1) This pressure does not appear to reflect a Mexican marihuana panic in the Southwest as Musto claims, and (2) the bill's clear sailing in Congress cannot be accounted for solely by this political pressure. Rather it must be recognized that the bill was not objectionable to most, both because it supported widespread common sense opinion of the time and because it was purely symbolic legislation. Certainly no Congressmen demanded increased appropriations to fund marihuana control.

> To Anslinger, Congress did not seem very concerned and "the only information they had was what we would give them in our hearings" (Musto, 1973:225).

It does appear that Congress was not very concerned. Apparently they recognized the public relations or symbolic nature of the Act. Also, those groups likely to be supportive of such legislation did not send representatives to the hearings in the House and Senate. The most plausible interpretation for their inactivity is that Anslinger did not feel it necessary to ask for their assistance, given the lack of Congressional opposition.

REFERENCES

Becker, Howard S.
  1963   *Outsiders.* New York: Free Press of Glencoe.

Bonnie, Richard J. and Charles H. Whitebread II
  1974   *The Marihuana Conviction: A History of Marihuana Prohibition in the United States.* Charlottesville: University Press of Virginia.

Dallas Morning News
  May 31, 1936–June 1, 1937

Denver Post
  May 31, 1936–June 1, 1937

Dickson, Donald T.
  1968   "Bureaucracy and morality: an organizational perspective on a moral crusade," *Social Problems* 16:143–156.

Edelman, Murray
  1964   *The Symbolic Uses of Politics.* Urbana: University of Illinois Press.

Gusfield, Joseph R.
  1963   *Symbolic Crusade: Status Politics and the American Temperance Movement.* Urbana: University of Illinois Press.
  1967   "Moral passage: the symbolic process in public designations of deviance," *Social Problems* 15:175–188.

Lindesmith, Alfred R.
  1965   *The Addict and the Law.* Bloomington: Indiana University Press.
  1975   Letter, August 21, 1975 in possession of the authors.

Los Angeles Times
  May 31, 1936–June 1, 1937

Musto, David F.
  1973   *The American Disease: Origins of Narcotic Control.* New Haven: Yale University Press.

New York Times
  May 31, 1936–June 1, 1937

New York Times Index
  1930–1935

Reasons, Charles E.
  1974   *The Criminologist: Crime and the Criminal.* Pacific Palisades, California: Goodyear.

U.S. Congress, House of Representatives
  1973a   Report No. 792 to accompany H.R. 6906, "The marihuana taxing bill." Seventy-fifth Congress, First Session, May 11.
  1973b   "Taxation of marihuana." Hearings before the Committee on Ways and Means. Seventy-fifth Congress, First Session on H.R. 6385, April 27, 28, 29, 30, and May 4.

U.S. Congress, Senate
  1937   "Taxation of marihuana." Hearing before a Subcommittee of the Committee on Finance. Seventy-fifth Congress, First Session on H.R. 6906, July 12.

Washington Post
  May 31, 1936–June 1, 1937

NEBRASKA'S MARIJUANA LAW: A CASE OF UNEXPECTED LEGISLATIVE INNOVATION

JOHN F. GALLIHER, JAMES L. MCCARTNEY

and

BARBARA E. BAUM
University of Missouri—Columbia

AUTHOR'S NOTE: *This investigation was supported by Biomedical Sciences Support Grant FR-07053 from the General Research Support Branch, Division of Research Resources, Bureau of Health Professions Education and Manpower Training, National Institutes of Health. We are grateful for the helpful criticism and guidance of Alfred R. Lindesmith, Nicholas Babchuk, Malcolm Spector and Edward Hunvald. An earlier version of this paper was presented at the annual meetings of the American Sociological Association, New York City, 1973. Readers will note that the anonymity of sources has been preserved throughout the article.*

The social processes involved in the development of criminal laws have been studied by several scholars (Jeffrey, 1957; Hall, 1952; Chambliss, 1964; Lindesmith, 1965; Sutherland, 1950; Becker, 1963). Generally, two major perspectives have guided these studies. One orientation has been the functionalist perspective (Pound, 1922, 1942; Durkheim, 1964) which stresses the emergence of moral consensus and the functional interdependence of the law with other institutions. Dicey (1920) suggests that public consensus is preceded by the origination of such ideas among elites, and is only later accepted by the mass of citizens. Such consensus, he claims, supplies the foundation for eventual legal change. An alternative view is the conflict orientation (Quinney, 1970; Vold, 1958: 203–219; Engels, 1972; Laski, 1935) which views law as the instrument through which one interest group dominates another. In the development of workman's compensation laws, Friedman and Ladinsky (1967) trace the history of conflict and eventual accommodation between workers and factory owners.

Both the functionalist and conflict orientations either explicitly or implicitly assume that people typically make rational decisions to maximize what they imagine will be their material gains. However, Edelman (1964) suggests that this assumption may not be correct, and that the political behavior of citizens often is determined not on the basis of their real or material interests, but on whether or not a given piece of legislation symbolically reassures them.

Within the sociology of law there have been more studies directed to the development of radically new legislation than to adjustments in existing statutes. Perhaps these latter instances are less dramatic, or it may be that they seem to be less clearly

Reprinted from *Law & Society Review* 8, no. 3 (1974), by permission of Blackwell Publishers, Ltd.

instances supporting the major theoretical perspectives. We have chosen to focus on the process of legal change as represented by the widespread phenomenon of alteration of drug laws controlling the possession of marijuana.

Becker (1963:121–146) and Dickson (1968:143–156) have written about the early history of marijuana control legislation, and have shown how the Federal Bureau of Narcotics successfully lobbied during the 1930's for the passage of legislation that would eliminate what it claimed to be the marijuana "drug problem." Although drug use appears to have been viewed earlier as an evil affecting the lower classes (Clausen, 1961:189–196), by the late 1960's, marijuana use had become fashionable among many middle and upper class college youths (Goode, 1970:35–40; 1972:36–37). With this new class of law violators, including the children of senators, judges, and other prominent citizens, the conditions were set for a reconsideration of the existing laws.

Late in 1968 and early in 1969, ten states changed their narcotics control laws to make the maximum penalty for possession of marijuana a misdemeanor, punishable by less than one year of confinement.[1] Nebraska was one of these first states to pass such legislation and, moreover, it established the lowest maximum penalty among these states. In fact, the maximum penalty of seven days, which was prescribed in Nebraska's law, was much lower than that stipulated in the bills of most other states which later passed similar legislation (National Organization for the Reform of Marijuana Laws, 1971).

Earlier, the accepted model for controlling drug usage had been one of increasing prescribed penalties (*see* Lindesmith, 1965:80–82; Clausen, 1961:215–217). Becker (1963:136) suggests that these attempts to suppress drug use are legitimized by the Protestant Ethic which proscribes loss of self-control, by traditional American values that disapprove of any action taken solely to produce a state of ecstasy, and by the humanitarian belief that all drugs enslave the user. The question that stimulated our research was why a traditionally conservative state such as Nebraska, which, we suspected, might reflect the values discussed by Becker, would be a leader in passing legislation reducing penalties for a vice such as marijuana use. Using either the consensus model, which views law as the product of compromise and shared values, or the conflict model, which sees law as the outcome of struggles between the interests of differing groups, one would not predict this development in Nebraska. We would not have predicted early consensus on such a radical departure in social control in this tradition-oriented state, nor would we have predicted that the proponents of reduced penalties would be strong enough to overcome a more conservative orientation in the control of drugs.

---

[1]The first states to pass such drug legislation were Alaska, August 4, 1968; Wyoming, March 7, 1969; New Mexico, April 2, 1969; Utah, May 13, 1969; Washington, May 23, 1969; North Carolina, June 23, 1969; Connecticut, July 1, 1969; Iowa, July 1, 1969; and Illinois, July 18, 1969 (*see* Rosenthal, 1969; Arnold, 1969:1, 60). The date of Nebraska's legislation, April 11, 1969, is missing from both of the above accounts.

PRELUDE TO THE NEW LAW

Before 1969, the penalties in Nebraska for possession or sale of marijuana consisted of a two- to five-year sentence in prison and a fine. Marijuana was classed along with opium derivatives and other narcotic drugs in legislation, modeled after the federal Harrison Act of 1914 (38 Stat. 785 as *amended*), and passed in 1943 (Rev. Stat. of Neb. ch. 28, §§451–470).[2] Drug abuse was a minor problem in Nebraska prior to the late 1960's. Newspaper reports in the state capital, a city of more than 100,000 population, list one case per year between 1950 and 1967 (*Lincoln Star,* 1950–1967). The Nebraska State Patrol (1970:3) recorded an average of 15 cases per year for the entire state between 1960 and 1967.

Late in 1967, numerous incidents of marijuana possession were recorded in the press, many of them involving college students. One prominent state senator (hereafter referred to as Senator C) spoke out publicly on the topic. His district, although primarily rural, had the third highest number of cases reported in the late 1960's (Nebraska State Patrol, 1970:14). He spoke at the state university in November 1967 and was rebuked by a group of students when he proposed spending money for undercover agents to deal with the "definite problem" of marijuana use on campus (DeFrain, 1967:5). Earlier in 1967, Senator C had been the sponsor of a law which expanded the 1943 drug laws to include depressant, stimulant, and hallucinogenic drugs, and established a narcotics control division in the state highway patrol (Legislative Bill 876, Ch. 161 at 460, June 7, 1967; henceforth LB 876).

In 1968, drug arrests in Nebraska increased sevenfold over the number in 1967 (Nebraska State Patrol, 1970:3). Many of the arrests involved students; but in the western, more rural part of the state, several out-of-state persons were arrested with substantial harvests of marijuana in the hundreds of pounds. Marijuana had grown abundantly in the state since World War I, when it was commercially harvested to produce rope fiber. One knowledgeable official at the Nebraska State Patrol estimated that there were 115,000 acres of marijuana growing wild in the state as late as 1969 (Thomas, 1969).

Response to the increasing number of arrests consisted primarily of statements of concern by some public officials and occasional newspaper editorials. Senator C felt that administrators at the state university were not taking the problem seriously (Senate Debate on LB 876, May 2, 1967). There was also mention of legislation to declare marijuana a noxious weed and to provide penalties for farmers who did not eradicate it on their property. Farmers vigorously opposed this, maintaining that such weed control was costly, time-consuming, and ultimately impossible (Wall, 1968:14). The issue was not raised again.

In 1969 Senator C introduced legislation (LB 8, 1969) that would permanently expel from college any student convicted of marijuana possession. It was amended to provide for a 30-day suspension from college, but, although it passed the legislature, it was vetoed by the governor. The veto prompted a public expression of outrage by

---

[2]The penalty prescribed under the 1943 Nebraska drug legislation was a fine of up to $3,000 and two to five years in prison.

the senator and an unsuccessful a[t]... ruary 25, 1969).

One day after introducing the suspe[n]... turn the veto (*Lincoln Journal*, February... bill (LB 2, April 11, 1969) which would ha[ve]... nator C had introduced another marijuana to a misdemeanor; and as amended,... the penalty for possession of sentence for first possession, and a mandatory d[i]...d for a maximum seven-day vative bill that we focus on in this paper. ...tion course. It is this inno-

PUBLIC RESPONSE TO LB 2

LB 2 was assigned to the Committee on Public Health an[d]... hearings were held on January 28, 1969. We reviewed newspaper[s]... fare and the first areas of the state, Omaha and Lincoln, the state capital, from Janu[ary] the two urban 1969. This included the period immediately preceding the bill's intro[duction] 1969 to June its consideration by the legislature and after its passage. We wanted to se[e] ...ion, during licly identifiable groups were lobbying for or against the legislation and ...hat pub-... ...hat the public reaction was to its passage. We expected that most of the interest in dru[g]s and related legislation would be concentrated in these two cities since they had recorded the greatest increase in drug arrests, and since both had several colleges in addition to a university.

We found no debate about the bill in the press either by politicians or citizens. The newspapers merely noted that the bill was being considered. It quickly passed the unicameral legislature without a dissenting vote, and was signed into law by the governor with little commentary thereafter. A total of three short articles appeared within six months of the bill's passage, all supporting the educational provision of the legislation. We also reviewed the newspaper from January to June 1969 in the small town where Senator C lived, to see the reaction of his constituents. As with the urban newspapers, the local paper simply noted the bill, but made no editorial comment.

LEGISLATIVE HEARINGS

Another reflection of lack of concern with this legislation is that only one witness came to the public hearings. A county attorney argued in favor of the new law as more reasonable and humane than treating "experimenting" with drugs by young people as a felony (Public Hearings on LB 2, January 28, 1969:4).[3]

The sponsor of the bill, Senator C, was from a rural area of the state and was well-known for being one of the most conservative members of a very conservative legislature. Considering his previous record for introducing tough drug bills (LB 876 and LB 8), he hardly seemed the type of person to introduce such lenient legislation. Nevertheless, the records of public hearings, legislative debate, and our personal interviews with Senator C revealed quite clearly that his motivation for introducing the bill was punitive and not humanitarian. His argument to the senate, supported indirectly by the prosecutor at the public hearings, was that too many people had

---

[3]Prosecuting attorneys are called county attorneys in Nebraska.

for possession of marijuana. Prosecutors ...ng people under a law requiring what these ...ere a punishment.

> ...oo severe . . . to the point where we nullified what we ...rts in many cases would not enforce the penalties (Public Hearings on LB 28, 1969:1).

> ...of this state and the courts that would hear these charges feel ...n the case of possession for the first time is too strong and irregardless [sic] ...e evidence, generally speaking, they will not enforce it (Senate ...dary 21, 1969:350).

> ...felony was so great, it was the belief of the County Attorneys that they wasted ... time trying to enforce it, because the judges would not apply the felony pen... (Senate Debate on LB 2, March 18, 1969:744).

To en...re that those found in possession of marijuana would receive some punishment, Senator C advocated a reduction in the penalty to a point that he felt would seem reasonable to those enforcing the law.

> With the 7 day penalty for the possession of a nominal amount, the court will rather promiscuously [sic] based on the evidence, apply these penalties (Senate Debate on LB 2, March 18, 1969:744).

While the sponsor's motivation was clear, it still was not evident why Nebraska was one of the first states to pass this type of legislation, why it was supported by other legislators, and why no public opposition emerged to this legislation.

CRITICAL EVENTS

To further our understanding of the events involved in the bill's passage, the two senior authors interviewed key informants, including several other members of Nebraska's unicameral legislature, newsmen covering the legislature for both local newspapers, and a legislative reporter for a local radio station. Selected civil servants were also interviewed, including several county attorneys, the head of the state police narcotics division, and the head of the legislative drafting group, an agency of the state legislature which assists elected representatives in writing bills. A professor from the University of Nebraska Law School who specializes in criminal law and two defense attorneys in narcotics cases were also interviewed, as well as the ex-governor under whose administration the bill was passed. We also interviewed several of the former administrative aides to the ex-governor.[4]

---

[4] Perhaps because of pride in their state's trend-setting legislation, all respondents seemed eager to be interviewed and readily made their files available. Moreover, we found that each respondent volunteered the names of other people who might have some information relevant to our questions, and these other respondents volunteered yet another set of names. In this serial sample selection, we eventually found that no new names were being mentioned and felt we had contacted all knowledgeable respondents.

The law professor recalled that a few months before the legislation had passed, a county attorney's son had been arrested for possession of marijuana. He felt this might have had some influence on the bill's success. Checking out his lead through back issues of the newspapers in the state capital, we found that, indeed, in August 1968, six months before the new marijuana control bill passed, the son of an outstate county attorney was arrested in the state capital where he was a student at the state university, and charged with possession of marijuana. The county attorney resigned his office to serve as his son's defense attorney, and in a press release he vowed to fight to change what he considered a harmful and unjust law (*Lincoln Journal*, August 13, 1968). Another university student arrested with the county attorney's boy was the son of a university professor. The county attorney's son was represented at first by his father, but soon his father hired a prominent Democratic lawyer who was later to become president of the Nebraska Bar Association. The university professor's son was represented by a popular Republican ex-governor who had declined to run for re-election. According to the outstate county attorney, these lawyers were intentionally selected as the most politically powerful bipartisan team of attorneys in the state. With regard to using this influence, the ex-governor said, "We recognized the case on our clients was air-tight so [we] figured it was best to attack the law." He wrote a draft of a first-offense marijuana possession misdemeanor law, and, after discussing the issue with the county attorney who was prosecuting the two boys, sent him the proposal.

This county attorney said that during the fall of 1968 he felt compelled to prosecute his colleague's son in part because, in his judgment, the boys had quite a large amount (one ounce) of marijuana in their possession. He claimed to have had no enthusiasm for his task, yet he indicated that he never considered not enforcing the law. Undoubtedly, the unusual publicity created by this case narrowed his options. The notion of a marijuana misdemeanor law provided him with an option in handling his colleague's son's case, and he said that, more importantly, it provided an avenue for getting more convictions in other drug cases. He said that, in enforcing the felony law, "We felt compelled to reduce charges to all sorts of ridiculous things such as disturbing the peace." Reducing the penalty to a misdemeanor would result in more convictions on appropriate charges since judges and juries would be more willing to convict if penalties were lowered. He said that the County Attorneys Association unofficially endorsed the idea because the prosecutors from Lincoln and Omaha had experienced special difficulties in getting convictions in drug cases. Since large quantities of drugs had not yet penetrated the other areas of the state, the other county attorneys were not as concerned. The Association, therefore, did not go on record in favor of such legislation for fear of appearing to take a pro-marijuana position. Nevertheless, the county attorney said, they were all concerned about the potential of a felony conviction for "college kids just experimenting with marijuana"—a concern reflected in the testimony of the county attorney who testified at the public hearings. In short, the county attorneys wanted a more nearly just and enforceable law, one that both should be and could be enforced. The county attorney in Lincoln sent a tentative version of the bill to the state legislative drafting group and contacted a friend in the legislature, Senator C, asking him to sponsor the bill. In making this request, he argued that, if penalties were reduced, it would help get more convictions. Senator C agreed to sponsor the bill.

Just prior to introducing the misdemeanor marijuana bill, Senator C introduced another bill (Public Hearings on LB 8, January 27, 1969) which would have suspended college students for life from any Nebraska college or university, state or private, upon conviction of possession of marijuana.[5] The day after the school suspension bill was introduced, Senator C introduced the county attorney's misdemeanor bill. No one except a TV newsman (Terry, 1969) characterized this legislator's proposal as being soft on drug offenses; certainly none of his colleagues in the legislature did. To think of this man introducing a permissive piece of drug legislation was beyond credibility, given his general conservatism and longstanding and well-known hostility toward drug use. Not only had he introduced anti-LSD legislation and the punitive college suspension bill, but he also had argued that the misdemeanor legislation would make it harder on drug users.[6] With these strong credentials, he hardly could be accused of being permissive on the drug issue.

Yet, even the punishment-oriented sponsor of the bill recognized the wisdom of leniency for at least some of the middle and upper classes. During the public hearings on the college suspension bill, a member of the firm of the ex-governor representing the professor's son spoke against the suspension bill and in support of the misdemeanor bill which the legislator had publicly promised to introduce. Senator C was unusually courteous and respectful of him and publicly volunteered to make the misdemeanor bill retroactive to cover the ex-governor's client (Public Hearings on LB 8, January 27, 1969:12), which he later did (Senate Debate on LB 2, March 18, 1969:745).

CONCLUSION

Nebraska was one of the first states to reduce first-offense possession of marijuana to a misdemeanor, and several events and conditions seem to explain its early

---

[5]The suspension period was amended to 30 days (Public Hearings LB 8, January 27, 1969:12), and was passed, aided by what was often characterized as Senator C's aggressive, overwhelming style (Senate Debate LB 8, February 4, 1969:105–08; February 21, 1969:345–51). The bill, however, was vetoed by the governor, and the outraged sponsor was only a few votes short of overriding the veto (Senate Debate LB 8, February 27, 1969:454–66).

[6]Two years before, in 1967, this legislator had introduced a bill creating penalties for possession of LSD and establishing a narcotics control division in the state highway patrol (LB 876, effective June 7, 1967). He justified this legislation in punitive and control terms (Public Hearings on LB 876, April 18, 1967; Senate Debate on LB 876, May 2, 1967).

As far as I am concerned, nothing can be too harsh for those people who pervade [sic] this step, because I can think of nothing more horrible, than to have a son or daughter of mine become afflicted with this habit . . . (and) . . . be unable to break themselves or himself of the habit (Public Hearings on LB 876, April 18, 1967:3).

Are you going to wait until it happens in your family, to your son or daughter becomes contaminated [sic] or maybe your grandchild or the kid next door. [sic] Are you going to wait till you have a vivid explanation of this thing or are you going to do something about it? I think drugs is [sic] the most terrible thing that can happen to the human mind. And I am not willing to sit still and not attempt to do something about it (Senate Debate on LB 876, May 2, 1967:1913).

lead. The timing of the county attorney's son's arrest was important, of course, as a triggering event. This case assumed special significance because of the prestige of the defense attorneys. The speed with which the unicameral legislature can respond to such incidents is also an essential element in this explanation. A unicameral legislature avoids the usual conflict between the two houses, which often delays and sometimes kills prospective legislation. Moreover, several informants mentioned that in Nebraska there was perhaps special reluctance to punish young people for using marijuana because it commonly grows wild in the state. Reflecting this attitude was an editorial in one of the Lincoln newspapers (Dobler, 1968:4), appearing approximately two months after the arrest of the outstate prosecutor's son, which discussed the long history of marijuana in the state. The editorial observed that the state had long endured the presence of large amounts of marijuana without serious disruption.

One of the most striking features in Nebraska's early lead, paradoxically, was the absence of any organized support for or opposition to this legislation. The only organization known to have supported this bill was the County Attorneys Association, and this support was unofficial, or at least not publicly announced. From newspaper reports it was clear that at least some students favored reducing or eliminating penalties for marijuana use, but we could find no evidence of any active support by students.[7] The bill quickly passed with *no* opposition. It could not have been predicted that a radically different and apparently lenient piece of drug legislation would go unnoticed in a state supposed to be very much influenced by the fundamentalist sentiments which justify punitive reactions to drug use (*cf.* Becker, 1963:136).

One explanation for both the absence of organized support as well as the unexpected lack of opposition may be that the felony marijuana law which had previously been used only on the lower classes was threatening to middle class families. Whether or not middle class parents continued to perceive marijuana as a harmful drug, the threat of a felony charge and a prison term for their children clearly was perceived as more harmful—a theme that emerged often in our interviews. This threat is clearly illustrated in the case of the prosecutor's son. In the search for support for the bill this type of interest is not visible as are organized groups, yet its influence in forestalling opposition may be no less real.

Both moral conservatives and liberals, for different reasons of course, supported the bill. The more liberal members of the state government, including the governor, backed the legislation as a remedy against sending "decent" college kids to the penitentiary for a "minor mistake." This opposition to severe punishment for marijuana possession reflects a widespread feeling, according to Lindesmith (letter in possession of authors) that victimless crime or morality legislation arbitrarily creates "criminals" who not only do not view themselves as such; but, more importantly, are not so viewed by much of the public because of the absence of external social harm.

Apparently the moral conservatives in the state legislature did not oppose this bill

---

[7]Because of his strong position on drugs and from other university-baiting positions, Senator C was not a popular figure on the state university campus. Perhaps this accounts for lack of student enthusiasm for his bill, or perhaps more likely, students might have viewed it as still too punitive to merit active support.

because its sponsor justified it as a vehicle for insuring a greater likelihood of punishment since the felony possession law was not being enforced. Hall (1952) suggests that in a similar fashion at the end of the Middle Ages in England, merchants lobbied for the elimination of the death penalty for property crimes since severe penalties, out of line with public sentiment, allowed property offenders to escape any punishment under the law. In drug cases, Lindesmith (1965:80–82) has also observed that, since felony convictions take more time in courts than do misdemeanors and are more difficult to get because of "technicalities," police will make fewer felony arrests and instead reduce charges to loitering or vagrancy. Also, with high minimum penalties, judges and prosecutors are likely to collaborate in avoiding imposition of the severe penalties by accepting guilty pleas to lesser charges. All of these things, apparently, were happening in Nebraska.

The issue of the seriousness of marijuana possession laws only developed with visible and seemingly widespread marijuana use among the middle and upper classes. As long as marijuana use appeared only among the poor, the problem of drug convictions didn't emerge for either conservatives or liberals. Only when confronting an increasing number of cases of middle class defendants did judges and juries begin to balk. While conservatives became angry with the leniency of the courts toward affluent defendants, liberals became worried and disgusted by the law's potential results, which included sending middle class defendants to prison.

Both moral conservatives and liberals recognized, for differing reasons, that severe penalties for possession of marijuana were not appropriate when the defendants were the children of middle class, affluent parents. Borrowing from the *consensus* and *conflict* models of legal change, we see that both conservatives and liberals *agreed* on the specific law although they fundamentally *disagreed* on the basic issue covered by the law. Perhaps most significantly, this consensus among diverse groups may offer some clues to understanding why a number of states in rapid succession passed similar legislation even though these laws represented a radical departure in controlling marijuana use.[8] Yet, contrary to the conflict orientation, no organized interest groups are in evidence in this case; and, unlike the functionalist perspective, there is no evidence of a massive opinion shift involved in this legislative change. For a complete understanding of these events, we must turn, as Edelman (1964) advises, to the symbolic properties of political events.

We see some parallels in our data with the argument by Warriner (1958) about the

---

[8]It is interesting to observe that most of the states that were in the initial group making a first offense of marijuana possession punishable only as a misdemeanor or at least giving this option to the court were in the west or western plains. Besides Nebraska, these states include Alaska, California, Iowa, Montana, New Mexico, North Dakota, South Dakota, Utah, Washington and Wyoming. Only Connecticut, Illinois and North Carolina are early passage states clearly not in this region. Aside from mere geographical proximity which makes the spread of ideas easily understandable, the agricultural and cultural characteristics of Nebraska undoubtedly exist to a degree in many of these other western states. Large quantities of open land where marijuana grows wild is one similarity. Since many of these states are predominantly rural in character, the concern with sending local (often country) boys to the penitentiary may have been widespread. Finally, many of these states are also predominantly rural Protestant so that punitive and repressive arguments in favor of reduction of penalties were likely to have been used.

symbolic functions of preserving official morality. In a small Kansas community he found inconsistencies between citizens' public expressions and private behavior regarding alcohol consumption. Publicly, they were uniformly opposed to drinking, yet most drank within the privacy of their homes. Irrespective of their behavior, citizens felt that it was important to give symbolic support to the community's normative structure. Public support for national prohibition, according to Gusfield (1963; 1967), was also mainly a result of an effort to give symbolic support to the values prescribing total abstinence. Gusfield distinguishes this *symbolic* function of the law from its *instrumental* or actual enforcement or control function. Edelman (1964) observes that often citizens are satisfied that their interests are being protected once relevant legislation is passed, even if it is not enforced. The mere passage of the law symbolizes to them that their values are being supported. This, apparently, was the case with national prohibition (Gusfield, 1963).

This distinction between the instrumental and symbolic functions of law seems ideally suited for an analysis of Nebraska's marijuana law. Using this distinction, it becomes clear that the senate sponsor of the misdemeanor marijuana bill essentially argued that it would be an improvement because of its instrumental features, *i.e.*, its ability to control. One unspoken, but no less real cost of this legislation was a certain loss of symbolic support for norms prohibiting drug use. Marijuana possession was still punishable under criminal law but the punishment was so light as to imply the offense was trivial. Those less condemning of marijuana use, on the other hand, gained some symbolic support for their position, and in fact made some instrumental gains as well because, while the probability of conviction might increase, the punishment was minimal. The basis for consensus on the legislation becomes clear: both moral conservatives and liberals gained something from this legal change.

Ironically, the pressure to enforce the law rather than to ignore it, as Edelman says so often occurs, was the result of the dramatic opposition to the law by the county attorney whose son was arrested. Because he was a prosecutor, he was in a special position to call public attention to his son's arrest. Moreover, his son was arrested in the state capital where state government and the mass media were centralized, which further served to publicize the case. Therefore, the other county attorney could not use the technique of ignoring the law to suit these specific interests. His options seemed limited by the publicity. The only course of action seemed to be a direct effort to change the relevant law.

It would appear that Senator C was taking a considerable chance of being labeled permissive regarding drug usage by introducing such legislation. He might have been protected from such criticism, however, by introducing the college suspension bill the day before. This emphasized his position on drugs, and, given the suspension bill's extreme provisions, absorbed most of the public and media attention. Like the county prosecutors, the senator made no statements to the press on behalf of the misdemeanor bill. Perhaps both the prosecutors and the senator were afraid of or at least uncertain of possible public reaction. However, the senator did have considerable commentary regarding the suspension bill and its ultimate veto. (See footnote 5.)

One possible interpretation of these events is that the senator intentionally introduced the suspension bill immediately prior to the misdemeanor bill in an attempt to distract the public and the media. Indeed, several respondents mentioned that the senator typically supports both extremes on an issue in an effort to protect himself from criticism. Another (not mutually exclusive) possibility is that those in the mass media felt that the bill was reasonable and they did not wish to arouse public indignation. Cooperation between the media and political officials is not uncommon, as Ross and Staines (1972) have concluded.

While the full impact of this legislation is not possible to assess so soon after its passage, some subsequent developments relevant to the legal change are apparent. In Omaha, which accounts for almost fifty percent of all drug offenses in Nebraska (Nebraska State Patrol, 1970:14), a city ordinance allowed cases involving possession of marijuana to be prosecuted in city courts as misdemeanors or, alternatively, under state law as felonies. Under the new state law county attorneys now have no option and must handle possession of marijuana as a misdemeanor. In Lincoln, where nearly one-fourth of all state narcotics cases are processed (Nebraska State Patrol, 1970:14), the prosecutor claimed that all marijuana possession cases are now prosecuted as such, while under the previous felony law guilty pleas were often accepted to lesser non-narcotic offenses such as peace disturbance.

During the first full year this law was in effect, arrests involving marijuana possession nearly doubled (Nebraska State Patrol, 1970:9). Even though arrests have rapidly escalated, a review of Omaha and Lincoln newspapers since the bill's passage indicates that neither student nor other groups have publicly protested, and there is no public argument that the law is oppressive. A maximum sentence of seven days is apparently acceptable, or at least tolerable. On the other hand, the bill's senate sponsor feels that most law-abiding citizens recognize that the increased arrests vividly demonstrate that the legislation which he introduced was badly needed. The lack of conflict regarding the consequences of the bill offers testimony to the symbolic and instrumental utility of the law. Moral conservatives may indeed feel, as Senator C speculates, that the new law offers more control as evidenced by increased convictions; those more tolerant of marijuana use may well regard the law as an instrumental and certainly a symbolic victory.

REFERENCES

Arnold, Martin (1969) "Varied Drug Laws Raising U.S. Fears," *New York Times* (August 17).

Becker, Howard S. (1963) *Outsiders.* New York: Free Press of Glencoe.

Chambliss, William J. (1964) "A Sociological Analysis of the Law of Vagrancy," 12 *Social Problems* 67.

Clausen, J. A. (1961) "Drug Addiction," in Robert K. Merton and Robert A. Nisbet (eds.) *Contemporary Social Problems.* New York: Harcourt, Brace and World.

DeFrain, John (1967) "Students Clash Over Narcotics," *Lincoln Journal* (November 21).

Dicey, A. V. (1920) *Lectures on the Relation Between Law and Public Opinion in England During the Nineteenth Century.* London: MacMillan.

Dickson, Donald T. (1968) "Bureaucracy and Morality: An Organizational Perspective on a Moral Crusade," 16 *Social Problems* 143.

Dobler, William O. (1968) "In Perspective," *Lincoln Star* (October 9).

Durkheim, Emile (1964) *The Division of Labor in Society.* New York: Free Press of Glencoe.

Edelman, Murray (1964) *The Symbolic Uses of Politics.* Urbana: University of Illinois Press.

Engels, Frederick (1972) *The Origin of the Family, Private Property and the State.* New York: International Publishers.

Friedman, Lawrence M. and Jack Ladinsky (1967) "Social Change and the Law of Industrial Accidents," 67 *Columbia Law Review* 50.

Goode, Erich (1970) *The Marijuana Smokers.* New York: Basic Books, Inc.

——— (1972) *Drugs in American Society.* New York: Alfred A. Knopf.

Gusfield, J. R. (1963) *Symbolic Crusade: Status Politics and the American Temperance Movement.* Urbana: University of Illinois Press.

——— (1967) "Moral Passage: The Symbolic Process in Public Designations of Deviance," 15 *Social Problems* 175.

Hall, Jerome (1952) *Theft, Law and Society.* Indianapolis: Bobbs-Merrill.

Jeffery, C. R. (1957) "The Development of Crime in Early English Society," 47 *Journal of Criminal Law, Criminology and Police Science* 647.

Laski, Harold J. (1935) *The State in Theory and Practice.* New York: Viking Press.

Lindesmith, Alfred R. (1965) *The Addict and the Law.* Bloomington: Indiana University Press.

National Organization for the Reform of Marijuana Laws (1971) "The Criminal Penalties Under the Current Marijuana Laws," Washington: National Organization for the Reform of Marijuana Laws.

Nebraska State Patrol, Division of Drug Control (1970) *Activity Summary, Drug and Narcotic Cases.* Lincoln: Nebraska State Patrol.

Pound, Roscoe (1922) *An Introduction to the Philosophy of Law.* New Haven: Yale University Press.

——— (1942) *Social Control Through Law.* New Haven: Yale University Press.

Quinney, Richard (1970) *The Social Reality of Crime.* Boston: Little Brown and Company.

Rosenthal, M. P. (1969) "A Plea for Amelioration of the Marijuana Laws," 47 *Texas Law Review* 1359.

Ross, Robert and Graham L. Staines (1972) "The Politics of Social Problems," 20 *Social Problems* 18.

Sutherland, E. H. (1950) "The Diffusion of Sexual Psychopath Laws," 56 *American Journal of Sociology* 142.

Terry, Lee (1969) KETV, Channel 7 News Observation, Omaha (February 27).

Thomas, Fred (1969) "Puffers Find Pot of Gold Under Nebraska Rainbow," *Omaha World Herald* (August 31).

Vold, George B. (1958) *Theoretical Criminology.* New York: Oxford University Press.

Wall, Millan (1968) "Farmers Oppose Declaring Marijuana a Noxious Weed," *Lincoln Star* (February 15).

Warriner, C. K. (1958) "The Nature and Functions of Official Morality," 64 *American Journal of Sociology* 165.

UTAH'S LIBERAL DRUG LAWS: STRUCTURAL FOUNDATIONS AND TRIGGERING EVENTS*

JOHN F. GALLIHER
University of Missouri–Columbia

and

LINDA BASILICK
Veterans Administration Hospital–Columbia, MO
University of Missouri–Columbia

Utah was one of the first states to reduce the penalty for first-offense possession of marihuana, as well as other drugs, to a misdemeanor. Such innovative legislation in Utah was not expected given the Mormon domination of the state legislature and Mormons' strict prohibition of drug use. To shed light on this development, interviews were conducted with a number of Mormon and non-Mormon citizens of Utah, including a variety of state officials. Other sources of information included Mormon Church documents, local newspapers and Utah state records including legislative floor debates. By distinguishing between legislative triggering events and relevant structural conditions it appears that the legislation was triggered by powerful special interest groups but seems to have been supported by many citizens in this unusually homogeneous state as a way of protecting their children. A corollary of the conflict perspective, which is supported by these results, is that consensus on lenient drug penalties is most easily achieved if the drug in question is not associated with a threatening minority.

It is now widely recognized by social scientists that the pharmacological characteristics of drugs do not alone determine the social definitions of the substances (e.g., see Goode, 1972). This awareness of the arbitrary nature of what is defined as a drug may help explain why considerable interest in the origins of drug control laws has recently developed. Knowledge of the political and cultural sources of specific drug laws promises to provide some reflection of the origins of widespread opinion about specific substances. The literature on the origins of drug prohibitions includes the well-known and widely cited work of Becker (1963) on the origins of marihuana legislation. Indeed most of the literature on the social origins of criminal laws deals with drug laws (Lindesmith, 1965; Musto, 1973; Helmer, 1975), and most of these studies of drug laws deal with one substance, marihuana (Dickson, 1968; Bonnie and Whitebread, 1974; Galliher et al., 1974; Reasons, 1974; Galliher and Walker, 1977).

*This research was funded by a grant from the Research Council of the Graduate School, University of Missouri-Columbia. Thanks are due Edward L. Kimball, Howard S. Becker, Allynn Walker and James L. McCartny for their help with several phases of this research.

Most states have revised their marihuana control laws within the past decade, reducing the penalty for first-offense possession from a felony to a misdemeanor. One of the first states to make such a change in its laws was Nebraska (Galliher *et al.,* 1974) where the bill to reduce penalties for marihuana possession was designed in part to insure more certain punishment of violators. Prior to reduction of the penalties, the bill's sponsor felt law enforcement agencies declined to proceed against violators due to the magnitude of the penalty. Indeed after the bill's passage, marihuana arrests increased greatly. Utah was also a leader becoming, on March 12, 1969, the third state to pass such legislation.

If a leadership role in such legislation was unexpected for Nebraska, it surely was for Utah. Utah is a contemporary Mormon equivalent of historical theocracies. Erikson (1966) claims that in another theocracy, the Massachusetts Bay colony, crisis periods arose from time to time when citizens lacked a clear notion of the group's collective self-identity. By punishing specific behavior, colonists asserted that as a part of their collective self-definition, they would not tolerate certain actions. In the case of Utah, much of the collective self-identity comes from a Mormon prohibition against not only tobacco and alcohol, but tea and coffee as well. The last two prohibitions obviously separate Mormons (Latter-day Saints) from most other Christians. Joseph Smith (*Doctrines and Covenants,* 1974:154–155), the LDS Church's founder, advocated these prohibitions as a means to protect the human body, and according to O'Dea (1957), the Church expends considerable effort to demonstrate the harmful effects of these substances. Surely in Utah, tolerance of marihuana would not be expected.

The Church opposition to drugs has been emphasized by Church President Spencer W. Kimball (1969) as well as numerous other Church leaders. As might be expected, the Mormon clergy's attitudes toward drug laws are much more restrictive than clergy from other religious groups. In a survey of Catholic, Protestant and Mormon clergy, Jolley (1972) found that a higher percentage of Mormons felt possession of such drugs as marihuana, amphetamines, LSD and heroin, should be punished as a felony. Non-Mormon clergy were more likely to choose either legalization or misdemeanor penalties.

The term *deseret* is widely used by Mormons as are the bee and beehive symbols, and all three are used to denote industry, hard work and perseverance. Mormons emphasize the importance of the family, as they do education, and believe that patriotism is a religious duty (O'Dea, 1957). However, Suchman (1968) found a radically different world view among drug users which he has called the "Hang-loose Ethic." The hang-loose ethic is irreverent toward Christianity and patriotism, legal and educational institutions, marriage, premarital chastity, and the right and competence of parents to make decisions for children—in short, it repudiates the Establishment. Such attitudes surrounding drug use directly contradict Mormon values, making Utah an unlikely place to find leadership in reductions in drug law penalties.

The conservative nature of the Mormon faithful is reflected in the Utah state government. Jonas (1961) reports that the Utah legislature is indeed very conservative and is typically 90–95 percent Mormon (Jonas, 1969) compared with only 70 percent of the population of the state which are Church members. Three-term Utah governor Calvin L. Rampton (1976) contends this Mormon overrepresentation in the state legislature is because Mormons vote for friends who are Church members. Rampton observes that not only are more Mormons elected, but LDS Church officials are especially likely to be elected. So the Utah legislature is not merely controlled by Mormons but by Church officials who would seem even more likely than other members to follow Church teaching.

Becker (1963) claims that prohibitionist drug laws have an essential structural foundation in traditional religious prohibitions against (1) becoming a slave to a drug; (2) loss of self-control; and (3) the experience of ecstasy states. All of these concerns regarding drug use in general, and marihuana in particular, should be found among Mormons in Utah. The research problem then is to explain why Utah's very morally conservative legislature moved so rapidly to reduce marihuana possession penalties. In a state like Utah, as in any theocracy, the linkage between morality and legislation should be relatively easy to trace compared to more morally and politically heterogeneous areas.

Two major theoretical perspectives are found in the studies of the social origins of law. One is the model illustrated in the works of Becker (1963) and Erikson (1966) which emphasizes moral consensus as the foundation of law. The other is the conflict perspective emphasizing the domination of one class by another using law as the vehicle for coercion (Chambliss, 1974; Musto, 1973; Helmer, 1975). For example, Musto demonstrates that prohibitionist drug laws are always aimed at controlling some threatening minority groups such as blacks, Asians, or Roman Catholics: "The most passionate support for legal prohibition of narcotics has been associated with fear of a given drug's effect on a specific minority" (1973:244). Helmer (1975) has also demonstrated that class conflict and the control of economic and racial minorities provide the basis for drug control legislation. But in fact there are few minorities of any kind in Utah. The 1970 census (U.S. Bureau of the Census) shows few blacks (6,617 or .06%) or Native Americans (11,273 or 1%), and Jonas (1969) cites evidence of only 46,766 Roman Catholics or approximately 4 percent. Therefore, the conflict model does not appear to be a likely aid in understanding Utah's marihuana laws both because of the homogeneous nature of this state and because the legal change seems to represent a reform rather than class conflict, denomination or repression.

These two theoretical positions are the focus of a continuing controversy among researchers. Conflict theorists are sometimes criticized for overemphasizing the role of powerful interest groups and coercion in the passage of criminal laws (Hagan and Leon, 1977). Those adopting a consensus perspective have been faulted for ignoring how powerful individuals and groups use criminal law to further their own interests though the oppression of others (Chambliss, 1974).

The tone of this debate clearly demonstrates that those on both sides of the issue feel their position alone is credible. Research on the origins of drug laws seldom reaches any agreement on the origins of the law, its meaning and significance (Galliher and Walker, 1977). However, it may be that part of this theoretical and substantive discussion is a result of overly simplified arguments. Apparently much of this confusion is a consequence of failure to distinguish between the structural foundations of criminal laws, such as traditional racial conflicts and racial composition of a society, as opposed to events triggering the passage of a specific law, such as the timely sponsorship of a bill by a powerful government official (Galliher and Walker, 1978; Balbus, 1977). Analysis of relevant structural characteristics of a society may require consideration of a relatively broad historical span, while triggering events typically consume a briefer period. For example, Becker (1963) emphasizes the lobbying efforts of Harry Anslinger, the Federal Bureau of Narcotics head, just prior to the passage of the Marihuana Tax Act of 1937; while Musto (1973) addresses a wider historical span in linking American drug prohibitions to traditional racial and ethnic antagonisms. Other laws such as delinquency legislation appear to have structural foundations in class oppression by the affluent, as Platt (1969) demonstrates in drawing on historical detail spanning several decades. Yet Hagan and Leon (1977) show that at the time of passage, such legislation was propelled by the sincere intention of its supporters to help children rather than coerce them. In either the case of drug or delinquency laws, researchers focusing on the structural foundations of legislation reach vastly different conclusions about a law's origins than those researchers studying the tactics and motivations of legislative sponsors. Complete understanding of any legislation, including drug laws, requires consideration of both triggering events and structural foundations.

The original objective was to study the origins of the 1969 misdemeanor marihuana law. Surprisingly, this law also provided misdemeanor penalties for possession of opium and cocaine, but was repealed in 1971. Moreover, in 1967, misdemeanor laws were passed for possession of LSD, barbiturates and amphetamines, which was as unexpected as the 1969 law. Therefore the objective of this research became the study of not just one isolated change in a drug law but the pattern of rapid legal change in Utah drug laws which began in 1969 and continued through 1971. We found, as did Berk *et al.* (1977), that it was not possible to study the origin of a single legal change in isolation from all others.

DATA SOURCES

To determine the origins of the legislation, a variety of existing documents were examined, including state and church records and newspapers, supplemented by interviews with a variety of Utah residents. We reviewed the two daily newspapers in Utah's largest city and state capital, Salt Lake City, where nearly one-half of the state's approximately one million citizens live. The newspapers are the LDS-owned *Deseret News* and the *Salt Lake City Tribune,* owned and managed by Roman Catholic laypersons. The papers were reviewed one year prior to each legal change in 1967, 1969 and 1971 and immediately after each change to determine the origins of, and response to, each law. (The legislature meets only every other year.) The purpose was to assess the political climate, important structural conditions and unique triggering events of each time period and especially to determine the number and type of articles on drugs, to identify important respondents for interviews, and to assess the role of the LDS Church in each legal change. LDS Church reports on drugs were reviewed as were similar official Utah state reports. The records of floor debates and sponsors' explanations of each bill were transcribed from tape recordings which are routinely made of Senate and House proceedings. Drug arrests in Salt Lake City were recorded to help determine the relationship between formal legal change and actual law enforcement. As Lindesmith (1965) has observed, there is often a great difference between a law's wording and its actual enforcement.

Elected officials were interviewed, including the bills' sponsors, legislative committee members who considered the legislation, the governor under whose administration all laws were passed, and the attorney general who was in office during much of this legislation. Law enforcement officials were also interviewed including city and supreme court judges, city and university vice control officers, the state drug enforcement director, and the assistant Salt Lake City prosecutor in charge of narcotics prosecutions. LDS Church officers were also interviewed including Church librarians and archivists, and the well-known historian, Leonard Arrington, who is the official LDS Church historian. Church officials were helpful in offering interpretations of the legal change and in locating Church position papers on drug use and control.

The sampling of knowledgeable officials in the state was both helped and hindered by what most respondents referred to as the "dominant Church" in Utah. Because of the cohesiveness of the LDS, informants always had someone else to recommend for interviews. The obvious weakness of this type of sampling is the bias toward only LDS informants. However, three distinguishable groups were interviewed: (1) non-Mormons, (2) Mormon faithful, and (3) Mormon apostates.[1] The sampling and interviewing were helped in yet another way by the Mormon faithful. These Mormons displayed uniform friendliness and exceptional readiness to cooperate with the interviews. Without minimizing their genuine goodwill, their cooperativeness in some cases seemed enhanced by the LDS commitment to proselytization. Religion in general and the role of the LDS Church in government was of necessity raised in the interviews; once it was, queries were sometimes made about the interviewer's religious preference. After learning that the interviewer was not a Mormon, informants at times began to discuss the good qualities of the LDS Church and to suggest conversion. For example, one key informant offered an invitation to lunch to continue his discussion of the Church and he promised to provide LDS literature and missionaries.

During the interviews, no conflict was found among various respondents' recounting of technical historic detail. Discrepancies did appear, however, in the interpretation of these historical events. Since the impact of the LDS Church on Utah drug laws was a topic of conversation, respondents always came to the point of referring to the LDS Church as "us" or "them." Non-LDS respondents typically provided a quite different analysis of the same legislation than did Church members. Both sets

---

[1]Mormon apostates include self-admitted deviants from Church rules and/or those widely recognized as such by others.

of responses can in turn be compared to explanations for specific legislation found in the Legislative Record. The information collected in the interviews was compared with data from existing records to check accuracy of respondent reports. Without the interviews, the researchers could not have known of all relevant documents. Moore (1974) suggests that secondary data sources, such as congressional committee hearings, provide better political drama than empirical evidence. Moreover, reliance on secondary data, typical of research on the origins of marihuana laws, is inadequate because there is no consensus on the interpretation and meaning of these records (Galliher and Walker, 1977).

We have attempted to avoid a narrow focus on only the attitudes and activity of legislative sponsors as triggering agents and have supplemented this with information on relevant structural characteristics. As Hall (1952:14) observes, information about structural features, such as "existing legal, social, political and economic institutions," is often reflected in the "common and recurring" events found over a relatively broad historical period, while "changes *within a short period of time* suggest the operation of individual, unique influences. . . ." The structural or institutional features of society provide the milieu within which these individual influences develop.

HISTORY OF EVENTS

Statutes

Until 1967, drugs and drug laws were apparently not an important issue for the Utah state legislature. In 1953, legislation was passed prohibiting the sale and possession of a wide variety of drugs and setting a penalty of up to five years. During the next legislative session in 1955, penalties were increased. In 1967, two drug control laws, which contradicted each other, were passed by the Utah state legislature. One law (HB 111) extended existing felony penalties to LSD while another (SB 86) made possession, sale and manufacture of LSD, barbiturates and amphetamines a misdemeanor punishable by a maximum of one year in the local jail.

In 1969, penalties were dramatically increased for most drug offenses. One bill (SB 143) dealt with narcotics including opium and coca products and also with marihuana. First-offense possession of these drugs was defined as a misdemeanor punishable by six months to one year in the local jail or probation. A second conviction for marihuana possession was punishable by six months to five years in prison. A second conviction for possession of the other drugs covered in SB 143 required five to twenty years. The other bill (SB 164) covered depressant, stimulant and hallucinogenic drugs and provided no possibility of parole and 60 days to ten years for first-offense possession.

In 1971 (SB 101) penalties were reduced for all drug offenses. For first-offense possession of any controlled substance, including marihuana, the maximum penalty was reduced from one year to six months in jail. For the second offense, the maximum was reduced from up to twenty years to one year in the county jail. Subsequent convictions were reduced from a maximum of twenty years to a maximum of five years in prison. All these bills passed both houses of the Utah legislature either unanimously or at least by wide margins reflecting the homogeneity of this group. Since

1971, legislative changes have been limited to a few minor technical modifications of the state's drug control statutes.

Background Information on Statutes

1967 Legislation. In 1967 there was a short explanation in the Legislative Record by the Senate sponsor of SB 86 which provided for misdemeanor penalties for possession of LSD, barbiturates and amphetamines. "There are no laws yet to control these drugs and I've read in the February 15th *Deseret News* that a local police lieutenant says drugs are becoming a problem here" (Senate, February 21, 1967). The bill was then passed unanimously. The contradictory bill (HB 111) which extended felony penalties to possession of LSD was explained in the House by its sponsor as a way to provide some legal control of LSD (House of Representatives, February 6, 1967). During 1966–1967, both newspapers appeared to be only minimally concerned with drug abuse (*Tribune*—5 articles, and *Deseret News*—10). The slight concern that existed was focused mainly on LSD. This was a period of initial study and reflection on the issue of drug abuse according to the *Deseret News* reports.

In the index to Publications of the LDS Church, from January 1, 1961 through May 31, 1967, no articles on drugs were recorded. From June 1, 1967 through December 31, 1970, 33 articles are recorded including a major address in October 1969 to the 139th semiannual Church general conference by President David O. McKay (1969) condemning drug use. Finally, from January 1, 1971 through December 31, 1975, 39 articles on drugs appear. These patterns suggest that it was not until mid-1967, after the 1967 drug legislation had been passed, that it suddenly dawned on the Church leadership that a "drug problem" existed which affected the life of the Church.

All respondents agreed that SB 111 which extended legal coverage to LSD was required for the reasons its House sponsor declared, simply that no prior laws existed to control LSD. However, on the issue of SB 86 which stipulated misdemeanor penalties for LSD, amphetamines and barbiturates, the LDS and non-LDS opinions divided. Most LDS respondents mentioned that their Church bends over backwards not to impose its values on others for fear of being criticized as undemocratic. One of the bill's Senate sponsors who identified himself as a member of the LDS Church said: "There is so much feeling that the Mormon Church pushes things down other people's throats that we bend over backwards to be fair and not inflict [sic] our standards on others." Non-Mormons, however, observed that in March of 1967 the people and legislature of Utah merely felt that no drug problem existed in their state and therefore high penalties were not required. The attorney who drafted SB 86 put it this way: "At the time [1967] the Salt Lake City police said that they knew of one addict and a little glue-sniffing. The Utah law was a response to California's and New York's drug problems, not Utah's." Another local attorney said: "The law [SB 86] was simply a first step. The effects of amphetamines and barbiturates were obscure at the time here." And finally, the former governor observed: "That law was designed just to draw people's attention to it—an introductory law." The pattern of drug arrests in Salt Lake City, 1962–1976, also shows few drug problems in 1967. In 1970 and 1971 there was a great increase in arrests and then a leveling off. The most dramatic

TABLE 1
Salt Lake City Drug Arrests, 1962–1976

Year	Total Drug Arrests*	Marihuana Arrests**	Non-Marihuana Drug Arrests
1962	9		
1963	23		
1964	21		
1965	51		
1966	81		
1967	131		
1968	146		
1969	218		
1970	280	110	170
1971	513	110	403
1972	510	315	195
1973	434	334	100
1974	537	393	144
1975	449	346	103
1976	440	261	179

* Annual Reports, Salt Lake City Police Department, Salt Lake City, Utah.
** Drug arrests since 1970 specified as marihuana only.

numerical increase is in 1971. Marihuana arrests reflect the greatest increase in 1972 while non-marihuana arrests show a bulge in only 1971.

1969 Legislation. In 1969, SB 164 and SB 143 were introduced which dramatically increased penalties for most drug offenses except first-offense possession of opium, cocaine and marihuana. The argument of the bill's sponsor was that high minimum penalties were generally required because the courts had misused their "broad discretion" (Senate, SB 143, February 24, 1969). Originally these bills contained felony penalties for first-offense possession of all drugs, but SB 143 was amended. First-offense possession penalties for the drugs covered in SB 143, opium, cocaine and marihuana, were amended and reduced to a misdemeanor, but felony penalties were retained in SB 164 covering depressant, stimulant and hallucinogenic drugs.

The pattern of drug arrests shows large increases from 1967 to 1969. It is understandable that concern about drugs was growing at this time in the state legislature, local newspapers and LDS Church publications. In 1968–1969, more articles appeared on drugs (*Tribune*—18, *Deseret News*—74) and both newspapers noted the high social class and youth of many users and the dramatic increase in overall drug use. However, almost half of the *Deseret News* drug-related articles focused on a battle the newspaper had waged against a liquor-by-the-drink referendum. Both the *Salt Lake City Tribune* and later the *Deseret News* voiced editorial opposition to the original blanket minimum penalties for first-offense drug possession, the *Tribune* doing so by quoting a prominent local psychiatrist, a juvenile court judge and a Salt Lake City attorney (Halliday, 1969). The head of the local state university's Department of Psychiatry was quoted:

This could be destructive, crippling many lives. Treating users as felons and confining them in prison would cause a great deal more harm than the good to be obtained from any deterrent effect of the measures.

The Head of the Committee on Dangerous Drugs and Narcotics of the Utah Bar Association (Halliday, 1969) said: "We would run the risk of classifying vast numbers of our children as felons, with the extremely serious consequences that brand carries." He noted that a felony conviction would mean loss of civil rights, the right to vote, rights of admission to many colleges, to government employment and employment in many private concerns. The attorney continued, "The requirement for mandatory minimum prison terms displays a lack of confidence in the courts and in the appropriate use of discretionary power by the judges." A local juvenile court judge (Halliday, 1969) said, "The courts involved should be given discretion to handle each case according to its degree of seriousness and rehabilitation potential. . . ." While the *Deseret News* did not attempt to pressure the legislature to change the original legislation as did the *Tribune,* it did give editorial support to the legislation once it was amended and passed:

> When critics objected to the mandatory jail sentence that had been provided by the drug control bills before the Utah legislature, they performed a useful service.
>
> California tried mandatory sentences only to find that court convictions and penalties fell off, even though drug abuses were increasing. Evidently, judges and juries hesitated to send youthful first offenders to prison where they could be brutalized by experienced criminals and induced to make crime a way of life.
>
> As a result, the Utah bills were modified to give the courts more discretion in sentencing so that drug users could be rehabilitated rather than hardened (1969, March 10:12A).

No complaint was made in either newspaper about reduced penalties for opium or excessive penalties for barbiturates and amphetamines.

The reasoning behind the 1969 misdemeanor provision for marihuana, opium and cocaine also elicited diverse opinion from LDS members and non-Mormons in the interviews. Non-Mormons had the following observations about the origins of the 1969 drug legislation. The assistant county attorney explained the lack of public reaction to the misdemeanor provisions: "The legislature masked this change with massive increases in other penalties." The *Tribune* newsman who wrote an article critical of the original high penalties for possession of drugs observed that:

> As a liberal I'm glad that I feel my story stopped the bill in its tracks. The author of the bill came to me and asked "what will you settle for?" I was concerned with the high mandatory penalty for marihuana possession.

An attorney who lobbied in the Utah Senate for reduction in penalties for drug possession explained the lack of opposition:

There was no Church commitment to the law as originally drafted. Also the Utah Bar Association had a committee in charge of studying drug laws at the time and they had not been consulted about the bill. The Bar committee chairman was offended and also lobbied for the reduction on marihuana. Marihuana was the symbol of our concern. It was our major concern because that was the drug for which amateurs were being arrested. If the Senate hadn't originally passed such an outrageous marihuana penalty the misdemeanor law might not have passed so soon. We merely asked the senators if they really wanted to sentence people who are really not criminals—kids and so on. "These are your kids after all," we told them.

However, we also asked the Senate to reduce the other penalties [in SB 143] for heroin and cocaine. We were surprised that the Senate would reduce these penalties. We didn't feel that barbiturates and amphetamines [in SB 164] were a problem of excessive penalties since police and courts were more severe for marihuana and heroin. That is, the laws against amphetamines and barbiturates are not severely enforced because they are not associated with any counter-culture.

Another attorney involved in the lobbying effort said:

We sat down with the legislators and said that this would only put kids in the state prison at a youthful age and hurt them. We also pointed out that the courts would be reluctant to convict in marihuana possession cases since the marihuana problem was hitting middle-class families and Mormon youth. For example, I was a federal magistrate judge at the time when a prominent Utah banker's son was arrested for possession of large quantities of marihuana.

Other explanations came from Mormon respondents in several occupational roles—state representative, vice squad captain, Senate committee member and the bills' co-sponsor. All emphasized that the LDS Church attempted not to force its values on others but also echoed the enforcement problems. For example, a vice squad captain explained: "The Church doesn't force through laws to prove that we are not bigots . . . Also we want realistic laws, juries won't enforce strong marihuana laws." And, the 1969 bills' LDS Senate co-sponsor claimed that with felony marihuana penalties: "We would be punishing kids, and anyway, judges wouldn't enforce it." In all, three themes are reflected in these interviews: (1) LDS claims of tolerance of other groups' behavior; (2) concern for the young, especially LDS young people; and (3) the unwillingness of the courts to enforce punitive drug possession laws.

1971 Legislation. On April 4, 1969, approximately two weeks after the 1969 drug law passed and the state legislature adjourned, the Utah governor appointed a Citizen Advisory Committee on Drugs. The main purpose of the Committee was to study Utah's drug problem and make recommendations for the control of drugs. According to the former governor who appointed the committee:

There was at the time [1969] a growing concern with drugs in Utah among the citizens and their elected representatives and the 1969 drug legislation reflected this concern. The committee's task was to determine to what extent these concerns were justified.

The committee distributed a statewide anonymous questionnaire to high school and college students and also held hearings on the drug abuse problem in Utah and issued its report in September 1969. Some of the study's conclusions were:

> If marihuana is included in a survey, then it can be said that no junior or senior high school in Salt Lake City has not had drugs. The age is lowering when arrests can be made in the sixth grade (Governor's Citizens Advisory Committee, 1969:9).

> There has been a 300 percent increase in the past two years in drug abuse admissions at the State Hospital (Governor's Committee, 1969:16).

> Economic status is no deterrent to obtaining drugs and youngsters of all economic levels are involved (Governor's Committee, 1969:18).

> High school students in Utah report that 33.7 percent of them can obtain drugs quite readily, while 31.6 percent *think* [emphasis added] they can do the same thing (Governor's Committee, 1969:21).

Based on testimony from the Salt Lake City Chief of Police, the Committee concluded that the mandatory minimum sentences in the 1969 drug laws resulted in judges throwing out cases in some instances (Governor's Committee, 1969:27). The Committee recommended that discretion be returned to the courts by dropping mandatory minimum sentences so consideration could be given to "the nature and seriousness of the offense, the prior record of the offender and other relevant circumstances" (Governor's Committee, 1969:30–31). The Committee also specifically recommended lowering the penalty for possession of marihuana (Governor's Committee, 1969:32).

After the 1969 legislature adjourned, the Utah Bar appointed a committee composed of judges, prosecutors and defense attorneys to make recommendations for the revision of Utah's criminal code. Immediately after the Advisory Committee Report on Drug Abuse was published in September 1969, the governor asked the Bar committee as its first order of business to make recommendations for the revision of Utah's drug control statutes. The Bar committee proposed the 1971 legislation (SB 101) and the Committee representative defended the legislation before the Utah legislature as follows (Senate, March 1, 1971):

> It was the feeling that there are a lot of people and young people [sic] who are experimenting and it didn't make a lot of sense to throw 18 and 19 year old kids who are merely experimenting in prison for terms where they may come out hardened criminals.

The 1971 bill (SB 101) dropping the mandatory minimum penalties for all drug offenses was justified by its Senate sponsor as necessary because judges refused to cooperate with the old law. He observed: "This bill gives the judges the permission to exercise some discretion in the case of young people and people who are first offenders" (SB 101, Senate March 1, 1971). During the floor debate, it was also mentioned that the Salt Lake County Prosecuting Attorney supported the bill.

In 1970–1971 there was a slight increase from 1968–1969 in *Tribune* drug-related articles (23) and a decrease in the *Deseret News* (26). Again the evidence of a drug epidemic among the young was presented. The theme of the affluence of drug users continued. Neither newspaper had as yet developed a clear editorial policy for dealing with drug abuse.

Unlike the interviews regarding the reasons for earlier drug legislation, now there appears nearly complete consensus regarding the reasons for the 1971 drug law. While the theme of LDS tolerance continues, the common interpretation of the 1971 drug legislation was that the 1969 law had to be scrapped because it was not enforceable due to its overly high penalties which could not and should not be levied against youthful offenders. The attorney who represented the Utah bar on behalf of the proposed 1971 legislation observed:

> With lesser penalties available defendants will plead guilty and get probation. So with lower penalties you get more convictions by [guilty] pleas and more supervision. The 1969 legislature was taking our high school kids and putting them with men who were rapists and big drug dealers. These criminals were treated the same as our sons and daughters.

The assistant county attorney put it this way:

> The [1971] law was passed very quietly with judges, prosecutors and defense attorneys behind it. Practitioners dealing with the law know better than to believe that high penalties increase crime control—they simply find the defendant not guilty.

A vice squad captain complained that: "Even if we had a case that was a lead-pipe cinch, we couldn't get a jury conviction." In fact, the former governor observed:

> The [1969] drug study showed widespread drug use in Utah—more than people thought—in all school ages. But marihuana is not worse than alcohol so a jury would not convict what they saw as misguided kids.

A former city narcotics officer claimed: "After the 1969 law passed, enforcing the law became easier because with the high penalties we didn't bother with users and only went after dealers." In other words, the law worked well only because the police made fewer arrests by ignoring possession cases. As indicated earlier, marihuana arrests do show the greatest increase in 1972 while non-marihuana arrests show a considerable bulge in 1971, the year the 1969 laws were repealed. So the high minimum penalties of the 1969 laws may have discouraged drug arrests as the police officer suggested. As might be expected given the high number of drug arrests, LDS concern continues to be reflected in a large number of Church publications on drugs during the early 1970's.

CONCLUSION

Jonas claims that the influence of the Mormon Church on Utah politics is systematically exaggerated by a variety of observers:

> Both Mormon and anti-Mormon leaders would prefer to have it popularly understood that the Church has a great deal of control. It is useful propaganda for both sides. Mormon leaders do not want publicized that they do not have the control their predecessors had . . . The anti-Mormons want to use the alleged power of the Church in politics to turn persons, both Mormons and non-Mormons, against the institution in order to minimize the influence which it can or does exert in Utah politics (1969:373).

Since the LDS Church influence is typically overestimated, it seems unlikely that our findings of limited Church activity on these drug laws are a consequence of research error or oversight.

All available evidence (including the Legislative Record, newspapers, LDS publications, interviews, and arrest patterns) suggests that no drug crisis existed in Utah in 1967, which allowed relatively lenient drug legislation to pass without congressional or citizen opposition. The LDS publications, including the *Deseret News,* indicate that in early 1967 the Church was not yet aware of any major drug problem influencing the Church, and interviews indicate this was also true of the Utah state legislature. Berk *et al.* (1977:40) report a narcotics crisis in California as early as 1961. The long lag in drug use in Utah is not unlike other "national, political and economic trends [that] seem to reach and enter Utah later than other states" (Jonas, 1969:373). It may also be that some legislators and citizens did not realize misdemeanor penalties were being passed because a contradictory felony law was also passed during the same session.

However, the argument that Mormons bend over backwards not to impose their values is not supported by the documents available concerning the 1969 laws. The 1969 drug bill, SB 164, which was the companion to the legislation covering marihuana possession (SB 143) increased to high levels the total penalty structure. Though LDS informants' beliefs in their tolerance may be genuine, it seems understandably exaggerated by them. Also, in 1969, the state suffered through a tough fight by the LDS Church against liquor-by-the-drink which was waged in part by the Church owned-and-operated *Deseret News.* A wide variety of issues are seen by the Church leadership as moral problems requiring Church intervention into government affairs ranging from Sunday closing laws, abortion (Kimball, 1977), and the ERA (Wohl, 1977). This being true, how can one explain the easy passage of this 1969 bill and lack of Church opposition and even support in the *Deseret News* for the marihuana misdemeanor provision? One obvious explanation is that, except for a few provisions, this was a very restrictive bill. Moral conservatives could rejoice in this legislation which escalated penalties for many other drug offenses. Also the *Deseret News* editorial indicates that a primary reason for Church support for elimination of high mandatory marihuana penalties was that this would increase the probability of conviction. However the same *Deseret News* editorial supported judicial discretion in sentencing due to a concern for protecting "youthful first offenders" from "experienced criminals" so the former can be "rehabilitated rather than hardened." These themes of punishment and protection of offenders dominated legislative considerations as well.

The historical record suggests that the governor and the legal community did not wait for evidence that the 1969 legislation was not effective before working against it. Immediately after the 1969 legislature was adjourned, the Governor appointed a committee to investigate the drug problem in Utah and make legislative recommendations, and the Utah Bar Association at his urging did the same. The Governor's Committee Report found drug use widespread among Utah youth rather than limited to a small deviant minority and recommended repeal of the 1969 laws. Evidence of the Utah Bar Association's antagonism to the 1969 laws was found in legislative records, in newspaper quotes from a Utah Bar Association officer, and in interviews. Since the 1969 legislation was explicitly designed to strip certain attorneys—judges and prosecutors—of their traditional professional discretion, this undoubtedly helped solidify Bar opposition. The argument of the legal profession was that higher penalties reduced the probability of punishment; and indeed after the law was passed in early 1971 reducing drug penalties, the number of drug arrests nearly doubled. As in Nebraska (Galliher *et al.,* 1974) it appears that the police in Utah were more willing to make arrests once the penalties were reduced and the perceived likelihood of prosecution and conviction increased.

As was true of the 1969 laws, the bill in 1971 was passed by the Utah legislature both to punish and protect drug users. Having already declared its opposition to high minimum penalties in drug laws in 1969, the Church's publications now stated no position. The themes of punishment and protection appear again in Nebraska (Galliher *et al.,* 1974) where a powerful conservative state legislator sponsored a radical decrease in the marihuana possession penalty for the stated purpose of increasing the percentage of convictions in such cases, but also incidentally to *protect* a prosecutor's son who had been arrested. It might be tempting for some observers to claim that legislators and others in Utah and Nebraska conceal their true motivations in an effort to pacify observers of diverse persuasions. Rather than looking for hidden motivations, it is probably safest to take respondent explanations at face value. These respondents indeed appear to want both punishment and protection of drug users. They want punishment, but only that punishment they see as appropriate for these youthful and often affluent law violators—not long prison sentences.

The Church could still have easily justified a strong stand against easing the penalties for possession of marihuana and other drugs. The Church's inactivity can be understood by the absence of any threatening group linked to drug use in Utah. If tough drug laws were to be passed and enforced, they would be used not against some threatening racial or ethnic minority, since few minorities live in Utah, nor against a specific economic class, but against all "our kids." This theme was repeated in many interviews and recorded testimony in the House and Senate, in the report of the Citizen Advisory Committee on Drugs, and in news stories. Mormons should be inclined to reduce penalties for drug offenses which would be imposed on their young because of the unusual emphasis and value they place on children (O'Dea, 1957). Moreover, since the anti-war movement and student revolt never flourished in Utah, the symbolic association of marihuana-smoking with counter-culture life styles mentioned by Suchman (1968) was never given a full opportunity to develop in Utah—no symbolic minority was created. As a vice squad captain said: "We never had an anti-war movement or student revolt. The professors and kids at the University of Utah and Brigham Young University are very conservative."

Although the moral net of prohibition that the LDS Church throws over the state of Utah is very broad, it did not extend to the drug laws of the late 1960's and early 1970's which reduced many penalty provisions. The 1967 legislation apparently was not seen as relevant for the Church, while opposition to the 1969 and 1971 reductions would have compelled the Church to attack its own children—something unthinkable for them. The high minimum penalties can make it more difficult for criminal justice officials to use their discretion, as Cicourel (1968) has demonstrated they usually do on behalf of youths from dominant social groups. In the case of the Nebraska legislation (Galliher *et al.,* 1974) the bill was triggered by the arrest of a prosecutor's son and indeed was made retroactive to the date of the arrest. These studies also jointly suggest that the recent widespread reduction in marihuana penalties is a corollary of the conflict perspective's claims regarding the use of drug laws for minority oppression. The conclusion is that consensus on lenient drug penalties is most easily achieved if the drug in question is not associated with a threatening minority. And while the legislative process in Nebraska was speeded by its unicameral legislature, the swiftness of Utah's legislative response seems facilitated by the homogeneous character of its legislature.

The triggering events for the laws passed in 1969 and 1971 reflect the influence of powerful interest groups. In 1969 some punitive legislation was attacked and ultimately modified due to the editorial position of the *Salt Lake City Tribune.* The 1971 legislation was to a great extent a product of the efforts of the Utah Bar Association and the Citizen Advisory Committee on Drugs which was composed of prominent Utah citizens. While the triggering events reflect the power of specific groups there is abundant evidence from existing records and interviews with a variety of Utah citizens that there was wide support for such changes to protect "our kids." The usual attempt to stigmatize and isolate marihuana and other drug users, which Goode (1972) notes, did not occur in Utah probably because of the conventional character of local young people. The homogeneity of opinion is, of course, a consequence of homogeneity in the state's demographic characteristics. While much of our data concerns triggering events, we also included information on structural characteristics. Evidence of the latter is reflected in Utah's demographic profile as well as historical detail not narrowly limited to events immediately preceding introduction and passage of each drug bill. The use of demographic information and historical detail such as the Mormon campaign against liquor-by-the-drink and the recurrent leniency found in Utah drug laws has helped sensitize us to the meaning and significance of specific triggering events. The previous lack of conceptual distinction between triggering events and structural foundations, together with the consequent theoretical imprecision, has until now made the legal change found in Utah and Nebraska difficult to anticipate or interpret.

REFERENCES

Annual Report: Salt Lake City Police Department
  1962–   Salt Lake City, Utah
  1976

Balbus, Isaac D.
  1977   "Commodity form and legal form: An essay on the 'relative autonomy' of the law."
          Law and Society Review 11:571–588.

Becker, Howard S.
  1963   *Outsiders.* London: The Free Press of Glencoe, Collier-Macmillan Ltd.

Berk, Richard A., Harold Brackman and Selma Lesser
  1977   *A Measure of Justice: An Empirical Study of Changes in the California Penal
          Code, 1955–1971.* New York: Academic Press.

Bonnie, Richard J. and Charles H. Whitebread II
  1974   *The Marihuana Conviction: A History of Marihuana Prohibition in the United
          States.* Charlottesville: University Press of Virginia.

Chambliss, William J.
  1974   "Functional and conflict theories of crime." New York: MSS Modular Publica-
          tions, Module 17.

Cicourel, Aaron V.
  1968   *The Social Organization of Juvenile Justice.* New York: Wiley.

Deseret News
  March 1, 1966–March 31, 1967
  March 1, 1968–March 31, 1969
  March 1, 1970–March 31, 1971

Deseret News (editorial)
  1969   "Don't kill drug bills with false charges." March 10:12A.

Dickson, Donald T.
  1968   "Bureaucracy and morality: An organizational perspective on a moral crusade."
          Social Problems 16:143–156.

Doctrine and Covenants
  1974   Salt Lake City, Utah: The Church of Jesus Christ of Latter-day Saints.

Erikson, Kai T.
  1966   *Wayward Puritans: A Study in the Sociology of Deviance.* New York: Wiley.

Galliher, John F., James L. McCartney and Barbara Baum
  1974   "Nebraska's marijuana law: A case of unexpected legislative innovation." *Law and
          Society Review* 8:441–455.

Galliher, John F. and Allynn Walker
  1977   "The puzzle of the social origins of the marihuana tax act of 1937." *Social Prob-
          lems* 24:367–376.
  1978   "The politics of systematic research error: The case of the Federal Bureau of Nar-
          cotics as a moral entrepreneur." *Crime and Social Justice* 10:29–33.

Goode, Erich
  1972   *Drugs in American Society.* New York: Alfred A. Knopf.

Governor's Citizens Advisory Committee
1969   Report on Drug Abuse. Utah. September.
Hagan, John and Jeffrey Leon
1977   "Rediscovering delinquency: Social history, political ideology and the sociology of law." *American Sociological Review* 42:587–598.
Hall, Jerome
1952   *Theft, Law and Society.* Indianapolis: Bobbs-Merrill.
Halliday, Robert S.
1969   "Expert criticize severity of drug bill's penalties." *Salt Lake City Tribune.* March 2.
Helmer, John
1975   *Drugs and Minority Oppression.* New York: Seabury Press.
Jolley, Jerry Clyde
1972   "Clergy attitudes about drug abuse and drug abuse education: A case study." *The Rocky Mountain Social Science Journal* 9:75–82.
Jonas, Frank H.
1961   "Utah: Crossroads of the west." Pp. 273–302 in F. H. Jonas (ed.), *Western Politics.* Salt Lake City: University of Utah Press.
1969   "Utah: The different state." Pp. 327–379 in F. H. Jonas (ed.), *Politics in the American West.* Salt Lake City: University of Utah Press.
Kimball, Edward L.
1977   Letter in possession of authors, March 29.
Kimball, Spencer W.
1969   *The Miracle of Forgiveness.* Salt Lake City: Bookcraft.
Latter-day Saints Church Index to Publications
January 1, 1960–December 31, 1975.
Lindesmith, Alfred R.
1965   *The Addict and the Law.* Bloomington: Indiana University Press.
McKay, David O.
1969   "Address to the 139th semi-annual Church conference." *Improvement Era* 72: 29–31.
Moore, William Howard
1974   *The Kefauver Committee and the Politics of Crime 1950–1952.* Columbia: University of Missouri Press.
Musto, David F., M.D.
1973   *The American Disease: Origins of Narcotic Control.* New Haven: Yale University Press.
O'Dea, Thomas F.
1957   *The Mormons.* Chicago: University of Chicago Press.
Platt, Anthony M.
1969   *The Child Savers: The Invention of Delinquency.* Chicago: University of Chicago Press.
Rampton, Calvin L.
1976   "Suggested remarks to Interstate Business and Professional Association." Los Angeles, California, December 13.

Reasons, Charles E.

1974   *The Criminologist: Crime and the Criminal.* Pacific Palisades, California: Goodyear.

Salt Lake City Tribune

March 1, 1966–March 31, 1967

March 1, 1968–March 31, 1969

March 1, 1970–March 31, 1971

Suchman, Edward A.

1968   "The 'hang-loose' ethic and the spirit of drug use." *Journal of Health and Social Behavior* 9:146–155.

U.S. Bureau of the Census

1970   Census of Population. General Population Characteristics. Final Report PC(1)-B46 Utah. Washington, D.C.: U.S. Government Printing Office.

Utah House of Representatives

1967   Hearings, HB 111, February 6.

Utah Senate

1967   Hearings, SB 86, February 21.

1969   Hearings, SB 143, February 24.

1971   Hearings, SB 101, March 1.

Wohl, Lisa Cronin

1977   "A Mormon connection?: The defeat of the ERA in Nevada." Ms. 68–70, 80, 83–85.

SYMBOLIC SEVERITY IN THE LAND OF EASY VIRTUE: NEVADA'S HIGH MARIHUANA PENALTY*

JOHN F. GALLIHER
University of Missouri, Columbia

and

JOHN RAY CROSS
Minot State College

Nevada is the only state where first-offense possession of the slightest amount of marihuana is a felony, punishable by up to six years imprisonment; ironically the state permits casino gambling and prostitution. News reports, government records, and interviews with public officials show that in Nevada marihuana and other drug use is continually, but incorrectly, blamed on tourists, and high penalties are thought necessary to control these outsiders. While it is recognized that the high penalties are seldom enforced, respondents said that their existence gives the state a more respectable image.

Since 1968, the penalty for first-offense possession of marihuana has been reduced to a misdemeanor in every state except Nevada, where first-offense possession of even the smallest amount of marihuana remains a felony, punishable by up to six years in prison. Assistance in understanding Nevada's high marihuana penalty can be found in Gusfield's (1963; 1967) study of the passage of national prohibition of alcohol. The United States' total prohibition of alcohol is similar to Nevada's high penalty for marihuana possession. Gusfield indicates that such prohibitionist legislation contains both instrumental and symbolic properties. The instrumental role of law involves its actual enforcement effects. Symbolic aspects of law require only promulgation or public announcement.

Evidence that symbolic properties are paramount is reflected in widespread violation of a law while little effort is directed toward enforcement. Gusfield found evidence of this symbolic role of law in the national prohibition of alcohol. To some extent, the mere existence of the law satisfied the middle classes, for it expressed their status frustrations. Gusfield assumes that (1) those who are pacified most by symbolic legislation are those who promulgate such laws; and (2) symbolic legislation has no instrumental uses and serves solely an expressive role.

Both of the preceding assumptions, however, seem open to question in Edelman's (1964) analysis of anti-trust legislation. He claims these laws were passed with the active support of corporation leaders to reassure a second group, an angry public,

*The authors thank James McCartney, Edward Hunvald, and James Galliher for their help. Correspondence to: Department of Sociology, University of Missouri, Columbia, MO. 65211.

that past abuses by business were no longer possible, even though the laws were seldom enforced. Here the symbolism served the instrumental purpose of allowing business leaders to retain the considerable freedom they had traditionally enjoyed. This suggests that unenforced laws do not necessarily demonstrate a purely symbolic role for legislation; rather, lack of law enforcement may be instrumental as well. While Gusfield's analysis of symbolic legislation sensitizes one to self-delusion, Edelman's treatment prepares the observer for calculated manipulation and deceit.

One contemporary and extreme example of legal prohibition is found in Nevada where casino gambling, relatively rapid marriages and divorces, and prostitution are legal, but where the penalty for possession of marihuana is the highest in the United States. The primary objective of this research is to explain this contradiction and explore the degree to which it is resolved through consideration of the instrumental and symbolic properties of laws.

DATA COLLECTION

Interviews were conducted during July, 1978, in Reno, Las Vegas, and Carson City with past and present members of the Nevada Assembly (lower house) and Senate, past and present civil servants, police officials, judges, prosecutors, defense attorneys, and news writers. Another source of information was the legislative record, including hearings and floor debates. Newspapers in Carson City (the state capital), Reno, and Las Vegas also were reviewed for articles concerning alcohol, drugs, divorce, marriage, prostitution, gambling, and the Nevada economy. All copies of daily papers in Carson City, Reno, and Las Vegas were read for the following time periods: April, 1930, through March, 1931; December, 1967, through November, 1968; and April, 1970 through March, 1971. These are periods immediately preceding the major legislative events under scrutiny. In 1931, Nevada legalized gambling and also established a short waiting period for divorce. In 1968, a state-wide lottery proposal failed, and in 1971, prostitution was prohibited under state law in Las Vegas alone. The 1967–1971 period was selected because during this time most states reduced their first-offense marihuana possession penalties to misdemeanor levels.

NEVADA'S MORALS LEGISLATION

Gambling, Divorce, and Prostitution Laws

To understand the patterns of lawmaking in Nevada, one must realize that the state's problems of survival were magnified during the 1930's when mining, its basic industry, was declining because of the decreasing price of silver, placing the local economy in great distress. In response to economic pressures, in 1931 the Nevada legislature lowered the waiting period for divorce from three months to six weeks (*Las Vegas Evening Review,* 1931; Nevada State Statutes, 1931b) and legalized casino gambling (*Las Vegas Evening Review,* 1930; Nevada State Statutes, 1931a). However, Nevada prohibited lotteries because they represented a possible source of competition to casino gambling (*Reno Evening Gazette,* 1968). Also, dog racing was legalized recently, but only in counties with less than 100,000 population (Nevada

State Statutes, 1977). Respondents explained that this precludes direct competition with the Reno and Las Vegas casino industries. News stories (*Las Vegas Review Journal,* 1970d; 1970e) and interviews also characterized prostitution as acceptable because of its capacity to generate revenue. Prostitution is prohibited by state law only in Las Vegas (Nevada State Statutes, 1971) to protect the casino industry both from a bad reputation and from competition for tourists' money (Skolnick, 1978). Local ordinances prohibit prostitution in several other areas of the state where casino gambling is concentrated, including Reno and Carson City.

Seriousness of the Nevada Drug Problem

In 1968, a Las Vegas newspaper lamented the fact that marihuana use by young people was rising rapidly (*Las Vegas Review Journal,* 1968h). While in 1965 there were only 40 known addicts in Nevada (*Las Vegas Review Journal,* 1968b), later in the decade the number of narcotics cases in Reno increased more than 300 percent in one year (*Las Vegas Review Journal,* 1968a). In Las Vegas, the district attorney "called for an end to school as 'sanctuaries for crime' saying that hall monitors are being organized in local schools to protect students . . . from other students" (*Las Vegas Review Journal,* 1970b). The Carson City Parent Teachers Association started a drug prevention program that included kindergarten children (*Carson City Nevada Appeal,* 1968), and a candidate for sheriff claimed that drugs were being sold to third graders (*Carson City Nevada Appeal,* 1970). Frequent news reports of massive drug raids in the state involving large numbers of suspects and massive amounts of illegal drugs appeared in Nevada's newspapers.

In 1970, 46 Las Vegas residents died from drug-related causes, according to the coroner (*Las Vegas Review Journal,* 1970k). During the same year, two Las Vegas physicians and three pharmacists were charged in two separate drug cases (*Las Vegas Review Journal,* 1970a; 1970j). In Las Vegas, 34 percent of senior high and 18 percent of junior high students used some type of narcotics (*Las Vegas Review Journal,* 1971b). The situation was seen as so severe that Howard Cannon, United States Senator from Nevada, asked the U.S. Bureau of Narcotics and Dangerous Drugs to send agents to assist the Las Vegas school district in fighting drug abuse (*Las Vegas Review Journal,* 1970i).

In 1969, a legislative study of the Nevada drug problem found an epidemic of drug use among middle- and upper-class youths and clung to the belief that future research ultimately would prove the addictive qualities of marihuana (Legislative Commission, 1969). Figures indicating increases in drug use, especially by students, are comparable to the results of a 1969 legislative study in Utah, yet there we do not find the intense concern that existed in Nevada (Galliher and Basilick, 1979).

During this period of intense concern with drugs a candidate for sheriff in Las Vegas was arrested on two occasions for marihuana possession. In 1970, a candidate for the state legislature was arrested for marihuana possession (*Las Vegas Review Journal,* 1970f; 1970h; *Reno Evening Gazette,* 1970b). In the same year, the sons of two Nevada state legislators were arrested and one convicted for possession of drugs including marihuana (*Reno Evening Gazette,* 1970a; 1970d).

Source of the Drug Problem

The 1969 Nevada legislative study determined that outsiders ultimately were responsible for the drug problem in the state.

> It appears that drugs are introduced into Clark County from Los Angeles and Mexico, while the Washoe County, Ormsby County, and Douglas County problem stems from the Lake Tahoe, Sacramento and San Francisco areas (Legislative Commission, 1969:6).

In spite of numerous arrests of prominent local residents, Nevadans continued to blame the high crime rate in the state on non-residents, especially Californians. The Carson City district attorney, who was the Republican candidate for attorney general, claimed that most crimes were committed by Californians and others from out of state, while the crime rate among Nevadans was low (*Reno Evening Gazette*, 1970c). The director of the Nevada State Crime Commission agreed that tourism was a substantial cause for the state's high crime rate (*Las Vegas Review Journal*, 1970g). In 1971, it was noted that Nevada's crime rate had jumped 175 percent in one decade, and this was blamed in part on increases in tourism (*Las Vegas Review Journal*, 1971a). However, the newspaper reports of the residential location of those arrested for drug offenses in 1967–1968 and 1970–1971 demonstrate that most were not from California, nor even from out of state. Fifty-nine percent of those arrested in 1967–1968 and 65 percent in 1970–1971 had a Nevada address.

In 1975 a comprehensive research report based on official arrest and conviction records was prepared by the state government to assess the magnitude and nature of crimes committed in the state by non-residents (Department of Adult Parole and Probation, 1974–1975). The study demonstrated, as does our tally of news reports, that non-residents made up a minority of those charged or convicted of crimes, including drug offenses. But the mere fact that such a comprehensive research project even was conducted reflects the concern in Nevada regarding the criminal behavior of non-residents.

Our interviews, the legislative records, and statements in the press, show that Nevadans continued to blame outsiders for their drug problems. Many respondents said that high drug penalties in Nevada were designed to keep out drug traffickers from California:

> California is only 13 miles away. There is the conscious thought that Nevada has stiff drug penalties to give Californians a warning to stay on your side (district attorney).

> We do have a serious problem with California people around the lake [Tahoe] area [which is half in Nevada]. There is no law enforcement around the lake in California and so we have a constant problem with pushers (circuit court judge).

A Las Vegas narcotics officer said: "We don't have local kids using drugs; we mainly are making arrests on transients." The director of legislative research said: "Most drug offenders aren't Nevadans but are Californians, since this is a tourist state and California has so many people, so close."

Law Enforcement Reaction to the Drug Problem

Arrest records from Nevada's two major population centers, Reno and Las Vegas, indicate that between 1972 and 1977 less than eight percent of those arrested in Las Vegas for narcotics offenses were ultimately convicted as charged. While Reno keeps no conviction data, it records the type of drug involved in each narcotics arrest. These indicate that while the total number of drug arrests remained fairly constant during the six-year period from 1972 through 1977, the proportion of marihuana arrests decreased from 75 percent in 1972 to 15 percent in 1977.

Information from the Nevada Department of Parole and Probation indicates that, of 214 persons convicted of possession of marihuana in 1974, only 14 were sentenced to prison (Campos, 1975). In 1978, there were only 13 prison sentences for marihuana possession and these were "special cases" involving other criminal charges (Campos, 1978).

Our respondents mentioned that high drug penalties gave the state a more respectable image than it might have had otherwise, given its notorious reputation for gambling and prostitution.

> We are scared to death that we might look so wide open and permissive to outsiders with our gambling, and all, that the federal government might outlaw everything here. High drug penalties, even though we don't use them, make us look better (district attorney).

> I was once a public defender and what is important here is law and order rhetoric, but most drug possession cases are dropped by the cops and the law is not enforced. (Las Vegas newspaper editor).

> The rest of the nation is always looking at us. Being a gaming state we must keep a high profile. The federal government is always looking into gaming (member of the Assembly).

> Las Vegas has had a bad image and so the penalty has been kept high so our image won't be hurt and business won't be damaged (Las Vegas narcotics officer).

> The state is subject to criticism for open drinking and gambling and so we try to fight the image as a wide open state and so we are tight on drugs. This need for image management in Las Vegas, of course, fits with the conservatism in the state (Reno Circuit Court judge).

The head of the legislative research department stated: "High drug penalties are a relief valve for not being able to deal with other moral issues with force." A member of the Assembly agreed: "There is a collective guilty conscience associated with gaming. The attitude is that, yes, we have gaming but we control it and we have no other sins." High marihuana penalties serve a symbolic or image-management purpose whether or not the law can be enforced effectively.

Proposals for Controlling the Drug Problem

Given the crisis atmosphere as well as the focus of blame on non-residents, one can understand why, in 1967, the speaker of the Nevada Assembly criticized the plans of some state legislators to reduce marihuana penalties: "Change from a felony to a misdemeanor for first-offense possession would lead to more importation of marihuana into Nevada" (*Reno Evening Gazette,* 1967). The Reno district attorney said the legislative proposal appeared to be supporting the belief that marihuana was not as bad as it used to be, and added: "Lessening of the penalty for first-offense possession of 'pot' might have a psychological impact increasing illegal use" (*Reno Evening Gazette,* 1967).

In 1968, the Clark County Democratic Party Committee voted against lowering penalties for marihuana possession (*Las Vegas Review Journal,* 1968c; 1968g) as did an ad hoc, anti-drug citizens group (*Las Vegas Review Journal,* 1968f). In 1970, the Nevada State Narcotics Officers Association opposed reduction of penalties for first-offense marihuana possession (*Las Vegas Review Journal,* 1970c). Some state officials argued for the establishment of a state bureau of narcotics (*Las Vegas Review Journal,* 1968d; 1968e). In 1971, the Nevada Senate passed a bill allowing schools to expel students arrested for drug violations (*Carson City Nevada Appeal,* 1971).

During the 1977 session of the Nevada legislature, the Assembly held extensive hearings on two bills (AB 253 and AB 280) that would have reduced the penalties for possession of marihuana. Neither bill was reported out of committee, but the arguments presented at the hearings show recent thinking on drugs. A number of witnesses argued that the law should be changed because, while it consumed a lot of police time and energy, it still could not be enforced. The president of the Nevada Peace Officers Association testified:

> Judges are not sending people to prison for six years as the present law calls for for smoking a joint of grass. . . . As a consequence, the law, as it stands is being subverted. It's being met with a lot of cynical amusement by the young people today (Assembly Judiciary Committee, 1977:25).

The director of parole and probation complained:

> We have a very, very low percentage of convictions right now. . . . Half of the jurors have experimented with marihuana, they aren't going to convict this guy for a marihuana cigarette if the possible punishment is six years in [the] Nevada State Prison. But if it's a misdemeanor, they might just do it (Assembly Judiciary Committee, 1977:41).

An attorney representing the American Civil Liberties Union agreed with the president of the Nevada Peace Officers Association, that the high marihuana penalties not only result in inefficient use of the law, but in fact subvert the law. He claimed that judges attempt to liberalize the marihuana law by creating loopholes in the laws of search and seizure; as a consequence, violent criminals are freed because of such technicalities (Assembly Judiciary Committee, 1977). However, the Nevada legislature ignored advice from most of the expert witnesses and decided to be tough on crime by retaining high marihuana penalties (*Reno Evening Gazette*, 1973).

Interview data dramatize the fact that much of the intense concern with marihuana reflected in the 1967–1968 and 1970–1971 Nevada newspapers continued to influence drug control policies. A member of the assembly explained the difference between gambling and marihuana: "We feel gaming is an industry, not a vice like drugs. We don't feel gaming is bad since we don't engage in it—it doesn't hurt us." The president pro tem of the Senate said: "Marihuana is bad but alcohol is a fact of life. . . . If we would reduce penalties for drugs, the Nevada state government would be encouraging drug use." A member of the Assembly explained: "Gambling and drinking are a financial boon to the state but marihuana doesn't generate any revenue."

The majority leader of the Senate recalled: "Drug penalties in Nevada have been increased in the last 20 years and there is no sentiment at all in Las Vegas [his district] to decrease penalties." Another senator claimed: "You can't connect gambling and prostitution with liberalism—we are tough on all crime in Nevada." The head of the legislative research department agreed: "This is the most conservative legislature in the United States and this shows up in our drug laws." A number of police officers, judges, and other state officials emphasized the conservative character of Nevada, its citizens and legislature.

SUMMARY AND CONCLUSIONS: MORALS LEGISLATION WITHOUT MORALITY

Across all types of issues including prostitution, prohibition, divorces, lotteries, casino gambling, and drug use, economic considerations rather than morality have played the central role. It is either the divorce–marriage business, or the gambling industry, or tourism in general that is in jeopardy; in recent years there has been an on-going crisis over drugs.

Why have other conservative states such as Utah (Galliher and Basilick, 1979), Nebraska (Galliher *et al.,* 1974), and Mississippi (Mississippi General Laws, 1977; Reinhold, 1977) been leaders in reducing marihuana and other drug penalties, while Nevada is the only state where first-offense marihuana possession is still a felony? Leaders in the first three states thought that local youth were the primary drug users. Nevada kept its high penalties due to the type of actors blamed for the drug problem. News reports of arrests indicated that most drug law violations were local and often high-status individuals, although the opinion was expressed in interviews and legislative reports that outsiders, or "transients," were responsible for Nevada's considerable drug problem. As Musto (1973) has demonstrated, the most repressive drug control laws typically are aimed at some threatening "outsiders" or minority—blacks, Mexicans, or Chinese.

The maintenance of high marihuana penalties served as a symbol to show that Nevadans are not totally without moral standards. Blaming outsiders for the local crime problem also helps avoid moral responsibility. The fact that lawmakers know that there are few arrests or convictions demonstrates that they view the legislation as a symbolic device rather than as a means of punishing criminal offenders. Nevada maintains the symbol of a high marihuana penalty for public consumption, yet seldom enforces the law which would require severe action against local citizens. In fact, the actual punishment of marihuana users in Nevada is not greatly different from other states with much lower formal penalties. In recent years, while penalties have been lowered drastically in other states, there has been a corresponding decline in marihuana arrests and convictions in Nevada.

The importance of symbolism for a group obviously depends on who it believes is watching; in Nevada many respondents claimed that the whole nation watches activities in their state. As in anti-trust legislation, the producers of the symbols attempt to manipulate others whom they see as potential consumers of these symbols. Nevada lawmakers recognized that the maintenance of a law-and-order image could protect their gambling industry from external controls. The high marihuana penalty in the state is more than a reflection of self-delusion or status frustrations, and has a symbolic as well as an instrumental role even if the law seldom is enforced.

REFERENCES

Assembly Judiciary Committee
    1977   Minutes, March 7. Carson City, Nevada.

Campos, A. A.
    1975   Memo to the Nevada Assembly Judiciary Committee, March 17. Carson City, Nevada.
    1978   Personal Communication, August 14.

Carson City Nevada Appeal
    1968   "PTA program on narcotics." September 10:3.
    1970   "Sheriff hopeful makes drug claim, Humphrey denies it." August 27:1.
    1971   "Senate overrides Laxalt veto on expulsions for drug users." January 21:4.

Department of Adult Parole and Probation
    1974–   Non-Resident Offender/Victim Impact on Crime in Nevada. Carson City, Nevada.
    1975

Edelman, Murray
    1964   *The Symbolic Uses of Politics.* Urbana: University of Illinois Press.

Galliher, John F. and Linda Basilick
    1979   "Utah's liberal drug laws: Structural foundations and triggering events." *Social Problems* 26 (February):284–297.

Galliher, John F., James L. McCartney, and Barbara E. Baum
    1974   "Nebraska's marihuana law: A case of unexpected legislative innovation." *Law and Society Review* 8 (Spring):441–455.

Gusfield, Joseph R.
    1963   *Symbolic Crusade: Status Politics and the American Temperance Movement.* Urbana: University of Illinois Press.
    1967   "Moral passage: The symbolic process in public designations of deviance." *Social Problems* 15 (Fall):175–188.

Las Vegas Evening Review
    1930   "Clara's games may force law change in state." October 4:5.

1931   "Farewell Nevada! Kiss divorces goodbye: Cuba to have 30-day divorce statute."
        February 20:1.
Las Vegas Review Journal
    1968a   "Reno dope cases quadruple." June 20:5.
    1968b   "Drug problems heard." June 29:4.
    1968c   "Democrats fight easing penalty on marihuana." July 30:3.
    1968d   "State Bureau of Narcotics suggested." August 5:4.
    1968e   "Fike favors Narcotics Bureau here." August 9:4.
    1968f   "Moms fight soft dope law." August 19:9.
    1968g   "Demo Central Committee asks strong dope laws." August 24:2.
    1968h   "More youths going to 'pot'." August 31:11.
    1970a   "Jury finds pharmacist guilty on two illegal drug charges." April 18:3.
    1970b   "Schools as crime sanctuaries must be stopped, says Franklin." April 24:13.
    1970c   "State narco men reduce penalties." May 4:5.
    1970d   "Reno prostitution nothing startling to Bill Raggio." July 13:11.
    1970e   "Love blooming in Reno, federal probe indicates." July 14:5.
    1970f   "Man arrested in 'pot' case seeks election as sheriff." July 15:3.
    1970g   "Nevada's high crime rate linked to tourism, FBI report reveals." August 18:13.
    1970h   "Candidate for sheriff arrested." August 21:1.
    1970i   "2nd narcotics agent sent to local office." September 2:10.
    1970j   "Arraignment is set for doctors, pharmacists nabbed in drug case." September
            17:6.
    1970k   "Drugs linked to 46 deaths of Las Vegans." December 20:33.
    1971a   "Nevada crime rate rises 175 percent." January 5:3.
    1971b   "7,000 LV pupils use drugs." January 13:1.
Legislative Commission of the Legislative Counsel Bureau
    1969   "Illegal Narcotic and Drug Use in Nevada." Bulletin No. 80 (January). Carson City,
            Nevada.
Mississippi General Laws
    1977   House Bill 72, Chapter 482 (April 15):922–927.
Musto, David F.
    1973   *The American Disease: Origins of Narcotic Control.* New Haven: Yale University
            Press.
Nevada State Statutes
    1931a   Assembly Bill 98, Chapter 99 (March 19):165–169.
    1931b   Assembly Bill 137, Chapter 97 (May 1):161–162.
    1971   Senate Bill 214, Chapter 14 (February 25):11–13.
    1971   Assembly Bill 630, Chapter 505 (May 13):1038–1040.
Reinhold, Robert
    1977   "Smoking of marihuana wins wider acceptance." *New York Times,* May 23:29, 46.
Reno Evening Gazette
    1967   "What about legalization of marihuana or lower penalties?" December 27:19.
    1968   "Private lottery proposal attacked by Nevada Chamber leaders." October 29:5.
    1970a   "Drug charge dropped against legislator's son." July 22:23.

1970b   "Candidate, wife arrested in drug case." August 6:17.
1970c   "Nevada crime up 18.5 percent." August 17:2.
1970d   "Senator's son is convicted in marihuana case." August 19:1.
1973   "Nevada's 1973 legislature continues 'tough on crime' tradition." June 11:2.
Skolnick, Jerome H.
1978   House of Cards: The Legalization and Control of Casino Gambling. Boston: Little Brown and Company.

DISSONANCE AND CONTRADICTIONS
IN THE ORIGINS OF MARIHUANA DECRIMINALIZATION

ALBERT DICHIARA

and

JOHN F. GALLIHER

The movement for removal of criminal penalties for possession of marihuana in the United States provides an important case study of the causes and process of decriminalization. Between 1973 and 1978, 11 states reduced criminal penalties for possession of small amounts of the drug, but the reform movement was fragile, brief, and limited to a few states. This case study suggests that reform was driven in part by "moral dissonance" resulting from the arrest of high-status offenders. Although public opinion has always been deeply divided on decriminalization of marihuana possession, a narrow "policy window" was created in the 1970s by the expressed concern of political leaders about the effect of arrest on high-status youths and the support of law enforcement agencies interested in efficient use of limited resources. Even after the window for reform closed at the end of the 1970s with a shift in national leadership, deep moral ambivalence renders criminalization symbolic and police place a low priority on marihuana arrests.

Many have observed that the 1970s was a period when a wide variety of deviant groups and their supporters began to mobilize to challenge popular stereotypes and to demand an end to discriminatory treatment (see, e.g., Weitzer 1991). The decriminalization of marihuana represents one part of this pattern. Previous research on the origins of criminal laws justifiably has been criticized for analysis of isolated case studies of one particular law, which Hagan (1980) claims has resulted in confusion in attempts to explain a law's passage. The study reported here attempts to avoid this problem by analysis of the legislative process in 11 states which, over a five-year period, removed jail sentences for possession of small amounts of marihuana. These laws, sometimes collectively referred to as "decriminalization," often specify that offenders are to be issued summons like those for traffic offenses rather than being taken into custody.

Such laws were passed in 11 states and cover about a third of the American population: Oregon in 1973; Alaska, Maine, California, Colorado, and Ohio in 1975;

The authors are grateful to William Chambliss, James Orcutt, James Galliher, Rea Galliher, Steven Murphy, and the *Law & Society Review* anonymous reviewers for assistance with various phases of this study. This research was funded by a grant from the Research Council of the Graduate School, University of Missouri–Columbia. An earlier version of this article was presented at the American Sociological Association annual meetings, Atlanta, August 1988. Address correspondence to John F. Galliher, Department of Sociology, University of Missouri-Columbia, Columbia, MO 65211.

Reprinted from *Law & Society Review* 28, no. 1 (1994), by permission of the Law & Society Association.

Minnesota in 1976; Mississippi, New York, and North Carolina in 1977; and Nebraska in 1978.[1]

If the 1970s was a period of liberal change, the 1980s was generally regarded by participants in government as a more conservative era (Kingdon 1984). In any case, no states have decriminalized marihuana since 1978, and in 1990 Alaska "recriminalized" the drug.

Our study sought the political and cultural sources of these laws through a description and analysis of the legislative process, as well as analysis of the ultimate stalling of the decriminalization movement.

TOWARD A THEORY OF DECRIMINALIZATION

Lempert (1974:1) has noted that little attention has been devoted to the problem of decriminalization and attempted to move "toward a theory of decriminalization" by identifying the initial pressures for such legal change, as well as distinguishing the pressures from their empirical consequences. He observed that pressure for decriminalization occurs to the extent high-status individuals are identified as violators of the law. His reasoning is that deviant, law-violating behavior creates a "moral dissonance" whereby an actor is simultaneously seen as having high social status and low moral status (p. 5). Lempert further reasoned: "If moral dissonance is to induce legal change it will have to work on a relatively large number of individuals. For this to happen, observed dissonant behavior must be widespread" (ibid.).

This widespread moral dissonance causes problems for law enforcement, reflecting not so much the irrelevance of the law but rather deep divisions of opinion and intense political conflict. A statute may be repealed "at a time when the moral principle embodied in the statute is still of compelling importance to many members of society" (p. 3). We here will demonstrate that the pressures leading to marihuana decriminalization had precisely the origins Lempert predicted.

As useful as Lempert's ideas may be, they tell us nothing about why particular marihuana policy alternatives emerged when they did and why they ceased to appear relevant by the 1980s. Kingdon (1984:174–75) has helped our understanding of the fleeting temporal quality of this legislative ebb and flow by observing that "policy windows, the opportunities for action on given initiatives . . . open infrequently. . . . Despite their rarity, the major changes in public policy result from the appearance of the opportunities." But when "the window opens, it does not stay open long. An idea's time comes, but it also passes" (p. 177). Kingdon also explained that if a proposal fails, people may be unwilling to invest more time and energy in the endeavor, or changes in key political leadership may make such proposals less feasible.

---

[1]This research intentionally omitted South Dakota, which enacted a decriminalization law effective in April 1976 as part of a general revision of the state's criminal code but repealed it 11 months later. We did not include this statute in our analysis because (1) unlike the other decriminalization statutes, this law was never accepted as a relatively permanent part of the state's criminal code, and (2) South Dakota kept no records of public hearings or legislative debate, making the analysis used for the other states impossible.

Supplementing Lempert's theory of decriminalization in this way draws attention away from an exclusive interest in the social status of the deviant and toward broader issues involving state and national politics and the activities of moral entrepreneurs. In addition, we consider the specific behaviors causing moral dissonance, the indicators of this problem, the events that focus public attention, and the policy alternatives available.

Burstein (1985:193) has observed that while "social scientists tend to divide themselves into those who study the causes of legislative change and those who study the consequences," in the real world the "law itself is neither an end nor a beginning, but rather an intermediate stage in the political process." Thus, while Lempert implied that decriminalization solves the problem of moral dissonance, another type of moral dissonance is actually created by legal reforms themselves. As an illustration, Chambliss (1979:7–8) has concluded that in any historical period law is created to help resolve the existing "contradictions, conflicts, and dilemmas. . . . The most important of these dilemmas and conflicts are those that derive from the economic and political structures of the times," but that "[o]ften, resolutions of particular conflicts and dilemmas not only create further conflicts, but also spotlight other contradictions which may have been dormant," leading to further resolutions.

We demonstrate that while decriminalization laws resolved certain conflicts, the legislation produced additional conflicts or moral dissonance all its own when behavior considered by some to be immoral was no longer severely punished, thereby setting the stage for the stalling of the movement toward decriminalization. Our view is that decriminalization as a policy alternative, and marihuana decriminalization in particular, represented a unique historical moment in the evolution of criminal sanctions. The ideological, social, and political basis for decriminalization opened a narrow and tenuous "policy window," and thus the viability of this policy was limited and quickly supplanted by de facto decriminalization. We also demonstrate that the effects of these laws were primarily symbolic, and thus it should not be surprising that another type of symbolic response, de facto decriminalization, was a commonly accepted alternative that addressed conflicting social-class and political interests more adequately than statutory change. According to these formulations, a theory of decriminalization and its consequent contradictions must include consideration of the national mood, political leadership, concerns of interest groups, especially law enforcement and drug users, as well as public opinion.

ESTABLISHING MORAL DISSONANCE

The social and economic costs of enforcement of prohibition of alcohol are legendary. During the 1920s there was a growing perception that the authorities' attempts to enforce prohibition were leading to disrespect for law in general and to a total breakdown in the social order (Kyvig 1979). Repeal promised an end to the diversion of police from the arrest of "casual" law violators (Engelmann 1979:35), an easing of the hopeless clogging of the courts and prisons, and an elimination of "thou shalt nots" that are so tempting to the young (p. 191). Similar problems in law enforcement have also been central to the history of marihuana prohibition.

During the first half of the 20th century, marihuana use was concentrated among Latin Americans (LaGuardia Commission on Marihuana 1944), African Americans, the Greenwich Village "beat" community, and jazz musicians (Polsky 1967). These usage patterns are of general significance, for research on alcohol prohibitions (Gusfield 1963), opium laws (Morgan 1978), and other drug legislation (Musto 1973; Helmer 1975) indicates that the most severe punishment is reserved for those instances where a substance is publicly associated with a threatening minority group. During the 1960s, however, patterns of marihuana use began to change. By 1970 Goode reported survey data indicating that marihuana smokers were likely to be urban, college graduates in their early 20s. By 1977, 60% of those aged 18–25 had used this substance (Abelson & Fishburne 1977). A survey in 1979 (Fishburne et al.) indicated that 68% of those aged 18–25 reported that they had used marihuana. In addition, 69% of whites, 62% of all others, and 73% of those with college training had used the drug. These figures indicate not only that marihuana use increased dramatically during the 1970s among those 18–25, but that the increase especially occurred among middle-class, college-educated whites—a totally different picture from what existed during the 1930s. These demographic changes in the typical marihuana user provided the key social context for the reform of marihuana laws.

Given what is known about the relationship between patterns of drug use and penalty structures, it was not completely surprising that, coincident with these changing patterns of marihuana use, several states reduced marihuana possession penalties to misdemeanor levels, among them Nebraska (Galliher et al. 1974) and Utah (Galliher & Basilick 1979). The increasing risks of arrest for affluent young people were critical ingredients in the passage of these new laws, especially in homogeneous states where drug use was not associated with any local minority group (Galliher et al. 1974; Galliher & Basilick 1979). A statewide survey in Utah revealed widespread marihuana use by young people of nearly all ages and all social classes (Galliher & Basilick 1979:291): "Economic status is no deterrent to obtaining drugs and youngsters of all economic levels are involved," the survey concluded. An attorney who supported reduction in drug penalties explained to the Utah state senate: "These are your kids, after all." Another attorney involved in the lobbying effort said: "We also pointed out that the courts would be reluctant to convict in marihuana possession cases since the marihuana problem was hitting middle-class families and Mormon youth."

In Nebraska a prosecutor's son was arrested for marihuana possession, and his lawyers lobbied with a state legislator for misdemeanor penalties retroactive to the date of his arrest. Prior to the law's passage, the Nebraska State Highway Patrol recorded an average of only 15 marihuana possession cases per year; after the change, arrests rose precipitously (Galliher et al. 1974).

By the late 1970s, Nevada was the only U.S. state retaining felony penalties for possession of the slightest amount of marihuana. Yet, just as was originally true in Nebraska, these severe penalties could not be enforced. In 1974, of the 214 persons convicted for marihuana possession, only 14 were actually sentenced to prison. In 1978, only 13 were sentenced to prison, and these were all "special cases" involving other criminal charges (Galliher & Cross 1982:383). The president of the Nevada Peace Officers complained in legislative hearings on misdemeanor penalties: "Judges are not sending people to prison as the present law calls for for smoking a joint of grass. . . . As a consequence, the law, as it stands today is being subverted. It's being met with a lot of cynical amusement by the young people today" (ibid., p. 384). The experience in both Nebraska and Nevada suggests that the police desired a law that could be enforced when felony penalties began to be widely seen as inappropriate for marihuana users increasingly concentrated in the middle and upper classes. Similar evidence of difficulties in marihuana law enforcement from across the United States were disclosed in a federal report published in the early 1970s (National Commission on Marihuana & Drug Abuse 1972).

PUBLIC OPINION AND AGENDA SETTING

Burstein (1985) has demonstrated that the weight of intensely held public opinion made the federal Equal Employment Opportunity legislation possible; this was not the case with marihuana decriminalization. Over all, public opinion is not necessarily the most important consideration (Kingdon 1984). Those most intensely interested are specialists in a given policy arena, who often emphasize "equity and efficiency" (p. 140). Assuming the significance of moral dissonance in the enforcement of marihuana laws, the relevant values and beliefs were those of political leaders, since the general public has been divided about evenly on this issue and thereby stalemated. For example, the 1977 Gallup Poll found 53% supported decriminalization; in 1980, 52% favored the idea; in 1985, 46% did so. This deep division of opinion may reflect an ambivalence arising from a recognition that while use marihuana may be immoral and may represent a health hazard, incarceration of marihuana users is not a reasonable response. Thus public opinion can be said to have made marihuana decriminalization a legitimate issue, but did not ensure its legislative success.

Conservative columnist William F. Buckley (1972) was among the first nationally prominent figures to endorse decriminalization. More significantly, prestigious groups and people associated with law enforcement such as the American Bar Association (MacKenzie 1973), U.S. Attorney General William Saxbe,[2] and FBI Director Clarence Kelley[3] lent their support to decriminalization. The reasons included the massive costs to law enforcement, the impossibility of deterring marihuana use, and the social cost of ruining a person's future employment opportunities with an arrest. Kelley said it might be better "not to prosecute for possession of marihuana, but spend greater attention and time on those who sell" marihuana and other drugs. First President Ford, and then President Carter, lent the prestige of their office to the cause of decriminalization, claiming that their primary motivation came from their children. President Ford claimed: "More people are hurt by criminal laws against marihuana use than are hurt by the drug itself."[4] Later President Carter asked the Congress

---

[2]"Pot Statement Expected," *Columbus Evening Dispatch,* 15 Nov. 1974, p. B9.
[3]"Get Sellers, Kelley Says," *Atlanta Constitution,* 24 June 1975, p. 6A.
[4]*Columbus Evening Dispatch,* 15 Nov. 1974 (cited in note 2).

to decriminalize marihuana possession (Wooten 1977).[5] No longer could it be said that marihuana was simply a minority-linked drug, and these changes in attitude and usage patterns were to play a role in future attempts to alter the method of its legal control. Both U.S. senators and representatives argued that middle- and upper-class college students, on the road to professional careers, should not be incarcerated for marihuana possession because such users would lose respect for a law their experience tells them is incommensurate with the danger of the drug (Peterson 1985).

A POLICY WINDOW OPENS

Beginning in the 1960s policymakers increasingly began to view deviance as being magnified by official reactions (Empey 1978). Thus a series of programs designed to limit the negative effects of official sanctions were enacted (Olson-Raymer 1984). Among those were laws to abolish the indeterminate sentence (Dershowitz 1976), as well as laws to decriminalize status offenses in California and New York (Rubin 1985). And official opinion on marihuana reflected in government reports also began to change. Initially, during the early 1960s, and before, when the effects of marihuana were studied by government agencies, its users were often described as was stated in the President's Advisory Commission on Narcotics and Drug Abuse (1963) as "frustrated, hopeless, maladjusted" and as exhibiting "psychological dependence" (pp. 1, 4). But by the late 1960s, we see evidence of the beginnings of moral dissonance when marihuana was described by the President's Commission on Law Enforcement and Administration of Justice (1968:13) as merely a "mild hallucinogen" and by the 1970s a federal commission described the marihuana user as "essentially indistinguishable from their non–marihuana-using peers by any fundamental criterion other than their marihuana use" (National Commission on Marihuana & Drug Abuse [NCMDA] 1972:41). The Comprehensive Drug Abuse and Prevention Act of 1970 reduced the federal marihuana possession penalty to a misdemeanor and also required reports to Congress on marihuana and other drugs.

In accordance with the latter provision of this legislation, in 1972 the NCMDA, drawing on advice from experts in a variety of fields appointed by President Nixon, released its report. It minimized the health risks of marihuana use and urged that public possession of one ounce or less of marihuana (the usual purchase amount) be decriminalized, subject only to confiscation, and that public use remain a criminal offense punishable by a $100 fine. Surveys conducted by the commission found that only a minority of prosecutors and judges viewed marihuana possession penalties as a deterrent and that police seldom attempted to seek out such law violators. Instead these surveys found that law enforcement viewed such prohibitions as too costly, claimed they created discrimination in enforcement, and ruined the lives of those arrested. At this point there seemed to be no difference between the demands of affluent marihuana

---

[5]"Carter Asks Congress to Decriminalize Marihuana Possession; Cocaine Law is Studied," *New York Times,* 15 March 1977, sec. 1, p. 15; "Administration Urges Marihuana Decriminalization," *South Mississippi Sun* (Biloxi-Gulfport), 15 March 1977.

users and the requirements of law enforcement efficiency. Much as the 1931 report of the Wickersham commission was instrumental in discrediting national prohibition of alcohol by describing the law as both ineffective and the source of political corruption (Kerr 1985), the key triggering event in decriminalization was the 1972 NCMDA Report. Beginning the next year and extending into 1978, 11 states passed laws modeled closely after its recommendations (Table 1).

DATA SOURCES

We reviewed all issues of a major daily newspaper in each state we studied for a year prior to, and immediately after, the passage of the decriminalization law to assess the type of political environment in which each law passed. In addition, we secured numerous articles that dealt with marihuana and marihuana offenses from private collections and library holdings in the states involved. We also explored legislative records of floor debate and/or public hearings. The quality and amount of such information available varied greatly across the states, but at least some such information was available for all states. In Mississippi and North Carolina we conducted interviews with key informants to supplement our analysis of existing records that appeared to give an incomplete picture of the legislative process. In addition, we contacted the legislatures in all states that did not decriminalize marihuana to locate existing records of the introduction of relevant bills, as well as committee hearings and floor debate on any marihuana reforms.

THE PUZZLING PATTERNS OF MARIHUANA DECRIMINALIZATION

A survey of some of the earliest of these marihuana laws found great variation in the legislative process of decriminalization from state to state, with no apparent logic to the pattern (National Governors' Conference 1977). Decriminalization in Maine, California, and Ohio was preceded by extensive legislative staff research, but such research was also conducted in New Jersey where the legislation failed. In Ohio and Maine decriminalization was part of an overall criminal code revision that diverted

TABLE 1

Provisions of State Marihuana Possession Decriminalization Laws

State	Year	Title of Law	Maximum Penalty	Amount of Marihuana
Oregon	1973	Violation	Up to $100—1st offense	Up to 1 oz.
Alaska	1975	Misdemeanor	Up to $100	Up to 1 oz. (in public)
Maine	1975	Civil violation	Up to $200	"Usable Amount"
Colorado	1975	Petty offense	Up to $100	Up to 1 oz.
California	1975	Misdemeanor	Up to $100	Up to 1 oz.
Ohio	1975	Minor misdemeanor	Up to $100	Up to 100 grams
Minnesota	1976	Petty misdemeanor	Up to $100—1st offense	"Small Amount"
Mississippi	1977	Noncriminal	$100–$250—1st offense	Up to 1 oz.
New York	1977	Violation	Up to $100—1st offense	Up to 25 grams
N. Carolina	1977	Misdemeanor	Up to $100—1st offense	Up to 1 oz.
Nebraska	1978	Civil offense	$100—1st offense	Up to 1 oz.

attention, to a degree, from the marihuana penalty changes. But in Colorado and California successful decriminalization bills stood alone, and in Iowa and New Jersey decriminalization bills failed despite being part of a general criminal code revision. In Minnesota, Ohio, and California, the survey reported an individual or interest group was of primary importance, but in other states they were not important factors. The press was typically supportive of decriminalization, but this was true in states that passed, as well as those that did not pass, such laws. The severity of existing penalties was an important influence in California and Colorado, but in Minnesota experience with previous penalty reductions made decriminalization more palatable. In none of these states did the National Organization for the Reform of Marihuana Laws (NORML), the only national organization lobbying for decriminalization, make a visible and constructive contribution to the decriminalization process. The limited significance of this organization is apparently a result of the ineptitude of its leadership (Anderson 1981). Interest groups cannot always control the course of the debate; in addition, the efforts of opposing interest groups often cancel each other out (Kingdon 1984).

The states that passed decriminalization laws had quite diverse political, cultural, and demographic characteristics. Some of these states (Minnesota, Oregon, and New York) are well-known liberal enclaves. But some are conservative (e.g., Nebraska, Mississippi, and North Carolina). And every region of the nation is represented: the West (California, Oregon, Colorado, and Alaska); the East (Maine and New York); the Middle West (Nebraska, Minnesota, and Ohio); and the South (Mississippi and North Carolina). There are populous states (Ohio, California, and New York) as well as sparsely populated states (Maine, Nebraska, and Alaska). Some of the states have heterogeneous populations, with sizable numbers of African Americans or Hispanics (among them New York, California, Mississippi, and North Carolina). Some states are relatively homogeneous (e.g., Oregon, Minnesota, Nebraska, and Maine; U.S. Bureau of the Census 1980). These variations in the demographic characteristics of decriminalization states are curious because some research leads us to believe that the demographic characteristics of a state will, to a considerable extent, determine the local response to drug use (Musto 1973; Galliher et al. 1974; Galliher & Basilick 1979). These puzzling patterns parallel the variations across the states in the process by which decriminalization laws were passed.

DECRIMINALIZATION HISTORIES

Polsby (1984) distinguished between laws on the basis of how quickly they are passed. Some laws are passed with dispatch, especially if there is a close association between the source of the ideas and the agencies responsible for enforcing the law. Other laws involve a much longer process and may require considerable research to attempt to determine the consequences of the policy change. Jacob (1988) has also observed that legislation can involve a routine process or can be associated with considerable conflict. According to Jacob (p. 11), "those who seek to use the routine policy process define their proposals in as narrow terms as they can." The experiences of both the states that decriminalized marihuana as well as those that failed to do so reflect these differences in speed and conflict.

Routine Policy Change

The decriminalization policy window was open only five years and ultimately ended with a significant shift in the national mood and change in presidential administrations. Nonetheless, the legislation begun in the early 1970s seemed full of promise for providing significant policy changes. Oregon was the first state to pass a decriminalization law—in 1973. Before the law was changed, conviction for possession of less than one ounce of marihuana was a misdemeanor and could be punished with a $1,000 fine, a one-year sentence, or both.[6] Possessing more than one ounce was a felony, and could incur a $2,500 fine and/or a 10-year sentence. However, these penalties existed only on the statute books, and a local paper noted many instances in which they were not actually enforced, particularly against juveniles.[7] The conservative Republican hog-farmer legislator who introduced the bill in the state legislature compared marihuana's dangers and penalties with that of alcohol and other drugs:

> "Having explored all the basic components of the marihuana situation, I am convinced we could and should take steps to decriminalize its use. Prohibition was not the answer to our alcohol problem in 1919, nor is it the answer to the marihuana problem in 1973."
> He sat down amid an ovation (Anderson 1981:122).

Later the legislator noted that public views toward marihuana were changing and that he had received very few letters objecting to his position, while the great majority supported his stand.[8] A local prosecuting attorney announced that less emphasis would be placed on marihuana enforcement and more on hard drugs and drug trafficking. He ordered local law enforcement authorities to begin issuing citations to marihuana users instead of putting them in jail.[9] This apparently involved no political risk, as no opposition to his ideas surfaced. Later, the prosecutor testified in support of such legislation in at least four other states (Alaska, Maine, Ohio, and Minnesota), and was greeted warmly in all four.

In Ohio, the Oregon prosecutor assured legislators that decriminalization had caused no perceptible increase in the use of the drug.[10] An Ohio federal court overturned a marihuana *sale* sentence of 20–40 years as cruel and unusual, and therefore "unconstitutional" (*Downey v. Perini* 1975).[11] This court decision provided a legal mandate for new Ohio marihuana legislation. A physician was quoted as saying: "We

---

[6]"Obvious, Subtle Effects of Pot Using Described," *Eugene Register-Guard,* 6 Oct. 1972, p. 4A.

[7]"Marihuana Costs Man $200 Fine," *Eugene Register-Guard,* 7 March 1973, p. 4D; "Youth Pays Fine for Possessing Pot," *Eugene Register-Guard,* 9 March 1973, p. 5A; "Court Dismisses Marihuana Case," *Eugene Register-Guard,* 18 March 1973, p. 3A; "Drug Sentence Put Off One Year," *Eugene Register-Guard,* 3 April 1973, p. 4A.

[8]"Drug Penalty Bill Passed by House," *Eugene Register-Guard,* 22 June 1973, p. 13A.

[9]"Hard Drug Crackdown Set," *Eugene Register-Guard,* 15 March 1973, p. 1C.

[10]"Marihuana Legislation Subject of Panel at Fair," *Columbus Evening Dispatch,* 1 Sept. 1974, p. A2.

[11]"Pot Case—Alleged Vendetta by Police Here Led to Overturning Ohio Statutes," *Cleveland Plain Dealer,* 28 July 1975, p. 14A.

just want to end the agony of arrest records for teenagers found with small amounts of marihuana."[12] A former police chief of Toledo declared that the money spent on marihuana arrests was wasted.[13]

Along with U.S. Attorney General Saxbe, a Republican and an Ohio native, who as we noted above supported decriminalization,[14] there were other similar proponents in Ohio. A wealthy Republican whose family owned a Columbus (the state capital) newspaper, several television and radio stations, hotels, and much of Ohio's largest bank eventually supported the bill. He had easy access to every state official, and he drew on it when necessary. He showed a film to the state legislature about a young marihuana smoker whose parents had found some marihuana in his room. Horrified, they called the police and had him arrested to save him from the drug. He was in fact sentenced to prison where he was soon gang-raped. Then he hanged himself in his cell (Anderson 1981:166). After this presentation the bill had no trouble passing.

In Colorado the state attorney general indicated that he supported reduced marihuana penalties because marihuana cases were clogging the courts and wasting money.[15] A split state supreme court "reluctantly" upheld the conviction of four defendants for selling marihuana. Two justices asserted that when marihuana is misclassified as a narcotic, "the classification lacks a fundamental rational basis and is unreasonable and is constitutionally offensive" (*People v. Summit* 1974:855 (Lee, J., dissenting)). A *Denver Post* editorial strongly endorsed the legislative efforts to lower the marihuana penalties by reclassifying marihuana as a "dangerous drug" rather than a "narcotic."[16] The Colorado legislation was supported by conservatives, and an ultra-conservative in the senate even proposed total legalization.[17] In the senate, the Republican sponsor of the bill to decriminalize possession summarized the prevailing mood, admitting that marihuana was dangerous, but "any person has the right to go to hell any way he chooses so long as he doesn't hurt anybody else."[18]

In April 1975 under a new city ordinance, the Denver prosecutor started giving tickets for marihuana possession rather than making arrests. During house hearings, another Colorado prosecutor said: "We simply can no longer in the criminal justice system expend taxpayers' money and lawyers' and investigators' time chasing the pot smoker around the dormitory" (debate in the Colorado House, 20 Feb. 1975). The Denver prosecutor's office reported that in 1972–73 only 7 marihuana cases in the city ended with sentences to prison out of 2,200 marihuana-related cases, at a total cost of $1,650,000. A deputy district attorney observed that the law was selectively enforced and was "the single most destructive force in society—in terms of turning our children against the system."[19]

---

[12]*Columbus Evening Dispatch,* 1 Sept. 1974 (cited in note 10).
[13]Ibid.
[14]*Columbus Evening Dispatch,* 15 Nov. 1974 (cited in note 2).
[15]"Marihuana Law Change Viewed—MacFarlane Supports Leniency," *Denver Post,* 16 Dec. 1974, p. 30.
[16]"Moderating Marihuana Laws" (Editorial), *Denver Post,* 27 Feb. 1975, p. 26.
[17]"Decriminalization Effort—Conservatives Back 'Pot' Proposals," *Denver Post,* 10 April 1975, p. 2.
[18]"Liberalized Laws—Senators Debate Bill on Marihuana," *Denver Post,* 2 May 1975, p. 3.
[19]"Testimony Favors Easing 'Pot' Law—Senate Judiciary Hearing," *Denver Post,* 9 April 1975, p. 18.

In Maine, the Oregon prosecutor testified once again about his state's decriminalization law in legislative hearings:

> [S]tudies indicate that use of marihuana has not increased in the state since then. Tremendous amounts of time and money have been spent trying to enforce the marihuana laws. . . . As a law enforcement officer, I am vitally concerned with the best use of the limited resources of the criminal justice system.[20]

Others testifying in favor of the revised code included a mother of seven who said several of her children had "problems because of marihuana use, but she wouldn't want to see them jailed."[21] A state legislator noted that in 1974 a total of 1,700 were arrested in the state for possession of marihuana.[22]

A former Republican state attorney general, head of a criminal code revision commission, put decriminalization in the new code. He defended a statement in the new code that marihuana was less harmful to our society than tobacco and alcohol, declaring that the latter two drugs cause many more deaths and havoc in people's lives than marihuana.[23] According to the local paper, the new code was an attempt to restrict the law "to instances where enforcement is to be encouraged and the prohibitions to be taken as representative of community judgments that are widely and strongly held. . . . Otherwise the already badly overextended law tends to squander . . . law enforcement and court resources."[24] A house member also noted that it would be easier to prove possession under this code because a civil offense is not subject to the same strict rules of evidence as are crimes.[25]

A 28 March 1975 *Kennebec Journal* editorial supported the efforts of the commission to abolish the criminal penalty for marihuana possession, "a move we have supported in the past and do again."[26]

> What hypocrites we can be without even conscious thought! We shy away from decriminalizing marihuana possession because it carries the name drug, and hug to our bosoms the cocktail hour because its image is social. Yet there are 450,000 under-21 alcoholics in this country; alcohol is responsible for one-half of traffic fatalities, accounts for one-third of all suicides and has some part in one-half of the 5,500,000 arrests made yearly. The marihuana cigarette will never match those figures, but we're afraid to look truth in the eye.[27]

We should recall that the Governors' Conference Report on state marihuana laws observed in 1977 that previous penalty reductions made decriminalization a relatively

[20]"Pot Decriminalization Aired," *Kennebec Journal*, 28 March 1975, p. 1.
[21]Ibid., p. 2.
[22]Ibid.
[23]"Lund Defends Marihuana Decriminalization," *Kennebec Journal*, 3 March 1975, p. 1.
[24]"Criminal Code Revision: A New Balance," *Kennebec Journal*, 3 March 1975, p. 1.
[25]"Bigelow Bill Dies in House," *Kennebec Journal*, 10 June 1975, p. 10.
[26]"A Polarizing Issue" (Editorial), *Kennebec Journal*, 28 March 1975, p. 4.
[27]Ibid.

easy process in Minnesota. A 1973 law had made the maximum penalty 90 days in jail and a \$300 fine. A decriminalization bill sponsor was quoted as saying: "There are a lot of young people in my district who smoke pot. . . . Enforcement of the present law involves an awful lot of expense, and . . . people who otherwise lead perfectly normal lives go to jail."[28] Another sponsor had "seen kids subjected to the criminal justice process, seen the disruption of their lives and the threat of jail hanging over them."[29] A legislative supporter concluded:

> My main interest is to put out accurate information to the public. We've got to give them the truth. . . . We've been putting out untruthful stuff the past 100 years—so much so that kids don't believe anything. I mean we've been telling people that pot-smoking will shrink your brain and turn you into a rapist.[30]

A local judge testified at the senate hearings that he favored decriminalization because of the time it would save the courts (Minnesota Senate Judiciary Committee 1975a). And a district attorney claimed: "As a prosecutor it is my feeling that the efforts of our police departments could be better utilized in investigating more serious crimes" (Minnesota House Judiciary Committee 1975). A Minnesota sheriff agreed: "I am against marihuana, however I feel the enforcement is not always constant. The new law, the way it's set up, could be more consistent . . . I don't have a large department . . . things could be speeded up" (Minnesota Senate Judiciary Committee 1975b). And a senator observed that police look the other way "from the use of marihuana by kids" (ibid.). Also, a 1973 study discovered that only 21 persons were confined in the state for marihuana possession, even though 40% to 50% of all Minnesota high school students had used the drug (Minnesota Senate Debate 1975).[31]

Nebraska was one of the pioneers in lowering marihuana possession penalties with a 1969 law that reduced the penalty for first-offense possession of marihuana to a maximum seven-day jail sentence; on subsequent offenses the sentence merely doubled (Galliher et al. 1974). Thus, like Minnesota's decriminalization, the move to decriminalization was not a major legislative step. A Nebraska state senator reasoned that a massive amount of police time could be saved by decriminalization: "A policeman, for the same amount of time, effort and money, could be dealing with ten or twelve individuals" (Nebraska Senate 1978). The Nebraska Supreme Court acknowledged that the costs of enforcing the marihuana laws exceeded the benefits (*State v. Kells* 1977).[32] A survey of rural Hall County found 57% favored decriminalization.[33] The people, the press, and the legislature in Nebraska showed little interest in this

---

[28]"Present Law Held Useless," *St. Paul Dispatch*, 21 April 1975, pp. 19, 21.
[29]"Knoll Says Law has 'Bad Effects,'" *St. Paul Dispatch*, 21 April 1975, pp. 19, 21.
[30]Ibid.
[31]"Marihuana Law Isn't Enforced, Study Says," *St. Paul Dispatch*, 21 April 1975, pp. 19, 21.
[32]"Marihuana Arrest in Home Legal, Nebraska Supreme Court Rules," *Lincoln Journal*, 2 Nov. 1977, pp. 1, 17.
[33]"Laxer Pot Laws Said Favored," *Lincoln Journal*, 24 Feb. 1978, p. 7.

law. As one state senator argued: "Particularly [if] a minor or young person has done wrong smoking marihuana, you don't destroy their career for the rest of their life" (Nebraska Senate 1978).

Alaska was the first state to enact misdemeanor marihuana possession penalties in 1968. Alcohol and alcoholism were widely recognized as the main social problem in the state. This was true even though a local attorney estimated that half the school children in the Anchorage area had used marihuana.[34] The Republican governor claimed that he opposed legalization of marihuana, but said, "I can certainly appreciate the hypocrisy in the manner we treat booze and, by comparison, marihuana."[35] The attorney general was also quoted as favoring the bill. The Commissioner of Public Safety in Alaska said in endorsing decriminalization: "Nobody in law enforcement objects to lessening the penalty for the possession of small amounts for an individual for his own use. [I have] no objection to doing away with jail time and lowering the fine" (Alaska House 1975). He admitted that such a change would save his resources, but said that even without the change his officers did not attempt to seek out marihuana users.

But the Anchorage newspaper bitterly opposed the decriminalization bill and published seven editorials in the year prior to decriminalization attacking the bill and its supporters. One editorial referred to it as "the odious measure," "the ugly mess," and "the garbage in the door."[36] The paper and the Republican candidate for the U.S. Senate attempted to make this the key issue in the election,[37] but few apparently listened and the Republican lost the election by a wide margin.

Shortly after the state legislature had passed the decriminalization bill, the Alaska Supreme Court ruled that private use and possession of marihuana were a constitutional right:

> There is no adequate justification for the state's intrusion into the citizen's right to privacy by its prohibition of possession of marihuana for personal consumption in the home. . . . The state cannot impose its own notions of morality, propriety, or fashion on individuals when the public has no legitimate interest in the affairs of those individuals. . . . It appears that the use of marihuana, as it is presently used in the United States today, does not constitute a public health problem of any significant dimensions. It is, for instance, far more innocuous in terms of psychological and social damage than alcohol or tobacco.[38]

In North Carolina, in 1977, a liquor-by-the-drink bill was hotly debated in the state legislature, thoroughly covered by the press, and ultimately defeated. By comparison, the marihuana decriminalization bill that passed that same year was covered

---

[34]"Supreme Court Receives Case on Marihuana," *Anchorage Daily Times,* 16 Oct. 1974, p. 2.
[35]"Marihuana Bill Moves to Vote," *Anchorage Daily Times,* 13 April 1975, p. A7.
[36]"No Marihuana Veto: Double-Dealing" (Editorial), *Anchorage Daily Times,* 24 May 1975, p. 4.
[37]"Gravel Hits Lewis, Press," *Anchorage Daily Times,* 3 Oct. 1974, p. 2.
[38]"Court Dilutes Pot Law: Ruling Says Constitution Protects Use in Home," *Anchorage Daily Times,* 27 May 1975, pp. 1, 2, referring to *Ravin v. State* (1975).

in only seven news reports. Even so, editorial opinion on decriminalization in the local press was sharply divided.[39] As early as the mid-1960s it was reported that drug use was increasing in the state's colleges,[40] and that marihuana use in particular was even more common among whites than among African Americans.[41] The press reported on what was called "High Noon" at the University of North Carolina in Chapel Hill. Several hundred students routinely gathered at noon to smoke marihuana at the campus bell tower.[42] A senate supporter recalled in an interview:

> There was tremendous disparity from Chapel Hill to Rose Hill. In Rose Hill you can make corn liquor but with a joint you're going to jail for two years. After football games in the Bell Tower at Chapel Hill as many as 15,000 smoked marihuana with the State Bureau of Investigation, local and county police watching. Do the same thing in Anderson, North Carolina, in the mountains and you were gone.

Another senator commented: "Last summer my nephew was busted for smoking marihuana . . . and due to the fact that maybe I've got somebody with clout over there, this kid got off fairly easily" (North Carolina Senate 1977). By contrast he cited the case of another "young boy" who was sentenced to prison for marihuana possession and murdered while there. Another senator observed: "I do not believe that the majority of the people of North Carolina support the concept that fifty or sixty kids in North Carolina ought to be imprisoned for doing what thousands of others have done without any punishment at all" (ibid.).

The director of corrections noted the state's prison overcrowding and asserted that there should be no imprisonment for alcohol and drug violations.[43] Soon a state commission confirmed that the state prisons were too crowded and therefore faced the threat of federal court intervention and control.[44] The threat was real since such intervention had already occurred in Mississippi. Another article noted that North Carolina led all states in the percentage of its population in prison.[45] A local judge was quoted as saying: "When drug use was restricted to young hippies, we could talk about THEM. When it hits the neighbor down the street, it's US. It's not what we can do about THEM, now it's what we can do for US."[46]

On the basis of such concerns, a liberal Democratic state representative began pressing the attorney general to support a decriminalization bill. In July 1977 the attorney general finally supported the bill and justified it as a means of concentrating on hard drug sales, of relieving prison crowding, and of avoiding placing kids in

[39]"No Glib Solutions Needed," *Fayetteville Times,* 9 March 1977; "Rufus Shouldn't Let 'Young Kids' Fool Him," *Goldsboro News-Argus,* 4 March 1977; "Decriminalization?" *Shelby Star,* 7 March, 1977.
[40]"Drug Usage May Be on Rise at State's Colleges," *News & Observer* (Raleigh), 19 Dec. 1965.
[41]"A Profile of Users of Hard, Soft Drugs," *News & Observer* (Raleigh), 24 March 1974.
[42]"High Nooners' Photographed," *News & Observer* (Raleigh), 16 Jan. 1975.
[43]"Prison Aid is Urged by Jones," *News & Observer* (Raleigh), 21 July 1976, p. 11.
[44]"Prisons Face Threat of Federal Control," *News & Observer* (Raleigh), 8 Feb. 1977, p. 19.
[45]"N.C. Prison Rate Highest in Nation," *News & Observer* (Raleigh), 25 May 1977, p. 19.
[46]"Pot in N.C.: It's Becoming No Big Deal," *News & Observer* (Raleigh), 4 July 1977.

prison with "professional felons." Just prior to the passage of the marihuana law, there were several stories of arrests in North Carolina involving massive amounts of drugs, including one case involving 25 tons of marihuana,[47] making it apparent that the local criminal justice system had its hands full with major dealers.

Various law enforcement representatives in all these states expressed support for decriminalization laws both to ensure the most efficient use of law enforcement resources and to protect the young. The list of supporters included prosecutors, state and federal judges, attorneys general, and the police. As Polsby (1984) has predicted, legislation passed quickly if those who would enforce new legislation also supported it. Although there were some differences across the states, decriminalization was never elevated to a critical political issue because the existing marihuana laws were not routinely enforced. There was widespread opinion among those directly involved that marihuana was not that dangerous, at least when compared to heroin, alcohol, or even tobacco. Since the drug was increasingly being used by affluent youngsters, it seemed rational that law enforcement should be explicitly freed to concentrate on more serious offenses, including more potent drugs. Much as Lempert (1974) predicted, decriminalization in these states was associated with "moral dissonance" stemming from widespread "dissonant behavior," leading in turn to obvious problems in law enforcement. In only two of these states could we locate evidence of opposition from the press. Missing was evidence of intense political conflict. This collective experience demonstrates Kingdon's (1984:176) point that "when the issue has a serious chance of legislative or other action, then advocates become more flexible, bargaining from their previously rigid positions, compromising in order to be in the game." It also illustrates Jacob's (1988) contention that a routine legislative process is easier to achieve if the initiative is narrowly defined: the successful bills all called for decriminalization of only possession, and only possession of small amounts of the drug, and most bills only called for this on the first offense. Instead of conflict, there were often-stated concerns that went unchallenged about the impact of law enforcement on the lives of the young.

Protracted Political Conflict

In a minority of the states that were successful in passing marihuana decriminalization bills, the legislative process involved sometimes rancorous political conflict. The fact that the process of decriminalization was so protracted and difficult, as well as so seldom successful, demonstrates that routinization was the key to success. Later we will demonstrate that when marihuana reforms were not presented in a routine manner, the initiatives always failed. No better example of protracted conflict can be found than in Mississippi where there were increasing numbers of arrests of young people for marihuana possession during the mid-1970s. Middle-class youths were sometimes convicted of marihuana possession, with some judges giving no prison sentences and some giving the maximum possible penalty of one to three

---

[47]"N.C. Now Major Importing Point for Pot Smugglers," *Durham Sun,* 12 Jan. 1976.

years. The senate sponsor of the decriminalization bill said: "We're putting children in jail and ruining their lives,"[48] and "your children and your neighbor's children are in severe jeopardy."[49]

One state legislator who was often associated with the Far Right supported decriminalization because of this disparity. In two separate cases in January 1977, involving the smuggling of tons of marihuana into Mississippi, ten out-of-state men were fined but given no jail sentences.[50] This prompted a flood of editorials and letters to the editor in papers across the state and included references to the obvious disparity in the handling of young people in the state compared with that for major drug dealers.[51] This harshness was especially outrageous because the state prison had been under federal court order since 1975 to reduce its crowding. This was a special problem for Mississippi because it is such a poor state and could not easily afford to build new prisons. A county sheriff, who was president of the Mississippi Sheriff's Association, agreed with the idea of decriminalization, and he said that his office "already concentrates on drug pushers rather than users. . . . If we were to round up everybody in [this] county who has smoked marihuana and send them to prison, . . . I don't know that we would have enough left to hold Sunday school."[52] Still, law enforcement and legislators were deeply divided on this issue.[53]

Mississippi was one of the first states to adopt prohibition of alcohol in 1908 and did not repeal it until 1966. From the lessons learned from alcohol prohibition, a young, conservative Republican president of a family-owned insurance company concluded that it was grossly unfair to treat young marihuana users differently from those who had used alcohol openly in Mississippi during prohibition. He traveled around the state speaking to individuals and groups, including state legislators, and also arranged hearings on decriminalization bills in 1975, 1976, and 1977. He displayed little concern about his personal reputation, which was sometimes under attack. For example, he was accused of being a drug dealer,[54] and a local newspaper implied that he had a financial interest in plans to manufacture marihuana cigarettes once the drug was legalized.[55]

But this business executive strategically mentioned that he was not in favor of marihuana use but only opposed to putting young marihuana users in prison. In a "Letter to Parents" he wrote: "We do not advocate or encourage the use of marihuana. . . . We do advocate a non-criminal, civil fine or citation approach to possession

[48]"Bill to Reduce Penalty to Be Debated," *Mississippi Press* (Pascagoula), 9 Feb. 1977.

[49]"Bill Reducing Marihuana Penalty Dealt Crushing Blow by Senate," *Natchez Democrat,* 10 Feb. 1977.

[50]"Officials Fear Mild Punishments Will Deter Drug Crackdown Efforts," *South Mississippi Sun* (Biloxi-Gulfport), 14 Jan. 1977; "11 Tons of Pot Seized in Giant Coast 'Bust,' " *Jackson Daily News,* 4 Oct. 1976.

[51]See, e.g., "Letter to Editor," *Daily Herald* (Biloxi-Gulfport), 10 Feb. 1977.

[52]"Marihuana Penalty Revision Draws Mixed Reviews," *Daily Journal* (Tupelo), 3 March 1977.

[53]Ibid.; "State Marihuana Law May Come before Senators," *Enterprise Journal,* 11 Feb. 1977; "One Down, One Still to Come," *Jackson Daily News,* 11 Feb. 1977; "House Approves Bill to Relax Pot Laws," *Mobile* (Alabama) *Register,* 11, Feb. 1977; "Senate Approves Marihuana Reform," *South Mississippi Sun* (Biloxi-Gulfport), 11 March 1977.

[54]"Slander and Worse," *Delta Democrat Times* (Greenville), 5 May 1975.

[55]"Playboy and Pot," *New Albany* (Miss.) *Gazette,* 12 June 1975.

of small amounts."[56] He also emphasized the long list of conservatives and establishment organizations supporting decriminalization and eventually convinced the director of the Mississippi Bureau of Narcotics to publicly support the bill. The latter told the state legislature (Mississippi Joint Judiciary Hearings 1977): "It is a bill that we could live with. . . . Our major thrust today is toward heroin, cocaine, amphetamines, barbiturates. . . . I personally feel that alcohol is much more physically damaging to the body than marihuana." After defeats in 1975 and 1976 a decriminalization law was finally passed in 1977. This third bill was no doubt helped by the light sentences given to major drug smugglers earlier that year, but the big difference appears to have been the support of the top drug enforcement official in the state. In an interview the young executive recalled his protracted negotiations with the leaders of the state Bureau of Narcotics:

> I spent several hours on many occasions at the Mississippi Bureau of Narcotics Office talking with the Director and his division heads. They kept saying they didn't arrest kids for possession and I kept saying, let's make your policy into law. After several drafts of the proposed bill, the Director said he could live with it except for the wording "civil offense." He crossed out the "civil" and put in "misdemeanor." I crossed out "misdemeanor" and said let's just leave it an offense. That is how the final draft came about.

Here we have a first-hand account of the process of selling decriminalization to law enforcement.

In California prior to decriminalization, state law provided for penalties of up to 10 years for simple possession. From the outset, the *Los Angeles Times* favored marihuana reform, giving it a great deal of coverage in dozens of articles. The 25 June 1974 paper presented a strong editorial urging senate passage of the assembly bill.[57] The chiefs of police from San Diego and San Francisco indicated that the law merely codified what they had been doing all along—that for years they had only given citations to marihuana users.[58] Prosecutors in Colorado and Oregon had made similar admissions. But the Los Angeles police chief referred to supporters of decriminalization as "irresponsible, no-good sons of bitches" and "pot peddlers,"[59] and " 'it is obvious that a 15 percent philosophical minority who believe in a licentious and libertine existence are going to force it on all of us, even if it kills us.' He predicted that the new law will lead to a doubling of the number of heroin addicts in the state within a year."[60] Earlier, then Governor Ronald Reagan had vetoed decriminalization bills on several occasions because he felt that reducing the penalty would give the "impression to young people that it isn't to be feared. They're going to seize on this as encouragement."[61]

---

[56]*George County Times,* 24 April 1975.
[57]"Reducing the Marihuana Penalty" (Editorial), *Los Angeles Times,* 25 June 1974, pt. 2, p. 6.
[58]"Police Differ on Possible Impact of Marihuana Law," *Los Angeles Times,* 26 Dec. 1975, pt. 2, pp. 1, 2.
[59]"Davis Predicts Outcry on 'Pot,' " *Los Angeles Times,* 2 May 1975, pt. 2, p. 1.
[60]"Davis Hits Signing of 'Pot' Bill, Predicts Crime Wave," *Los Angeles Times,* 11 July 1975, pt. 1, p. 3.
[61]"Reagan Warns against Easier 'Pot' Penalties," *Los Angeles Times,* 5 Dec. 1974, pt. 1, p. 32.

In 1972 there were 73,000 arrested and 150 in prison for marihuana offenses in California—at an annual cost of $100 million (California Senate Select Committee on Control of Marijuana 1974:92, 96, 123). In May 1975 the assembly defeated a decriminalization bill but narrowly passed it in June. All Republicans voted against the bill both times and tried to make it a major partisan issue. The conflict was intense, and the charge was even made before a legislative committee that funding for pro-reform witnesses came from communists.[62] An assembly Republican told the press: "If the Democrats want to pass that bill and foster San Francisco morals on California, . . . they ought to get full credit for it. Ring it around their necks."[63] The Republicans saw what they regarded as a good political issue. Said their leader in the assembly: "Republicans ought not to be a party to taking the first step toward the legalization of marihuana."[64] Four previous attempts had failed: statewide referendum attempts in 1972 and 1974 and vetoes of decriminalization bills by Reagan in 1973 and 1974. It was not until Governor Reagan left office that a bill passed the state legislature and was signed into law.

In New York by 1977, according to a survey of New York City judges, it had become clear that the notoriously tough Rockefeller drug laws passed in 1973 had not deterred illegal drug use (Raab 1977). A congressional committee studied New York City's public schools and found a marked increase in all drug use, including marihuana (Burks 1977). During the assembly debate there were dire predictions for the chain smoker of marihuana: "One year of cannabis smoking, 20 cigarettes a day, can produce sinusitis, pharyngitis, bronchitis and emphysema and other respiratory conditions" (New York Assembly 1977a). All these alleged horrors were just too much for one member of the assembly to endure in silence: "It really bothers me to hear somebody talk about recreational drugs. You might as well talk about recreational cancer because the debilitating effect of drugs are far worse" (ibid.). The small Conservative party nearly killed the bill by bullying conservative Republicans into joining their opposition, but then backed away after criticism by William F. Buckley for its "unthinking traditionalism."[65]

New York assembly members claimed: "No judge is convicting, no jury is convicting, the law is not working" (New York Assembly 1977a); "One judge that I know of in Upstate New York . . . refused to impose the penalties and publicly stated it. And, all the people in the 7th Judicial District knew that he refused to impose the penalties, and they elected him to the supreme court of this state" (New York Assembly 1977b). A member of the New York assembly who was also a police officer reported:

> In ten years in the New York City Police Department I never experienced or met anybody that had mugged somebody to get the money to buy marihuana. I never found any-

[62]"Bill to Ease State Marihuana Penalties Clears Key Panel," *Los Angeles Times*, 12 Feb. 1975, pt. 1, pp. 1, 25.
[63]"Bill to Ease 'Pot' Law Moves to Assembly Floor," *Los Angeles Times*, 30 April 1975, pt. 2, pp. 1, 3.
[64]"Bill to Relax 'Pot' Law Hits Roadblock," *Los Angeles Times*, 8 May 1975, pt. 1, pp. 3, 31.
[65]"Justice Done, Undone, Done in: No Pot Luck," *New York Times*, 29 May 1977, sec. 4, p. 14.

body that was addicted to marihuana. . . . Forcing a police officer to go out and lock somebody up for having marihuana causes them to be hypocritical because he knows that if the case is brought to court that the probability of anybody being prosecuted is practically nil. (New York Assembly 1977a)

In the New York Senate it was reported that there were 27,644 marihuana possession arrests in the state in 1975 and 20,961 in 1976—at a total cost of $52 million (New York Senate 1977). An editorial on 30 April 1977 stated, "The imperatives for reform are clear."[66]

In both New York and California it was obvious that marihuana possession penalties did not deter marihuana use even though massive numbers of arrests were made at great expense. The question was, could young people be protected from the law and could law enforcement be protected from collapse? Yet the bills were the subject of protracted conflict and nearly failed to pass because in both states the opposition to decriminalization was represented by an organized interest group. In California and Mississippi there were deep divisions of opinion among local law enforcement. In Mississippi the legislation took three years of intensive lobbying in spite of the obvious problems of crowded prisons and hanging judges, and was ultimately passed only when the director of the Mississippi Bureau of Narcotics was convinced to support the bill. In these three states we again see the law enforcement problems and widespread dissonant behavior Lempert (1974) predicted, but here we also see the intense political conflict that he imagined would be associated with all such legal changes. In these three states concern for young people was not prominently mentioned and, in any case, did not immobilize opposition to decriminalization. The importance of including in our analysis the total cohort of decriminalization states, avoiding isolated case studies as cautioned by Hagan (1980), now becomes apparent. By including the total group of decriminalization states, we can distinguish between conditions that are incidental to marihuana decriminalization and those that are essential.

THE NARROW WINDOW OF OPPORTUNITY MISSED: THE FAILURE TO PASS DECRIMINALIZATION BILLS DURING THE 1970S

In 1978 the eminent criminologist Jerome Skolnick confidently predicted: "It is conceivable that in the next ten years marihuana will be virtually decriminalized in this country" and that some states would do the same with heroin and cocaine (Skolnick & Dombrink 1978:194). But by 1979 the movement to decriminalize marihuana had come to an end. Just as Kingdon (1984) claimed, the policy window closed just as quickly as it had opened. In 1973 a writer in *Harper's* had expressed certainty that marihuana would be *legalized* in Iowa by 1980, preceded by decriminalization in 1976, as this was an idea "whose time had come" (Bourjaily 1973:13). But the effort to pass a decriminalization bill failed in Iowa (National Governors' Conference 1977). In 1976 it was predicted that Illinois and New Jersey would decriminalize

---

[66]"Melting the Marihuana Glacier" (Editorial), *New York Times,* 30 April 1977, pt. 4, p. 20.

marihuana possession (Post 1976). Illinois never passed such a law, and developments in New Jersey provide an example of how quickly the situation changed. By 1978 proponents of decriminalization in New Jersey had the support of legislative leaders, the state's governor, and attorney general, as well as the endorsement of a legislative study commission (Sullivan 1974; Waldron 1978). Even so, such legislation got nowhere in the 1979 legislature or thereafter.

Records of floor debate and committee hearings indicate that many of the 39 states which did not pass marihuana decriminalization bills never seriously considered marihuana reform legislation. For example, decriminalization legislation was not even introduced in some states, among them Texas (National Governors' Conference 1977), Alabama (Adams 1993), Florida (Helms 1993), Kentucky (Cummins 1993), Idaho (Silvers 1993), Delaware (Gross 1993), Montana (Foley 1993), Arizona (Muir 1993) and Nevada (Galliher & Cross 1983). In other states, decriminalization bills never got out of committee and left no record of public hearings or floor debate. For example, in Maryland decriminalization bills were introduced in 1973, 1974, and 1976, but the closest a bill came to being reported out of committee was a 4–4 deadlock in the Senate Judiciary Committee in 1978 (Garland 1981).

In some areas failure of marihuana reforms seems to have been a consequence of how the issue was originally framed because legal change seemed to require a specific formula for success. No matter what the traditions of the local political culture, if the bills proposed violated the narrow boundaries of successful decriminalization legislation, the initiatives inevitably failed. For example, in Virginia a legislative subcommittee recommended removing jail terms for marihuana possession and *cultivation* (Edwards, 1979). The proposal got nowhere. Suggesting that cultivation be treated the same as simple possession apparently was beyond the bounds of possible reform. In Maryland one bill introduced in the Senate Judiciary Committee in 1974 would have "eliminated all penalties" for possession of marihuana (Barker & Walsh 1974). Marihuana reform bills introduced thereafter were all scuttled, including a 1977 initiative to study legislation to "fully legalize marihuana" (Baker 1977). In Seattle in 1974 voters rejected by a 2 to 1 margin an initiative that would have legalized marihuana possession.[67] All subsequent attempts at marihuana reform in Washington State were stalled. In Louisiana a 1972 "proposal was introduced . . . to study the feasibility of *legalization* or decriminalization of marihuana" (emphasis added), which failed by more than a 2 to 1 margin (National Governors' Conference 1977: pt. I, p. 215). Subsequent 1976 decriminalization bills in both the House and the Senate died in committee. The only marihuana reform bill reported out of committee was debated in the Senate and amended to include jail terms; thus the concept of decriminalization was dead (National Governors' Conference 1977).

Other states had similar experiences. A 1977 Oklahoma bill (H.B. 1268) providing for the "*legal* possession of four ounces or less" died in committee (emphasis added). In Washington, D.C., a task force appointed by the mayor advised legalizing

---

[67]"Around the Nation," *Washington Post*, 28 March 1974, p. A10.

marihuana use and possession (Claiborne 1973), and thereafter marihuana reforms were stymied in spite of support from the D.C. Medical Society (Feinberg 1973). A 1972 Michigan bill would have *legalized* use of marihuana in a private residence (H. 6051). Similar bills were reintroduced in Michigan in 1973/74, 1975/76, and 1977/78, with no success. A *Chicago Tribune* headline reported on a "Stormy Session on Marihuana Bill" where a proposal to *legalize* possession of marihuana in private residences was defeated in the Illinois House Judiciary Committee.[68] Thereafter several decriminalization bills were introduced, but all failed. In 1974 the Massachusetts state senate approved plans for a public referendum to "legalize marihuana" that got nowhere.[69] In addition that year, bills that would have *legalized* possession and *sale* of marihuana in Massachusetts were introduced (H. 3406, H. 3587). In subsequent years decriminalization bills failed, even though there was support from law enforcement (Buckley 1975) and 54% of those polled in the state in 1978 supported decriminalization (Clark University Department of Government 1978). If *legalization* seemed to be one word to avoid, *sale* of marihuana was another.

In some states, failure of decriminalization initiatives appeared to result not only from the terms originally used to propose marihuana reforms but also as a consequence of who was sponsoring the legislation. In Kansas the *Topeka Journal* reported about a bill that would have decriminalized possession of less than two ounces of marihuana, sponsored by a Democratic legislator from Lawrence, the home of the University of Kansas.[70] The paper reported that in past sessions the legislator had "attempted outright legalization, and much broader decriminalization" measures. His picture appeared with the article, showing him with shoulder-length hair and a heavy beard. Given his historical support for more sweeping marihuana proposals as well as his appearance, it was not surprising that this and his later even more modest decriminalization proposals failed.[71]

In Wisconsin multiple, wide-range marihuana reform bills were introduced in 1971, 1973, 1975, 1977, and 1979. All these bills would have eliminated prohibitions for possession and use as well as *sale* of the drug. The sponsor of these bills was a liberal African American, Democratic house member whom the press described as "outrageous" and as one who "loved to shock the system."[72] Early in the marihuana debate he argued: "[i]f a person wants to take a joint to make life more palatable, we shouldn't say he can't."[73] This line of reasoning predictably triggered angry responses, including one from a house colleague who said: "As far as I'm concerned intoxication is a sin."[74] Along with marihuana reform, the maverick legislator defended the legalization of all drugs, prostitution, gay rights, and abortion on

---

[68]23 April 1975, p. 1A.
[69]"Marihuana Vote Urged," *New York Times,* 26 April 1974, p. 31.
[70]"Marihuana Law Revision Proposed," *Topeka Journal,* 26 Jan. 1977.
[71]"Pot Backers Go for 6th Try," *Wichita Eagle,* 11 March 1979.
[72]"The OUTRAGEOUS Mr. Barbee," *Milwaukee Journal, Insight Magazine,* 16 April 1972, pp. 24, 25.
[73]"Barbee Presents Case for Legalization of Marihuana," *Capital Times* (Madison, WI), 29 April 1971, p. 19.
[74]Ibid.

demand. The *Milwaukee Journal* noted with considerable understatement that the "mortality rate of such unorthodox bills is high."[75] This legislator, however, remained undeterred, for he felt that even if his bills were not passed, their mere introduction was "educational."[76] Like the legislator in Kansas, he seemed to be the wrong messenger, with the wrong message. The difference in his approach and that of the conservative Republican in Mississippi who said he did not "advocate or encourage the use of marihuana" could not have been greater. Not only was the marihuana policy window open for a short period, but it only allowed for narrowly circumscribed reforms. It did not extend to sale of marihuana and did not include the legalization of possession. Successful reforms also required some maintenance of the message that marihuana use was improper. The many tactical errors appear to have been based on the mistaken presumption of imminent radical change reflected in the predictions of Skolnick and others mentioned above.

THE DEMISE OF DECRIMINALIZATION IN THE 1980S

If the 1972 NCMDA Report provided the form as well as the timing of the states' decriminalization laws, perhaps we should again look to the federal level to understand why only 11 states passed such laws and why none did so after 1978. What seems important, if not essential, to this legislation is federal leadership. That leadership was briefly available during the Ford administration and early in the Carter administration, but missing prior to that time and thereafter. Until his resignation in 1974, President Nixon had consistently opposed decriminalization of marihuana, even after the publication of his commission's report, which he rejected.[77] After Nixon left office and until 1978 there was considerable agreement among national political leaders on the desirability of marihuana decriminalization. However, this changed after marihuana use by Carter White House staff was reported. Carter was besieged by further charges of drug use among senior White House staff being leaked to the press. The Republican Senate minority leader called for an official investigation by the Justice Department into drug use among White House staff (Smith 1978). President Carter gave no support to decriminalization thereafter, undoubtedly in part because partisan political conflict with Republican opposition had not been the usual path to success, and Carter could have been expected to know that a partisan political conflict on marihuana decriminalization without wholehearted Republican support would be hard to win.

At the time marihuana decriminalization bills were being passed, Skolnick (1978:27–28) observed: "Basically, the strategy of decriminalization has been to reduce penalties for the socially acceptable and powerful users." Yet with "concepts like decriminalization . . . we solve some problems, but create new ones." Skolnick (1978:28) quotes from the NCMDA report: "[I]t is painfully clear . . . that the

---

[75]*Milwaukee Journal, Insight Magazine,* 16 April 1972, p. 25 (cited in note 72).
[76]"Barbee Calls His 'Far-out' Bills Educational," *Capital Times,* 28 June 1973, p. 15.
[77]"Transcript of the President's News Conference on Foreign and Domestic Matters," *New York Times,* 25 March 1972, p. 12.

absence of a criminal penalty for private use is presently equated in too many minds with approval. . . . The commission regrets that marihuana's symbolism remains so powerful, obstructing the emergence of a rational policy." At least in this regard, Skolnick and the commission were prophetic. The symbolism of marihuana use remained a powerful part of the legislative equation.

Even as early as the late 1970s, the views political leaders expressed began to change. In 1977 Dr. Robert DuPont, the former drug-policy advisor to the Nixon and Ford administrations, reversed his earlier support for decriminalization and advocated de facto decriminalization in its place.

> On the substantive merits of the issue, everybody is for decriminalization. But the real issue is symbolic. Nobody wants to have anyone, young or old, go to jail for possession of small amounts of marihuana. But being in favor of decriminalization is seen by the majority of the public as being in favor of pot. . . . It is possible to eliminate jail as a threat for simple possession of marihuana without favoring decriminalization. This is the way out! In fact, as a nation we have already done that. . . . Those who now go to jail are the sellers of marihuana. (Anderson 1981:312)

De facto decriminalization has the added advantage of being a means of avoiding the rancorous conflict that surrounded decriminalization bills in New York, California, and Mississippi.

Additional evidence concerning de facto decriminalization emerges when government records of incarceration and arrest are compared with survey data on frequency of marihuana use. If it is assumed, as some respondents argued, that the primary concern in decriminalization hinges on the issue of incarceration, then it is necessary to determine the levels at which incarceration is actually used. In 1984 questionnaires were mailed to all state departments of correction asking for the number of inmates in the state prison system whose most serious crime was marihuana possession. The 43 states responding reported a total of 2,729 prisoners, for an average of about 65 per state. Given such small numbers, one can understand why a sense of urgency or widespread dissonance was missing.

The incarceration figures can also be compared with arrest figures. The *FBI Uniform Crime Reports* between 1977 and 1992 indicate that total drug arrests nearly doubled, while marihuana possession arrests have declined by nearly a third. In 1977 marihuana possession arrests accounted for 61% of all drug arrests; in 1986, 36% of all drug arrests; by 1992 this figure had dropped to 25%. These figures show that the police no longer are swamped primarily by marihuana possession cases, and that over these three decades there has been a steady decrease in the emphasis on marihuana possession enforcement compared to other drugs. Thus the sense of urgency regarding the bureaucratic benefits flowing from marihuana reform has vanished. Still, compared with the about 300,000 marihuana possession arrests made annually, the numbers incarcerated for marihuana possession are minuscule and give real evidence of de facto decriminalization.

The relatively constant number of marihuana possession arrests is mirrored by levels of marihuana use that remained relatively stable between the 1970s and the

1980s. For example, in 1976 approximately 52% of high school seniors had ever used marihuana. In 1980 the figure had increased to 60% but had dropped again by 1985 to 54%, about the same level as found in 1976 (Bachman et al. 1986). One possible explanation for the decreasing support for the decriminalization movement is that states passing such laws might have routinely experienced consequent increases in marihuana use. No such evidence exists. There were similar patterns in the frequency of marihuana use in decriminalization states compared with those without such laws (Johnston et al. 1981). The decreased proportions of all drug arrests involving marihuana and scant use of incarceration cannot be attributed to there being far fewer marihuana users or much less marihuana in circulation. Given the widespread use of marihuana reflected in survey results, these arrest and incarceration figures suggested some de facto decriminalization. Yet they also indicated that the process was not quite complete, contrary to the claims of DuPont.

If de facto decriminalization indicates *how* the legislative reform has been stalled, the question that remains is *why* it occurred and at this particular time. Himmelstein (1986) has observed that by the 1980s, or even earlier, local parents' groups concerned about marihuana began to form, the New Right emerged as a major antimarihuana force, and federal officials no longer supported decriminalization. He concluded: "Which is cause and effect is hard to say" (p. 10). The 1980s ushered in a new conservative Republican administration. In 1986 President Reagan attempted to initiate a "national crusade" to combat the drug epidemic, which he said was "a repudiation of everything America is" (Pasztor 1986). This crusade is consistent with Reagan's opposition to decriminalization while he was governor of California, given his fear of sending the wrong message to potential users. To this was added Mrs. Reagan's cant, "Just Say No to Drugs." More recently, the Bush administration's director of drug control policy, William Bennett, joined the crusade in criticizing skeptics like economist Milton Friedman and former Secretary of State George Shultz for their observations that the nation's drug control policies were not enforceable. Bennett was unswayed by these difficulties. "I remain an ardent defender of our nation's laws against illegal drug use and our attempts to enforce them because I believe drug use is wrong" (Bennett 1989). When a federal judge called for legalization due to his first-hand observations of the collapse of drug law enforcement, Bennett responded by asserting that this argument was as "morally atrocious as it ever was."[78] Bennett, like DuPont, apparently preferred unenforced legislation as opposed to actual decriminalization because of the symbolic power criminal penalties provide even if unenforced. The cornerstone of the Bush administration's efforts to control illegal drugs is found in its voluminous *National Drug Control Strategy* published in 1989. No mention was made there of decriminalization of marihuana, and only feeble recommendations were made for marihuana control, including increased intelligence in foreign drug-producing countries and stepped-up crop eradication.

---

[78]"Bennett Says 'No' to Drugs," *Kansas City Star,* 14 Dec. 1989, p. 1.

Yet the failure of decriminalization produced additional dissonance and contradictions. "[R]esolutions of particular conflicts," as Chambliss noted (1979:7–8), "create further conflicts." To understand these problems, it is important to emphasize that the academic community was of little direct significance in this dispute because there was comparatively little debate about the definition of marihuana or the degree to which it is a dangerous drug. Just as in the 1930s when expert medical testimony was ignored in federal marihuana legislation (Galliher & Walker 1977), the impact of physicians in the decriminalization process seemed blunted by the fact that even as early as the 1970s marihuana was already widely recognized as something other than a very dangerous drug. During the 1980s the medical picture remained unchanged. In 1988 a Drug Enforcement Administration (DEA) administrative law judge ruled that marihuana was "one of the safest therapeutically active substances known to man" (Isikoff 1988), with no evidence of a single cannabis-induced fatality and thus the drug should be made available for legitimate medical purposes such as the treatment of glaucoma and the nausea resulting from chemotherapy in cancer patients (Drug Enforcement Administration 1988). "But the DEA rejected its own judge's opinion and stands firm that doctors shall not prescribe marihuana."[79] In 1989 the Director of the Office of National Drug Control Policy, William Bennett, publicly admitted that marihuana was no more dangerous than alcohol but still saw no reason to support any legal changes.[80]

Alaska, the only state to have repealed a decriminalization law, did so by referendum in 1990 after the state legislature had consistently refused to recriminalize marihuana, knowing that, if enforced, any such statute would be overturned by the state supreme court (Boyko 1990). The Anchorage Bar Association also had unanimously voted to oppose recriminalization because of problems of selective enforcement. But shortly prior to the referendum vote, William Bennett traveled to Alaska to offer his support.[81] Unlike the state bar association, the minority whip of the state assembly was not concerned with actual enforcement of the measure, which called for up to 90 days in jail and a $1,000 fine. He was quoted as claiming:

> [P]eople like me understood that the law is more than just putting people in jail. It has
> other functions as well. The law is a witness. The law is a testament to our values. It
> describes what we believe is right and wrong. It sets an example for our children and
> that's why it passed.[82]

Another leader of the drive to recriminalize marihuana said the voters should be congratulated for "sending out a strong message against drugs."[83] Yet another leader said, "what I am hoping to achieve with this law is to begin to tell our young people,

---

[79]"60 Minutes," CBS News, 1 Dec. 1991.
[80]*Kansas City Star,* 14 Dec. 1989, pp. 1, 2 (cited in note 90).
[81]"Showdown over Pot-Smoking in Anchorage, Alaska," Donahue Show, NBC News, 16 Nov. 1990.
[82]Ibid.
[83]"Alaska: Mowing the Grass," *Time,* 19 Nov. 1990, p. 47.

'This stuff is harmful. It is hurting you.' And we will begin, hopefully not only to change the attitudes of the children, but the attitudes of the parents."[84] Thus, all supporters appeared to agree that the vote itself sent a symbolic message and that was the critical issue rather than actual enforcement.

SUMMARY: THE CONTINUING CONTRADICTIONS OF MARIHUANA CONTROL

The problem addressed here concerns the origins of marihuana decriminalization, both its inception and its lapse into de facto decriminalization. Two factors seem important—bureaucratic, law enforcement problems and moral dissonance. The first played a major role in decriminalization, while the second was a factor both in the origins of decriminalization legislation and in the symbolic form this reform eventually took in de facto decriminalization, which avoids jail terms without formal legal change. Marihuana decriminalization provided what initially seemed to be an ideal resolution to the conflict between the drug use of affluent Americans and the requirements of law enforcement. Among the 11 decriminalization states, there were very few instances of severe press opposition. Yet the immediate significance of the mass media in and of itself is less important than might be imagined because across the nation, even in states that never decriminalized marihuana, press reports during the 1970s became increasingly sanguine about marihuana and its users (Himmelstein 1983; Shepherd 1979). If the scientific evidence remained unchanged, the mass media in the 1980s largely ceased making distinctions between marihuana and other drugs, thereby playing a role in a resurgent "drug frenzy" (Ehrenreich 1988:20). And all successful decriminalization bills had some law enforcement support, as Scheerer (1978) also found in the Netherlands. Our results are much like Inciardi's (1981), who also noted that decriminalization drives were propelled through state legislatures largely by efforts aimed at increasing law enforcement efficiency. Such instrumental considerations often dominate the agenda of local officials, responsible as they are for local social order. After the first wave of decriminalization laws had been passed, the structural foundations for decriminalization remained unchanged and compelling. There were still large numbers of affluent marihuana users and police forces that were more overwhelmed every year.

While scientific facts were not significant considerations in the demise of decriminalization, neither bureaucratic considerations nor social class interests sealed the fate of this legislative movement, and we uncovered no evidence of changing public opinion. As Himmelstein (1986:3) has observed, "that marihuana received only partial approval suggests that impact of the social status of the actor on the moral status of the act is limited." Given the history of alcohol prohibition, many observers undoubtedly have been surprised that the widespread use of marihuana by affluent Americans has not resulted in its legalization. Unlike the failure of alcohol prohibition, marihuana prohibitions remain on the books in most states in spite of

---

[84]Donahue Show, NBC News, 16 Nov. 1990 (cited in note 81).

widespread marihuana use by the middle and upper classes and in spite of the over-whelming demands on law enforcement resulting from the 1980s crack epidemic.

The different histories of these two prohibitions can best be explained by the nature of the prohibitions themselves, as well as other demographic characteristics of alcohol and marihuana users. Alcohol prohibition only put legal controls on manu-facture and distribution, not on possession. Therefore, public use of alcohol by those of all ages was common during Prohibition and speak-easies abounded, both broad-casting the failure of this national policy. For marihuana, manufacture, distribution, *and possession* are all prohibited. And while marihuana use has occurred in public at rock concerts and other similar events, it has more often been a private event. Because most marihuana use occurs in private, the failure of the current legal policy is not so obvious, allowing officials to persist in the illusion of the efficacy of these legal controls even in the face of survey data showing massive use. Moreover, while alcohol is used by all age groups, marihuana is used primarily by young people and thus can be dismissed as the product of immaturity and youthful indiscretion. Gus-field (1981:184) has noted that the intense conflict over marihuana legislation sym-bolized the struggle of the "authority of adult culture and its power over youth" during a historical period "when adult public values were under attack in wide areas, including sex, work goals, public decorum, and dress." Our data suggest that only prominent concern for young people could neutralize this conflict and allow decrim-inalization legislation to pass without partisan controversy. No one political party, for example, was willing to cede to another a monopoly on concern for the young.

The theory of decriminalization began with the assumption that such legislation originates in a moral dissonance created by the law violation by high-status individ-uals. Lempert (1974:5) predicted that "if moral dissonance is to induce legal change . . . observed dissonant behavior must be widespread." Marihuana use and the consequent threat of arrest was widespread across America. Thus, such dissonance was equally widespread and developed in states in all regions of the nation, among large and small states, homogeneous and heterogeneous states, conservative and lib-eral states, and clearly was not idiosyncratic to any particular political and cultural mix. This is true, even though Lempert notes that decriminalization laws may be passed at a time "when the moral principle embodied in the statute is still of com-pelling importance to many." This was clearly the case with marihuana decriminal-ization, and thus a new moral dissonance was created by the decriminalization laws themselves, since those who continued to argue that marihuana use belonged in the same moral realm as use of other illegal substances were now concerned that the new laws provided insufficient penalties. Just as Burstein (1985:193) noted, the passage of a law does not represent the end "but rather an intermediate stage in the political process." The persistence of prohibitionist moral principles explains the bitter leg-islative battles in some decriminalization states, the failure of most states to pass decriminalization legislation, and recriminalization efforts in still others. In King-don's (1984:174) words, marihuana reform bills could only take advantage of a very narrowly defined and strictly limited "policy windows" with only clearly circum-scribed justifications.

Indicators of a problematic condition form the most immediate basis for policy change. Selective enforcement of marihuana laws, nominal sentences for large-scale dealers, the arrest of affluent users, and the fears of parents of youthful marihuana users all served to focus attention for a time on the legal controls rather than the drug use itself. Kingdon (1984) has demonstrated that policy initiatives at first circulate informally within communities of policy specialists. As the marihuana policy crisis reached its height, the National Commission on Marihuana and Drug Abuse in 1972 recommended decriminalization as a minor incremental reform that would solve the existing law enforcement problems while not raising the ire of President Nixon. It is important to remember that no other "recreational" drugs were seriously considered as candidates for reform. This demonstrates weak support for decriminalization as a foundation for penal policy. In addition, Kingdon referred to the importance of the national mood in any policy change. For marihuana reforms, it is significant that President Nixon had left office and was eventually replaced by the more reformist Carter administration. Yet after one Carter term, the nation seemed to veer to the right led by President Reagan.

As early as 1974 it had become clear that even while most opponents of decriminalization agreed that marihuana users should not be imprisoned, they preferred de facto decriminalization and "a minimum penalty . . . to make it clear to young people that society . . . does not approve of [marihuana] use" (Himmelstein 1983:105). The problem with decriminalization as a solution to these practical problems, as Ronald Reagan had said while he was still governor of California, was that it indicated that marihuana was not really a dangerous drug. Since the consequences of marihuana decriminalization were primarily symbolic, another type of symbolic policy was seen as the required response. Both Edelman (1964) and Chambliss (1979) argue that symbolic law is often a vehicle for such a resolution of conflicting political and economic needs. De facto decriminalization offered an ideal resolution of this additional conflict that developed as a consequence of the decriminalization laws themselves. In the final analysis the real differences for law enforcement and, for most marihuana users, in the consequences of de facto versus de jure decriminalization are not that great. De facto decriminalization is an effective means of reducing the moral dissonance inherent in the arrest of high-status individuals while still retaining the presence of criminal penalties. Since law enforcement has only finite resources, if legislatures refuse to set law enforcement priorities, police will do it for them. Legislators are seldom interested in taking political risks. Thus the obvious symbolic advantages of de facto decriminalization tip the balance.

REFERENCES

Abelson, Herbert I., & Patricia M. Fishburne (1977) *National Survey on Drug Abuse.* Rockville, MD: National Institute on Drug Abuse.

Adams, Anne (1993) "Report of Legislative Analyst," Alabama Legislative Reference Service, Montgomery, AL, 16 March.

Alaska (1975) House Judiciary Committee, S.B. 350, 1 May.

Anderson, Patrick (1981) *High in America: The True Story behind NORML and the Politics of Marijuana.* New York: Viking Press.

Bachman, Jerald G., Lloyd D. Johnston, Patrick M. O'Malley, & Ronald H. Humphrey (1986) "Changes in Marihuana Use Linked to Changes in Perceived Risks and Disapproval." Monitoring the Future, Occasional Paper No. 19. Ann Arbor: MI: Institute for Social Research, Univ. of Michigan.

Baker, Donald P. (1977) "Md. Delegate Backs Study on Easing Marijuana Law," *Washington Post,* 23 Feb., p. C7.

Barker, Karlyn, & Edward Walsh (1974a) "Md. Senate Unit Kills 2 Bills to Cut Marijuana Penalties," *Washington Post,* 1 March, p. B10.

Bennett, William S. (1989) "A Response to Milton Friedman," *Wall Street Journal,* 19 Sept., p. A30.

Bourjaily, Vance (1973) "Marijuana Politics: Iowa, 1973," *Harper's Magazine,* August, p. 12.

Boyko, Edgar Paul (1990) "Showdown over Pot-Smoking in Anchorage, Alaska," Donahue Show, 16 Nov.

Buckley, John J. (1975) Remarks of Middlesex County Sheriff before the Human Services and Elderly Affairs Committee, 13 March, Massachusetts State Legislature.

Buckley, William F., Jr. (1972) "The Spirit of the Law," *National Rev.,* 8 Dec., p. 1348.

Burks, Edward C. (1977) "House Panel Finds Big Rise in Drug Use in New York's School-children," *New York Times,* 8 Feb., sec. 1, p. 15.

Burstein, Paul (1985) *Discrimination, Jobs, and Politics: The Struggle for Equal Employment Opportunity in the United States since the New Deal.* Chicago: Univ. of Chicago Press.

California Senate Select Committee on Control of Marijuana (1974) *Understanding the Social Costs of Marijuana.* Sacramento: California Legislature.

CBS News (1991) "60 Minutes," 1 Dec.

Chambliss, William J. (1979) "Contradictions and Conflicts in Law Creation," in S. Spitzer, ed., 2 *Research in Law and Sociology: A Research Annual.* Greenwich, CT: JAI Press, Inc.

Claiborne, William L. (1973) "Mayor's Task Force Advises Legalizing Marijuana Here," *Washington Post,* 6 March, p. A1.

Clark University Department of Government (1978) "Majority Supports Decriminalization of Marihuana," Released July 14, State Library of Massachusetts.

Colorado (1975) House Judiciary Committee, H.B. 1027, 20 Feb.

Cummins, Leslie (1993) "Report of Legislative Research Commission," Frankfort, KY, 24 Feb.

Dershowitz, Alan M. (1976) "Criminal Sentencing in the United States: An Historical and Conceptual Overview," 423 *Annals of the American Academy of Political & Social Science* 117.

Edelman, Murray (1964) *The Symbolic Uses of Politics.* Urbana: Univ. of Illinois Press.

Edwards, Paul G. (1979) "Reduced Pot Penalties Asked," *Washington Post,* 20 Jan., p. B2.

Ehrenreich, Barbara (1988) "Drug Frenzy," *MS,* November, pp. 20–21.

Empey, LaMar T. (1978) *American Delinquency: Its Meaning and Construction.* Homewood, IL: Dorsey Press.

Engelmann, Larry (1979) *Intemperance: The Lost War against Liquor.* New York: Free Press.

Federal Bureau of Investigation (1977–92) *Uniform Crime Reports.* Washington, DC: GPO.

Feinberg, Lawrence (1973) "D.C. Doctors: Legalize Use of Marijuana," *Washington Post,* 21 Nov., p. C2.

Fishburne, Patricia M., Herbert I. Abelson, & Ira H. Cisin (1979) *National Survey on Drug Abuse: Main Findings.* Rockville, MD: National Institute on Drug Abuse.

Foley, Jodie Ann (1993) "Report of Archival Technician," Montana Historical Society, Helena, MT, 6 April.

Galliher, John F., & Linda Basilick (1979) "Utah's Liberal Drug Laws: Structural Foundations and Triggering Events," 26 *Social Problems* 284.

Galliher, John F., & John Ray Cross (1982) "Symbolic Severity in the Land of Easy Virtue: Nevada's High Marihuana Penalty," 29 *Social Problems* 380.

———— (1983) *Morals Legislation without Morality: The Case of Nevada.* New Brunswick, NJ: Rutgers Univ. Press.

Galliher, John F., James L. McCartney, & Barbara E. Baum (1974) "Nebraska's Marijuana Law: A Case of Unexpected Legislative Innovation," 8 *Law & Society Rev.* 441.

Galliher, John F., & Allynn Walker (1977) "The Puzzle of the Social Origins of the Marihuana Tax Act of 1937," 24 *Social Problems* 367.

Gallup Poll (1977) "Public Would not Legalize Marijuana Now, but Decriminalization Wins Support," *Gallup Opinion Index,* Report No. 143 (June).

———— (1980) "Opposition to Legalization of Marijuana Unchanged," *Gallup Opinion Index,* Report No. 179 (July).

———— (1985) "Public Resists More Liberal Marijuana Laws," *Gallup Report,* Report No. 241 (Oct.)

Garland, Eric (1981) "Legal Marihuana: An Idea Going Up in Smoke," *Baltimore Magazine,* Jan., p. 63.

Goode, Erich (1970) *The Marijuana Smokers.* New York: Basic Books.

Gross, Randy L. (1993) "Report of Archivist Supervisor," Bureau of Archives and Records Management, Delaware Department of State, Dover, DE, 2 April.

Gusfield, Joseph R. (1963) *Symbolic Crusade: Status Politics and the American Temperance Movement.* Urbana: Univ. of Illinois Press.

———— (1981) *The Culture of Public Problems: Drinking-Driving and the Symbolic Order.* Chicago: Univ. of Chicago Press.

Hagan, John (1980) "The Legislation of Crime and Delinquency: A Review of Theory, Method, and Research," 14 *Law & Society Rev.* 603.

Helmer, John (1975) *Drugs and Minority Oppression.* New York: Seabury Press.

Helms, James (1993) "Report of Division of Library and Information Services," Florida Department of State, Tallahassee, 15 March.

Himmelstein, Jerome L. (1983) *The Strange Career of Marihuana: Politics and Ideology of Drug Control in America.* Westport, CT: Greenwood Press.

———— (1986) "The Continuing Career of Marihuana: Backlash . . . within Limits," 13 *Contemporary Drug Problems* 1.

Inciardi, James A. (1981) "Marijuana Decriminalization Research: A Perspective and Commentary," 19 *Criminology* 145.

Isikoff, Michael (1988) "Administrative Judge Urges Medicinal Use of Marijuana," *Washington Post,* 7 Sept., p. A2.

Jacob, Herbert (1988) *Silent Revolution: The Transformation of Divorce Laws in the United States.* Chicago: Univ. of Chicago Press.

Johnston, Lloyd D., Patrick M. O'Malley, & Jerald G. Bachman (1981) *Marihuana Decriminalization: The Impact on Youth, 1975–1980.* Monitoring the Future, Occasional Paper, No. 13. Ann Arbor: Institute for Social Research, Univ. of Michigan.

Kerr, K. Austin (1985) *Organized for Prohibition: A New History of the Anti-Saloon League.* New Haven, CT: Yale Univ. Press.

Kingdon, John W. (1984) *Agenda, Alternatives, and Public Policies.* Boston: Little, Brown & Co.

Kyvig, David E. (1979) *Repealing National Prohibition.* Chicago: Univ. of Chicago Press.

LaGuardia Commission on Marihuana (1944) *The Marihuana Problem in the City of New York: Sociological, Medical, Psychological, and Pharmacological Studies.* New York: LaGuardia Commission on Marihuana, New York City.

Lempert, Richard (1974) "Toward a Theory of Decriminalization," 3 *Et Al.* 1.

MacKenzie, John P. (1973) "Bar Moves on Drug, Sex Laws," *Washington Post,* 9 Aug., pp. A1, A12.

Minnesota House Judiciary Committee (1975) Hearings on H.F. 749, 1 April.

Minnesota Senate Judiciary Committee (1975a) Hearings on H.F. 749, 21 March.

———— (1975b) Hearings on H.F. 749, 11 April.

Minnesota Senate (1975) Debate, H.F. 749, 12 May.

Mississippi Joint Judiciary Committee (1977) Hearings on Controlled Substances Act, 1 Feb.

Morgan, Patricia A. (1978) "The Legislation of Drug Law: Economic Crisis and Social Control," 8 *J. of Drug Issues* 53.

Muir, Louise (1993) "Report of Library, Archives and Public Records," Phoenix, AZ, 8 April.

Musto, David F. (1973) *The American Disease: Origins of Narcotic Control.* New Haven, CT: Yale Univ. Press.

National Commission on Marihuana & Drug Abuse (1972) *Marihuana: A Signal of Misunderstanding.* Washington, DC: GPO.

National Governors' Conference Center for Policy Research & Analysis (1977) *Marijuana: A Study of State Policies and Penalties.* Washington, DC: U.S. Department of Justice.

NBC News (1990) "Showdown over Pot-Smoking in Anchorage, Alaska," Donahue Show, 16 Nov.

Nebraska Senate (1978) Debate, L.B. 808, 7 April.

New York Assembly (1977a) Debate, 16 May.

———— (1977b) Debate, 27 June.

New York Senate (1977) Debate, 28 June.

North Carolina Senate (1977) Debate, H.B. 1325, January 29.

Olson-Raymer, Gayle (1984) "National Juvenile Justice Policy: Myth or Reality," in S. H. Decker, ed., *Juvenile Justice Policy: Analyzing Trends and Outcomes.* Beverly Hills, CA: Sage Publications.

Pasztor, Andy (1986) "Reagans Issue Call for Crusade against Drugs," *Wall Street Journal,* 15 Sept., p. 64.

Peterson, Ruth D. (1985) "Discriminatory Decision Making at the Legislative Level: An Analysis of the Comprehensive Drug Abuse Prevention and Control Act of 1970," 9 *Law & Human Behavior* 243.

Polsby, Nelson W. (1984) *Political Innovation in America: The Politics of Policy Initiation.* New Haven, CT: Yale Univ. Press.

Polsky, Ned (1967) *Hustlers, Beats, and Others.* Chicago: Aldine Publishing Co.

Post, Penny (1976) "Joint Effort," *Seventeen,* Feb., p. 30.

President's Advisory Commission on Narcotics & Drug Abuse (1963) *Final Report.* Washington, DC: GPO (Nov.).

President's Commission on Law Enforcement & Administration of Justice (1968) *Task Force Report: Narcotics and Drug Abuse.* Washington, DC: GPO.

Raab, Selwyn (1977) "Stiff Antidrug Laws Held No Deterrent," *New York Times,* 2 Jan., sec. 1, p. 1.

Rubin, H. Ted (1985) *Juvenile Justice: Policy, Practice and Law.* 2d ed. New York: Random House.

Scheerer, Sebastian (1978) "The New Dutch and German Drug Laws: Social and Political Conditions for Criminalization and Decriminalization," 12 *Law & Society Rev.* 585.

Shepherd, R. Gordon (1979) *Science News of Controversy: The Case of Marijuana.* Journalism Monographs. No. 62, August. Lexington, KY: Association for Education in Journalism.

Silvers, Carol (1993) "Report of State Documents Coordinator," Idaho State Library Boise, Idaho, 26 Feb.

Skolnick, Jerome (1978) *House of Cards: The Legalization and Control of Casino Gambling.* Boston: Little, Brown & Co.

Skolnick, Jerome H., & John Dombrink (1978) "The Legalization of Deviance," 16 *Criminology* 193.

Smith, Terence (1978) "Carter Orders White House Staff to Follow Drug Laws or Resign," *New York Times,* 25 July, pp. A1.

Sullivan, Ronald (1974) "Study Asks Easing of Marijuana Law," *New York Times,* 12 Oct., p. 67.

Time (1990) "Alaska: Mowing the Grass," 19 Nov., p. 47.

U.S. Bureau of the Census (1980) *Census of Population: General Population Characteristics.* Washington, DC: GPO.

U.S. Office of National Drug Control Policy (1989) *National Drug Control Strategy.* Executive Office of the President. Washington, DC: GPO, September.

Waldron, Martin (1978) "Trenton Topics," *New York Times,* 21 March, p. 75.

Weitzer, Ronald (1991) "Prostitutes' Rights in the United States. The Failure of a Movement," 32 *Sociological Q.* 23.

Wooten, James T. (1977) "Carter Seeks to End Marijuana Penalty for Small Amounts," *New York Times,* 3 Aug., pp. A1.

CASES CITED

People v. Summit, 183 Col. 421, 517 P.2d 850 (1974).

Downey v. Perini, 518 F.2d 1288 (1975).

Drug Enforcement Administration, U.S. Department of Justice. Opinion and Recommended Ruling, Findings of Fact, Conclusions of Law and Decision of Administrative Judge: In the Matter of Marihuana Rescheduling Petition. Docket No. 86-22, 6 Sept. 1988.

State v. Kells, 199 Neb. 374, 259 N.W.2d 19 (1977).

Ravin v. State, 537 P.2d 494 (1975).

LEGISLATION CITED

Alaska Statutes. "Depressant, Hallucinogenic and Stimulant Drugs," Ch. 12, p. 21, October 1975.

California, Statutes of. Ch. 248, p. 641, 9 July 1975.

Colorado, Session Laws of. Ch. 115, pp. 433–437, 1 July 1975.

Oklahoma. H.B. 1268 (1977).

Massachusetts. H. 3406, "Penalty Removal for Possession," Social Welfare Committee (1974).

Massachusetts. H. 3587 "Legalize Sale of Marihuana," Social Welfare Committee (1974).

Maine, Laws of. Ch. 499 at 1368, effective 1 March 1976 (1975).

Michigan. H.B. 6051, "Permits Private [Marihuana] Use in Residence" (1972).

Minnesota, Laws of. Ch. 42, p. 101, 11 March 1976.

Mississippi, Laws of. Ch. 482, p. 922, 1 July 1977.

Nebraska, Laws of. Legislative Bill 808, 20 April 1978, p. 817.

New York, Laws of. Ch. 360, 29 June 1977.

North Carolina, Laws of. Ch. 862, p. 1178 (1 July 1977).

Ohio, Laws of. H.B. No. 300, p. 2324, 1 July 1976 (1975).

Oregon, Laws. Ch. 680, p. 1521, 22 July 1973.

South Dakota, Laws of. Ch. 158, p. 227, 1 April 1976.

South Dakota, Laws of. Ch. 188, p. 233, 24 March 1977.

U.S. Congress (1970) Comprehensive Drug Abuse Prevention and Control Act of 1970, Public Law 91-513, 84 Stat. 1236 (1970), vol. 1, pp. 1236–96.

PROHIBITION OF BEER IN ICELAND: AN INTERNATIONAL TEST OF SYMBOLIC POLITICS

HELGI GUNNLAUGSSON

and

JOHN F. GALLIHER

Beer has been prohibited in Iceland since 1915, but wine has been legally imported since 1922, as have all other alcoholic beverages since 1934. Since 1932, ten unsuccessful attempts have been made to repeal the beer prohibition. Using the records of parliamentary debates, newspaper reports, opinion poll results, and interviews, we examine the degree of fit between this legislation and Gusfield's model of linkage between status politics and symbolic legislation (Gusfield, 1955, 1963, 1967). We also identify the type of demographic and economic settings that appear to create an environment that encourages symbolic politics.

I. INTRODUCTION

In a study of the Woman's Christian Temperance Union (WCTU), Gusfield (1963) observed that in the early 1900s national prohibition of alcohol in the United States was largely the result of the efforts of middle class, rural Protestants who felt that they were losing their position of dominance in American society. As America was becoming more urban, more Catholic, and more secular, the prohibition law "established the victory of Protestant over Catholic, rural over urban, tradition over modernity, the middle class over both the lower and upper strata" (Gusfield, 1963: 7). Total abstinence was seen by the rural Protestants as the solution to lower class poverty so common, for example, among the urban European-Catholic immigrants in the early 1900s. Much of the motivation claimed by those supporting Prohibition was an "attempt to alleviate suffering though humanitarian actions by those in advantageous positions or to reform the habits of the suffering as a way to the improvement of both their character *and* their material situation" (Gusfield, 1955: 223). The significance of Prohibition was that "it marked the public affirmation of the abstemious, ascetic qualities of American Protestantism" (Gusfield, 1963: 8). Gusfield (ibid., pp. 16–19) observed that status politics typically involve a struggle over symbols to secure deference, while class politics are usually characterized by a conflict over material issues.

An earlier version of this paper was read at the annual meeting of the American Sociological Association, September, 1986, New York, New York.

The authors are grateful for the help of Kenneth Benson and Edward Hunvald in various phases of this research.

Reprinted from *Law & Society Review* 20, no. 3 (1986), Blackwell Publishing, Ltd.

Even though the prohibition law in America was widely violated and only grudg-ingly and selectively enforced, its mere existence demonstrated the superiority of the rural Protestant way of life. Symbolic legislation does not depend upon law enforce-ment for its effect, unlike what Gusfield (1967) calls instrumental legislation, which actually attempts to control human behavior. Signs of symbolic legislation are found when there is a law that is obviously unenforced and even unenforceable or that appears on its face to make no real difference in the lives of those it is supposed to benefit (ibid.).

Even in the case of America's alcohol prohibition, some of the law's middle class supporters hoped that it would serve the instrumental purpose of controlling worker behavior. (Timberlake, 1966: 80). Contrary to Gusfield's claims, however, in using the illustration of America's alcohol prohibition it is difficult to see a clear distinc-tion between class conflict and status conflict for both types of conflict involve the domination of the working class by higher social strata. Furthermore, in both the United States and the United Kingdom there is some evidence that allegedly sym-bolic legislation also has instrumental qualities, and that in the United States class and class conflict seem to infect even alcohol, opium, and marihuana prohibitions, situations in which one might imagine that class interests would be minimal, at least when compared to laws involving such issues as antitrust violations, legal control of factories, and other property rights.

Like Gusfield, Edelman (1964) found a symbolic role for law in American antitrust legislation. The mere passage of these laws in the late nineteenth century appeased Americans who were greatly concerned over the rapidly growing power and abuses of American corporations, even though these laws have in fact almost never been used to control business. Nevertheless, Gusfield's distinction between instrumental and symbolic legislation seems inadequate to describe the legislative events taking place in antitrust legislation, since these unenforced, or symbolic, laws served the instrumental purpose of reassuring an angry public that past abuses of business leaders were no longer possible. Similarly, Carson's (1975) study of the origins of the United Kingdom's Factories Regulation Act of 1833 found both instrumental and symbolic origins of this legislation. Leading manufacturers had instrumental reasons for supporting this attempt to improve factory working condi-tions, including the fact that these new requirements might have forced many smaller manufacturers out of business, thereby reducing competition. Yet initially these man-ufacturers were not enthusiastic about the legislation because of its symbolic signifi-cance, which appeared to condemn all manufacturers. Thus Carson claims, "An exclusive empirical dichotomy between the two [instrumental and symbolic] is likely to be misleading . . . [since] most attempts to make law probably contain elements of both" (ibid., p. 136).

A parallel development was found in California's first opium law, passed in 1875, which used the symbol of moral inferiority as an instrument to divide the working class (Morgan, 1978). White workers were coopted when convinced of their superi-ority to the Chinese. Once the labor market could no longer absorb both white and Chinese workers, the latter were accused of being immoral opium users who required stern criminal penalties to control their corrupt appetites. The 1875 law was aimed at removing the Chinese from the labor force and is associated historically with strict controls on Chinese immigration. Once the Chinese laborers were no longer needed, they lost the protection they had received earlier from members of the business community. Other researchers have found that a symbolic role of law likewise applies to American marihuana prohibitions, which are routinely defended by legislators but, like alcohol prohibition laws before them, almost never enforced (Himmelstein, 1983). Still, Himmelstein observes, "Symbolic politics may also affirm domination of various kinds—economic, political, and ideological" (ibid., p. 17). Galliher and Cross (1982; 1983) found, for example, that in the state of Nevada, where gambling and prostitution are legal—the penalties for the possession of marihuana were the highest in the United States. While these high penalties were almost never enforced, local observers claimed the law was an effort of lawmakers to demonstrate, or *symbolize*, to others that, even with legal prostitution and gambling, Nevadans were not without some moral values. The state feared that federal interference could threaten the gambling industry on which its economy depends. Nevada's marihuana penalties, while seldom enforced, were thus seen as instrumental in protecting the state's reputation and hence its economy.

In sum, then, existing evidence of symbolic law is confounded by evidence of instrumentalism, perhaps because of the facts of social stratification in the societies thus far studied. If we are to locate an environment where purely symbolic legislation is enacted, it perhaps would have to be a society where social class is not so pervasively important as it is in the United States or the United Kingdom. In the Western world, it is impossible to locate a better candidate for this study than Iceland. This is the only European nation never to have had a nobility. All citizens are white, totally literate, and over 95 percent Lutheran; there is total government financing for all education and virtually all medical care. Among these people social or economic stratification is seen as being of relatively little importance (Grimsson and Broddason, 1977).

There is evidence that unenforced, symbolic legislation exists in Iceland in the form of beer prohibition, which has been in effect since 1915. The prohibition of all other alcoholic drinks has been abolished (wine in 1922 and other beverages in 1934). Moreover, "near beer" of 2¼ percent alcohol is legal, but on ten occasions since 1932, proposals to increase the percentage to between 3.5 percent and 4.5 percent have been defeated. The differences between the law and suggested alternatives are so modest that the continuing debate seems to reflect the operation of symbolic concerns rather than material interests.

Among the questions that can be raised about Iceland's beer prohibition are what possible effect can such an isolated and minute prohibition have on material well-being when all other alcoholic beverages have been legally available for over 50 years, and what does this law indicate about Icelandic cultural and social systems? More specifically, we will explore the question of whether this legislation represents purely symbolic politics, such as described by Gusfield, or whether it also contains instrumental qualities. In addition, we will examine the degree to which this legislation is a reflection of status or class conflict.

II. DATA TYPES

Interviews were conducted by Helgi Gunnlaugsson with past and present members of Iceland's Parliament during the summer of 1984, and records of Parliament were collected from the beginning of the national debate on alcoholic beverages in 1909. A review was made of newspaper reports of sessions of Parliament in 1934, 1953, 1960, 1965, and 1984 during which major discussions of beer proposals developed. Data from surveys on citizen attitudes to various issues related to beer prohibition were also reviewed.

III. THE HISTORY OF PROHIBITIONIST SENTIMENT

Based on the results of a national poll in 1908, the Parliament of Iceland voted in 1909 to cease the importation of all alcoholic beverages. At the time, this small nation had no domestic commercial brewing. Lawmakers believed that their actions made them the first nation in the Western world to pass such prohibition legislation. But it was not until 1915 that a ban on sales went into effect, and this grace period between 1909 and 1915 was designed to enable alcohol distributors to dispose of their remaining stocks. Complete prohibition remained in effect for only seven years, from 1915 until 1922. Even so, some discussion later arose in Parliament over the fact that alcohol consumption during this period was obvious and was presumed to be from illegal home-brewed beverages.

After only a seven-year attempt at total prohibition, the law was modified as a result of economic pressures from the Spanish, who demanded that Iceland resume the importation of Spanish wine in return for the continued Spanish importation of Icelandic fish. Under such economic pressure, the Icelandic Parliament agreed to this exception to its prohibition law.

Perhaps feeling uncomfortable with such a gerrymandered law, in 1928 Parliament decided that a national poll should determine the future of prohibition, just as was done in 1908. A poll was finally conducted in 1933, and the majority of those surveyed supported the repeal of prohibition. Given the exception already provided for Spanish wine, it seemed reasonable, at least to some members of Parliament, that other exceptions were plausible. Thus in 1932 and 1933 two proposals were introduced in the lower house of Parliament to allow the brewing of beer with up to 4 percent alcohol. They were justified as attempts to abolish illegally brewed liquor, which was characterized as very harmful, especially when compared to beer, which was thought to be the least harmful of all alcoholic beverages. Local beer brewing, it was also argued, could prevent the loss of foreign exchange caused by importing Spanish wine.

However, neither proposal succeeded because the opposition was formidable. For example, the chief physician of Iceland vigorously opposed the measures, arguing that beer would be especially harmful to the working class and to the young since "many workers and even children would tend to abuse beer because it's a relatively cheap substance" (*Iceland Parliamentary Documents of the Hearings,* Vol. A (1932), at 1290). The prime minister also opposed this legislation, saying, "I totally disagree that consumption of beer is harmless, beer inevitably will evoke longing for alcohol, especially among youngsters, the working class and students. It would even be more useful to allow importation of heavy liquor to Iceland than allow brewing of beer" (ibid., pp. 1280–1281). Over the next fifty years these same arguments involving the defense of the young and workers would appear again and again.

A. *The End of Prohibition and the Beginning of the Beer Battles*

In 1934 legislation was introduced in Parliament to allow the importation of all alcoholic beverages. But the ban on local production of alcoholic beverages would remain in effect, with a separate provision, however, to allow the local brewing of beer if Parliament should approve it in a later separate vote. Proponents argued that beer brewing would both increase revenues to the state and create a successful profession for many Icelanders (*Morgunbladid*, 1934). The opponents of the repeal of prohibition countered by saying that this argument revealed a serious inconsistency in the 1934 proposed bill, which in one place stated that the production of alcohol was prohibited but in another indicated the possibility of brewing beer. With the law's opponents capitalizing on this alleged inconsistency, the provision allowing for a later vote on beer brewing was expelled from the legislation. Beer was thus singled out for special consideration almost by chance, first by pro-beer members of Parliament (MPs) and then by those opposed to alcohol, who seized on the alleged inconsistency to prevent a complete loss of prohibition. The final version of the bill, which was ultimately passed, allowed the importation of all alcoholic beverages except beer, which was still prohibited unless it contained less than 2¼ percent alcohol. One of the first, and certainly one of the most influential, to speak against ending the prohibition on beer was an MP who was both a farmer and a temperance leader. His argument that beer is an especially dangerous alcoholic beverage because it is used as a stepping stone to harder liquor has been used repeatedly over the past 50 years:

> The youth starts to drink beer and gets acquainted with the influence of alcohol. This develops step by step, the influence of beer becomes not enough, which leads to drinking strong liquor. But it is evident that beer evokes the longing for drinking alcohol. . . . Although we may allow the importation of strong liquor to Iceland, it is important to prohibit beer. . . . It's very important to prevent such a disaster, especially a disaster to the young people (*Iceland Parliamentary Documents of the Hearings*, Vol. B, No. 7 (1934) at 2110–2111).

A socialist member of Parliament also argued that working people in Iceland would be those most injured by beer and that they were especially vulnerable to its effects due to their Viking blood:

> Those with the lowest income, living under poor social conditions, have a great tendency to soothe their pain with alcohol drinking. . . . But why is alcohol legal? It is because alcohol production is a big profession, controlled by powerful capitalists and can't therefore be easily abolished . . . Icelanders are not able to use alcohol as civilized persons, their nature is still too much of the Viking kind, they get too excited and brutal, with alcohol usage. The Parliament should be like a father to a child, knowing what

is best for its welfare. . . . Poor people will start to drink beer, because it's the cheapest alcohol. But when beer has been consumed for a while, it leads to consumption of hard liquor (ibid., pp. 2157–2158, 2226).

A supporter of beer importation observed that it would be very strange to prohibit beer while allowing the importation of liquor since beer is less harmful than other, stronger alcoholic beverages. This argument has been used repeatedly by proponents of the end of beer prohibition for fifty years, but to no avail. In 1934 the new prime minister recalled that he had been the sheriff of Reykjavik, the capital of Iceland, when the importation of Spanish wine was resumed, and noticed no increase in the amount of drunkenness compared to the period before total prohibition, when all types of alcoholic beverages had been available. He added that "it's a strange regulation to prohibit brewing of beer, when importation of strong liquor has been allowed" (ibid., p. 2093). However, during the debate the prime minister switched his position and soon spoke against legalized beer (ibid. pp. 2237–2238). Paralleling his change of heart, the votes on the bill repealing prohibition in both houses were very lopsided, thirteen to three in the upper house and twenty-four to eight in the lower house. It appears that the willingness of almost all in Parliament to exclude beer from the bill helped its passage, for this provision was used as a bargaining point between the opposing sides. The supporters of repeal apparently decided to compromise on the issue of beer to help ensure the passage of the rest of the bill.

The largest daily newspaper in Iceland, the *Morgunbladid* in Reykjavik, strongly supported the repeal of prohibition, including the repeal of beer prohibition. There were forty-three press reports on prohibition during the year prior to its partial repeal, many of which (37 percent) described home brewing and the accidents it caused. Some also described the total failure of prohibition in the United States. An article in the late fall of 1934 concluded that it made no sense to ban beer: "The ban of beer is ridiculous, everyone should understand that dangerousness of alcohol increases with alcohol content" (*Morgunbladid,* 1934).

In 1947 the beer issue surfaced again. A member of the lower house of Parliament introduced legislation to allow the local brewing of 4 percent beer as a means to decrease the consumption of hard liquor and to raise new tax revenues for building hospitals from domestic and export beer sales. The proposal was not taken seriously by most members of Parliament and it did not come to a vote. Opponents capitalized on an apparent contradiction in the bill's objectives: to decrease alcohol consumption and at the same time to increase tax revenues from alcohol sales (*Iceland Parliamentary Documents of the Hearings,* Vol. A, Nos. 69–71 (1947), at 196, 198).

Undaunted, in 1952 the proponents of beer were back again, in the upper house with a proposal for a national referendum on beer. However, this proposal was removed from suggested legislation by the minister of justice. It was at this time that opposition to a national referendum as a means of settling the beer issue first appeared. In 1953, as an indirect method of repealing the prohibition of beer, there was an effort in the upper house to limit the legal definition of alcohol to include only beverages with over 3.5 percent alcohol. There was considerable dispute as to how the bill, as worded, proposed to measure the percent of alcohol in beer. Opponents claimed that the law proposed a new method of measuring alcohol content, whereas if the traditional method were used the actual alcohol level would be closer to 4.4 percent than 3.5 percent. This alleged attempt was seen as a subterfuge and angered many members of Parliament, especially in the lower house. It did not pass.

During the same session another bill was introduced in the lower house, this one to allow local brewing of 4.4 percent beer. The opponents of beer again capitalized on the apparent subterfuge in the earlier bill, and it was also defeated. Parliament did, however, pass legislation allowing alcohol to be brewed for export and for use on the NATO air force base in Keflavik, after it was argued that beer exports would help the economy, as had happened in Denmark and Holland, which were famous for their beers. There was apparently no moral concern about brewing beer for the consumption of others, only concern about the effect on Icelanders. The newspapers published thirty-two articles on the beer issue in the year prior to the introduction of these two proposals and endorsed the suggestion of a national referendum (*Morgunbladid,* 1953).

In 1954 a new government agency was created called the Council of the Government Against Alcohol (CGAA). This agency is financed through taxes on alcohol sales and its purpose is "to fight against abuse of alcohol and abolish the misfortune which follows abuse of alcohol" (Alcohol Law, *Laws of Iceland* (1954); Alcohol Law, *Laws of Iceland* (1969)). In an interview with Helgi Gunnlaugsson in 1984, the manager of the CGAA explained the agency's opposition to allowance of beer:

> There are several reasons why we oppose allowance of beer in Iceland. The most important one, however, is that experience in Iceland and other countries shows that any lenience of the alcohol law increases alcohol consumption in general. Thus, it is very likely, that allowance of beer, will not only be an addition to the present types of alcohol consumption in Iceland, but will also lead to an increased consumption on the whole. . . . We're no amateurs, we only provide scientific facts, based on reliable sources from different countries.

Over the years the CGAA has continued this line of reasoning, and its position has had a major impact on members of Parliament who in recent years have frequently used this argument against the allowance of beer.

In 1960 another proposal for brewing beer with up to 3.5 percent alcohol was introduced in the upper house with the rationale that the beer ban "was an insult to the Icelandic peoples' sense of liberty and civilization" (*Iceland Parliamentary Documents of the Hearings,* Vol. C, No. 1 (1960), at 443). The bill's sponsor argued that brewing could help the economy through domestic beer sales and exportation, and also claimed that "people don't perceive they are violating the law [by making home-brewed beer] because prohibition of beer does not coincide with their sense of justice" (ibid., p. 410). These arguments notwithstanding, the proposal was again defeated. The stepping-stone argument surfaced again, as did the notion that beer is a special threat to workers. Another agreed, citing the horrible situation in the United Kingdom: "All factories and dock yards have to lock up their workers during working hours and especially take care not to let anyone out until the pubs are closed" (ibid., p. 447). Yet another opponent told the following tale of woe: "A few days ago I witnessed a thirteen-year-old school boy saying that kids his age really needed this beer to get up in the morning to go to school. This boy also believed it to be handy for the homes, because then they didn't have to bother about preparing coffee or tea, just grab the beer from the kitchen shelves" (ibid., p. 438). Perhaps wearying some of this issue, the *Morgunbladid* devoted only twenty-five articles to the topic during the year prior to Parliament's deliberations. But the paper did editorialize, citing majority opinion and chemical reality: "It is a common fact that most people want to use alcohol, thus one immediately realizes how ridiculous it is to allow liquor but ban beer, which is healthier than liquor" (*Morgunbladid*, 1960).

In 1965 a bill was introduced in the lower house to allow the brewing of 4.5 percent beer. The proposal was defeated, however, as was a proposal for a national referendum on beer. During the year prior, the *Morgunbladid* had published twenty-three articles on beer, but seems to have given up on this issue and did not take an aggressive editorial position, as it had previously. Still, the paper did observe that "allowances of beer could become a major source of income for the state" (*Morgunbladid*, 1965b). The paper also described a new brewery in northern Iceland with "perfect natural conditions for brewing beer" (*Morgunbladid*, 1965a), and a Danish brewery that was very profitable and paid considerable taxes to the state (*Morgunbladid*, 1966b). Three articles questioned a regulation instituted by the minister of financial affairs in December 1965 that allowed ship and airplane crews to bring beer back to Iceland for their private use, asking "Why are seamen allowed to bring in beer, when it's not allowed here in Iceland?" (*Morgunbladid*, 1966a). These crews could bring in up to twenty-four bottles of beer if they had been out of the country for less than twenty days, and forty-eight bottles if gone for over twenty days. Before the decision, this had been the informal practice for a number of years.

Three years later, in 1968, another national referendum was proposed, again in the lower house, but again also defeated. In 1977 a national referendum was proposed in the lower house and then defeated once again. (One member of Parliament later claimed that the beer issue was a "petty issue" and that it was therefore ridiculous to waste a national referendum on this proposition (*Iceland Parliamentary Documents of the Hearings*, No. 27 (1983–84), at 6387).

In parliamentary hearings during the late fall of 1983 a proposal for a national referendum on beer was introduced one more time, with the following preamble: "It sounds awfully strange to ban the sale of the weakest substance of all alcohol beverages, but allow sales of hard liquor. It sounds similar to a ban of aspirin, but allowance of morphine" (Preamble to Proposal Number 138, *Iceland Parliament*, (1983)). This time the bill was introduced in both houses (*Iceland Parliamentary Documents of the Hearings*, No. 17 (1983–84), at 3335). In spite of these pleadings, the bill never came to a vote. Opponents argued that surveys were better measures of public opinion, and one said: "I doubt the usefulness of direct democracy like a national referendum and I believe they don't have any future. In the western world, a much better choice has appeared, attitude surveys, which are utilized to reveal the will of the people" (ibid., p. 3338). During these same hearings in the early spring of 1984, a proposal was introduced in the lower house to allow the local brewing and importation of beer, but the proposal was not discussed. Fifty-five articles on this issue had appeared in the *Morgunbladid* during the prior year, with the newspaper supporting a national referendum. When it became apparent that the national referendum was to be defeated, a headline in the paper called it "Perfunctory Work in Parliament" (*Morgunbladid*, 1984b).

IV. PUBLIC OPINION AND PARTY POLITICS

Nationwide surveys on the beer issue in Iceland have indeed become increasingly common in recent years, and there has been a steady increase in support for beer sales. In 1977, 57 percent opposed beer sales in Iceland (Hagvangur, 1977); in the summer of 1983, 53 percent wanted beer sales (Haadarson, 1983); and by the fall of 1983 the figure had risen to 63.5 percent (Hagvangur, 1983). Those most supportive of beer have been the young and urban, with approximately 83 percent of those between the ages of twenty and twenty-nine and 68 percent of those in the Reykjavik area supporting legal beer by 1983. In March of 1984, 74 percent of all Icelanders surveyed supported the idea of a national referendum on the beer issue (DV, 1984).

Opponents of beer sales clearly distrust direct democracy through referendums or even survey results. In our interviews in 1984, one member of Parliament complained about the press, perhaps thinking of Iceland's largest paper, which has always supported the repeal of beer prohibition, for its distortion and manipulation of public opinion: "Nowadays, it is nothing but pure propaganda in newspapers that heavily influence people's minds. That's why so many support allowance of beer in the surveys, because papers carry so much propaganda for alcohol consumption. I believe therefore, we should not take these surveys too seriously." Another added: "Propaganda of newspapers for increased consumption of alcohol has affected the public's mind. But I still believe that the majority of the public is against beer, surveys that indicate the opposite are most likely false." He said this even though he was the MP who had been quoted several months earlier during parliamentary debate as favoring surveys over a national referendum. One member of Parliament complained: "If a referendum is to be conducted, how should we protect the rights of the minority?"

An MP who was a supporter of a national referendum and legalized beer observed: "Opponents believe such direct democracy threatens their interests. There is also a strong distrust of voters, especially among MPs who come from rural areas." Proponents of legal beer cited the hypocrisy of allowing those who go abroad to bring in twelve half-liter cans of foreign beer or to purchase twenty-four bottles of Icelandic beer through the duty-free store upon reentering Iceland. The first privilege was allowed by the minister of financial affairs in 1979 and the second in 1984 after complaints were made about the unfair privileges of airplane and ship crews. Moreover, a "beer" is sold in Iceland's bars, which is made by mixing the legal 2¼ percent "near beer" with liquor. A few years ago this practice was started in several Reykjavik bars, and the government prosecutor has held this to be legal since both the 2¼ percent near beer and the whiskey are legal substances (*Morgunbladid*, 1984a). The decision of the minister of financial affairs to allow travelers to bring in foreign beers or to purchase one case of Icelandic beer at the duty-free store for their personal use is nicely suited to permit the relatively affluent middle classes, who have the finances to travel abroad frequently, to have a steady supply of beer while denying it to the less affluent. This policy is consistent with the professed fear of the effect of beer upon workers. The deputy sheriff of Reykjavik discussed the impossibility of controlling beer consumption: "The police occasionally arrest people for brewing beer in their households. We find these people mostly through drunken drivers who maintain they've been drinking beer. But on the whole, we can do very little against this. Materials for brewing beer are sold everywhere legally."

From the various parliamentary votes on the prohibition of beer over the years, it is clear that the Progressive Party, which is predominantly rural, and the two socialist parties (Socialist Democratic Party and People's Alliance), which traditionally represent workers, have provided most of the opposition to beer proposals. Most of the support for beer has come from the largest single political party, the Independence Party; with 38 percent to 42 percent of the vote, it represents the urban middle class and is endorsed by the *Morgunbladid*. In the three actual votes on the issue of beer that have taken place, the Independence Party provided 73 percent of the support for beer proposals, and the socialists and the Progressives provided 80 percent of the opposition.

V. ECONOMIC AND DEMOGRAPHIC FOUNDATIONS OF ICELANDIC LAW

The population of Iceland increased nearly threefold in the sixty years from 1910 to 1970, with farming and the rural areas of the country experiencing rapidly declining numbers as approximately half of the rural population was lost in those years (see Table 1). All these figures demonstrate that although the urbanization process in Iceland began later than in the United States, it has been more rapid (Table 2).

Table 1 also shows that in 1910 the area around the capital of Reykjavik represented only approximately one-fifth of the nation's population, while in 1970 it represented over half of the total population. One reflection of how different the Reykjavik area is from the rest of the nation is that the next largest city has less than a tenth of

TABLE 1

Demographic and Economic Characteristics of Iceland, 1910-70

	1910	1930	1950	1970
Total population	85,183	108,861	143,973	204,578
Reykjavik area population*	17,595	37,188	70,648	119,822
Rural population	54,141	44,952	33,453	28,739
Percent rural	63	42	23	14
Percent agricultural	48	35	24	12
Percent fishing	15	15	11	6
Percent industrial workers	12	20	32	37

Source: Grimsson and Broddason, 1977, pp. 153 and 170.
*Includes Reykjanes

TABLE 2

Demographic and Economic Characteristics of the United States, 1910-70

	1910	1930	1950	1970
Percent rural	54	44	36	27
Percent agricultural	31	21	11	4
Percent industrial workers	28	24	29	27

Source: United States Department of Commerce, 1975: 11, 126–127, 137.

that region's population. This is an important distinction because, as we noted above, it is predominantly in the capital area that a majority desires to end beer prohibition.

The reappointment of Parliament to reflect these remarkable population shifts has, however, been slow in coming. In 1934 and again in 1959 Parliament reapportioned itself. But even so the votes in rural Iceland currently clearly count for more than those in urban areas. This is especially true in the capital, for while only 25 percent of Parliament is from the Reykjavik city proper, approximately 40 percent of the total population lives there. In 1908 and 1933 there were national referendums on alcohol, but not later. The unrepresentative nature of Parliament explains the growing reluctance of this body to rely on a direct referendum to settle the issue of beer or anything else. Thus even in such a small, ethnically, racially, and religiously homogeneous nation there is still opposition to direct democracy.

VI. CONCLUSION

It is curious that for all the appeal and apparent utility of the analysis of symbolic laws, there have been only a few attempts to determine whether or how such ideas are applicable in other nations besides the United States (for example, see Carson, 1975). The implication of much of this research is that only Americans are so fundamentalist, puritanical, and shallow as to be pacified by such symbolic drug or alcohol legislation; certainly the generally more secular and sophisticated Europeans would not be so submissive. The goal of the present research has been to see if such an analysis could be useful in understanding legislative action in other than an American setting.

This case of beer prohibition in Iceland is especially interesting because among alcoholic beverages, beer is less widely prohibited than whiskey. This distinction is a result of the general recognition that beer is not as potent as other alcoholic beverages. Just as beer was claimed to be a stepping stone to hard liquor and therefore especially dangerous to young people just beginning to drink, marihuana has often been alleged to be particularly dangerous as a stepping stone to the use of harder drugs among the young (Kaplan, 1970: 232; Himmelstein, 1983). The special irony is that in Iceland beer has been routinely associated with hard liquor, which has not been prohibited by law for over fifty years.

According to Gusfield's reasoning, it is very clear that the Icelandic law is an instance of symbolic legislation because the difference in the alcohol content of legal near beer, compared to the proposed changes, ranges from only 1 percent to 2 percent alcohol. Moreover, beer is already widely available in Iceland—ban or no ban. Those citizens who travel abroad are allowed to bring in beer for their personal use; a "beer" composed of liquor and near beer is sold in some Reykjavik bars; and home-brewed beer is widely made with no limitations on the percent of alcohol except the preferences of the brewer. This is largely an unenforceable law, which Gusfield (1967) has indicated to be a sure indication of symbolic legislation, even though the proponents of the law are certain that it serves to control drinking behavior.

During the late nineteenth and early twentieth centuries, the United States was experiencing the rapid industrial expansion that would occur in Iceland approximately fifty years later. During this rapid American industrial development, national prohibition of alcohol was enacted, as were special laws and special courts to deal with the problems of young people—the juvenile codes and the juvenile courts. These laws were a consequence of what has been called the "child-saving movement" (Platt, 1977). Although cloaked in the language of helping and protecting lower class youth, such legislation was ideally suited to ensure that developing capitalism would in the future have the type of disciplined work force that it required. This same rationale was used in the United States for the defense of alcohol prohibition.

In the United States ethnic conflict has been related to class conflict, and both have been associated with alcohol prohibition, which was opposed by labor unions. By comparison the temperance position of the socialist parties and the Labor Union of Iceland, which represents workers in all industries, has its roots in the rapid industrialization of Iceland. Most Icelandic workers and union leaders have relatively recent rural origins and thus have been opposed to alcohol. Moreover, some union leaders received their initial experience in political organizations through participation in the temperance movement (Einarsson, 1970). In Iceland there are no ethnic groups and there has been little economic stratification and class conflict. The country's labor unions have their origins more in an attempt to imitate similar movements in Western Europe and North America rather than in local class conflict (ibid.; Kristjansson, 1977). Since Iceland's labor unions were essentially borrowed from abroad rather than being created by local class conflict, these organizations came closer to representing status groups rather than class interests.

Like the "child savers" and prohibitionists in early twentieth-century America, the opponents of beer in Iceland have continued to base their opposition to this substance for almost 60 years on its dreaded effects upon workers and young people, the workers of the future. Even though economic stratification and class conflict have not been pronounced in Iceland, one might get the impression that they were from the seemingly paternalistic references to the workers' special weaknesses and needs. In Iceland, however, even the representatives of labor unions and the socialist parties have repeatedly emphasized the weakness of the workers, the very people they represent, apparently because of Icelanders' "Viking blood." This has given an unexpected strength to the last vestiges of Icelandic prohibition. In contrast to the unions, the representatives of the urban middle classes have always seen beer and other alcohol as simply commodities to be exploited for the income they can generate for industry, employment, and tax revenues for the state.

Rural Icelanders are losing their numerical strength, just as rural American Protestants did earlier. Yet rural Icelanders maintain some sense of power through the law in an unrepresentative parliament, and, in the instance of beer prohibition, they have had the support of the political parties of the workers and unions. Beer prohibition is thus a means of demonstrating rural domination in the face of population odds attendant to the rapid changes that have occurred in Iceland's economic and social system. Such a protracted conflict in Icelandic politics has obscured class, or material, interests because during most of this century there has been only the most rudimentary class system in the country (Grimsson and Broddason, 1977). Since economic stratification developed much later in Iceland compared with other Western democracies, in the past its parliament has been easily deflected from material issues to status conflicts. Industrialization likewise came later than in other Western countries, and developed much more rapidly due to the influence of these other nations. The rural domination of parliament, its beer prohibition, and the contemporary prohibitionist sentiment of labor unions are dramatic reflections of the resulting cultural lag.

The ambiguous mixture of class and status conflict that existed in the American prohibition movement, in which the alcohol-status conflict seemed closely aligned with the class conflict between capitalists and workers, is absent in beer prohibition in Iceland. Unlike the case of American prohibition, in Iceland the middle classes clearly want no prohibition laws forced upon workers and do not accept the logic of workers' special vulnerability to alcohol. Thus Iceland's beer prohibition has its foundations in the local social structure that created the conditions for social conflict between rural citizens and workers on the one hand and the urban middle class on the other. This particular conflict differs from conventional class conflict because in Iceland a rural, working class coalition controls the urban middle class. This suggests an urban-rural status conflict unlikely to be found in most other Western nations.

Most of the studies of symbolic law reviewed above recognized the importance of the perception of actors involved in these legislative events. There were discussions of the perceptions of Nevada lawmakers, English manufacturers, American corporate leaders, and white workers and business leaders in California during the late nineteenth century. All of these studies, to some degree, show a business group operating according to class interests. While Timberlake (1966) found influential business interests in the case of American prohibition, Gusfield (1955, 1963, 1967) missed any instrumental qualities in the perceptions of the WCTU members he interviewed. But just as surely as American prohibitionists believed in the positive effects of the law they advocated, proponents of beer prohibition in Iceland remain firmly convinced of its instrumental qualities in controlling drinking behavior and thus struggle unceasingly on its behalf. Surely social scientists can all agree with the time-honored dictum that if people believe a thing to be true, it is real in its consequences. And so it is with alcohol prohibition in both the United States and Iceland.

Moreover, Icelandic beer prohibition probably does make the substance more difficult to secure, for beer must either be home-brewed or imported in small amounts. Prohibition supporters understandably believe that Icelanders drink less because of beer prohibition. Therefore, even in the extreme case of beer prohibition in Iceland, while it is clearly not the result of class conflict, it is still something other than a totally symbolic law. Making the distinction between the instrumental and symbolic origins of law, as Gusfield (1955, 1963, 1967) has done, seems inadequate, because no laws appear to have totally symbolic origins, even in Iceland where status conflict rather than class conflict has been the norm.

VII. POSTSCRIPT

The beer prohibition in Iceland shows no sign of ending. During the summer of 1985 a bill to allow the importation and brewing of beer and one to authorize a national referendum on the prohibition were introduced. As with all earlier bills of these types, both were defeated.

REFERENCES

Carson, W.G. (1975) "Symbolic and Instrumental Dimensions of Early Factory Legislation: A Case Study in the Social Origins of Criminal Law," in R. Hood (ed.), *Crime, Criminology and Public Policy.* New York: The Free Press.

DV (1984) Survey findings published in the daily newspaper "DV," March 5.

Edelman, Murray (1964) *The Symbolic Uses of Politics.* Urbana: University of Illinois Press.

Einarsson, O. R. (1970) *The Origins of the Icelandic Labor Union.* Reykjavik: M.F.A. (Cultural and Educational Association of Workers).

Galliher, John F., and John R. Cross (1982) "Symbolic Severity in the Land of Easy Virtue: Nevada's High Marihuana Penalty," 29 *Social Problems* 380.

——— (1983) *Morals Legislation without Morality: The Case of Nevada.* New Brunswick: Rutgers University Press.

Grimsson, O. R., and T. H. Broddason (1977) *The Icelandic Society.* Reykjavik: Social Sciences Department of the University of Iceland, and Orn and Orlygur.

Gusfield, Joseph R. (1955) "Social Structure and Moral Reform: A Study of the Woman's Christian Temperance Union," 61 *American Journal of Sociology* 221.

——— (1963) *Symbolic Crusade: Status Politics and the American Temperance Movement.* Urbana: University of Illinois Press.

——— (1967) "Moral Passage: The Symbolic Process in Public Designations of Deviance," 15 *Social Problems* 175.

Hagvangur Ltd. (1977) "The Majority of Icelanders Opposes Beer" *VISIR* (March 10) 8.

——— (1983) "A Total of 63.5% Favor Beer Sales in Liquor Stores" *Morgunbladid* (November 20) 48.

Hardarson, Olafur (1983) Unpublished. Social Sciences Department of the University of Iceland.

Himmelstein, Jerome L. (1983) *The Strange Career of Marihuana: Politics and Ideology of Drug Control in America.* Westport, CT: Greenwood Press.

Kaplan, John (1970) *Marihuana—The New Prohibition.* New York: World Publishing Company.

Kristjansson, S. (1977) *Icelandic Labor Unions, 1920–1930.* Reykjavik: Social Sciences Department of the University of Iceland, and Orn and Orlygur.

Morgan, Patricia A. (1978) "The Legislation of Drug Law: Economic and Social Control," 8 *Journal of Drug Issues* 53.

Morgunbladid (1934) "The New Beer Ban" (November 28) 3.

———— (1953) "New Alcohol Law Passed in Parliament During This Session" (October 3) 8.

———— (1960) "Beer" (November 12) 10.

———— (1965a) "New Brewery in Akureyri Next Year" (December 1) 32.

———— (1965b) "Beer" (December 18) 14.

———— (1966a) "Beer to Seamen?" (January 30) 6.

———— (1966b) "721 Million Bottles of Carlsberg Beer" (February 18) 14.

———— (1984a) "The State Prosecutor Declares that the So-called 'Beer' is Different from Beer" (May 10) 2.

———— (1984b) "Perfunctory Work in Parliament" (May 12) 24.

Platt, Anthony M. (1977) *The Child Savers: The Invention of Delinquency,* 2nd ed. Chicago: University of Chicago Press.

Timberlake, James H. (1966) *Prohibition and the Progressive Movement: 1900–1920,* Cambridge, MA: Harvard University Press.

United States Department of Commerce (1975) *Historical Statistics of the United States: Colonial Times to 1970,* P. 1. Washington, DC: Bureau of the Census.

GOVERNMENT DOCUMENTS CITED

ICELAND PARLIAMENTARY DOCUMENTS OF THE HEARINGS,

———— Vol. A (1932).

———— Vol. B, No. 7 (1934).

———— Vol. A, Nos. 69–71 (1947).

———— Vol. C, No. 1 (1960).

———— No. 17 (1983–84).

———— No. 27 (1983–84).

Alcohol Law, *Laws of Iceland* (1954).

———— (1964).

Preamble to Proposal Number 138, *Iceland Parliament* (1983).

TIMOTHY LEARY, RICHARD ALPERT (RAM DASS) AND THE CHANGING DEFINITION OF PSILOCYBIN*

COLIN WARK** and JOHN F. GALLIHER***

ABSTRACT

Background: This research focuses on the events leading to the 1968 U.S. federal prohibition of psilocybin. It is a study of duelling moral entrepreneurs—Timothy Leary and Richard Alpert vs. the Harvard University Administration. The goal is to show how the primary active compound in an ostensibly harmless fungus (the psilocybin mushroom) became controversial in less than a decade.

Methods: We used books, newspapers, magazine articles and previously unpublished materials (including documents from the Harvard Archives) to analyze Leary and Alpert's lives and careers through the early 1970s.

Results: The prohibition of psilocybin in the U.S. was largely a product of Leary and Alpert's involvement in the "Harvard drug scandal" and their transformation from Harvard professors to countercultural icons. They tested the substance on a variety of human subjects and in doing so piqued the interest of Harvard undergraduates while drawing condemnation from other faculty and Harvard administrators. This case is theoretically interesting because unlike most illegal drugs, psilocybin was never linked to a threatening minority group, but to some of the nation's most privileged youth.

Conclusion: The Harvard administrators were not really moral entrepreneurs but Leary and Alpert clearly were. Although they were far from being prohibitionists, they were self-righteous crusaders on different but equally holy missions for the good of young and minority Americans. Ironically, due to their successes the possession of psilocybin was criminalized under United States federal law in 1968 (Pub. L. No. 90-639, Stat. 1361 1968 and Boire, 2002). This case study demonstrates that crusaders can be successful in changing culture even when laws are passed in futile attempts to control their behaviour, just as Leary predicted.

The objective is to study the transition of psilocybin from a non-threatening substance to a dangerous drug from 1957 to 1968 when it was prohibited under U.S. federal criminal law. The principals in this history are Harvard Professors turned countercultural icons Timothy Leary and Richard Alpert (later Ram Dass). This paper is organized thematically and addresses a variety of topics including the early psilocybin experiences of Leary, Alpert, and R. Gordon Wasson as well as Leary and Alpert's psilocybin research and the ensuing controversy. We draw on mass media, audio and video recordings

---

*Thanks are due to Jay Gubrium, Wayne Brekhus, Victoria Johnson and Ted Koditschek for help with an earlier draft of this manuscript.
**Texas A&M University-Kingsville, Department of Psychology and Sociology, MSC 177, 700 University Blvd, Kingsville, TX 78363-8202, United States
***Missouri University-Columbia, United States

Reprinted from *International Journal of Drug Policy* (2009), Elsevier B.V.

(primarily of talks by Leary and Alpert) and also audio and print records found in the Harvard University Archives, to see the picture that emerges from these three sources. The original analysis of the mass media and many of the audio and video recordings can be found in *Outlawing Magic Mushrooms: The Prohibition of Psilocybin in the United States* (Wark & Galliher, 2007). This article is a study of duelling moral entrepreneurs. According to Becker (1963, p. 148) the moral entrepreneur;

> is fervent and righteous, often self-righteous. They typically believe that their mission is a holy one. . . The crusader is not only interested in seeing to it that other people do what he thinks is right. He believes that if they do what is right it will be good for them. Or he may feel that his reform will prevent certain kinds of exploitation of one person by another.

Becker (p. 148) also noted that "the prohibitionist serves as an excellent example" of the moral entrepreneur citing as examples the membership of the Woman's Christian Temperance Union (WCTU) and the zealot Harry Anslinger who was the long-time head of the Federal Bureau of Narcotics (FBN). According to Becker, Anslinger and the FBN drummed up much of the basis for the U.S. federal criminalization of marihuana as did the WCTU for national alcohol prohibition, yet others argue that crusades are triggered by attempts to control threatening minority groups. Musto (1999) has argued that prohibitionist drug laws have targeted the behaviour of blacks, Asians, Hispanics or others but ignored Anglo drug use. We examine the role moral entrepreneurs played in the changing definition of psilocybin and its ultimate U.S. federal prohibition. This became complicated and ironic and we demonstrate that Harvard University psychologists Timothy Leary and Richard Alpert were moral entrepreneurs but more diverse in background and orientation than those imagined by Becker. Their moral entrepreneurship consisted of extolling the virtues of psilocybin and, in the case of Leary, denouncing the educational, religious and legal Establishment. These efforts led to greater restrictions on the drug. The Harvard Administrators were moral entrepreneurs because they warned the Harvard community and others of the dangers of psilocybin. Dyck has claimed that "discussions about LSD had shifted from a medico scientific context to a social and cultural one concerned with the perils of drug use" and that the drug's "path from medical marvel to modern menace is far from unique" and includes other substances such as opium based on social concerns with the youth movement of the 1960s (2008, pp. 10, 120). This is precisely what happened in the case of psilocybin. In addition, psilocybin was often confused with LSD. For example, a 1965 New York Times article discusses an experiment in which researchers (Leary and Alpert among them) gave psilocybin to theology students. The article refers to psilocybin as an "LSD-type drug" and begins by asking the reader "Can mind-expanding drugs, like LSD . . . give people mystical experiences?" (Osmundsen, 1965).

WRITTEN HISTORY OF PSILOCYBIN BEGINS WITH R. GORDON WASSON

Hallucinogens entered popular culture in 1957 when R. Gordon Wasson, a vice president of J.P. Morgan published an article in Life Magazine describing his experiences with "divine mushrooms" in Mexico (1957, p. 101). He described visions of "mountains" and "rivers", claimed that the experience was "astonishing" and that it left him "awestruck" (Wasson, pp. 101, 109–110).

At this time *Life* magazine did not condemn the mushrooms, nor did R. Gordon Wasson. Instead he wrote a straight-forward article describing his personal visions and experiences with what later became known as psilocybin mushrooms. He said that they did not appear to be addictive and even mentioned their potential medical applications. In 1960 Oxford Professor Robert Graves wrote that he "wholeheartedly" supported Wasson's assessment (p. 10). A year later Graves wrote (1961, p. 127): "My single experience of psilocybin was wholly good: an illumination of the mind, a re-education of sight and hearing, and even touch." The writings of Wasson and Professor Graves gave no indication of what would happen in years to come.

A recent study seems to confirm the predictions made by Harvard psychologists Leary and Alpert in the early 1960s that with the right set and setting, psilocybin can have profound and positive psychological effects. The study was conducted primarily by researchers at the John Hopkins School of Medicine and funded by the National Institute of Drug Abuse. Similar to Leary and Alpert's studies at Harvard the researchers administered the drug in a setting that they described as "a living room-like environment." To create a mindset favourable to the experience participants "were encouraged to focus their attention inward by lying down on. . .[a] couch and wearing an eye mask. . .[as well as] headphones through which classical music was played" (Griffiths, Richards, Johnson, McCann, & Jesse, 2008, p. 2). When asked about their psilocybin experience 14 months later the majority of participants indicated that in terms of spiritual significance and positive behaviour change, the drug session had a profound impact on their lives. In reflecting on the results the authors conclude that:

> When administered under supportive conditions, psilocybin occasioned experiences similar to spontaneously occurring mystical experiences that, over a year later, were considered by volunteers to be among the most personally meaningful and spiritually significant experiences of their lives and to have produced positive changes in attitudes, mood, altruism, behaviour and life satisfaction (Griffiths et al., p. 11).

It is ironic that the Griffiths' study emphasized the importance of "set and setting" given that this is one of the primary reasons why Leary and Alpert's research was questioned.

Researchers have recently begun studying the usefulness of psilocybin for treating a variety of medical and psychological conditions including obsessive compulsive disorder (Moreno, Wiegand, Taitano, & Delgado, 2006), cluster headaches (Sewell, Halpern, & Pope, 2006), and anxiety related to terminal cancer (Brown, 2006). Yet psilocybin prohibition is still viewed as a critical problem in many countries. In late 2007 protestors in Amsterdam rejected the Dutch government's prohibition of "hallucinogenic mushrooms" ("Dutch Protestors", 2007). This followed similar bans by Ireland in 2006 ("Sale and Possession", 2006), the UK in 2005 ("Magic Mushrooms Ban", 2005), Japan in 2002 ("Japan Culls Magic", 2002), and Denmark in 2001 ("Netherlands Bans", 2007). The prohibition of psilocybin in the U.S. preceded the actions of these European and Asian nations by several decades. Our research suggests that during the sexual revolution and antiwar movement of the

1960s the efforts of Leary and Alpert (later Ram Dass) created a combustible mixture that quickly led to the U.S. pioneering this prohibition.

Soon after Wasson's experience Dr. Timothy Leary picked up the story of these mushrooms. Leary was a Berkeley trained psychologist who read Wasson's article shortly after being appointed lecturer in Clinical Psychology at Harvard University in 1959. Despite his academic successes, Leary questioned his career choice and was experiencing a mid-life crisis (Lee & Shlain, 1985). Leary tried the mushrooms during a trip to Mexico in 1960. Leary ate psilocybin mushrooms and was greatly impressed calling the event "'above all and without question the deepest religious experience of [his] life'" (Lee and Shlain, p. 73). Leary soon helped to start a research program called the Harvard Psilocybin Project (Weiner, 2002). He was joined by an Assistant Professor named Richard Alpert who had come to Harvard in 1958. Alpert's first encounter with psilocybin was, like Leary's, a profound experience.

RESEARCH INITIATIVES WITH PSILOCYBIN

Leary and Alpert were affiliated with Harvard's Department of Social Relations and their project was to be sponsored by the university's Center for Research in Personality. Although there was no indication that psilocybin was addictive the university pressured Alpert to keep it away from undergraduates after hearing that students had experienced "acute psychoses" after taking hallucinogens (Dowling, 1977; Mayer, 1963; Weil, 1963). When Leary and Alpert started their psilocybin research most of the subjects had a positive experience. In 1961 they gave the drug to prisoners for rehabilitation purposes with reportedly positive effects on recidivism (Leary et al., 1965). By mid-1964 they had "administered over four thousand doses of psychedelic drugs" (Alpert & Leary, 1964, p. 42; Weil). Leary believed that drug research "should be conducted with subjects rather than on subjects" (Gordon, 1963, p. 36). Some argued that Leary and Alpert's ability to collect data on the effects of psilocybin would be compromised by their own consumption of the drug. In the fall of 1961 they gave the drug to several graduate students creating increasing hostility among the Harvard faculty (Gordon).

Leary and Alpert tried to increase knowledge of hallucinogens by starting a group called the "International Federation for Internal Freedom" (IFIF) (Weil, 1963, p. 46). They asked Harvard undergraduates to join and form research cells which would allow them to obtain hallucinogens (Weil). The IFIF published a journal called *The Psychedelic Review* and organized a commune in Newton, Massachusetts. The neighbours of the commune were upset, often complaining that residents would come and go at all hours (Mayer, 1963). Moreover students were acquiring hallucinogens through mail order and from a black market near Harvard ("Harvard Ousting Aide", 1963).

RICHARD ALPERT AND RALPH METZNER'S EXPERIENCES WITH PSILOCYBIN

Alpert believed that psilocybin was a sacrament. Alpert spoke of the impact of his first psilocybin experience by pointing to his chest and stating "From then on in here is the cue" (Lemle, Fierce Grace documentary, 2001). Alpert first took psilocybin in early 1961. He was initially frightened by the drug's effects but he soon felt a sense of fulfilment and peace that academics had not provided. As Alpert continued to take psilocybin he spent his time with others who had done the same. Harvard psychology graduate student Ralph Metzner's first dose of psilocybin taught him about the limits that society had placed on his awareness. Metzner had a profound experience while looking at garbage and throwing snow (Timothy Leary, LSD Science and Experience video, n.d.).

While discussing his termination from Harvard at a press conference (to be presented later) Alpert stated that he, like others around him, had questioned his own sanity. Nevertheless he felt that he should continue studying psilocybin (Baba Ram Dass: One Man's Journey to the East lecture, 1971). Alpert seemed comfortable rejecting Harvard and he claimed that Leary's influence was decisive. "I was thrown out of Harvard because of Tim's revolutionary spirit. He frightened me because he was so free" (The Last Dance video, n.d.). Ram Dass stated that he was someone whom Richard Alpert would label as crazy (Baba Ram Dass at Stephens College lecture, 1973).

BETTER LIVING THROUGH CHEMISTRY AND CHRISTIANITY

In 1962 Leary and Alpert tried to create a religious experience for 20 seminary students by giving them psilocybin inside a chapel on Good Friday. They may have known that this would cause conflict. Taking on Christianity by equating the presence of God with a chemical substance was risky behaviour. Leary had talked to the students about psilocybin, describing it as a way to explore unfamiliar territory and "a new breakthrough for humanity." Ten students took psilocybin and ten took a placebo (Ranen, Power & Control Part 2 documentary, 2005). Ben Thornberg, a subject, claimed that taking hallucinogens was respectable especially when compared to getting drunk. Further, Leary was a respected psychologist (Ranen, Power & Control Part 3 documentary, 2005). Harvard's ultimate refusal to support the Psilocybin Project did not surprise Leary. Metzner recalled Leary saying "expecting. . . . Harvard to sponsor research in consciousness expanding drugs would be like expecting the Vatican to sponsor research in aphrodisiacs" (Lemle, Fierce Grace documentary, 2001).

EARLY REACTIONS OF HARVARD'S SOCIAL RELATIONS DEPARTMENT

An annotated bibliography on psilocybin from the Harvard Medical School contains 87 entries published between 1958 and 1991 in English, German and French (Rinkel, n.d.). There are studies of the drug's influence on spiders, rats and the physiology and behaviour of humans. This demonstrates the immediate and significant impact of the discovery of the drug. Moreover, a manuscript by Ralph Metzner, George Litwin, and Gunther Weil titled "The relation of expectation and setting to psilocybin reactions" states that the psilocybin project was partially funded by a grant from the Laboratory of Social Relations. The support given by this organization (led by the famous social psychologist Robert Freed Bales) in addition to the project's association with the prestigious Center for Research in Personality shows that this was at least initially considered a legitimate scientific undertaking (Metzner, Litwin, & Weil, n.d.).

Harvard University's Archives indicate that the Chair of Harvard's Social Relations Department, David McClelland reported on October 8, 1961: "[Psilocybin] Initiates begin to show. . . a feeling of being above and beyond the normal world [since] the inner world of fantasy is valued more than the outer world of social reality. [And] The research group has repeatedly stated (based on what appears to be scanty evidence) that taking psilocybin under benign circumstances cannot possibly have any bad effects yet the effects mentioned seem sufficiently prominent to warrant some caution" especially for experimenters who frequently take the drug in the course of their research (McClelland, 1961). Over a year later (December 19, 1962) McClelland wrote to Ralph Metzner. He had read a draft of Metzner's paper on psilocybin and told him "My general impression of the report is that you are not analyzing your data objectively." And said "I would be grateful if you removed my name from the acknowledgements" (David C. McClelland Papers a). Approximately 6 months later (June 10, 1963) McClelland wrote to Harvard graduate student George Litwin after reading another version of the paper. He noted the need to control for the "author's favourable bias. . .[ignoring] an average negative effect—increases in depression, anxiety." He said that he hoped that Metzner would keep polishing the paper "rather than take the easy way out of publishing it in *The Psychedelic Review*" (David C. McClelland Papers b).

In the letter to Litwin McClelland expressed the belief that "people who take [psilocybin]. . .regularly or frequently do change or are different. . .they differ in what they experience during ingestion and this represents to me a personality change of a major order. Thus people who start taking it should be told in advance that they are likely to see God, feel differently about the Universe, become different from other people, etc." McClelland continued by showing his frustration with the cliquish atmosphere that had grown among those who took psilocybin: "I use the word alienation to describe this change because their [people who ingest psilocybin] associative patterns become permanently altered and different from those common among lesser mortals who do not consume the divine mushroom. They develop an appetite for finding God that grows and grows." McClelland expressed concern for Litwin and urged him to stop taking hallucinogens and to stay away from Leary, Alpert and their IFIF colleagues in Mexico. Leary and Alpert had ignored his advice: "Perhaps you can understand why I have great anxiety about your going to Mexico to take more of these drugs in August. I tried over and over again to warn Tim [Leary] and Dick [Alpert] against so many ingestions, just as I am warning you now—but to no effect" (David C. McClelland Papers b, 1963).

HARVARD ADMINISTRATORS AND DUELLING MORAL ENTREPRENEURS

Likely based on McClelland's opinion by late 1961 Harvard College Dean John U. Monro and the director of the Harvard University Health Services – Dr. Dana L Farnsworth – had demanded that Leary and Alpert stop using undergraduates as research subjects (Mayer, 1963; Weil, 1963). In early 1962 Leary and Alpert's studies were discussed in the campus newspaper *The Harvard Crimson*. Moreover another faculty member demanded during a meeting that Leary and Alpert alter their research methods or abandon the Psilocybin Project. A student reporter was at the meeting and the exchange appeared on the front page of *The Crimson* the following day (Mayer). In the fall of 1962 Farnsworth and Monro published statements in *The Crimson* alerting students to the dangers of hallucinogens (Weil). Moreover at least one faculty member argued that study participants had formed a "cult" (Gordon, 1963, p. 37). Psilocybin was first mentioned in the *New York Times* on November 29, 1962 when Monro and Farnsworth stated that undergraduates were showing interest in psilocybin and LSD—drugs that "'may result in serious hazards to the mental health and stability of even normal persons'" ("Harvard Men," 1962).

The Harvard administration was concerned and the Department of Social Relations was worried about its reputation (Mayer, 1963). The university began to "peel . . . layer after layer of apparent intellectual respectability from this spiritual Disneyland" (Mayer, p. 73). Then, in April 1963 Leary left town without notice and was fired for neglecting his teaching duties ("Harvard Recalls Statement," 1966; Weil,1963). Mean while the Harvard Administration had been using undergraduates to build a case against Leary and Alpert. A student claimed that Alpert had given him psilocybin in 1962 and on May 27, 1963 Alpert was fired ("Harvard Ousting Aide," 1963; Weil).

MEXICO, MILLBROOK AND THE LAW

Soon after Leary and Alpert were fired from Harvard, the IFIF moved its activities to a hotel in Zihuatanejo, Mexico. Several weeks later the Mexican government forced them to return to the U.S. and the group moved to a large estate in Millbrook, New York where they continued experimenting with hallucinogens and entertained guests that included famous artists, intellectuals, and musicians (Lee & Shlain, 1985; Mansnerus, 1996; "Mexico Ousts 20," 1963). According to Lee and Shlain (p. 99) "Millbrook was a constant party, but one infused with a sense of purpose and optimism. The residents saw themselves as a vanguard of a psychic revolution that would transform the entire society." Leary was arrested for marihuana possession on three occasions, once in Texas in 1965, once at the Millbrook estate in 1966 and once again in California in 1968 ("Leary, Wife and Son," 1970; "Ousted Lecturer Jailed," 1965; Playboy, 1966, p. 95). In 1966 he drew a 30-year prison sentence and a $30,000 fine from the Texas case (Zion, 1966). Leary and his friends were evicted from Millbrook in 1968 ("Dr. Leary and Followers," 1968).

In 1969 Leary's Texas conviction was ruled unconstitutional by the U.S. Supreme Court ("What's News," 1969), yet he received 1–10 years for the California case. Leary soon escaped from his minimum-security California prison and went to Algeria where he received political asylum ("Timothy Leary, Drug Advocate," 1970; "What's News," 1970). Leary travelled to Europe, Asia and Africa before being forced to return to the U.S. while in Afghanistan ("Leary Flown to U.S.," 1973). He received 5 years for his prison escape and was paroled 3 years later ("Leary, Once an LSD Advocate," 1976; "Timothy Leary Sentenced," 1973). Leary spent the next 20 years lecturing to college students and died in 1996 at age 75 (Mansnerus, 1996). Alpert went to India in 1967, returned as a Guru with a beard and a robe and spent several decades on the lecture circuit (Davidson, 2000; Levine, 1976). From these media sources it seems that Leary and Alpert were moral entrepreneurs who personified countercultural values and were clearly vanquished by the establishment.

LEARY FOUGHT THE LAW AND THE LAW WON

In 1963 Leary noted the legal uncertainties surrounding hallucinogen research. He believed that "tolerance" and "patience" were the keys to solving the social conflicts of the 1960s and argued "we're not going to solve these problems by shouting at other people and not listening. . .[or] by passing laws or by putting young people in jail" (Timothy Leary at Millbrook—Interview part four, n.d.). He further stated "I see myself as a bridge between the middle age generation of whisky drinking, book readers and this new generation who have been brought up on new forms of energy like television, [and] psychedelic drugs" (Timothy Leary at Millbrook—Interview part three, n.d.). Leary predicted that people would soon have to be licensed to take hallucinogens—having shown that they can use them responsibly. He labelled the freedom to use hallucinogens as "the fifth freedom" and equated it with the right to control one's own nervous system. He discussed plans to open training centres that would help people use hallucinogens to improve their lives (Leary, Individual in the College Community lecture, 1963).

According to other sources Leary and Alpert parted in late 1964. Leary's legal troubles contrasted with Alpert's transformation into the spiritual leader Ram Dass. In a conversation with Ram Dass Leary stated: "from a cultural social point of view. . . I'm getting badder and badder and badder and you're getting gooder and gooder and gooder. I have 5,000,000 dollars on my head and you're practically Billy Graham." Ram Dass summarized his differences with Leary: "his models of the universe aren't mine. I'm much more into mysticism" (Baba Ram Dass at KOPN radio station interview, 1973).

Leary stated laws prohibiting marihuana and other "sacred substances" were unconstitutional and as sacraments their use was not illegal (Leary interview, KDNA radio station, 1970). He blamed a "middle class, middle brow bureaucracy" for the prohibition of marihuana and hallucinogens and the resulting imprisonment of young people and minorities (Leary interview, KDNA radio station). While Leary was on trial in California the judge called him "the most dangerous man in America" (Perry & Perry, The Drug Years: Feed Your Head documentary Part 2, 2006). Undaunted, Leary said "I'm insulted when people call me are bel. Fuck you. I'm smarter, I'm better educated, better looking than most of those stabbing me" (Paul Krassner Interviews Timothy Leary 1995 Part 6). He equated formal education with a dangerous drug and urged students to drop out of school (The Drug Years: Feed Your Head documentary Part 2). He told them: "Go out closer to reality to direct experience." (Leary, Individual in the College Community lecture, 1963).

HARVARD LAW SCHOOL

In 1966 Leary was invited to a Harvard Law School symposium on the control of LSD. Leary demonstrated again his intellect, sense of humour and utter disregard for religious, political or educational authority. He spoke of the distinction between the sacred and the secular:

> I have a great fondness and respect for Harvard. However, Harvard is a secular institution and my business has to do with the sacred or the religious. I'm going to talk tonight about God and man and law and about the relationship between these two issues: What should we render to society? And what must we insist on preserving to our self and our sense of divinity? (Leary, Harvard Law School lecture, 1966)
>
> Leary also argued that as a representative of a religion: A sacrament puts you in a different state of consciousness. But there's really very little external danger to sacraments. We have to say 'LSD is dangerous when compared to what'? The statistics tell

us that every year one thousand college students kill themselves, while the number of suicides attributable to LSD are perhaps between 5 and 10. What is natural to me are botanical species which interact directly with the nervous system and what I consider artificial is four years at Harvard and the Bible and St. Patrick's cathedral and the Sunday school teachings. Anything is possible because your consciousness creates it all. I can create a world in which I am Napoleon or [Harvard President] Nathan Pusey and you can't pass a law against my believing it (Leary, Harvard Law School lecture, 1966).

SUMMARY AND CONCLUSIONS

Alpert and Metzner's experiences with psilocybin were playful and peaceful, seemingly nothing that should have caused alarm. Even when being terminated by Harvard Alpert seemed to be at peace, seemingly aided by this experience. The details of the research with divinity students shows that it was conducted in a Christian chapel, on seminary students on the holiest of days, Good Friday. Leary challenged the ability of the law to control drug use and declared that educational institutions were intellectually bankrupt. In the final analysis it is not surprising that he was singled out and set up for drug arrests since he had become a public enemy of American political, legal, religious and educational systems. He was a true counter-cultural symbol. Alpert and Leary became moral entrepreneurs much as Becker (1963) described. They had a national stage where Leary broadcast the immorality of the educational, religious and legal opposition. To those in the mainstream Leary was undoubtedly seen as a symbol of the enemy. By 1968 the war on drugs, on young people and the Vietnamese mandated to many policy makers that psilocybin should be criminalized under federal law.

Harvard's archives demonstrate that McClelland was concerned about his academic career and likely the reputation of psychology at Harvard. He was obviously worried about the health and careers of Leary's followers. Other university administrators were worried about Harvard's reputation, the health of Harvard undergraduates, and faculty research methods. Leary and Alpert were determined to push the limits at Harvard and in the end Leary simply left.

The Harvard drug scandal became part of a process that culminated in 1968 and parallels prohibition of LSD and international prohibition of psychedelic drugs (Dyck, 2008). Though Leary and Alpert parted ways they converge in the late 1960s. Becker's (1963) theory of moral entrepreneurs can be loosely applied to the Harvard administrators in 1962, as well as to Alpert and Leary, but later applies even more to Leary and Alpert's activities and their increasingly radical ideas. They were clearly moral entrepreneurs, Leary the anarchist and Ram Dass the Guru. Although they were far from being prohibitionists, they were self-righteous crusaders on different but equally holy missions for the good of young and minority Americans. Leary and Alpert became involved in the drug and anti-war movement of the late 1960s. People using hallucinogens were labelled by much of America as a danger to society. LSD and marihuana were linked to psilocybin, antiwar activism, and non-conventional lifestyles, with Harvard administrators long forgotten. This research demonstrates that moral entrepreneurs are not necessarily prohibitionists but the pressure from their efforts may lead to new legal prohibitions. Due to the actions of Alpert and Leary the possession of psilocybin was criminalized under United States federal law in 1968 (Pub. L. No. 90-639,

Stat. 1361 1968 and Boire, 2002). Leary, Alpert and their followers clearly frightened law enforcement authorities and members of the Establishment. This case study demonstrates that crusaders can be successful in changing culture even when laws are passed in futile attempts to control their behaviour, just as Leary predicted.

STATUTE

Public Law, No. 90-639, Statute 1361, 1968.

REFERENCES

Alpert, R., & Leary, T. (1964). Reply with rejoinder. *Esquire, 61*, 42, 44, 50, 54.

Baba Ram Dass. (Speaker). (1971). *Baba Ram Dass: One man's journey to the East* [Lecture] (Cassette Recording). San Rafael, CA: Big Sur Recordings, Duplicated by Superscope.

Baba Ram Dass. (Speaker). (1973). *Baba Ram Dass at KOPN* [Interview] (Compact Disc). Columbia, MO: KOPN Radio Station.

Baba Ram Dass. (Speaker). (1973). *Baba Ram Dass at Stephens College* [Lecture] (Compact Disc). Columbia, MO: KOPN Radio Station.

Becker, H. S. (1963). *Outsiders: Studies in the sociology of deviance*. New York: The Free Press.

Boire, R. G. (2002). *Sacred mushrooms and the law*. Berkeley, CA: Ronin.

Brown, S. (2006, December 7). Researchers explore new visions for hallucinogens. *Chronicle of Higher Education*, 53, A12. Retrieved May 29, 2009, from http://www.maps.org/sys/nq.pl?id=1118&fmt=page.

David C. McClelland Papers a, Box 94. (1962, December 19). *David C. McClelland to Dr. Ralph Metzner*. Harvard University Archives, Cambridge, MA.

David C. McClelland Papers b, Box 94. (1963, June 10). *David C. McClelland to Mr. George Litwin*. Harvard University Archives, Cambridge, MA.

Davidson, S. (2000, May 21). *The Dass effect. The New York Times Magazine*. Retrieved May 29, 2009, from http://www.nytimes.com/library/magazine/home/20000521mag-ramdass.html.

Dowling, C. (1977, December 4). Confessions of an American guru: Ram Dass. *New York Times*, pp. 41–43, 136–149

Dr. Leary and followers told to vacate estate. (1968, February 20). *New York Times*, p. 20.

Dutch protesters make bid to save "magic mushrooms." (2007, October 27). *Reuters*. Retrieved May 29, 2009, from http://www.reuters.com/article/worldNews/idUSL2748299520071027.

Dyck, E. (2008). *Psychedelic psychiatry: LSD from clinic to campus*. Baltimore: The Johns Hopkins University Press.

Gordon, N. (1963, August 15). The hallucinogenic drug cult. *The Reporter*, 29, 35–43.

Graves, R. (1960). *The Greek myths: 1*. New York: Penguin.

Graves, R. (1961). *Oxford addresses on poetry*. London: Cassell and Company.

Griffiths, R. R., Richards, W. A., Johnson, M. W., McCann, U. D., & Jesse, R. (2008). Mystical-type experiences occasioned by psilocybin mediate the attribution of personal meaning and spiritual significance 14 months later. *Journal of Psychopharmacology*, 22, 621–632.

Harvard men told of mind-drug peril. (1962, November 29). *New York Times*, p. 18.

Harvard ousting aide in drug case. (1963, May 28). *New York Times*, p. 60.

Harvard recalls statement. (1966, March 12). *New York Times*, p. 25.

Japan culls magic from mushrooms. (2002, May 13). BBC News. Retrieved May 29, 2009, from http://news.bbc.co.uk/1/hi/world/asia-pacific/1984498.stm.

Leary flown to U.S. in custody. (1973, January 19). *New York Times*, p. 39.

Leary, once an LSD advocate, paroled. (1976, April 21). *New York Times*, p. 56.

Leary, T. (Speaker). (1963). *Timothy Leary: Individual in the college community: His commitments and his works* [Lecture] (Compact Disc). Ellensburg, WA: Central Washington University.

Leary, T. (Speaker). (1966, November 4). *Timothy Leary Lecture at Harvard University Law School forum on LSD: Methods of control*. Retrieved July 19, 2008, from: http://www.law.harvard.edu/students/orgs/forum/audio.html.

Leary, T. (Speaker). (1970). *Timothy Leary interview* (Compact Disc). St. Louis, MO: KDNA Radio Station.

Leary, T., Metzner, R., Presnell, M., Weil, G., Schwitzgebel, R., & Kinne, S. (1965). A new behavior change pattern using psilocybin. *Psychotherapy: Theory, Research and Practice, 2*, 61–72.

Leary, wife and son guilty of marijuana possession. (1970, February 21). *New York Times*, p. 47.

Lee, M. A., & Shlain, B. (1985). *Acid dreams: The complete social history of LSD: The CIA, the sixties, and beyond*. New York: Grove Press.

Lemle, M. (Producer/Director). (2001). *Ram Dass: Fierce grace* [Documentary]. USA: Zeitgeist Films.

Levine, R. M. (1976, April 22). The pizza and the path: Ram Dass's U.S.A. *Rolling Stone*, 42–47, 76, 78, 80, 82, 84, 85.

Magic mushrooms ban becomes law. (2005, July 18). BBC News. Retrieved May 29, 2009, from http://news.bbc.co.uk/2/hi/uk_news/4691899.stm.

Mansnerus, L. (1996, June 1). Timothy Leary, pied piper of psychedelic 60s, dies at 75. *New York Times*. pp. 1, 12.

Mayer, M. (1963). Getting alienated with the right crowd at Harvard: Drugs in the yard; and where, mother is your wandering son tonight? *Esquire*, 60, 73, 141, 142, 144

McClelland, D. C. (1961, October 8). *Some social reactions to the psilocybin research project*. David C. McClelland Papers a, Box 94. Harvard University Archives, Cambridge, MA.

Metzner, R., Litwin, G., & Weil, G. (n.d.). *The relation of expectation and setting to psilocybin reactions: A questionnaire study*. Unpublished manuscript, David C. McClelland Papers, Box 94. Cambridge, MA: Harvard University Archives.

Mexico ousts 20 in drug research: Bars psychic tests led by former Harvard teacher. (1963, June 15). *New York Times*, p. 17.

Moreno, J. A., Wiegand, C. B., Taitano, E. K., & Delgado, P. L. (2006). Safety, tolerability and efficacy of psilocybin in 9 patients with obsessive-compulsive disorder. *Journal of Clinical Psychiatry*, 67, 1735–1740.

Musto, David F. (1999). *The American disease: Origins of narcotic control* (3rd ed.). New York: Oxford University Press.

Netherlands bans hallucinogenic mushrooms: Lawmakers tighten nation's drug policy after girl's suicide. (2007, October 12). *MSNBC*. Retrieved May 29, 2009, from http://www.msnbc.msn.com/id/21269227/.

Osmundsen, J. A. (1965, May 15). Harvard study sees benefit in use of mind drugs. *New York Times*. p. 64.

Ousted lecturer jailed in Laredo on drug charge. (1965, December 24). *New York Times*, p. 15.

Paul Krassner interviews Timothy Leary 1995 Part 6. (2009). *From Nancy Cain's video archives*. Retrieved May 25, 2009, from http://www. youtube.com/watch?v=xQW1ChD3Z34.

Perry, D. H., Perry, H. (Producers), & Perry, H. (Director). (2006). *VH1 documentary: The drug years feed your head (1967–1971) Part 2 Timothy Leary.* Retrieved July 19, 2007, from http://youtube.com/watch?v=4ZTaanUpK24.

Playboy interview: Timothy Leary, a candid conversation with the controversial ex-Harvard professor, prime partisan and prophet of LSD. (1966, September). *Playboy, 13,* 93, 95, 102, 104, 106, 110, 112, 250, 251, 254, 255.

Ranen, A. (Documentarian), Power & control—LSD in the sixties part 2 (2005). Retrieved May 25, 2009, from http://www.youtube.com/ watch?v=47vt5Z5wxol&feature=related.

Ranen, A. (Documentarian), Power & control—LSD in the sixties part 3 (2005). Retrieved May 25, 2009, from http://www.youtube.com/ watch?v=vNODtfw0K3o&feature= related.

Rinkel, M. (n.d.). *Annotated bibliography: Psilocybin.* Medical Department, Sandoz Pharmaceuticals. Hanover, NJ. Max Rinkel Papers, Center for the History of Medicine, Harvard Medical School.

Sale and possession of magic mushrooms banned. (2006, January). *RTÉ News.* Retrieved May 29, 2009, from http://www.rte.ie/news/2006/0131/mushrooms.html.

Sewell, R. A., Halpern, J. H., & Pope, H. G. (2006). Response of cluster headache to psilocybin and LSD. *Neurology, 16,* 1920–1922.

The Last Dance (n.d.). Retrieved May 25, 2009 from http://www.youtube.com/ watch?v=ifB9InfAPRw.

Timothy Leary at Millbrook—Interview part three [Video] (n.d.). Retrieved May 25, 2009, from http://www.youtube.com/watch?v=y22py0Qf80o.

Timothy Leary at Millbrook—Interview part four [Video] (n.d.). Retrieved May 25, 2009, from http://www.youtube.com/watch?v=eaEWk2dAecE.

Timothy Leary, drug advocate, walks away from coast prison. (1970, September 14). *New York Times,* p. 14.

Timothy Leary LSD science and experience [Video]. (n.d.). Retrieved May 25, 2009, from http://www.dailymotion.com/video/x2hr5n_dr-timothy-leary-a-lsd-science_and_short films.

Timothy Leary sentenced to up to five years in escape. (1973, April 24). *New York Times,* p. 12.

What's news. (1969, May 20). *Wall Street Journal,* p. 1.

What's news. (1970, October 21). *Wall Street Journal,* p. 1.

Wark, C., & Galliher, J. F. (2007). *Outlawing magic mushrooms: The prohibition of psilocybin in the United States.* Saarbrucken, Germany: VDM Verlag Dr. Muller.

Wasson, R. G. (1957, May 13). Seeking the magic mushroom. *Life, 42,* 100–109.

Weil, A. T. (1963, November 5). The strange case of the Harvard drug scandal. *Look, 27,* 38–48.

Weiner, T. (2002, May 8). The place for trips of the mind-bending kind. *New York Times,* A4.

Zion, S. E. (1966, March 16). Convicted user of marijuana to appeal on religious basis; Dr. Leary used plant as "key" to widen his experience—calls it "harmless". *New York Times,* 55.

ABOLITION AND REINSTATEMENT OF CAPITAL PUNISHMENT DURING THE PROGRESSIVE ERA AND EARLY 20TH CENTURY*

JOHN F. GALLIHER,** GREGORY RAY***
and BRENT COOK***

ABSTRACT
Ten American states abolished the death penalty between 1897 and 1917, but by the end of the 1930s, eight of these states had reinstated capital punishment. Not surprisingly, many of these abolitionist states were relatively homogeneous. Information ranging from individual motivations and tactics to the economic trends and the demographic characteristics of an area were drawn on to analyze developments in each state. Existing records indicate that most of the initial abolition laws had the support of the state's governors or a major local daily newspaper. While abolition was associated with economic boom, reinstatement occurred during economic recession and depression. Along with such issues of social context, reinstatement was triggered by the threat of lynchings and political radicals, since abolition gave those outside of government a monopoly on lethal violence.

1. INTRODUCTION

Historians generally agree that the Progressive Era encompassed the first two decades of the twentieth century.[1] A growing fear of communists, foreigners and other minorities at the end of World War I brought the era to a close.[2] The most significant production of this short period was a long list of reform legislation designed to protect the public. New laws regulating business activities included anti-trust legislation,[3] the Pure Food and Drug Act, the first Workman's Compensation Act,[4] laws limiting the hours and conditions of employment for women and children, and minimum aid to dependent children.[5] Other Progressive Era legislation included female

---

*The authors are grateful to Hugo Adam Bedau, Michael L. Radelet, Philip Mackey, Eli Zaretsky, Mark Gaylord, anonymous reviewers for comments on an earlier version of this paper and to Steve Chippendale for help with reviewing some of the newspapers used in this research. Presented at the Law and Society Association meetings in Amsterdam, 1991.
**Professor of Sociology, University of Missouri, Columbia. Ph.D. (Sociology), Indiana University, 1967; M.A., Indiana University, 1964; B.A., University of Missouri, Kansas City, 1961.
***M.A. candidate at the University of Missouri, Columbia.
[1]George E. Mowry, The Progressive Movement 1900–1920: The Reform Persuasion (1958).
[2] Arthur S. Link & William B. Calton, American Epoch: A History of the United States since 1900, Vol. I: The Progressive Era and the First World War 1900–1920 (4th ed. 1973).
[3]Mowry, *supra* note 1; Murray Edelman, The Symbolic Uses of Politics (4th ed. 1973).
[4]Thomas K. McCraw, *The Progressive Legacy, in* The Progressive Era 181–201 (Lewis L. Gould ed., 1974).
[5]Mowry, *supra* note 1.

suffrage,[6] alcohol prohibition,[7] federal drug controls,[8] state juvenile codes,[9] and probation and parole statutes.[10]

A debate continues as to what forces pressed for these legislative reforms. While some view these laws as resulting from the demands of the urban working classes,[11] others have found that the middle classes were largely responsible for generating these reforms.[12] Still others contend that these reforms were elite-inspired and controlled.[13] Additional research notes the involvement of women,[14] journalists,[15] government bureaucrats[16] and intellectuals.[17] Moreover, some view the Progressive Era as a period of significant and lasting accomplishments,[18] while others view the reforms as short-lived and insignificant.[19] Thus, while there is general agreement concerning the time period covered by the Progressive Era, there is comparatively little agreement regarding the sources of the period's legislative innovations or the significance of these reforms.

Progressive Era legislative reforms, especially those changes in criminal law, have attracted considerable attention. However, the Era's numerous death penalty laws largely have escaped analysis. The *Annals of the American Academy of Political and Social Science* published three short essays in 1952 on capital punishment abolition laws enacted during the Progressive Era. One page of this compilation reveals that the governor of Oregon supported a public referendum on abolition because of his objections to lethal retribution and difficulties in securing convictions in death penalty cases.[20] The abolition and reinstatement of the death penalty in Washington is covered in three pages.[21] Four pages are devoted to the abolition and the subsequent

---

[6] McCraw, *supra* note 4.

[7] Joseph R. Gusfield, Symbolic Crusade: Status Policies and the American Temperance Movement (1963).

[8] Alfred R. Lindesmith, The Addict and the Law (1965).

[9] Anthony M. Platt, The Child Savers/The Invention of Delinquency (2d ed. 1977).

[10] David J. Rothman, Conscience and Convenience: The Asylum and its Alternatives in Progressive America (1980).

[11] Michael P. Rogin, *From Below, in* The Progressive Era 20–30 (Arthur Mann ed., 2d ed. 1975).

[12] George E. Mowry, *From Above, in* The Progressive Era 13–19 (Arthur Mann ed., 2d ed. 1975); The Age of Reform: From Bryan to F.D.R. (Richard Hofstadler ed., 1972).

[13] Gabriel Kolko, The Triumph of Conservatism: A Reinterpretation of American History, 1900–16 (1963); Samuel P. Hays, *The Upper Class Takes the Lead in* The Progressive Era 79–93 (Arthur Mann ed., 2d ed. 1975).

[14] Gusfield, supra note 7; Paula Baker, *The Domestication of Politics: Women and American Political Society, 1780–1920, in* Women, the State, and Welfare, 55–91 (Linda Gorden ed., 1990).

[15] Christopher Lasch, The New Radicalism in America [1889–1963]: The Intellectual as a Social Type (1965); John Hagan & Jeffrey Leon, *Rediscovering Delinquency: Social History, Political Ideology and the Sociology of Law,* 42 Am. Soc. Rev. 587, 587–98 (1977); Robert M. Crunden, Ministers of Reform: The Progressives' Achievement in American Civilization 1889–1920 (1982).

[16] Lindensmith, *supra* note 8.

[17] Christopher Lasch, The True and Only Heaven: Progress and its Critics (1991).

[18] McCraw, *supra* note 4.

[19] Kolko, *supra* note 13.

[20] Robert H. Dann, *Capital Punishment in Oregon,* 284 Annals Am. Acad. Pol. & Soc. Sci. 110, 110–14 (1952).

[21] Norman S. Hayner & Hohn R. Cranor, *The Death Penalty in Washington State,* 284 Annals Am. Acad. Pol. & Soc. Sci. 101, 101–04 (1952).

reinstatement process in Missouri.[22] Bedau[23] gathers even smaller scraps of information in a few sentences about the legislative processes in four states that reinstated capital punishment during this period (Washington, Colorado, Missouri and Oregon), but falls far short of collecting enough material necessary for a complete understanding of these events.

Moreover, an encyclopedic history of changing criminal penalties of the period, *Conscience and Convenience: The Asylum and its Alternatives in Progressive America*,[24] comprehensively addresses Progressive Era reforms in criminal law and philosophies of punishment, but omits the death penalty. According to Rothman, the reforms included "probation, parole, and the indeterminate sentence; the juvenile court and the outpatient clinic; and novel designs for the penitentiary, the reformatory, and the insane asylum."[25] Rothman does not address capital punishment changes, even though ten states abolished capital punishment between 1897–1917: Colorado (1897), Kansas (1907), Minnesota (1911), Washington (1913), Oregon (1914), South Dakota (1915), North Dakota (1915), Tennessee (1915), Arizona (1916) and Missouri (1917). Of these ten states, eight reinstated capital punishment between 1901–1939: Colorado (1901), Arizona (1918), Tennessee (1919), Missouri (1919), Washington (1919), Oregon (1920), Kansas (1935) and South Dakota (1939). Bedau, the dean of capital punishment researchers, noted that: "One is also more curious to know what accounts for the reintroduction of the death penalty in several states no more than a few years after it had been abolished. Surprising though it may be . . . the full story has never been told."[26] Maintenance of these reforms would have helped keep the United States in step with the widespread abolition movement in Europe, instead of having laws consistent with nations such as South Africa and Iran.

A. *The Social Context of Capital Punishment*

Those studying the social origins of law usually acknowledge the significance of the general social context of legislation.[27] More specific "focusing events,"[28] including crises or disasters, call attention to a given problem to be addressed by particular legislation. The objective of this study is to describe both the social structural context and the focusing events of these abolition and reinstatement laws during the first three decades of the twentieth century. Significant elements of the general social context of criminal laws include the economic and demographic makeup of the relevant political jurisdiction.[29] The death penalty has been traditionally administered in a

---

[22]Ellen E. Guillot, *Abolition and Restoration of the Death Penalty in Missouri*, 284 Annals. Am. Acad. Pol. Soc. Sci. 105, 105–09 (1952).

[23]Hugo A. Bedau, The Death Penalty in America (3d ed. 1982).

[24]Rothman, *supra* note 10.

[25]*Id*. at 3.

[26]Bedau, *supra* note 23, at 22.

[27]Herbert Jacob, Silent Revolution: The Transformation of Divorce Law in the United States (1988); John W. Kingdon, Agendas, Alternatives, and Public Policies (1984).

[28]Kingdon, *supra* note 27.

[29]Richard A. Berk et al., A Measure of Justice: An Empirical Study of Changes in the California Penal Code, 1955–1971 (1977).

racist fashion,[30] and states with the highest concentrations of non-white citizens have used the death penalty most frequently.[31] It therefore should come as no surprise that, whatever may be the unique triggering events in the history of the death penalty in any particular state, most of these Progressive Era abolitionist states had very small non-white populations. Only two of the abolitionist states contained more than five percent minority citizens (Table 1). In general, the absence of minorities renders the states with homogeneous populations conducive to lenient or less severe criminal penalties.[32]

The economic context also plays a critical role in the genesis of death penalty reforms. Most of these abolition laws were passed during the economic boom immediately preceding American entry into World War I.[33] Moreover, analysis of other time periods also shows that economic factors often influence death penalty policies. Rusche and Kirchheimer[34] have traced the development of punishment in Europe since the Middle Ages. They noted that while fines were a frequent punishment during the early Middle Ages, in the later Middle Ages fines were replaced by a harsh system relying heavily on capital punishment. Associated with these changes in penal practice were the deteriorating economic conditions from the early to late Middle Ages. The increasing inability of the poor to pay fines led to a search for alternative punishments. Rusche and Kirchheimer concluded that criminal punishment in any era must provide conditions that are worse than the lot of the poorest free people if such punishment is to serve as a deterrent.

TABLE 1

Percent of Non-whites in Abolitionist States, 1897–1917.

State	Year of Abolition	Percent Non-white*
Minnesota	1911	.7
North Dakota	1915	1.2
Colorado	1897	1.5
Oregon	1914	2.5
Washington	1913	2.6
Kansas	1907	3.1
South Dakota	1915	3.3
Missouri	1917	5.0
Arizona	1916	12.0
Tennessee	1915	21.0

*Source: U.S. Bureau of the Census, 1900–1920.

[30]William J. Bowers et al., Legal Homicide: Death as Punishment in America, 1864–1982 (1984).
[31]U.S. Department of Justice, *Capital Punishment* (1973).
[32]John F. Galliher & Linda Basilick, *Utah's Liberal Drug Laws: Structural Foundations and Triggering Events*, 26 Soc. Probs. 284 (1979).
[33]The Progressive Movement: 1900–1915 (Richard Hofstadler ed., 1963); Joseph S. Davis, The World Between the Wars, 1919–1939: An Economist's View (1975).
[34]George Rusche & Otto Kirchheimer, Punishment and Social Structure (1939).

During the eighteenth century the American colonies averaged approximately twelve capital offenses compared to more than 200 in England. The relatively low number of such statutory offenses in America was due to the scarcity of labor; that there were any such offenses at all was due to the scarcity of prison space.[35] More recently, Adamson[36] has noted the importance of economics in changes in United States' penal policy from the 1790s through the early twentieth century. He shows that during economic booms, the convict population was a resource to be exploited through such policies as a convict labor system, but during recessions, these same convicts became a threat that encouraged reliance on capital punishment. Correspondingly, not only were abolition bills passed during a period of economic boom, but most of these states that reinstated capital punishment did so during the economic recession following World War I or during the 1930s. This article will demonstrate that expressed humanitarian motivations of reform-minded legislators pressing for abolition of capital punishment are not necessarily inconsistent with a structural analysis of law, linking such legislation to the changing economic fortunes of a society.

B. Statement of the Problem and Data Sources

Census data and indicators of economic trends provide information on the social context. In addition to a search for the social context of legislation, our analysis includes idiosyncratic focusing events for specific laws. To learn more about the precise process of these legislative events, we drew on any existing records of legislative debate and public hearings, as well as any materials in the archives of individual state historical societies. These materials include the correspondence of governors and other elected officials, state agency reports and previously published materials dealing with capital punishment reform. We also reviewed every issue of a major daily newspaper in each state for one year prior to a particular bill's passage. We developed an initial narrative based on newspaper accounts and then supplemented and modified the initial sequence of events, as necessary, by drawing on the additional materials. Newspaper accounts were especially important because most young states were not able to develop mechanisms of generating detailed official records of the legislative process. This was especially true of sparsely populated states in the West and Great Plains. Nowhere is this better illustrated than in Arizona, which became a state in 1912 and by 1920 had a population of only 334,000. As a very new state, Arizona had neither sufficient time nor the tax base necessary to establish organizations that produced formal and detailed records of legislative deliberations.

We will deal with both the behavior of specific lawmakers, as well as the broad historical economic trends largely unrelated to any specific individual. These obvious demographic and economic patterns compel us to recognize different levels of analysis, which "cover a range from the individual to the world system with aggregates,

---

[35]Louis Filler, *Movements to Abolish the Death Penalty in the United States,* 284 Annals. Am. Acad. Pol. & Soc. Sci. 124 (1952).
[36]Christopher Adamson, *Toward a Marxian Penology: Captive Criminal Populations as Economic Threats and Resources,* 31 Soc. Probs. 435 (1984).

groups, corporate social systems, organizations, communities, institutions, states, and societies somewhere in between."[37] Only by considering *both* "the interactions within the social system and the conditions under which the social system operates" can the sources of deviant behavior and its punishment be understood.[38]

While social scientists typically study either the origins of law or the consequences of law, in reality, "[t]he law itself is neither an end nor a beginning, but rather an intermediate stage in the political process."[39] Considering the pervasive legislative and legal maneuvering, Calabresi and Bobbitt ask:

> Why do we move restlessly from one system which proves inadequate to another? The answer is, we have come to think, that a society may limit the destructive impact of tragic choices by choosing to mix approaches over time. Endangered values are reaffirmed. . . . More important, . . . the deep knowledge that change will come again carries with it the hope that values currently degraded will not for all that be abandoned.[40]

In addition to this juggling of values, once laws are created to resolve specific conflicts, they "not only create further conflicts, but also spotlight other contradictions which may have been dormant."[41] These new conflicts lead in turn to further resolutions. The most important of these conflicts involve issues of social context and are "those that derive from the economic and political structures of the times,"[42] including market conditions, profits and the control of labor. It is through multiple levels of analysis that contradictory consequences of specific laws become apparent.

We will demonstrate that while abolition resolved certain conflicts, the legislation produced additional conflicts of its own. The conflicts were exacerbated by economic recession and set the stage for additional policy changes. This analysis should allow us both to understand more about the structural origins of modern death penalty laws and their abolition, and to add to our understanding of the sources and consequences of Progressive Era ideology.

Sample design is also of critical importance. Hagan[43] argues that since most research on the social origins of law has focused on isolated case studies, generalization is impossible. This reliance on isolated case studies in all probability has contributed to the long-term and unproductive dispute involving the conflict and consensus perspectives.[44] To avoid this problem, Galliher et al.[45] analyzed the origins

---

[37]Pat Lauderdale et al., *Levels of Analysis, Theoretical Orientations and Degrees of Abstraction*, 21 Am. Sociologist 32 (1990).

[38]*Id.* at 35.

[39]Paul Burstein, Discrimination, Jobs, and Politics: The Struggle for Equal Opportunity in the United States Since the New Deal 193 (1985).

[40]Guido Calabresi & Philip Bobbit, Tragic Choices 197 (1978).

[41]William J. Chambliss, *Contradictions and Conflict in Law Creation*, 2 Res. Law & Soc. 8 (Steven Spitzer ed., 1979).

[42]*Id.* at 7.

[43]John Hagan, *The Legislation of Crime and Delinquency: A Review of Theory, Method and Research*, 14 Law & Soc'y Rev. 603 (1980).

[44]Chambliss, *supra* note 41; John F. Galliher & Allynn Waltzer, *The Puzzle of the Social Origins of the Marihuana Tax Act of 1937*, 24 Soc. Probs. 367 (1977).

[45]John F. Galliher et al., Searching for the Origins of the 1970s Marihuana Decriminalization Movement, Presented at the Annual Meeting of the American Sociological Association in Atlanta, GA, August 1988.

of the entire set of eleven state marihuana decriminalization laws passed during the 1970s, the cessation of such legislation during the 1980s, and eventual moves to recriminalize this drug during the 1990s. Such a series of legislative events is also found in the abolition and reinstatement of the death penalty by several states during the early twentieth century.

II. ABOLITION

A. Support from Governors

1. Kansas

There were fifty-seven murders mentioned in published articles in the *Topeka Daily Capital* in the year prior to death penalty abolition in 1907. According to one historical account, a total of nine persons had been executed under state law prior to 1907.[46] The first legal execution occurred in 1863 and the last in that century in 1870. Governor Edward W. Hoch signed the law abolishing capital punishment on January 30, 1907.[47]

Kansas passed a statute establishing a death penalty for first-degree murder in 1872. The statute required that the sentence be carried out "by hanging by the neck, at such time as the governor of the state for the time being may appoint, not less than one year from the time of conviction."[48] A former pardon attorney has observed:

> For many years the Kansas death sentence was [an] anomalous formality because the statute provided that a person was taken to the Penitentiary and there confined at hard labor until the governor should sign his death warrant—which few governors did. Thus we had the death sentence as imposed by the court which everybody knew meant imprisonment for life.[49]

In fact, no governor had signed a death warrant under the provisions of this statute.[50]

Governor Hoch claimed that it was largely at his insistence that the 1907 legislature repealed the death penalty.[51] That year, he explained his position in a personal letter: "The fatal defect of the capital punishment theory is that it cheapens life instead of magnifying it as its votaries have believed. The criminal usually takes life hurriedly without much deliberation, but the law takes plenty of time and does it deliberately."[52] As early as 1905, the Governor had pledged to resign rather than to sign a death warrant against any prisoner. He said: "The hanging of a human being, whether it be legalized or not, is a relic of barbarism."[53] Apparently many Kansans agreed with the Governor, for prior to abolition the paper noted in a headline that it

---

[46]Louise Barry, *Legal Hangings in Kansas,* 18 Kan. Hist. Q. 279 (1950).
[47]1907 Kan. Sess. Laws 188.
[48]Kan. Stat. Ann. § 82 (1901).
[49]*Kansas Office of Director of Penal Institutions,* 1966 State Office Bldg., Topeka, KS (Rev. 1966).
[50]Barry, *supra* note 46.
[51]*Id.*
[52]Letter from Governor E. W. Hoch to Robinette Scheier, *Kansas State Historical Society* (Mar. 23, 1907).
[53]*Hoch Would Resign First,* Kansas City Star, Dec. 9, 1905, at 1.

was "Hard to get Jury in Murder Case."[54] The article added: "After the regular panel was exhausted sixty new jurymen were summoned without completing the jury. The sheriff is now summoning twenty five more men." This difficulty demonstrates that a large number of Kansans simply had no stomach for imposition of the death penalty.

2. Washington

Washington executed fourteen individuals between 1904–1910.[55] In the year immediately preceding abolition, eighteen murders occurred. The most dramatic account of a murder spawned the following headline: "Saloon Man Kills Two Peace Officers; Then Ends Own Life."[56] Prior to abolition of the death penalty, the *Times* published editorials condemning violent crimes,[57] but the paper took no position on capital punishment: "Nor has human experience determined the issue absolutely. It is not definitely established that the abolition of capital punishment encourages murders—or that the continuance of the practice discourages them."[58]

Later that year, it was reported by the press that four convicted murderers had been executed on the same day in Oregon. This prompted the warden of the Washington state penitentiary to announce his opposition to the death penalty and to predict its eventual abolition in Washington.[59] Governor Lister's records indicate that in December 1914, he became an honorary vice president of the Anti-Capital Punishment Society of America, just one of many such abolitionist organizations created during the Progressive Era.[60] Finally, the local paper reported: "The death penalty for murder in the state of Washington is a thing of the past. Governor Lister today signed H.B. 200, whereby it [the death penalty] is relegated to history."[61]

3. South Dakota

According to the *Pierre Daily Capital-Journal,* from statehood in 1889 through 1915, 103 murders and five executions occurred in South Dakota.[62] The state executed one individual during the months preceding death penalty abolition in 1915— a black man was hanged for allegedly murdering a woman and her child.[63] Meanwhile, the press reported five murders during the year leading up to death penalty abolition. The most sensational of these was a double murder; the headline read: "Geddes Couple Murdered: Wealthy Man and His Stenographer Killed and Burned—Great Excitement Prevails."[64] The article warned that "the feeling was so

---

[54]*Hard to Get Jury in Murder Case,* Topeka Daily Capital, Sept. 23, 1906, at 1.
[55]Daniel Evans, *Persons Executed at Washington State Penitentiary 1904–1963* (on file with the Washington State Historical Society).
[56]*Saloon Man Kills Two Peace Officers; Then Ends Own Life,* Seattle Times, Aug. 25, 1912, at 1.
[57]*An Atrocious Crime,* Seattle Times, Oct. 10, 1912, at 4.
[58]*The Death Penalty,* Seattle Times, Oct. 14, 1912.
[59]*Warden Reed Opposed to Capital Punishment,* Seattle Times, Dec. 13, 1912, at 2.
[60]Filler, *supra* note 35.
[61]*Death Penalty Abolished,* Seattle Times, Mar. 22, 1913, at 3; 1913 Wash. Laws Ch. 167, H.B. 200, at 581.
[62]*Death Penalty is Abolished,* Pierre Daily Capital-J., Feb. 1, 1915, at 1, 3.
[63]*Perkins Murderer Hung This Morning,* Pierre Daily Capital-J., Dec. 4, 1913, at 1.

intense today that it is believed that if any well founded suspicion is developed as to the author of the crime, a lynching would follow."[65]

The state legislative records indicate that "Governor Byrne in his [1913] inaugural address recommended the abolition of the death penalty."[66] A legislator subsequently introduced an abolition bill in the state House of Representatives. In introducing the proposal, the lawmaker read "a paper in which he cited a large number of authorities"[67] who supported abolition and gave "statistics from different states regarding the matter of homicides."[68] In support of his argument, he provided statistical information on homicide occurrence in various cities with and without the death penalty. During the period 1901–1910, Milwaukee has 56 homicides without a death penalty, while among cities with capital punishment, 1659 homicides occurred in Chicago, 1249 in New York City, 328 in Cincinnati, and 283 in Boston. Another supporter of abolition reminded his colleagues "that the divine commandment 'Thou shalt not kill,' applied to everybody."[69] One lawmaker, however, cautioned that repealing the death penalty would "encourage mob law instead of legal punishment of crimes."[70] The abolition forces carried the day, as the South Dakota legislature passed the abolition bill by a vote of 63–24.

During this debate, the *Pierre Daily Capital-Journal* argued that abolition of the death penalty was "sentimentalism gone to seed. As a matter of fact, there is not sufficient killing of men who ought to be 'exterminated'."[71] The newspaper also editorialized that capital punishment provides a deterrent, "but the repeal of the death penalty is not a demand of society as a whole but rather in line with the effete eastern society organized for protection of Indian rights, which are well known in this part of the country to be simple jokes."[72] An abolition supporter countered that:

> errors in conviction are only too likely in cases where public sentiment rules and the twelve men are only human. . . . The man with the money and a good lawyer was always able to get out better than the poor man with an attorney selected by the court. After a man was hanged . . . no evidence nor court order could bring him back, even though he was proven innocent.[73]

Another abolition advocate said "he was not swayed by maudlin sympathy, but opposed a cowardly assassination by the state in a way that exterminates rather than reforms." Yet another supporter of abolition plead, "now is the time to strike from our

---

[64]*Geddes Couple Murdered: Wealthy Man and His Stenographer Killed and Burned—Great Excitement Prevails,* Pierre Daily Capital-J., Apr. 18, 1914, at 1, 4.
[65]*Id.*
[66]South Dakota Vertical File.
[67]*The Legislature Today,* Pierre Daily Capital-J., Jan. 20, 1915, at 1.
[68]*Capital Punishment Contest,* Pierre Daily Capital-J., Jan. 20, 1915, at 1, 4.
[69]*The Legislature Today, supra* note 67.
[70]*Id.*
[71]*Capital Punishment Contest, supra* note 68, at 1.
[72]*Id.* at 4.
[73]*Death Penalty is Abolished, supra* note 62, at 1.

limbs the last shackles of barbarism."[74] He also noted that the state had pardoned and released twenty-one murderers, and none of these had committed another crime.[75] On February 15, 1915, the governor signed the death penalty abolition legislation.[76]

4. Oregon

Oregon executed twenty-four individuals from 1903–1914, averaging approximately two per year.[77] According to a report of a legislative lobbying group, in 1910 the Oregon superintendent of prisons reported that eighteen men had been executed in the state between 1903–1910, "the greatest number ever executed in any similar period in this state."[78] But this prison official added, "It does not appear that the increasing number of executions in this state has operated as a deterrent to the crime of homicide. . . . I am fully convinced that capital punishment should be abolished."[79] The next year, Governor Oswald West initiated the campaign to abolish capital punishment. Addressing the state legislature, the Governor reasoned, "[t]he desperate criminal, relying on the reluctance of the average juror and the caution of the court in the imposition of the capital sentence, is more willing to take a gambler's chance with death . . . than he would be to face the greater certainty of life spent behind bars."[80]

The *Portland Oregonian* reported thirty-six murders and one lynching in the year prior to abolition in 1914. An editorial condemned sympathy for accused criminals among public servants administering the law, accusing these officials of shirking their responsibilities to public safety.[81] Another editorial saw the death penalty as a deterrent because well-publicized executions "signified a triumph in part of law and order over an atrocious system. Their force as crime deterrents would have been largely lost by suppression of any important feature of the event."[82] Commenting on a recent case, the *Oregonian* acknowledged that with expensive legal assistance, the wealthy were never executed, and conceded that Oregon sometimes executed innocent people.[83] Yet the newspaper also maintained: "That these things are facts does not in itself justify abolishment of the noose any more than it justifies abolishment of penitentiaries."[84]

In 1912, Governor West postponed the executions of five murderers until after a referendum on the death penalty. The Governor reasoned: "he would cause all to be hanged at once, and thus make the people responsible for a gruesome and terrifying

---

[74]*Id.*
[75]*Id.*
[76]1915 S.D. Laws 335.
[77]Hugo A. Bedau, *Capital Punishment in Oregon, 1903–1964*, 45 Or. L. Rev. 1 (1965).
[78]Oregon Council to Abolish the Death Penalty, *The Abolition of the Death Penalty in Oregon, 1914*, at 1–2, May 14, 1964.
[79]*Id.* at 1.
[80]Dann, *supra* note 20.
[81]*Harry Thaw's Appeal*, Portland Oregonian, Mar. 16, 1914.
[82]*Guarding Sensibilities*, Portland Oregonian, Apr. 21, 1914.
[83]*With a Murder's Money*, Portland Oregonian, Dec. 22, 1914, at 6.
[84]*The Lesson*, Portland Oregonian, Jan. 5, 1915, at 8.

exhibition, unless the death penalty were to be abolished."[85] The *Oregonian* reacted: "It is a shocking accusation for a Governor to make against his own people that they are murderers because they would enforce the law."[86] An editorial criticized the Governor's decision to force another referendum on the death penalty almost immediately after a resounding defeat of abolition in 1912.[87] The voters, however, abolished capital punishment by 157 votes in the 1914 referendum.[88] The Governor deferred two executions until after the referendum,[89] and following the vote he stated, "the old barbarous system of capital punishment has been abolished."[90]

5. Arizona

Perhaps it should not be surprising that in this demographically heterogeneous state there were ten executions and fourteen murders mentioned in the *Tucson Citizen* during the year prior to abolition in 1916. In the *Citizen,* a short article noted that "within the last three weeks there have been eight executions for banditry and theft," without mentioning any names of those executed.[91] The death penalty apparently was so common that its use did not merit mention of the names of the deceased. According to a state historical society report, between 1910–1916, Arizona executed only Hispanics.[92] An editorial in the *Arizona Republican* noted that many Hispanics indeed felt that the death penalty was unfairly applied to their people.[93]

The Governor led the fight against death penalty in Arizona. Governor Hunt was quoted as claiming that no executions would take place in the state as long as he was governor.[94] And indeed, he granted 105 pardons, commutations and reprieves in his first term, eighty-five during 1912–13 alone. Furthermore, "[o]n 22 December 1914, Hunt notified the leaders of the Chicago-based Anti-Capital Punishment Society of America that he would accept the presidency of their organization."[95]

Prior to abolition, the Governor regularly awarded reprieves to condemned prisoners, actions that were rather unpopular at the time.[96] On March 12, 1912, Governor Hunt made the following remarks to the first legislature of the newly admitted state:

I subscribe, also, to the belief held by millions and yet increasing millions, that capital punishment is relic of barbarism; that the legalized taking of life is a straining of Christ's law which has no place in modern civilization. I subscribe to the belief that the

---

[85]*Busybodies Once More,* Portland Oregonian, Sept. 21, 1914.
[86]*Can a People Murder?,* Portland Oregonian, Nov. 26, 1914, at 6.
[87]*Busybodies Once More, supra* note 85.
[88]*No More Hangings, Verdict of Voters,* Portland Oregonian, Dec. 1, 1914, at 6.
[89]*2 Reprieves Possible,* Portland Oregonian, Aug. 5, 1914, at 4; *Death Penalty Stayed,* Portland Oregonian, Oct. 5, 1914, at 6.
[90]Dann, *supra* note 20.
[91]*Execution Squad Busy Now in Sonora,* Tucson Citizen, Jan. 28, 1916, at 5.
[92]*Executions in Arizona 1910–1965,* Arizona State Historical Society.
[93]David L. Abney, Capital Punishment in Arizona, 1863–1963 89 (1988) (unpublished M. Hist. thesis, Arizona State University).
[94]*Id.*
[95]*Id.* at 67.
[96]William L. Eaton, *The Death Penalty in America (1864–1933),* Arizona State Historical Society.

murderer may be punished through the medium of an awakened consciousness far more effectively than by breaking of his neck and hurling his soul into eternity; that a more fearful and effective example to others lies in the certainty of imprisonment than in the fleeting fear of death, a fear which temporarily has no place in the passion-heated or drunk-crazed brain. I therefore recommend the submission to the people of an amendment to the Constitution directed to the abolition of capital punishment.[97]

In 1913, the state legislature passed revisions of the penal code to restrict the Governor's independent pardon and reprieve powers, creating instead an independent board of pardons and paroles. The Governor vetoed the legislation. All of the state's newspapers except for the *Arizona Republican* criticized the Governor's actions.[98] In the *Citizen*,[99] there was a short article on the efforts to begin a recall of Governor Hunt. Later a *Citizen* editorial explained its reasoning for opposing the re-election of the Governor:

[He] has not enforced the law but has broken it repeatedly; among other instances, note his action in cases of criminals legally sentenced to death . . . he has vetoed bill after bill, passed by both houses. . . . He has initiated and promoted a freak prison policy at enormous expense to the state and very real danger to civilized society.[100]

Capital punishment advocates defeated an initiative petition abolishing the death penalty in 1914; however, a similar petition succeeded in 1916. The 1916 referendum passed by a margin of only 152 votes—18,936 to 18,784.[101]

B. Support of the Press and Prominent Citizens

1. Colorado

In the first state to abolish capital punishment during the Progressive Era, the abolition bill not only engendered the support of the Governor but also gained the support of the press. The *Rocky Mountain Daily News* reported twelve murders and three executions during the year prior to abolition in 1897. The three executions were performed on the same day in 1896, and a long front-page newspaper account included drawings of each man and descriptions of how each conducted himself prior to and during his execution. The article reported that one man had to be partially carried to the death chamber where he was to be hanged:

The look of pleading that came into his eyes, the deathly pallor of his face and the utter helplessness of his entire body would have melted the heart of any man. . . . Once in the brilliantly lighted room it was with the greatest difficulty that [he] could stand. He was

---

[97]*Id.* at 18.
[98]Abney, *supra* note 93, at 60.
[99]*The Move to Recall Governor Hunt,* Tucson Citizen, Dec. 11, 1915, at 4.
[100]*Reasons Why,* Tucson Citizen, Sept. 27, 1916, at 32.
[101]Bruce E. Babbit, *Arizona's Death Penalty,* Arizona State Historical Society.

placed before the platform upon which to step means death, and was given a chance to say what few last words he might. Speak he could not.[102]

The article concluded that in his case, "He has paid the penalty for his rash act [of killing a police officer] many times over, for his suffering had been intense and continuous ever since the date he entered the cell from which fate decreed he should leave only to meet his doom."[103]

A March 1987 article in the *Daily News* predicted that the Governor would sign death penalty abolition legislation.[104] On March 24, 1897, the *Daily News* reported:

H.B. 74, abolishing capital punishment, passed in about two minutes. . . . The Bill provides for life imprisonment in all cases now sentenced to capital punishment. The idea seems to be among those whose sentiment has modified on this point that it will do no harm to pass this law and observe its effects for two years.[105]

The same article continues: "The most striking thing about the senate session yesterday was probably the passage in committee of the whole of the . . . bill abolishing capital punishment, without discussion and by a large majority." It became law on March 29, 1897.[106] Legislative records indicate that in his Biennial Message, Governor Alva Adams gave the new law his enthusiastic blessing. While there were twelve executions in the state between 1890–1896,[107] the Governor reported that of the twenty-five murderers condemned to die in the state penitentiary, thirteen had been reprieved and thus, the death penalty carried little deterrent effect. He opined: "Nothing is so appalling to a criminal as certainty of a life sentence, with no hope of pardon."[108]

2. Minnesota

Twenty-six hangings occurred in Minnesota from 1858–1911.[109] A particularly significant execution occurred after a gay man killed his former lover and that individual's mother. The State staged a hanging on February 13, 1906, but the rope was too long and the man ended up on the floor. "Three deputy sheriffs immediately ran to the platform, hauled on the rope, and held the unfortunate man's feet off the ground for the fourteen and a half minutes it took to choke him to death."[110] The press gave extensive coverage to this grisly ordeal in spite of a 1895 law prohibiting publication of accounts of executions. Minnesota prosecuted, convicted and fined the press for this coverage. Yet perhaps because of such reporting, this man was the last person executed in Minnesota.

---

[102]*Three Men Executed at Canon City,* Rocky Mountain Daily News, June 27, 1896, at 1–2.
[103]*Id.*
[104]*Capital Punishment,* Rocky Mountain Daily News, Mar. 28, 1897, at 4.
[105]*Hanging To Be Stopped,* Rocky Mountain Daily News, Mar. 24, 1897, at 5.
[106]1897 Colo. Sess. Laws 135.
[107]Bowers, *supra* note 30.
[108]Governor Alva Adams, Biennial Message, Colorado State Historical Society, at 24–25.(1899)
[109]Walter N. Trenerry, *Murder in Minnesota: A Collection of True Cases,* Minnesota Historical Society (1962).
[110]*Id.* at 163.

The St. Paul newspaper reflected the local sentiment. The *St. Paul Dispatch* published thirty-five articles about separate murders, two death sentences and one life sentence during the year preceding abolition in 1911. An article, comparing St. Paul with other cities, downplayed area crime.[111] Later, another headlined, "Clean Week for Crime, Pinkerton Man Declares St. Paul Sets a Record—Few Arrests and Still Fewer Accidents,"[112] in spite of being the site of the state fair and a large convention. A *St. Paul Dispatch* editorial referred to the lack of prosecution of the meat trusts and complained of discriminatory criminal enforcement.[113]

Moreover, an article titled "To Abolish Death Penalty" quoted a county attorney who complained:

I wish somebody would start agitating for the abolition of capital punishment in this state. . . . The law allowing the imposition of the death sentence upon conviction of murder makes it practically impossible for the state to obtain the right sort of jury, and after the jury is secured the chances of conviction, even with the strongest evidence, are at a minimum. There are many men, otherwise competent to serve as jurymen, who honestly have conscientious scruples against taking a life into their hands. There are many more men of high character who, deliberately or otherwise, seize upon the death penalty as an excuse from serving.[114]

In sum, one author's appraisal is probably accurate: "It is fairly safe to say that capital punishment was never really popular in the state."[115] Minnesota abolished the death penalty on April 22, 1911.[116]

3. Missouri

The *St. Louis Post-Dispatch* reported seventy-nine murders and three death sentences during the year prior to abolition in 1917. On October 23, 1916, the paper headlined "Six Murders Since August 20 Unsolved."[117] At the time, Missouri was undergoing a widespread reform of its prison system.[118] The Prison Reform League lobbied for the termination of the antiquated convict labor system,[119] and a local judge demanded separation of the juvenile court from the criminal court system.[120] A *Post-Dispatch* editorial noted that in many states there was movement away from capital punishment and concluded: "Michigan presents an example of consistent and

---

[111]*Sees Less Crime Here,* St. Paul Dispatch, May 13, 1910, at 7.
[112]*Clean Week for Crime, Pinkerton Man Declares St. Paul Sets a Record—Few Arrests and Still Fewer Accidents,* St. Paul Dispatch, Sept. 9, 1910, at 16.
[113]*Why Not Punish All Criminals Alike?,* St. Paul Dispatch, Apr. 1, 1910, at 10.
[114]*To Abolish Death Penalty,* St. Paul Dispatch, Dec. 10, 1910, at 9.
[115]Trenerry, *supra* note 109, at vii.
[116]1911 Minn. Laws at 572.
[117]*Six Murders Since August 20 Unsolved,* St. Louis Post-Dispatch, Oct. 23, 1916, at 1.
[118]Guillot, *supra* note 22.
[119]*Gardner Hears Women on Prison Reform,* St. Louis Post-Dispatch, Nov. 24, 1916 at 3; *Senator Cook's Prison Bill,* St. Louis Post-Dispatch, Jan. 22, 1917, at 10.
[120]*Judge Grimm and the Juvenile Court,* St. Louis Post-Dispatch, Dec. 7, 1916, at 16.

long-continuing adherence to the principle that the taking of life under judicial order furnishes no safeguard not found in other forms of punishment."[121]

Representative O.B. Whitaker, a prominent Christian leader, writer and college president, introduced an abolition proposal in the state legislature.[122] On introducing the legislation, Whitaker passionately defended abolition as a means of dealing with the congestion of courts, easing the selection of jurors and removing the real possibility of sentencing the innocent to death.[123] After indications by the Governor that he would sign the bill into law, the Missouri legislature overwhelmingly approved abolition legislation on April 13, 1917.[124] The *Post-Dispatch* editorialized:

> The . . . bill abolishing the death penalty in Missouri was not passed reluctantly under the coercion of any public agitation or propaganda. In fact the approval of the measure was preceded by so little discussion in the Legislature as to come with surprise to very many Missourians. . . . What they have done is the more impressive because it is the deliberate expression of a slow-growing, mature conviction that the supreme penalty known to civilized law is not essential to the full protection of society. . . . Missouri is in good company in refusing longer to impose on its officials the repulsive duty of executing criminals. . . . Their experience shows that the substitution of life imprisonment does not increase the frequency of grave offenses.[125]

C. No Opposition and No Controversy

1. North Dakota

Between 1885–1905, North Dakota executed only eight persons.[126] During the year preceding abolition in 1915, the *Bismarck Daily Tribune* reported ten murders. In three murder convictions, a local court imposed one death sentence, one life sentence and one fifteen-year sentence. In none of the newspaper stories is there any evidence of hysteria, perhaps because many of these crimes involved domestic disputes. During legislative debate on the abolition bill a citizen petition was read, which stated: "Whereas, the death penalty is barbarous, ineffective in checking crime, contrary to the dictates of humanity, and violates the sacredness of human life, we, the undersigned, protest against the infliction of the penalty and make this appeal for the abolishment of capital punishment."[127] The House of Representatives passed Bill No. 33 unanimously, while the final Senate vote was 28–12. The bill included an emergency clause, putting it into effect immediately to avoid the execution of a convicted man already scheduled to hang.

---

[121]*Death Penalty in Disfavor,* St. Louis Post-Dispatch, Feb. 24, 1917, at 4.
[122]Guillot, *supra* note 22.
[123]*Opposes Capital Punishment,* St. Clair County Democrat, Mar. 15, 1917, at 1, 5.
[124]*Gardner Will Sign Bill Abolishing Death Penalty,* St. Louis Post-Dispatch, Mar. 19, 1917, at 1.
[125]*Missouri Abolishes Death Penalty,* St. Louis Post-Dispatch, Mar. 20, 1917, at 14.
[126]D.P. Gray, *Comment,* 54 North Dakota History 39 (Fall 1987).
[127]*Death Penalty Opposed,* Bismarck Daily Trib., Jan. 12, 1915, at 1.

D. *Prominent Citizens, Pro and Con*

1. Tennessee

Tennessee was the only state outside the West and Midwest to abolish capital punishment for murder during this era and the only southern state ever to have done so. Between 1909–1912, nine executions occurred in Tennessee.[128] The *Nashville Tennessean* described forty-five murders and one convicted murderer sentenced to death during the year prior to abolition in 1915. At the time abolition legislation was being considered, a *Tennessean* article headline indicated that the legislature had passed the abolition bill only after "vigorous debate."[129]

Bill proponents argued that after testing abolition, subsequent legislatures could determine how abolition was actually working compared to capital punishment.[130] A paid advertisement published just prior to the debate asserted that "Capital Punishment is Murder!"[131] A state senator summed up his tentative support of the abolition bill as follows: "I yield to no man in my devotion to womanhood. I find in states where we have capital punishment we find more lynchings. . . . I do not believe this bill will encourage mob law. Yet I know when a black brute commits the unspeakable crime he was certain to be slain, law or no law."[132]

The most prominent supporter of the abolition drive was Duke C. Bowers, a retired grocery merchant from Memphis, who was at least partially motivated by cases of innocent defendants executed in Tennessee.[133] He was influential enough to receive the following endorsement from the Mayor of Memphis in a letter to Governor Thomas Rye:

> Mr. Bowers has made a most heroic fight for this measure, at a great personal sacrifice of both time, energy and money. . . . That the bill is either good or bad is, of course, open to debate. At the same time, I think you will agree that it is at least worthy of a fair trial and, if at the end of two years, it is found bad its repeal should be accomplished without difficulty.[134]

Duke Bowers was so influential that the legislation was titled the "Duke Bowers' Bill."

In this, the most heterogeneous of abolitionist states, the public debate was predictably the most intense. Records of the state historical society indicate that a Tennessee attorney wrote to the Governor opposing abolition: "My son John was murdered on October 1, 1914 by two negro tramps. . . . These negroes have been

---

[128]Bowers, *supra* note 30.
[129]*Bowers' Bill is Passed in Lower House,* Nashville Tennessean, Mar. 6, 1915, at 1, 2.
[130]1915 Tenn. Laws 94.
[131]*Capital Punishment is Murder!,* Nashville Tennessean, Jan. 18, 1915, at 2.
[132]*Recess is Urged by Governor in Message to Salons,* Nashville Tennessean, Mar. 27, 1915, at 2.
[133]Hugo A. Bedau & Michael L. Radelet, *Miscarriages of Justice in Potentially Capital Cases,* 40 Stan. L. Rev. 21 (1987).
[134]Letter from E. H. Crump to Gov. Thomas Rye (Mar. 27, 1915) (on file with the Tennessee State Historical Society).

indicted and their case stands for trial May 4, 1915."[135] And a concerned citizen wrote to Governor Rye, pleading with him to veto the bill abolishing capital punishment. He focused on Tennessee counties on the Mississippi River "in which negroes are the thickest. . . . Now negroes fear nothing but death, and this law would increase the crimes of homicide among that race."[136] A Tennessee business leader agreed, citing problems in deterrence:

> We have a large negro population in our state, many of them are ignorant and brutal. I honestly think that there are thousands of them that would commit murder for ten dollars if they thought they would not be hung or electrocuted. These people and some whites do not fear the penitentiary. I know instances where negroes have expressed a desire to go to the penitentiary where they are better off than on the outside.[137]

Several writers threatened white savagery. A county attorney argued in a letter to the Governor that this law would "only encourage mob law. . . . [M]obs will at least try and execute all the negroes hereafter guilty of, or perchance charged with, murder in the first degree. . . . I think nothing but a sickly sentiment calls for any such a law."[138] A Tennessee State Committee member insisted: "The population of our county is three-fourths colored, and if this bill should become law it would be almost impossible to suppress mobs in their efforts to punish colored criminals."[139] A local bank executive agreed: "But to abolish the death penalty here in the state of Tennessee will cause men who are otherwise citizens who are the strictest for law enforcement [to be] law breakers."[140] An attorney stated that the bill would encourage "lynchings and murdering. With the large percent of colored. . . . The state legislature has simply let a false feeling of sentiment run away with their judgment."[141]

Although the media and law enforcement officers joined the opposition to abolition, the abolition bill became law early in 1915. Addressing the abolition proposal, an editorial from the *Somerville Falcon* warned: "Our people are as much opposed to violence as any people, but the very knowledge that there can be no legal execution will lead men to commit crimes for which civilized people will never submit."[142] Thirty-five Knoxville police officers signed a petition asking the governor to veto the

---

[135]Letter from Noble Smithson to Gov. Thomas Rye (Apr. 29, 1915) (on file with the Tennessee State Historical Society)

[136]Letter from D. J. Currie to Gov. Thomas Rye (Mar. 29, 1915) (on file with the Tennessee State Historical Society)

[137]Letter from John P. Williams to Gov. Thomas Rye (Apr. 7, 1915) (on file with the Tennessee State Historical Society)

[138]Letter from D. J. Caldwell to Gov. Thomas Rye (1915) (on file with the Tennessee State Historical Society)

[139]Letter from B.F. Murrell to Gov. Thomas Rye (Mar. 27, 1915) (on file with the Tennessee State Historical Society)

[140]Letter from C.A. Ross to Gov. Thomas Rye (Mar. 8, 1915) (on file with the Tennessee State Historical Society)

[141]Letter from S. E. N. Moore to Gov. Thomas Rye (Mar. 27, 1915) (on file with the Tennessee State Historical Society)

[142]*Kill the Bowers Bill By All Means,* Somerville Tennessee Falcon, May 7, 1915.

bill.[143] However, the abolition bill passed the legislature and became law on March 27, 1915, after the Governor failed to veto the bill until after the deadline required by state law.[144] The new law abolished capital punishment for murder, but the death penalty was retained for rape and for murder committed by a prisoner serving a life sentence.[145]

E. Summary of Abolition

As might be expected in states with different population sizes and characteristics, the number of recorded murders during the year prior to abolition greatly vary, from seventy-nine in Missouri to five in South Dakota. There also were large variations in the number of executions in these states during the year prior to abolition, from ten in Arizona to none in North Dakota. Thus, neither frequency of murders nor executions were determining forces behind abolition.

Earlier research in Missouri[146] and Oregon[147] noted the difficulty in securing convictions in death penalty cases, while the data marshalled here indicates that Colorado, Kansas and Minnesota had similar problems. Moreover, in eight of these ten abolition states, either the Governor or the press, or both, supported abolition. In Colorado, abolition had the support of both the Governor and the press, and it passed by "a large majority" and "in about two minutes." In five states, the Governor supported the cause, usually very forcefully. Several of these governors were acquainted with each other through their affiliation with the Anti-Capital Punishment Society of America. In Minnesota, the press supported abolition. In Tennessee, a local business leader worked alone without the support of the press or the Governor and appears to have been successful due to his prominence. And in North Dakota, no leaders seemed to actively support abolition, yet no one seemed to oppose it, and the abolition bill passed the state House, 80–0.

As with most of the other reforms enacted by Progressive Era legislation, it is difficult to interpret the significance of the bills to abolish the death penalty since eight of the ten abolition laws were promptly repealed. The best answer is that the abolition movement was at most a partial success, as Mann[148] has said was true of Progressive Era legislation in general.

Certainly, this movement was not a total failure. For example, it would be an oversimplification to say that abolition legislation, as Kolko has claimed for all Progressive Era reforms, was "Designed for and by Big Business."[149] While some Progressive Era bills may have been coercive of the general public (federal drug con-

---

[143]Letter from the Knoxville Police Department to Gov. Thomas Rye (Apr. 9, 1915) (on file with the Tennessee State Historical Society)

[144]1915 Tenn. Pub. Acts 181.

[145]*Id.*

[146]Guillot, *supra* note 22.

[147]Dann, *supra* note 20.

[148]The Progressive Era 202 (Arthur Mann ed., 1975).

[149]Gabriel Kolko, *Designed by and for Big Business, in* The Progressive Era 63–75 (Arthur Mann ed., 1975).

trols), or were not enforced in a way to protect the general public (antitrust laws), other legislation made an obvious and lasting change for the better in the lives of many ordinary working Americans (i.e., laws controlling working conditions and hours of employment, female suffrage).

Correspondingly, a class-conflict interpretation of death penalty abolition would not be entirely accurate. This legislation, supported by selected governors and the press, was ostensibly intended to help ordinary citizens, and only in the case of Tennessee do we find considerable elite opposition. On the other hand, while the personal motivations of legislative supporters were apparently humanitarian, the intensity of the abolition movement during an economic boom suggests a reluctance to execute American citizens when they could productively contribute to economic growth. And, like other Progressive Era reforms, enactment of death penalty abolition laws was concentrated during the economic boom years of 1914–1917; however, this progression abruptly stopped upon U.S. entry into World War I.

Elites may be most concerned about workers' welfare when the workers were badly needed for a booming economy. To produce at optimum levels workers must be happy, healthy, drug-free and above all else, alive. So, at least in part, economic forces may have contributed to the Progressive Era abolition movement. Thus, the origins of these abolition laws demonstrate the importance of both the nature of individual support as well as the social context of this legislation.

III. REINSTATEMENT

A. *The Legacy of Lynching*

1. *Colorado*

Colorado provided a foreshadowing of the transiency of abolition laws when the state reinstated capital punishment before any other states abolished the death penalty during the Progressive Era. With the passage of House Bill 71 on May 2, 1901, Colorado reinstated the death penalty after only four years of abolition. This measure became law without the Governor's approval.[150] At its inception, the abolition of the death penalty in Colorado was treated as a tentative change and an experiment. Immediately before abolition, it was remarked, "it will do no harm to pass this law [abolishing the death penalty] and observe its effects for two years."[151] Four years later, this experiment apparently had failed in the eyes of the legislature and the death penalty was reinstated.

Some have argued that several lynchings provoked Colorado's decision to reinstate the death penalty.[152] Bedau has written: "Colorado abolished the death penalty for a few years, but reinstated it in the face of what at the time seemed the threat of mob rule. In that state, public dissatisfaction with mere imprisonment . . . resulted in

---

[150]H.R.J. Res. 71, 1901 Colo. Laws 64.
[151]*Hanging to be Stopped, supra* note 105.
[152]J.E. Cutler, *Capital Punishment and Lynching,* 29 Annals Am. Acad. Pol. & Soc. Sci. 182 (1907).

lynchings during the abolition years."[153] Indeed, during the time period studied—May 2, 1900, to May 2, 1901—two lynchings occurred. Both of these lynchings were covered extensively in the *Rocky Mountain Daily News* and aroused a great deal of pro-death penalty sentiment. In the first lynching, a "mulatto" who was accused of shooting his wife and killing two young girls at an orphanage was hanged by a mob before thousands.[154] The *News* described the lynching as having the approval of the community, as expressed through direct public participation or non-interference. Furthermore, the *News* editorialized that this lynching was proof that the death penalty should be restored in Colorado:

> The people of Colorado and the next legislature might as well face the fact that in the absence of capital punishment, under the law it is inflicted through the angry mob violence whenever an especially atrocious crime is committed. . . . To prevent the recurrence of such horrors the death penalty should be restored in this state.[155]

There was also some concern with the effect that the lynching had on the state's image: "In the case of such crimes as those committed . . . a jury may be relied upon to fix the penalty at death, and the certainty that it will do so will stop the blackening of Colorado's fair name with lynchings."[156]

Only a few months later, another even more brutal lynching tainted Colorado's image. Preston Porter, a sixteen-year-old African-American charged by the local authorities with "outraging" and murdering a thirteen-year-old white girl, was burned at the stake before a large crowd in Limon.[157] Earlier, a reward of $2200 was offered for the capture of Porter "dead or alive and preferably dead."[158] While the citizens of Limon had originally planned to avoid torture in favor of a respectable hanging,[159] stronger passions prevailed and Porter was burned at the stake by a mob. The victim's father was allowed to strike the first match.[160] Law enforcement officials never filed charges against any of the lynchers, even though none wore masks.[161] Had there been an investigation of the lynching, the *News* was confident there would have been no convictions: "If indictments could be procured at all which is very doubtful, the trial or trials certainly would produce no convictions, and it is not impossible that a Lincoln County jury would attach a vote of thanks to the mob."[162]

In the days that followed Porter's lynching, the *News* printed numerous opinions concerning lynching. A former lieutenant governor stated:

---

[153]Bedau, *supra* note 23, at 10.
[154]*Hanged in Pueblo Before Thousands,* Rocky Mountain Daily News, May 23, 1900, at 1.
[155]*Restore Capital Punishment,* Rocky Mountain Daily News, May 24, 1900, at 4.
[156]*Id.*
[157]*Limon Lynching Told in Pictures,* Rocky Mountain Daily News, Nov. 18, 1900, at 1.
[158]*Capture of Fiend is Reported,* Rocky Mountain Daily News, Nov. 11, 1900, at 1.
[159]*Mob Much Disappointed,* Rocky Mountain Daily News, Nov. 16, 1900, at 2.
[160]*Limon Lynching Told in Pictures, supra* note 157.
[161]*The Porter Lynching,* Rocky Mountain Daily News, Nov. 26, 1900, at 1; *No Prosecution of Limon Lynchers,* Rocky Mountain Daily News, Nov. 26, 1900, at 1.
[162]*Let it Drop out of Sight,* Rocky Mountain Daily News, Nov. 23, 1900, at 4.

Capital punishment has been abolished in Colorado and the only resource left to an outraged citizenship is that which overtook Porter this afternoon at Limon. Lynch law may
be objectionable to some sentimentalists, but there was little of sentiment or pity in
Porter when he outraged and murdered Louise Frost.[163]

Similarly, a local pastor wrote: "In the first place, I think it was a mistake on the part
of the state to change the law. There should be capital punishment for such crimes.
It is largely the reason for the occurrence of lynchings of this sort."[164] In response
to these lynchings, the *News* editorialized: "The mature opinion of the *News* is that
the death penalty should be restored in this state."[165] According to the *News*, the
chief justifications for the reinstatement bill were the Frost murder and subsequent
Porter lynching.[166]

In the aftermath of Porter's crime, the citizens of Limon voted to have all
"negroes of bad character" leave town.[167] If they would not voluntarily leave, they
were to be "quietly escorted" across the border.[168] One local man explained:

Many of the men brought here by railroad companies are illiterate and brutal. They have
many of them been guilty of crime. We have before us an awful example [Porter] and
we cannot afford to take chances. Let them leave the country. There are enough white
men to do the work.[169]

Clearly this comment reflects a populist, racist sentiment triggered by economic
forces.

2. Arizona

Arizona reinstated the death penalty for first-degree murder on November 5,
1918. In a referendum initiated by the state legislature, 20,443 favored death penalty
reinstatement and only 10,602 were opposed.[170] This 2-to-1 margin in favor of death
penalty reinstatement was overwhelming compared to the 1916 abolition referendum
victory, which passed by a total of only 152 votes.[171] The *Phoenix Arizona Republican* noted the less-than-overwhelming original support for the abolition cause:

There was no discussion of the bill except by those who were advocating its adoption.
There was nowhere a voice raised against the abolition of the death penalty. While perhaps a large majority of the people were not really in favor of it, they were willing to
give it a trial.[172]

---

[163]*Citizens Express Themselves on the Burning of Porter,* Rocky Mountain Daily News, Nov. 17, 1900,
at 7.
[164]*What Ministers Think of Torture of Porter,* Rocky Mountain Daily News, Nov. 17, 1900, at 7.
[165]*The Death Penalty,* Rocky Mountain Daily News, Jan. 27, 1901, at 16.
[166]*Mob Much Disappointed, supra* note 159, at 2.
[167]*Id.*
[168]*Id.*
[169]*Id.*
[170]Ariz. Rev. Stat. Ann. §1 at 18.
[171]Eaton, *supra* note 96, at 48.
[172]Abney, *supra* note 93, at 93.

On May 13, 1917, one event occurred that probably influenced turning the tide against abolition. It involved the lynching of a murderer/rapist, who allegedly boasted that the state could not execute him since it no longer had the death penalty. A coroner's jury ruled that the lynching was a "justifiable homicide."[173] While the lynching may have been legally justified, it was interpreted as an embarrassment to the state by the *Tucson Citizen,* which felt that the lynching could have been averted if capital punishment had remained in effect:

> It matters not that [he] richly deserved the punishment meted out to him, the fact that there has been a lynching in Arizona, the first in a score of years, is bound to cast a blot on the fair name of the baby state. Governor Hunt and his followers always maintained that as long as Arizona tolerated legal execution, she had the blood of her citizens on her hands, and Governor Hunt did succeed for a number of years in preventing legal executions. Capital punishment was finally abolished and now we find Arizona with blood on her hands and those who took the life as a penalty for crime [are] beyond the pale of the law.[174]

Another significant case occurred on Christmas Eve 1917, when Louis Sundeen and several co-conspirators murdered a local business proprietor.[175] The *Citizen* reported that the men had "discussed the dangers which attended such an expedition and remarked that the worst that could happen to them was a sentence of life imprisonment."[176] Sundeen shuffle-danced while on the way to serve his sentence and made sarcastic remarks when he passed the murder scene in the custody of police officers.[177] Furthermore, Sundeen reportedly was merry the night before his sentencing, until sobered by the threat of a lynch mob. These events led the *Citizen* to conclude that "[t]here is but one answer to this question and this performance. It is capital punishment. Human life must be held more seriously in Arizona. The fear of life imprisonment has no effect on criminals like Sundeen who boasts of 'bumping them off every now and then'."[178] The public's dissatisfaction with abolition of the death penalty in Arizona was not unpredictable since Governor Hunt "had persuaded the public to end the death penalty based on an absolute correlation between abolition and a lower crime rate."[179]

3. Tennessee

Tennessee ended a four-year abolition period on January 27, 1919, when the Governor signed Bill 106 reinstating the death penalty for murder.[180] The events surrounding

---

[173]*Id.* at 96.
[174]Eaton, *supra* note 96, at 52.
[175]*Pastime Park Proprietor Slain; Four Arrested,* Tucson Citizen, Dec. 25, 1917, at 1, 5.
[176]*Arizona's Mistake,* Tucson Citizen, Jan. 13, 1918, at 5.
[177]*Id.*
[178]*Id.*
[179]Abney, *supra* note 93, at 110.
[180]1919 Tenn. Pub. Acts 5.

abolition foreshadowed this reinstatement. As noted earlier, passage of the 1915 measure abolishing the death penalty was achieved only after Governor Rye signed his veto too late to prevent enactment.[181] And the Memphis Mayor suggested in a letter to the Governor that abolition of the death penalty was worthy of a fair trial and conceded that "if at the end of two years, it is found bad its repeal should be accomplished without difficulty."[182] Thus, abolition in Tennessee began as a tentative experiment, similar to abolition in Colorado and Arizona. Indeed, the abolition experiment was so tentative that the state had retained capital punishment for some crimes. During the year prior to reinstatement, there were four legal executions in the state, three rapists and one previously convicted murderer who killed a fellow inmate.

In addition to the legal executions in Tennessee, three lynchings occurred. All involved African-American victims, and together the lynchings built momentum for the reinstatement movement. The first lynching was of an African-American man who had allegedly killed three white men, shooting two of them in the back. He was burned at the stake in front of a crowd of more than 1500 people.[183] Prior to burning the alleged murderer, hot irons were applied to his body for ten minutes in an unsuccessful attempt to draw a confession from him. The second lynching victim was an African-American bootlegger who allegedly shot and killed a local white sheriff.[184] The accused man's body was dragged by a mob through the streets, hanged for over an hour and burned in front of a large crowd. The final lynching reported prior to reinstatement was of another African-American man who was accused of raping a fifteen-year-old white girl.[185] He was shot and wounded by four white men who were present at the scene of the crime. He was then dragged back to the community and hanged and burned in front of sixty to seventy blacks forced to view the lynching.

These lynchings spawned community outrage. Several anti-lynching articles appeared in the *Tennessean* and concerned citizens formed a Law and Order League to combat lynching.[186] Significantly, racism and pragmatism often motivated anti-lynching crusaders. The *Tennessean* reported: "The lynching . . . yesterday, can but sow disunion among our people, undermine the morale of our negro troops, and lessen the effectiveness of our propaganda among the colored people for food production and conservation. It will, therefore, tend to prolong the war and increase the price in victory."[187] The paper also editorialized: "We are enlisting negroes in our armies by the hundred thousands and sending them to France to fight for us. The negroes furnish most of the labor for our farms and in our homes. We want them to stay in the South."[188] The Nashville Women's Suffrage Association endorsed the Law and Order League's stance against lynching in its charter: ". . . the negro race, being yet in a

---

[181]Tennessee Senate J., at 94 (1915).

[182]*See supra* note 134 and accompanying text.

[183]*Negro Murderer is Burned at the Stake by Mob,* Nashville Tennessean, Feb. 13, 1918, at 1.

[184]*Negro Slayer of Sheriff Hanged and Body Burned,* Nashville Tennessean, Apr. 23, 1918, at 1.

[185]*Negro Rapist Killed and Burned by Mob,* Nashville Tennessean, May 21, 1918, at 2.

[186]*Prevention of Mob Violence Proposed,* Nashville Tennessean, Apr. 24, 1918, at 2.

[187]*Lynching Evil to be Fought,* Nashville Tennessean, Apr. 25, 1918, at 8.

[188]*Interest in Law and Order Keen,* Nashville Tennessean, Mar. 7, 1918, at 3.

comparatively early stage of moral development, has a right to look to the white race for guidance and certainly for justice."[189]

4. Missouri

Missouri reinstated the death penalty on July 8, 1919, when the Governor signed Senate Bill 2, ending a two-year period of abolition.[190] Guillot argues that several sensational crimes spawned pro-death penalty sentiment.[191] One case involved the alleged killing of a sheriff by a jailbreaker. This crime aroused public sentiment to such a degree that the perpetrator was lynched by a mob shortly after being sentenced to life imprisonment. Some alleged that the lynching was a "plotted commentary on the refusal of the legislators to restore capital punishment."[192]

If so, the plan achieved its desired result. The state representative from the county where the lynching occurred circulated a pro-death penalty petition among his colleagues. Seventy-eight members of the House signed the petition, which was addressed to the Governor and urged "him to send a special message submitting to the legislature the question of restoring capital punishment" during an upcoming special session of the legislature. The petition stated that "in so doing that we will save the state of Missouri from the stigma of mob violence and reduce the number and viciousness of capital crimes."[193] Similarly, the St. Louis prosecutor argued, "I advocate return to the death penalty because I believe it in many cases would prevent mob violence."[194] The warden of the state penitentiary agreed.[195]

The other case mentioned by Guillot was a St. Louis robbery and murder. The city prosecutor's request for the Governor to consider death penalty reinstatement at the special session of the legislature was made the day following the robbery of a St. Louis bank and the killing of a police officer.[196] A telegram to the Governor read: "I respectfully request that in your call for a special session of the legislature you include for its consideration a recommendation that capital punishment be restored as punishment for various crimes as it previously existed. Numerous crimes of violence throughout the United States and in the city of St. Louis and the state of Missouri make this action imperative",[197] especially given what he saw as the "danger of the spread of Bolshevism."[198] Another facet of the bank robbery that fueled death penalty fervor was a statement made by the robbers after the crime:

---

[189]*Condemns Action of Estill Springs Mob,* Nashville Tennessean, Mar. 8, 1918, at 19.

[190]1919 Mo. Laws 778.

[191]Guillot, *supra* note 22.

[192]*Should Capital Punishment be Restored?,* St. Louis Post-Dispatch, June 8, 1919, at 1B.

[193]*78 of House Sign Plea for Death Penalty,* St. Louis Post-Dispatch, July 2, 1919, at 1.

[194]*Why M'Daniel Wants Return of Death Penalty,* St. Louis Post-Dispatch, Dec. 24, 1918, at 3.

[195]*No Lynching at Lamar if Mob Had Thought Punishment Adequate,* St. Louis Post-Dispatch, June 8, 1919, at 5B.

[196]*Policeman Wounded by Bank Robbers Dies; Two Men Confess,* St. Louis Post-Dispatch, June 13, 1919, at 1.

[197]*Id.*

[198]*Capital Punishment Only Deterrent of Certain Crimes Say Circuit Attorney and his Predecessor,* St. Louis Post-Dispatch, June 8, 1919, at 1B.

We went downstairs and looked out a rear window. There were policemen in the yard, too, and we went in the basement. [One] reportedly said: "What'll we do?" I said: "It's a case of life or death. We can get a life sentence for robbery and we can't get more than a life sentence if we shoot a policeman or two. They can't hang us. It's against the law in this state. So, we'd better shoot our way out."[199]

The special session of the state legislature passed a reinstatement bill 19–1 in the Senate and 87–19 in the House of Representatives only two years after a large legislative majority had abolished capital punishment.[200]

In 1919, the *Post-Dispatch* declared a "crime wave" in St. Louis and discussed its causes and cures. The paper blamed the alleged crime wave on unemployment,[201] inadequacies of policing[202] and abuses of the parole system.[203] Unemployment was clearly a problem in post-war St. Louis. The Mayor estimated that there were 20,000 unemployed in St. Louis and urged soldiers not to return to St. Louis in search of jobs.[204] Several letters to the editor from disgruntled soldiers looking for work appeared in the newspaper.[205] In spite of these high crime rates and apparent public sentiment favoring the death penalty, the *Post-Dispatch* was consistently opposed,[206] as was its rival the St. Louis *Globe-Democrat*.[207]

During the early years of the twentieth century, lynching was a growing phenomenon attracting greater and greater concern among both citizens and lawmakers at the state and federal levels.[208] Abolition served to create a monopoly on lethal violence for those outside of government and rendered lynching more difficult to control. Ironically, the relatively feeble punishments available to the state seemed to make lynching more attractive as a deterrent to crime.

B. Economic Recession and the Fear of Radicals

1. Washington

Washington reinstated the death penalty on March 14, 1919, when Governor Louis Hart signed Senate Bill 256 marking the end to a six-year period of abolition.[209] Both houses of the Washington legislature had strongly supported the reinstatement measure.[210] For the year prior to death penalty reinstatement in Washington, the *Seattle Times* recorded twelve murders. The victims included a

---

[199]*Policeman Wounded by Bank Robbers Dies; Two Men Confess, supra* note 196.
[200]*Hanging Bill Passed; Goes to Governor,* St. Louis Star, July 8, 1919, at 1–2.
[201]*Unemployment,* St. Louis Post-Dispatch, Mar. 19, 1919, at 22.
[202]*Many Robberies Due to Police Inefficiency,* St. Louis Post-Dispatch, Mar. 17, 1919, at 7.
[203]*The Crime Wave,* St. Louis Post-Dispatch, Mar. 12, 1919, at 22.
[204]*Mayor Wants Men Out of Work to Go Home,* St. Louis Post-Dispatch, Mar. 23, 1919, at 12.
[205]*No Work for Many Returned Soldiers,* St. Louis Post-Dispatch, Feb. 2, 1919, at 7.
[206]*Defeat the Hanging Bill,* St. Louis Post-Dispatch, Feb. 13, 1919, at 24; *Fickleness in Penal Policy,* St. Louis Post-Dispatch, Nov. 7, 1919, at 18; *Unemployment,* St. Louis Post-Dispatch, Mar. 19, 1919, at 22.
[207]*The Punishment of Crime,* St. Louis Globe-Democrat, July 5, 1919, at 10.
[208]Claudine L. Ferrell, Nightmare and Dream: Antilynching in Congress: 1917–1922 (1986).
[209]*Death Penalty Restored,* Seattle Times, Mar. 14, 1919, at 9; 1919 Wash. Laws 112.
[210]Hayner & Cranor, *supra* note 21; *Death Penalty is Voted by Senate,* Seattle Times, Mar. 8, 1919, at 5.

police officer[211] and a prosperous executive,[212] undoubtedly contributing to momentum for reinstatement. Hayner and Cranor argue that the reinstatement movement was also fueled by the fear of a crime wave following World War I, and the murder of the Industrial Insurance Commissioner in the capitol building by a man who boasted that the State could do nothing to him but board him for the rest of his life.[213]

Indeed, these deterrence issues were of central concern. At a legislative hearing, a lawmaker reminded that, "History told that great wars always were followed by an epidemic of murders and that crimes of violence could be expected."[214] He recalled that "while the legislature was in session two years ago Industrial Commissioner E.W. Olson was murdered in his office in the capitol building."[215] This legislator also alleged that victims had been trailed into Washington by murderers taking advantage of the lack of capital punishment in the state.[216] He pleaded with his colleagues to take steps "no longer to encourage the murder industry in this state."[217] Another legislator, who was also a member of the clergy, drew applause by citing the biblical argument that those who kill should be killed: "I say there is law to crush and obliterate the foul monster who stalks to kill, . . . I will hark back to the good book of Genesis."[218]

Further, parallel to the economic problems occurring in Colorado, Tennessee and Missouri, unemployment and Industrial Workers of the World (I.W.W.) union agitation were problems in Washington. Six to seven thousand people were out of work in Seattle, and several thousand workers were on strike. An estimated 120,000 individuals were without means of support and thousands of sailors would be returning home soon.[219] The director of Washington's federal employment service was particularly concerned: "How to take care of 40,000 idle members and at the same time obtain jobs for the returning soldiers and sailors is the serious problem now faced. How to feed this army of unemployed once their money runs out is still another."[220]

Beyond the threat of unemployment and poverty lay a deeper threat that was not noticed by the Mayor of Seattle:

> The so-called sympathetic Seattle strike was an attempted revolution. That there was no
> violence does not alter the fact. . . . The intent, openly and covertly announced, was for
> the overthrow of the industrial system; here first, then everywhere. . . . True, there were
> no flashing guns, no bombs, no killings. Revolution, I repeat, doesn't need violence. The
> general strike, as practiced in Seattle, is of itself the weapon of revolution, all the more
> dangerous because quiet. To succeed, it must suspend everything; stop the entire life

---

[211]*Slays Policeman: Has Record Here,* Seattle Times, Feb. 19, 1919, at 7.
[212]*Aged Oil Man Dies From Thugs Shot,* Seattle Times, Feb. 11, 1919, at 9.
[213]Hayner & Cranor, *supra* note 21.
[214]*Death Penalty is Voted by Senate, supra* note 210.
[215]*Id.*
[216]*Id.*
[217]*Id.*
[218]*Death Penalty in State is Restored,* Seattle Times, Mar. 12, 1919, at 9.
[219]*Army of Jobless Swelling, He Says,* Seattle Times, Jan. 22, 1919, at 5.
[220]*Id.*

stream of a community. . . . That is to say, it puts the government out of operation. And that is all there is to revolt—no matter how achieved.[221]

Clearly the I.W.W. menace was not taken lightly by city officials. The mayor swore in 2400 special deputies and the federal government sent almost a thousand sailors and marines to the city. The generally peaceful strike ended with raids and arrests in Socialist party headquarters. Thirty-nine members of the I.W.W. were jailed as "ringleaders of anarchy."[222]

2. Oregon

The 1914 Oregon abolition referendum had succeeded by a scant 157 votes, suggesting that future support for abolition would be tenuous at best. Indeed, Oregon ended its six-year period of death penalty abolition on May 21, 1920, when fifty-six percent of Oregon voters supported a constitutional amendment reinstating the death penalty.[223] This vote occurred after a special session of the legislature had decided that the capital punishment issue was of such a pressing nature that it warranted a statewide vote. The Governor spoke with urgency: "Since the adjournment of the regular session in 1919 a wave of crime has swept over the country. Oregon has suffered from this criminal blight, and during the past few months the commission of a number of cold-blooded and fiendish homicides has aroused our people to a demand for greater and more certain protection. . . ."[224] Apparently, the majority of Oregonians agreed.

One case which undoubtedly influenced some Oregon voters, occurred not in Oregon, but in nearby Centralia, Washington. It involved a shootout between American Legionnaires and local I.W.W. members, resulting in the death of four World War I veterans.[225] Although the cause of the deaths was uncertain, the union members were blamed and the Governor of Oregon endorsed the ultimate punishment: "I thank God the gallows tree still stands in the state of Washington."[226] Soon after these deaths, the Oregon American Legion endorsed the death penalty: "It is astonishing that so many people were misled five years ago by the foolish pleas of 'reformers' who sought to coax murderers not to murder by the assurance that the state would not hang them, but care for them all their lives, if they did murder."[227] The vast majority of the state prosecutors[228] and the Oregon Bar Association[229] supported reinstatement. Moreover, the state supreme court unanimously endorsed the death penalty while citing the Centralia murders.[230] During the debate on reinstatement, a lawmaker capitalized on

[221]Howard Zinn, A People's History of the United States 370–71 (1980).
[222]Id. at 370.
[223]1920 Or. Laws 46.
[224]Dann, supra note 20, at 111.
[225]Bedau & Radelet, supra note 133.
[226]Law of the Most, Portland Oregonian, Nov. 14, 1919, at 12.
[227]Back to Justice, Portland Oregonian, Nov. 19, 1919, at 12.
[228]State Prosecutors in Favor of Noose, Portland Oregonian, Nov. 30, 1919, at 14.
[229]Bar Urges Return of Death Penalty, Portland Oregonian, Nov. 19, 1919, at 4.
[230]Supreme Court in Favor of Hanging, Portland Oregonian, Nov. 27, 1919, at 7.

the fear of the I.W.W., charging that, "Statistics also show that in those states where capital punishment has been abolished the I.W.W. are quick to gather."[231] In short, in view of the post-World War I economic recession and consequent I.W.W. activism, many felt abolition of the death penalty was a reform the state could ill afford.

Another influential case in shaping many Oregonians' opinions concerning capital punishment was the murder of prominent welfare worker Mrs. Eunice Freeman. The murderer, Clarence Johnson, beat Mrs. Freeman to death with a gas pipe and reported at his trial: "I don't believe I'd have done it if I thought there was any chance of my hanging for it."[232] When asked if he thought that the lack of a death penalty in Oregon was responsible for a number of murders, Johnson replied: "Yes, that's the reason so many of these stunts are being pulled off."[233] After being sentenced to life imprisonment, Johnson smiled and thanked the judge while loudly clapping his hands. The judge informed Johnson: "I wish I might put you on bread and water for the rest of your life—in fact, hanging is too good for you."[234] According to the *Oregonian,* Johnson had sufficient cause to believe that he would be free again, considering that most life sentences lasted no longer than eight years.[235] This murder case particularly disturbed the prosecutor, who remarked:

> There has been a distinct suspicion, in the past that other crimes would have been prevented had there been a fear of capital punishment to deter the criminal, but this is the first complete substantiation we have had. I firmly believe Johnson would not have resorted to murder had there been the shadow of a noose over his head.[236]

Many Oregonians obviously agreed with the prosecutor and felt that imprisonment was not a sufficient deterrent. Only the death penalty could adequately prevent heinous crimes. Similar to the concern with lynching, in both Washington and Oregon citizens became concerned about non-governmental actors, such as the I.W.W., monopolizing violence in the absence of capital punishment. In the minds of many, this situation gave radical dissenters an unfair and unwarranted advantage.

C. Reinstatement During the Great Depression of the 1930s

1. Kansas

Governor Alf Landon's 1935 signature on House Bill 10 reinstated the death penalty in Kansas, ending a twenty-eight-year period of abolition.[237] The state House of Representatives approved the bill by a margin of 85–26, while the state Senate passed the bill by a vote of 24–15.[238] Interestingly, Kansas rarely used the death

---

[231]*Capital Punishment Bill is Introduced,* Portland Oregonian, Jan. 31, 1920, at 7.

[232]*Slayer Says Law Invited His Crime,* Portland Oregonian, Oct. 22, 1919, at 1.

[233]Id.

[234]*Johnson Sentenced to Serve Life Term,* Portland Oregonian, Oct. 23, 1919, at 9.

[235]*Not Closed,* Portland Oregonian, Nov. 29, 1919, at 8.

[236]*Slayer Says Law Invited His Crime, supra* note 232.

[237]1935 Kan. Laws 234.

[238]Theodore Heim, *Capital Punishment in Kansas,* (On file with the State Historical Society of Kansas) (1966).

penalty even when it was an option under state law. Prior to abolition in 1907, only nine persons were hanged under Kansas law. Moreover, all of these executions occurred between 1863–1870. And no executions occurred in Kansas for nine years after the death penalty was reinstated in 1935.[239]

According to Heim, the supporters of capital punishment in Kansas were primarily interested in reducing the number of violent crimes in the state. A state representative who introduced the death penalty measure stated that this punishment was necessary because of "the loss of lives in the state in the wave of crime."[240] One gruesome slaying undoubtedly contributed to the movement to reinstate the death penalty. In this murder case, two wealthy farmers and a neighbor were the victims of a band of thieves. One farmer died of a gunshot wound and the two other individuals were reportedly "severely injured by having butcher knives thrust down their throats and being forced to stand disrobed in the cold night air for several hours."[241] According to some legislators this particular slaying and resulting threatened mob action together showed the need for death penalty reinstatement in Kansas. Even so, the *Daily Capital* consistently opposed capital punishment: "It will not accomplish any purpose and will be a more or less discreditable backward step for this state,"[242] and: "Better a hundred guilty should escape than one innocent man should suffer punishment."[243]

2. South Dakota

The Governor's signature on House Bill 30 reinstated the death penalty in South Dakota after twenty-four years of abolition.[244] This bill had easily passed in the House of Representatives 58–15[245] and in the Senate 27–8.[246] The success of the 1939 death penalty reinstatement is particularly curious. Prior to the abolition of capital punishment in 1915, the death penalty had been meted out only nine times,[247] and in the year preceding reinstatement there were only four in-state murders recorded in the *Capital-Journal*.

One of these murders, however, incited emotional support for death penalty reinstatement. The kidnapping/sex-slaying of seventeen-year-old Betty Schnaidt "was so hideous that it has resulted in a nearly unanimous demand for the legalization of capital punishment in South Dakota."[248] Upon Schnaidt's disappearance, almost 5,000 people formed a search party, and when this party discovered her lifeless, bound and gagged body, a reward of $4,000 was offered for finding Schnaidt's slayer. The fact

---

[239]Barry, *supra* note 46.
[240]Heim, *supra* note 238, at 1.
[241]*Five Held, One Confesses in Reiter Slaying,* Topeka Daily Capital, Jan. 12, 1935, at 1.
[242]*Kansas and the Death Penalty,* Topeka Daily Capital, Jan. 18, 1935, at 6.
[243]*Cases of Capital Punishment,* Topeka Daily Capital, June 15, 1934, at 4.
[244]1939 S.D. Laws 30; *Governor Signs Companion Bills,* Pierre Daily Capital-J., Jan. 27, 1939, at 1.
[245]*Sponsors Expect Senate Passage, Executive Favor,* Pierre Daily Capital-J., Jan. 21, 1939, at 1.
[246]*Floor, Galleries Packed as Hot Debate Marks Passage of First Death Penalty Law Since 1915,* Pierre Daily Capital-J., Jan. 25, 1939, at 1.
[247]*Capital Punishment Carried Out Nine Times in South Dakota,* Pierre Daily Capital-J., Feb. 5, 1938, at 2.
[248]*The Capital Punishment Issue,* Pierre Daily Capital-J., Aug. 16, 1938, at 2.

that Schnaidt's killer, Earl Young, was a jailbreaker from Pennsylvania with a long record of prior offenses only added more fuel to the fire. *The Redfield Journal Observer* reported, "The kidnapping and murder of the girl at Sioux Falls again emphasizes the importance of watching out for the enemies of civilization."[249] Similarly, the *Potter County News* wrote, "There is little excuse for harboring the hardened type of criminal in penitentiaries at great expense to taxpayers only to be turned loose later to continue their dirty work."[250] One senator characterized gangsters and criminals as "yellow," stating that "they come to states where there is no capital punishment to perpetrate their crimes. They are afraid of the death penalty."[251]

The *Pierre Daily Capital-Journal* clearly pushed South Dakota towards reinstatement. The *Journal* published ten editorials concerning the death penalty during the year prior to reinstatement. Of these articles, seven specifically concerned the Schnaidt case. The paper ardently supported capital punishment: "The Governor and the legislature committed a crime against society when the old territorial capital punishment law was repealed . . . [so] vote against any constitutional officer or lawmaker candidate who is not favorable to reenactment of capital punishment law in this state."[252] The *Journal* asserted: "The picture of [the tattooed murderer] really suggests that cooking . . . is what his kind should receive, instead of a respectable hanging."[253] The *Journal* even published articles favoring lynching since the only lethal retaliation available was to those outside of government: "Lynching needs to be practiced more as in the days of the frontier building of our country."[254] "During the last 56 years the United States has had nearly 5,000 lynchings. If there were more lynchings the country would be better off."[255]

IV. CONCLUSION: REINSTATEMENT'S FOCUSING EVENTS AND SOCIAL CONTEXT

Zimring and Hawkins have argued that the recent experience in Europe demonstrates that public opposition to abolition generally wanes after a number of years without an actual execution.[256] Thus, the relatively rapid repeal of abolition laws in most of the states considered here robbed the abolition movement of what might have been a budding base of opposition to capital punishment in the United States. The position of the press concerning the death penalty was not a particularly crucial variable. The *St. Louis Post-Dispatch* and the *Topeka Daily Capital* were both strongly against death penalty reinstatement. The other newspapers ranged from ardently pro-death penalty (*Pierre Daily Capital-Journal*) to neutral (*Seattle Times*). As might be expected with such a large and diverse group of states, motivations for reinstatement varied somewhat from state to state. Those in a racially heterogeneous

---

[249]*Get Capital Punishment,* Pierre Daily Capital-J., Aug. 4, 1938, at 2.

[250]*Capital Punishment,* Pierre Daily Capital-J., Aug. 12, 1938, at 2.

[251]*Death Penalty Bill Ready for Executive O.K.,* Pierre Daily Capital-J., Jan. 26, 1939, at 1.

[252]*Capital Punishment, supra* note 250.

[253]*Memory of Schnaidt Case,* Pierre Capital-J., Aug. 30, 1938, at 2.

[254]*Capital Punishment,* Pierre Daily Capital-J., June 2, 1938, at 2.

[255]*Capital Punishment,* Pierre Daily Capital-J., Aug. 15, 1938, at 2.

[256]Franklin E. Zimring & Gordon Hawkins, Capital Punishment and the American Agenda (1986).

and relatively violent state, like Tennessee, could be expected to have had different motivations for reinstating the death penalty than a racially homogeneous state with a low rate of violent crime like South Dakota.

However, some significant patterns and several common themes and motivations for reinstating the death penalty did emerge. Statements made by non-repentant convicted murderers helped fuel death penalty reinstatement movements in Oregon, Washington, Missouri, Arizona and South Dakota. In each of these states, a convicted murderer publicly acknowledged that he might not have committed his crime had the threat of the death penalty existed. Some of these convicted killers even went so far as to smile and applaud while being sentenced to life imprisonment, and others bragged that the state would feed and care for them the rest of their lives. In some states, initial reluctance to abolish the death penalty foreshadowed reinstatement. This was clearly the case in Oregon, where abolition was approved by a margin of only 157 votes, and in Arizona, where the measure passed by a margin of only 152 votes. Some states even considered abolition an experiment. The death penalty could quickly be (and indeed was) reinstated if the "experiment" appeared to be failing.

Lynchings emerged as the most important common triggering event in reinstatement of the death penalty. Significantly, lynchings occurred in each of the four states with the shortest periods of death penalty abolition. Lynchings were usually committed by otherwise law-abiding citizens taking justice into their own hands. According to these individuals, if a legal death penalty did not exist as a deterrent, lynching was the only method of deterring criminals from committing heinous crimes. These lynchings often alerted officials that the public was unwilling to consistently support abolition. Ironically, belief that without capital punishment lynchings inevitably would occur caused many death penalty opponents to re-think their positions. To these individuals, the death penalty became the lesser of two evils. The resulting coalition of anti-lynching forces with traditional death penalty advocates virtually guaranteed reinstatement.[257]

Economics also played an important role in reinstatement. The end of the death penalty abolition movement coincided with the end of World War I and the start of the post-war economic depression.[258] With the exception of Colorado, reinstatement bills were passed during either the recession immediately following World War I or

---

[257]This is not to say that abolition actually caused anyone to be lynched, but rather, at most, that abolition provided a convenient rationalization for such lynchings. Studies have shown that lynchings occur whether or not capital punishment is in effect *See* Cutler, *supra* note 152; Charles David Phillips, *Exploring Relations Among Forms of Social Control: The Lynching and Execution of Blacks in North Carolina, 1889–1918,* 21 Law & Soc. Rev. 361–374 (1987); Louis P. Mansur, Rites of Execution: Criminal Punishment and the Transformation of American Culture, 1776–1865 (1989). Mansur demonstrates how elites in the 1800s pressed the idea of moving executions from public to private places to help maintain public order. Mansur, *supra.* The reactions to lynching were very similar. Lynchings, like public executions, were associated with disorder. Moreover, lynchings, like public executions, were widely felt to be disgraceful because they were public. In the final analysis, however, whether one considers lynching and its control, or the control of political radicals, abolition of the death penalty elevated such conflicts to issues of much greater concern than they had been earlier.

[258]Davis, *supra* note 33; Philip E. Mackey, Voices Against Death (1976).

during the Great Depression of the 1930s. And in many of these states, including Colorado, there is clear evidence of economic forces at work in the reinstatement process. There were frequent complaints about the job shortages and the threat of unemployed workers. In addition, since lynchings are typically a consequence of declining economic fortunes,[259] economic forces indirectly caused reinstatement through the increased frequency of lynchings. One should also note that the states that did not reinstate capital punishment, North Dakota and Minnesota, had the smallest percentage of non-white populations. The three states with the largest minority populations (Tennessee, Arizona, Missouri) all quickly reinstated the death penalty. In other words, the threat of a large minority population influenced reinstatement, and this threat may have been exacerbated by the economic recession.

To understand the "tragic choices" inherent in jumping from one legal solution to another in attempting to affirm competing values, and parallel contradictions such as vigilante violence emerging out of abolition movements, one must "cover a range from the individual to the . . . states"[260] and integrate these levels into the analysis. Only by considering both "the interactions within the social system and the conditions under which the social system operates"[261] can one understand these patterns of punishment of criminal behavior. Neither individual motivations nor societal level data taken alone demonstrate the development of such contradictions. The significance of the motivations behind a particular legislative process can only be understood fully within the social context of that process. Society used the death penalty not only to oppress minorities and protect the majority, but also as a repressive response to depression-era conditions of social dislocation and economic turmoil.[262] In periods of political stability without the threats of crime or economic disruption, the elites opposed to capital punishment were in a position to prevail. But emergence of these threats and the resulting politicization of the death penalty overwhelmed the influence of elites pressing for abolition. Society could ignore the misgivings of moral entrepreneurs, including governors, when faced with the threats of lynching and political radicals on the one hand, and economic depression on the other.

---

[259]E.M. Beck & Stewart E. Tolnay, *The Market for Cotton and the Lynching of Blacks, 1882–1930*, 55 Am. Soc. Rev. 526 (1990).
[260]Lauderdale, *supra* note 37, at 32.
[261]*Id.* at 35.
[262]Bowers, *supra* note 30.

"DEJA VU ALL OVER AGAIN:" THE RECURRING LIFE AND DEATH OF CAPITAL PUNISHMENT LEGISLATION IN KANSAS*

JAMES M. GALLIHER
University of Missouri-Kansas City

and

JOHN F. GALLIHER
University of Missouri-Columbia

After the U.S. Supreme Court's 1972 decision in *Furman v. Georgia* banning the use of capital punishment as then practiced, American states immediately began rewriting their death penalty laws. While most states rushed to enact new death penalty legislation, Kansas was not successful in these attempts until recently. Although a restricted death penalty bill became law in 1994, concerted efforts directed toward reinstatement occurred in 18 of 22 legislative sessions with consideration of 48 bills. This case study examines the Kansas legislative experience with death penalty politics. We describe an ambivalent history and tradition toward capital punishment, document the triggering events that affected the eventual passage after 22 years of debate, and discuss the legislation's symbolic nature for both supporters and opponents of capital punishment and how passage of a very restricted death bill was consistent with the cultural tradition of normative ambivalence in Kansas.

In the 1972 *Furman v. Georgia* decision, the U.S. Supreme Court effectively invalidated all existing American death penalty laws due to their capricious and arbitrary administration. Most state legislatures rushed to reinstate new death penalty laws they hoped would pass constitutional review. The subsequent Supreme Court decision in *Gregg v. Georgia* in 1976 was favorable. On January 17, 1977, state-sanctioned executions began again after a 10-year hiatus with the execution of Gary Gilmore in Utah.

Despite the rapid reintroduction of death penalty statutes in most jurisdictions and the ostensible public support for this sanction (Bohm 1991), prominent death penalty researchers predicted that America's long tradition of capital punishment had (or soon would) come to an end, much as it had in most other industrialized nations. In 1974 Bedau (1974:643) wrote that "we will not see another execution in this nation in this century" and Bowers (1974:29) confidently predicted the "abandonment of

---

*An earlier version of this paper was presented at the 1995 annual meeting of the Society for the Study of Social Problems in Washington, DC. The authors gratefully acknowledge the contributions of Joyce Hoyes, Sharon Hunt, and Phyllis Naragon for data gathering, coding, and verification. We express our appreciation to Rita Haley and her staff at the Kansas State Library for their helpfulness in locating archive materials and answering our many questions. We also thank the anonymous reviewers for their comments and suggestions.

executions in America." Even after executions had begun, Zimring and Hawkins (1986:157) remained optimistic: "we surmise that the last execution in the United States is more likely to take place in fifteen than in fifty years; and it is not beyond possibility that executions will cease in the near future." They noted that a theoretical basis for their prediction rested on Durkheim's (1984) assertions that repressive punishments are more typical of less developed societies. During the years since Zimring and Hawkins made this observation, there has been little evidence to support their prediction: between 1977 and 1986 there were 68 executions; between 1987 and 1996 there were more than 250 (NAACP 1996:3).

The question is: How could these prominent observers of American political culture be so wrong? And how could the patterns predicted by Durkheim have been of so little use in the analysis of American trends in punishment during the last part of the twentieth century? Nearly a decade after his overly-optimistic prediction, Bedau (1982:22) pondered the emerging punitiveness: "One is more than a little curious to know what accounts for the reintroduction of the death penalty in several states . . . no more than a few years after it had been abolished. Surprising though it may be . . . the full story has never been told."

While most states rushed to reintroduce death penalty statutes after the 1972 Supreme Court decision in *Furman v. Georgia,* the legislative debate in Kansas was an almost annual event for over 20 years, until eventual passage in 1994. The purpose of this research is to describe and explain this long delay and eventual passage.

THEORETICAL CONSIDERATIONS

Analysis of the dramatic differences among American states' death penalty laws invites distinctions across different theoretical levels (McGarrell and Castellano 1991; Castellano and McGarrell 1991; McGarrell and Castellano 1993). At the most microscopic level, one can consider the attitudes of individuals reflected in public opinion polls. In fact, state legislatures' rush to reinstate death penalty laws in the mid-1970s seemed entirely consistent with the prevailing shift in public opinion. The politicians' push to enact death penalty laws and also focus election campaigns on the issue appear to have "struck a responsive cord with the public" (Pierce and Radelet 1990–1991:722). In the years prior to the 1976 *Gregg* decision, public support for the death penalty increased dramatically, from 42 percent in 1966 to 65 percent in 1976 (Bohm 1991:116). Indeed, public opinion has been suggested as the primary reason the U.S. Supreme Court approved post-*Furman* death penalty laws (Haines 1996:54; Zimring and Hawkins 1986:66). As Haines (1996:54) has argued, "*Gregg v. Georgia* can be seen in large part as a surrender to vox populi."

Yet there is contradictory evidence regarding individual attitudes toward capital punishment. While polls consistently show strong support for the death penalty in the abstract, surveys also indicate that large majorities agree that it is typically imposed in an arbitrary manner (Bowers 1993). As a consequence, support drops precipitously when survey respondents are presented with a reasonable alternative such as life in prison without parole combined with restitution for victims' families

(Bowers 1993; McGarrell and Sandys 1996). Moreover, survey data in the U.S. show that there is less support for capital punishment among Southern residents compared to those in other regions, even though Southern states lead all others in the use of capital punishment, both before and after *Furman* (Bohm 1991). Perhaps this inconsistency is due to legislators overestimating their constituents' support for the death penalty (McGarrell and Sandys 1996). Surprisingly, fear of personal victimization appears unrelated to respondents' death penalty position (Fox, Radelet and Bonsteel 1990–1991; Warr 1995).

At this same microscopic theoretical level, triggering events can be identified which propel legislative action at a particular time and place, affecting the motivations and tactics of legislative opponents and supporters (Galliher and Basilick 1979; McGarrell and Castellano 1993; Marquart, Ekland-Olson and Sorensen 1994). Some of these events provide "the link between demands for action and public policy" such as the efforts of "moral entrepreneurs, media attention, election year politics, [and] sensationalized heinous crimes" (McGarrell and Castellano 1993:353). Of course, one clear contradiction is that, although some instances of strong public opinion and triggering events elicit punitive laws, others do not. And even in states with long traditions of abolition, public opinion leans heavily in favor of capital punishment (Koch and Galliher 1993).

At a macroscopic level, the focus is on the cultural factors generally conducive to legislation, often referred to as structural foundations (Galliher and Basilick 1979). According to McGarrell and Castellano (1993:349): "These are the overriding social structural and cultural factors that produce crime in society and guide society's response to crime." They include economic conditions as well as the local racial and religious composition. For example, social units characterized by heterogeneity, inequality, and economic decline are also associated with higher levels of interpersonal and intergroup conflict, increased rates of criminal law invocation, as well as increased demands for punitive responses to crime (McGarrell and Castellano 1993). Yet Michigan, the first American state to abolish capital punishment, is not only racially heterogeneous, but also has high levels of violent crime (Koch and Galliher 1993). Thus at this macroscopic level, contradictions can be just as obvious as at lower theoretical levels.

COMPARATIVE ANALYSIS AMONG AMERICAN STATES

While most states rushed to pass capital punishment laws, some did not. Those states that led the movement to restore capital punishment typically had long traditions of executions, especially those of the former Confederacy (Marquart, Ekland-Olson and Sorensen 1994). Zimring and Hawkins (1986:144) argued that: "a history of frequent executions . . . serves as a kind of precedent, reassuring political actors that their own participation is neither inhumane nor immoral . . . on grounds that, historically, executions do not violate local community morality." As such, the death penalty is a normatively accepted legal reaction to homicide and is consistent with the cultural traditions in these states. State governments in the Deep South have always shown great enthusiasm for capital punishment, with Georgia, Florida, and Texas the first three to propose language for constitutionally acceptable death penalty laws in 1972–73.

In addition, New York led all states in the number of prisoners executed prior to the death penalty moratorium beginning in 1967 (Bowers 1984). After *Furman,* its legislature passed death penalty statutes continuously between the 1970s and 1990s only to have them repeatedly vetoed by two Democratic governors (Zimring 1996). With the election of a new Republican Governor in 1994, New York reinstated the death penalty the following year. Even though the law easily passed, there clearly remained some ambivalence on the issue. This ambivalence in New York developed because the long debate itself created a special "sensitivity" to possible unfairness in the administration of capital punishment, especially when combined with governors' numerous vetoes which were widely recognized as the "moral high ground" (Zimring 1996:317). Indeed, opposition to the death penalty became respectable in that the sanction was no longer viewed as the only appropriate legal reaction to large numbers of homicides. According to Zimring (1996:317), this ambivalence is reflected in the nature of the legislation finally passed: "In drafting and debating a death penalty, the New York legislature eventually passed a law that established a minimum standard for a legally acceptable death sentencing system that is substantially higher than set forth by a state legislature anywhere else." The law applies only to narrowly defined crimes and requires constant vigilance on issues of effective legal counsel and racial bias in sentencing. After reviewing this statute, Weisberg (1996) estimated that no one will actually be executed under the law. The ambivalence in New York was resolved by passing a death penalty bill, but passing one that might never be used:

> The death penalty law itself was the symbolic victory desired, and the remote prospect of an execution was not a major issue. . . . The major focus of the effort was producing a legislative result. The campaign issue was a death penalty, not executions. (Zimring 1996:318)

Such unenforceable law has been termed symbolic legislation (Gusfield 1963).

If such ambivalence existed in New York, with its long history of frequent executions, ambivalence can be hypothesized to be even more pronounced in states with long periods of abolition and infrequent executions. Indeed, some states that have long traditions of abolition and few executions did not join the rush to reinstate the death penalty. These include longtime abolition states such as Michigan (Koch and Galliher 1993), Minnesota and North Dakota (Galliher, Ray and Cook 1992). Other states that executed relatively few before 1967 still do not have post-*Furman* death laws, including Rhode Island (Conley 1986), Iowa (Acton 1991), and Maine (Schriver 1990). Death bills in Michigan never are reported out of committee and are thus not the subject of legislative debate. In their 150 year experience with death penalty abolition, nearly all of Michigan's political leaders, including conservative Republicans, have supported this cultural and political tradition (Koch and Galliher 1993). In doing so they symbolize to others, and perhaps more importantly to themselves, the moral superiority of their state's government and people even while having one of the most decrepit and punitive prison systems in the nation and one of the nation's highest murder rates. Other jurisdictions still without a death penalty are Alaska, District of Columbia, Hawaii, Massachusetts, Vermont, West Virginia, and Wisconsin (NAACP 1996:1).

Kansas is another state with long periods of abolition punctuated by an occasional execution. Nonetheless, between 1973 and 1994, death penalty bills were the subject of almost annual legislative hearings and floor debate, were frequently passed by one or both houses, were vetoed by the governor on several occasions, and eventually became law in 1994. The question is: What would make this state with a long abolition tradition reinstate capital punishment after years of legislative debate? This research examines the legislative process surrounding reinstatement of the death penalty in Kansas between 1973 and 1994.[1] In so doing, it highlights those factors which influenced the legislative process and its eventual outcome. We will show how Kansas' normative ambivalence toward capital punishment was resolved by eventual passage of a capital punishment law. As was true in New York, the Kansas death penalty law was so narrow in scope that in actual practice it would cover few defendants in murder cases. Yet without even being invoked, the law serves to define the moral or cultural boundaries of the state much as Erikson (1966) found was true of the occasional execution of condemned witches in colonial Salem.

METHODS AND DATA SOURCES

This research on reinstatement of the death penalty in Kansas used several sources of information including: 1) all news articles and editorials on the death penalty from five newspapers [*Topeka Capital-Journal* (TCJ), *Hutchinson News* (HN), *Wichita Eagle-Beacon* (WE), *Kansas City Star* (KCS), and *Kansas City Times* (KCT)], between 1973 and 1994; and selected other state newspapers in 1993 and 1994 [*Johnson County Sun* (JCS), *Kansas City Kansan* (KCK), and *Olathe Daily News* (ODN)]; 2) minutes and other materials from House and Senate committee hearings on death penalty bills between 1973 and 1994; 3) governors' veto messages; 4) death penalty bills introduced between 1973 and 1994; and 5) official data on homicides and other violent offenses from the FBI's annual Uniform Crime Reports (1965–1993). The newspaper articles and editorials and the House and Senate committee minutes were used to trace the history of the legislative process, uncover triggering events, identify key supporters and opponents, and discover claimsmaking and motivations behind support and opposition to the death penalty.

---

[1]The experience in Kansas is clearly more interesting and dynamic than in New York. Since the 1972 *Furman* decision, both the Kansas and New York Legislatures frequently attempted to enact death penalty statutes. New York's legislature passed numerous death bills only to be vetoed each time by Governor Hugh Carey (1975–1983) and then Governor Mario Cuomo (1983–1995). The legislative action became perfunctory after a time with the same legislators delivering the same addresses before their colleagues in hearings and on the floor. Everyone knew that there would be no death bill signed into law by either Governor Carey or Cuomo. The situation in Kansas was much more complex and dynamic.

KANSAS EXPERIENCE WITH DEATH PENALTY LEGISLATION

From its territorial days, Kansas vacillated on the death penalty. There have been 24 prisoners hanged under state authority in Kansas since 1863 (WE 1977). Between 1872 and 1907, the state had a death penalty statute stipulation that the condemned person should be confined at hard labor for one year at which time the governor would sign a death warrant (WE 1976). No governor authorized a hanging during this period. On January 30, 1907, Governor Edward Hoch signed into law a bill abolishing capital punishment. Republican Governor Alf Landon's 1935 signature on House Bill 10 reinstated the death penalty after 28 years (Galliher et al. 1992). This law remained in effect until 1972 when all existing states' death penalty statutes were ruled unconstitutional in the *Furman* decision. Thus, Kansas experienced long periods of death penalty abolition, and executions have been relatively infrequent (Bowers 1984).

While advocates of capital punishment in the Kansas legislature were not successful in enacting a death penalty law until 1994, this was not due to their lack of effort. Indeed, legislative activity in the form of floor debates and committee hearings on capital punishment during these years in Kansas is equaled only by that in New York (Zimring 1996). In the 22 legislative sessions between 1973 (the year following the *Furman* decision) and 1994, there were 48 death penalty bills considered in 18 legislative sessions, with no death penalty activity in just four sessions: 1974, 1984, 1988, and 1993.

The discussion below summarizes this dynamic, volatile legislative history, beginning with the administration of Republican Governor Robert Bennett.[2] This legislative history is also summarized in Table 1. In some legislative sessions, passage of a common death penalty bill and signature by the governor seemed certain, yet it did not occur. At other times, death penalty bills were defeated while the legislature passed alternatives of long, mandatory prison sentences that met varied receptions by the governor. And finally, passage became a reality when death penalty legislative opponents compromised and agreed to a narrow death penalty bill that became law without action by a governor staunchly opposed to the death penalty.

The Bennett Years: 1975–1978

During the administration of Republican Governor Robert Bennett, there were four Senate votes on death penalty bills with two passing, and four House votes with three passing. However, there was no common death peanlty bill passed by both chambers. While there were Democrats and Republicans on both sides of the debate, the death penalty was a partisan issue from the beginning as indicated in Table 1. In both the Senate and House, a majority of Republicans supported the death penalty in 7 of 8 votes, while the majority of Democrats opposed the death penalty in all eight votes. The highlight of this period was a 25-year "death-in-prison" bill

---

[2]There was one death penalty bill (SB0082) passed (24–15) in the Senate in 1973 during the administration of Democratic Governor Robert Docking who served between 1967 and 1975. During Docking's last year in office in 1974, there was no legislative activity on the death penalty.

TABLE 1
Kansas Legislative Voting and Outcomes by Chamber and Political Party on Death Penalty and Imprisonment Bills, 1975–1994

Year	Bill*	Legislative Chamber	Percent Voting 'Aye' by Party Republicans	Democrats	Outcome Vote	Count	Governor's Action
The Bennett Years							
1975	HB2472	House	46	33	Failed	48–71	
1975	SB0503	Senate	58	36	Failed	19–19	
1975	HB2141	Senate	54	36	Failed	19–21	
1976	SB0740	Senate	69	21	Passed	21–10	
1976	SB0740	House	64	35	Passed	64–60	
1976	SB1027	Senate	72	36	Passed	23–16	
1976	SB1027	House	66	35	Passed	65–58	
1977	SB0156**	Senate	40	90	Passed	25–14	
1977	SB0156**	House	45	80	Passed	77–45	
1977	SB0156**	Senate	37	76	Passed	23–17	Vetoed
1978	HB2683	House	75	39	Passed	66–48	
The Carlin Years							
1979	HB2160	House	80	49	Passed	82–42	
1979	HB2160**	Senate	48	74	Passed	24–16	
1979	HB2160	House	80	41	Passed	78–47	
1979	HB2160	Senate	67	37	Passed	21–19	Vetoed
1980	HB2988	House	81	46	Passed	81–43	
1980	HB2988	Senate	67	37	Passed	21–19	
1980	HB2988	Senate	68	33	Passed	21–19	
1980	HB2988	House	82	46	Passed	81–42	Vetoed
1981	SB0456	Senate	79	40	Passed	25–14	
1981	SB0081	House	81	41	Passed	79–44	
1981	SB0081	Senate	47	33	Passed	23–15	Vetoed
1985	SB2135	House	78	40	Passed	78–46	
1985	SB2135	Senate	67	50	Passed	24–16	Vetoed
1986	HB2980	House	78	43	Passed	80–45	
The Hayden Years							
1987	HB2062	House	77	28	Passed	71–53	
1987	HB2062	Senate	58	25	Failed	18–22	
1989	SB0038	Senate	73	11	Failed	18–22	
1989	SB0077**	Senate	96	100	Passed	39–1	
1990	SB0077**	House	88	98	Passed	111–9	Signed
1990	SB0077	House	75	12	Failed	57–67	
The Finney Years							
1994	HB2578	House	88	19	Passed	70–55	
1994	HB2578	Senate	74	15	Passed	22–18	
1994	HB2578	House	74	10	Failed	54–69	
1994	HB2578***	House	88	15	Passed	67–58	

Notes:
*Some bills (e.g., HB2988 in 1980) were amended in the House and/or Senate and thus voted on more than once.
**Non-death penalty bills specifying long mandatory prison ("death-in-prison") terms.
***Became law without Governor Finney's signature.

(SB0156) passed in 1977 by both the House and Senate and sent to Governor Bennett who vetoed it. According to Governor Bennett, a strong proponent of capital punishment, the life-in-prison bill was not a suitable alternative to a death bill and its passage might make reinstatement of capital punishment more difficult. This life-in-prison bill also reflected partisan politics: most Democrats from both chambers supported it (House: 80%; Senate: 76%) while most Republicans did not (House: 45%; Senate: 37%).

The Carlin Years: 1979–1986

In 1979, Democratic Governor John Carlin took office in what would be the first of two 4-year terms. During his campaign against incumbent-Governor Bennett, Carlin, an avid opponent of capital punishment, stated that if he became governor he would nevertheless sign a constitutionally-valid death penalty bill (HN 1979). In 1979, the House and Senate took him at his word, passed a death penalty bill (HB2160) and sent it to him for approval. Much to the dismay of death penalty supporters, he would not sign it even though he did not question its constitutionality. Rather, he rejected it on moral grounds and announced that he would never sign such legislation. When queried years later about his campaign promise and 1979 veto, he stated: "When I ran for governor in 1978, a reporter asked me if I would sign a capital punishment bill even though I had always voted against it as a legislator" (TCJ 1994d). Carlin said that he would: "I was simply telling the truth" (HN 1994a). But after the death penalty bill was passed, "The magnitude of the decision hit me. For the first time I held the power of life and death in my hands, and I knew I couldn't sign it" (HN 1994a).

Proponents in both chambers passed death penalty bills again in 1980 (HB2988) and 1981 (SB0081) only to have them vetoed by the Governor. Despite Governor Carlin's staunch opposition to capital punishment, he was reelected in 1982 to a second term, the maximum allowed by state law. In the 1985 legislative session, capital punishment proponents again passed a death penalty bill (HB2135), and Carlin again vetoed this bill. The partisan nature of the debate remained evident during Governor Carlin's tenure: in 13 death penalty votes, Republicans as a group voted favorably 12 times, while the Democrats always voted in opposition.

The Hayden Years: 1987–1990

In 1987, Republican Governor Mike Hayden took office. Hayden had campaigned for office on a platform that emphasized the need for a death penalty. After being elected, Governor-elect Hayden remarked:

> I am a strong supporter of capital punishment. I'm going to call on the Legislature to enact it, and I would hope they would put a bill on my desk in March or April that would make it effective at least by July 1 next year. (KCT 1986)

In January, 1987, much to the delight of the new governor, the House passed a death penalty bill (HB2062) by a vote of 71–53. Yet, in a surprising outcome, the Senate defeated this same bill (18–22); six senators (two Republicans and four Democrats) changed their positive 1985 votes to negative votes in 1987. In 1989 Governor Hayden again pushed the legislature for a death penalty bill and, as happened two years before, the bill (SB0038) was defeated in the Senate. In lieu of a death penalty bill, the Senate passed (39–1) another "death-in-prison" bill (SB0077) providing a mandatory 40-years in prison before parole would be possible. In 1990, the House handed Governor Hayden another political setback by defeating a death penalty bill (57–67); this time, eight representatives (two Republicans and six Democrats) changed their positive votes to negative votes. The House now joined the Senate in passing the 40-year prison bill (SB0077) by an overwhelming margin (111–9), and the governor then signed that bill into law.

During the Hayden years the death penalty remained a partisan issue: across all four death penalty votes, Republicans voted favorably, while Democrats voted negatively. The only non-partisian support was for the 40-year prison bill; with its passage, one Democratic representative predicted: "death penalty politics will probably die the day the governor signs that [40-year] bill" (KCT 1990). While Governor Hayden signed into law the "hard-40" bill, he did so with some reluctance: "I would say the [death penalty] issue will be around until it's enacted. Among the people, it has not been resolved, and they'll continue to support it" (KCT 1990). When Governor Hayden ran for reelection in 1990, he lost to a strong death penalty opponent, Democrat Joan Finney. Given that there was now a mandatory 40-year prison alternative to the death penalty and a newly-elected governor who opposed capital punishment, death penalty politics in Kansas appeared to be over.

The Finney Years, 1991–1994

Except for isolated activities in House committees there was no organized effort to introduce death penalty legislation during the first three sessions of Finney's term as governor (1991–1993). At the beginning of the 1993 session, a Republican representative and strong advocate of capital punishment stated: "I haven't discussed it [the death penalty] with anybody, and nobody has talked to me about it," and "I don't know anybody who plans to bring it up." (TCJ 1993a). While no death penalty bill was proposed during this legislative session, the issue soon became an explosive one among lawmakers and citizens that would carry over into the 1994 legislative session.

On July 1, Stephanie Schmidt, a 19-year-old female college student was raped and murdered by a co-worker on parole for a previous rape conviction. The victim's parents lived in an affluent Kansas City suburb. There were immediate calls for reinstating capital punishment in Kansas. The *Topeka Capital-Journal* (1993b) declared that the perpetrator: "charged into battle armed with a murderous intent, a serpent-like cunning and a blaring criminal record" and that his prey was "[s]weet [and] unsuspecting Stephanie Schmidt," concluding: "The death penalty . . . would be a valuable tool in [this] case."

Legislators could not wait for the 1994 legislative session to begin. The *Wichita Eagle-Beacon* (1994a) observed: "Lawmakers are falling all over one another to get tough on crime. As expected, the return of the death penalty is the hot-button centerpiece for the tough talk." After amendments and compromise in House committees and on the floor, a death bill (HB2578) passed the House (70–55) and was sent to the Senate for consideration. The Senate amended this bill by restricting it to a handful of premeditated, intentional murders termed "the worst of the worst" (WE 1994d). Before the full Senate, the narrow death bill passed (22–18).

When the House refused to accept the Senate version, the issue was taken before a Senate and House Conference Committee to reconcile their differences. While most Senate members were apparently satisfied with a very narrow bill, dissatisfaction with the Senate version resulted in defeat (54–69) in the first House vote. Two weeks later, on the last day of the legislative session, the House accepted the Senate's restricted death bill (67–58) and sent it to the Governor (WE 1994i). Democratic Governor Joan Finney allowed the bill to become law without her signature. (In Kansas, a bill passed by both legislative chambers can become law without the governor's signature if s/he does not veto it within ten calendar days after the date of receipt.) Thus, after 22 legislative sessions and 48 death bills, Kansas became the 37th state to reinstate capital punishment.

STRUCTURAL FOUNDATIONS UNDERLYING KANSAS DEATH PENALTY LEGISLATION
States' Racial Composition and Death Penalty Laws

The five states (Texas, Florida, Virginia, Louisiana, and Georgia) that rushed most quickly to enact post-*Furman* death statutes, and subsequently accounted for 213 of 318 (67.0%) executions since their resumption in 1977 (NAACP 1996), have relatively large African-American populations, averaging 21.0 percent black (U.S. Bureau of the Census 1995:34,36). In contrast, Kansas has an African-American population of 6.1 percent. The 12 abolition states (excluding the District of Columbia) average 2.8 percent black (U.S. Bureau of the Census 1995:34,36). These figures demonstrate that racial composition is an important structural foundation for states' experience with capital punishment. (The exception is Michigan; despite having a relatively large black population, it was the first state to abolish capital punishment and has not had a death penalty as punishment for murder for approximately 150 years.) In the protracted Kansas death penalty debate, race was conspicuous by its absence as a contested issue. When considered at all, both sides were likely to argue for safeguards to prevent discrimination whether due to race, social class, or other defendant characteristics.

Normative Evaluations of Capital Punishment

Both informal polls and more systematic surveys show that Kansas, like other states, has a large majority favoring capital punishment (Bowers and Dugan 1994). The Republican Chair of the Senate Judiciary Committee stated that: "public pressure probably encouraged legislators" to continue introducing death penalty legislation (HN 1994d). Responding when asked why most House members favored a bill to reinstate the death penalty in the 1994 session, a Democratic representative replied: "I attribute it to public opinion polls." And, a Republican representative asserted that a death bill passed the House with a larger number of votes than expected because: "A great deal of the margin is legislators responding to how their constituents feel about the issue" (KCS 1994a). This seemingly stable and powerful public support provided the cultural and political environment for death penalty legislation, not merely the attitudes of isolated individuals. Yet, we noted earlier, contradictions in death penalty support. While citizen support may be a necessary condition for reinstatement of death penalty statutes, it clearly is not a sufficient condition. Even abolitionist states are likely to have large proportions of citizens who favor the death penalty (Koch and Galliher 1993). Alternatively, some U.S. states and other nations have abolished their death penalty laws without popular support (Zimring and Hawkins 1986).

Moreover, citizens who purportedly support capital punishment laws often express preferences for alternatives to the death penalty. This was true in Kansas at the time of the 1994 legislation; Bowers and Dugan reported that 85 percent of Kansans supported the death penalty (1994:1). Yet, support decreased to 42 percent when these same respondents were presented several alternatives; the other 58 percent favored either: life without parole, life in prison without parole plus substantial payments to victims' families from prison work, or life in prison plus substantial payments to victims' families from prison work, with a chance for parole after 40 years if payments were made in full (Bowers and Dugan 1994:9).

TRIGGERING EVENTS INFLUENCING DEATH PENALTY LEGISLATION
Sensational and Visible Homicides

While Kansas historically experienced relatively low homicide rates, these numbers do not typically galvanize the attention of the media, politicans, and the public, compared to specific acts of especially shocking violence. Indeed, sensational and brutal homicides can serve as important "triggering events." During the 1980s the crime-victims movement emerged and the crime victim became a "symbolic figure in the conservative agenda for building crime policy. These policies include[d] a return to the use of the death penalty" (Weed 1995:132).

This is clearly illustrated in the 1959 murders of four Clutter family members in rural Holcomb, Kansas. The Clutter family murders became symbolic of violent crime in Kansas, in large part due to Truman Capote's best-selling book, *In Cold Blood* (1959), and the movie by the same name. One Kansas newspaper stated: "Almost 35 years after the Clutter family homestead became a slaughterhouse, Kansas legislators debating the death penalty still speak movingly, almost intimately, of Herb, Bonnie, Nancy and Kenyon, the four victims no one can forget" (HN 1994b). A Republican representative observed: "It [the Clutter case] is like a Bible. We can look at it through our own lenses and substantiate our own viewpoints" (HN 1994b).

But Kansans pushing for reinstatement of the death penalty would not have to rely only on the earlier Clutter murders. During the 1994 legislative session, the *Wichita Eagle-Beacon* (1994c) noted: "The people most on legislators' minds were Kansans such as Stephanie Schmidt, raped and murdered last year . . . ; 9-year-old Nancy Shoemaker, abducted off a Wichita street in 1990 and later found strangled; and the

Clutter family." One Republican representative declared: "There is enough support for it across the state, primarily in connection with the Stephanie Schmidt situation. The time is right for it" (JCS 1993).

Gene Schmidt, Stephanie's father, speaking before a House committee asked rhetorically: "How many more Stephanies must we kill? When are we going to accept that the death penalty is in the hands of the criminals?" (KCS 1994b). He added that: "by voting no on the death penalty, you are voting to definitely execute innocent lives in the largest of numbers" (TCJ 1994a). In a March, 1994 story "Schmidt Crusade Getting Results," a Wichita newspaper reported that the Schmidts:

> have gone nationwide with their fight for tougher laws against sex offenders, appearing with such talk-show hosts as Larry King and Maury Povich. And they formed a not-for-profit corporation called Speak Out for Stephanie that will continue to lobby for tougher laws. (WE 1994h)

In addition, a Kingman couple, Bob and Joelene Fairchild, whose daughter, son-in-law, and two grandchildren were murdered in rural Reno County on November 5, 1993, led a petition drive in 1994 to reinstate capital punishment (KCK 1994). They collected approximately 22,000 signatures on a petition "demanding" reinstatement of the death penalty and testified before a House committee (WE 1994b).

Murder of young people, coupled with promotion of the death penalty by surviving family members, appears to have a powerful influence on death penalty politics. While earlier instances of horrific homicides could have served as triggering events, the two 1993 cases were followed by surviving family members becoming crusaders in the drive to reinstate the death penalty. These murders and political crusades clearly had an additive character, making these triggering events successful, where others had failed to secure legislative results.

Opposition to Capital Punishment and Eventual Compromise

In response to Stephanie Schmidt's murder, Governor Finney wrote:

> I, too, am appalled with the recent tragedy. . . . I am personally opposed to capital punishment; however, I believe that most Kansas citizens favor reinstatement of the death penalty. For this reason, should the Legislature pass a law to reinstate the death penalty, I would allow it to become law without my signature. (ODN 1993)

Responding to this letter, a Republican senator stated: "The death penalty will have a good chance to become law in 1994. . . . The governor has changed her position, and if the legislation passes, it can become law" (ODN 1993). The Republican Chair of the Senate Judiciary Committee concurred: "I had not heard of any talk of trying to reimpose capital punishment from my colleagues in the Legislature until I heard the governor's announcement" (HN 1994d).

Given the course of death penalty politics prior to Governor Finney's term in office, there was no reason to believe that a death penalty bill would become law during or after her term in office, even if a staunch death penalty supporter followed her as governor. After all, neither Governors Bennett (1975–1979) nor Hayden (1987–1991), strong advocates of capital punishment, had been able to entice majorities in both houses to submit a death bill for their signatures. In fact, both Republicans had lost elections for second terms to liberal Democrats who were vocal critics of capital punishment.

Why then would Governor Finney not veto a death penalty bill, especially since she testified against this proposed legislation before the Senate Judiciary Committee (TCJ 1994b)? According to Finney, she did not wish to break a campaign pledge to allow a death penalty bill to become law without her signature if the Legislature sent her one (WE 1994l). She also felt that the death penalty represented the collective will of Kansans (TCJ 1994b).

The bill that became law was approved by the Senate (22–18) only after amendments were introduced by a Democrat who had voted against previous death bills. He argued that: "if a death penalty law were to be enacted, I wanted it to be as narrow as possible, so that the flaws of capital punishment would be minimized" (HN 1994c). This bill also had the support of the Republican Senate President, who previously had voted against death bills: "I am basically a death penalty opponent" who along with 21 others voted for a narrow death penalty bill which passed the Senate (WE 1994g). If these two opponents had voted against this bill, there would not have been the votes necessary to pass it—it would have been defeated by a vote of 20–20.

Framing the Death Debate: Passage of a Narrow Bill

While enactment of this law can be viewed as an obvious victory for death penalty supporters, it can as easily be viewed as a symbolic victory for at least some death penalty opponents. The new law would apply to few potential offenders. The Legislature passed a very narrow bill that created the crime of "capital murder" (KCS 1994c; WE 1994f) allowing prosecutors to seek the death penalty for seven specific types of intentional or premeditated killing.[3] Kansas legislative researchers concluded that the Senate's bill might result in the death penalty being sought about three times a year (WE 1994e), while the Kansas Department of Corrections estimated that this number could be from two to five per year (HN 1994d). With an average of 141 homicides reported annually in Kansas between 1990 and 1993 (U.S. Department of Justice 1994), an estimated five capital cases amounts to approximately 3.5 percent. And, a spokesperson for the Kansas Department of Corrections said (HN 1994d) that only two of 29 inmates (6.9%) sent to prison for first-degree murder convictions in 1993 could have been charged with capital murder as defined by the newly enacted legislation. Coincidentally, a limited death bill would also make its enactment more affordable, with estimated costs of no more than $800,000 in the first fis-

---

[3]These are: 1) killing of a kidnapping victim, if that person was being held for ransom; 2) killing of a kidnapping victim under 14, if that victim was being held because the criminal intended to commit a sex crime; 3) killing of a victim of rape, criminal sodomy or aggravated sodomy; 4) killing for hire or participation in a murder-for-hire scheme; 5) killing of a prisoner or jail employee or inmate by a prisoner or jail inmate; 6) murder of a law enforcement officer; and 7) two or more killings committed at once or connected together or constituting parts of a common scheme (Kansas Statutes Annotated 21-3439).

cal year after passage (WE 1994e; KCT 1994; WE 1994k) and $770,000 the next year (WE 1994j).

While opponents generally have not been successful in resisting attempts to reinstate death penalty laws across the country, they have nonetheless been instrumental in influencing the terms of the debate. Specifically, death penalty opponents have "helped to make legal executions far less routine than they might otherwise be" (Haines 1996:149). This certainly appears to be the case in Kansas, with the passage of a narrow death penalty law.

DEATH PENALTY LEGISLATION: SYMBOLIC LAW OR INSTRUMENTAL LAW?

Even a cursory review of this legislative history powerfully reinforces the view, attributed to Clarence Darrow, that capital punishment and other such issues are not settled by reason but rather by prejudices, sentiments, and emotions, and, when they are settled, they do not remain settled (KCS 1979). The same observation was made time and again by Kansas newspapers and legislators; for example: "Another year, another governor, another legislature, and the death penalty will be before Kansas again" (KCS 1979). In fact, as noted above, the legislature considered 48 death penalty bills in 18 of 22 legislative sessions between 1973 and 1994.

The bill that ultimately passed in 1994 required the confluence of a number of events. Clearly the triggering events of greatest significance were the two highly-publicized murder cases in 1993—that of Stephanie Schmidt and the multiple murders of the young family in Reno County. They became even more politically influential because surviving family members lobbied for capital punishment legislation. Had it not been for these murders and family reactions, there likely would have been no death penalty legislation vote in 1994. After all, there had been no House or Senate vote since 1990, when a mandatory 40-year prison bill became law during the Hayden administration. This case study thus provides strong evidence for the hypothesized importance of triggering events in the legislative process (Galliher and Basilick 1979; McGarrell and Castellano 1993). They serve as a catalyst for receptive political actors to propose (or support) legislation even in jurisdictions whose cultural and structural foundations would seemingly mitigate such legislation.

In addition to these triggering events, passage came only after the House reluctantly compromised and agreed to a very narrow death penalty bill appealing to both fiscal conservatives and some death penalty opponents. And finally, there was the governor who—while opposed to capital punishment on moral grounds—disregarded the overwhelming opposition to the death penalty shown by her fellow Democrats in the House and Senate and allowed the bill to become law without her signature.

Symbolic Versus Instrumental Law

Edelman's (1964) study of the origins of anti-trust legislation and Gusfield's (1955, 1963, 1967) research on alcohol prohibition distinguish between symbolic law, designed to make a public statement of social condemnation, and instrumental law aimed at actually controlling behavior. Both authors claim that the laws in question served as prime examples of symbolic law. The Kansas experience illustrates that both the legislative process and its outcome can serve symbolic functions. Lawmakers knew full well that Governor Carlin (1979–1987), after his first veto in 1979, would not approve a death penalty bill; yet they went through annual rituals of public hearings, contentious debate, and pointless votes, sending three additional bills for his veto. As evidence that at least some lawmakers' votes served symbolic purposes, several Democrats and Republicans from both chambers changed their positive death penalty votes in 1985 (under Governor Carlin) to negative votes in 1987 and 1989 (under Governor Hayden). These lawmakers knew that Hayden, a staunch death penalty supporter, would sign a death bill. Some legislators ostensibly voted for death penalty bills when the governor opposed capital punishment, knowing that their vote was meaningless, but they switched their votes to avoid actually passing a death penalty bill under a pro-capital punishment governor.

Table 2 shows that, across administrations, Republicans' support for capital punishment legislation generally rose from the Bennett administration (.630) through the Finney administration (.810); while Democrats' support generally fell from the Bennett administration (.339) to the Finney administration (.148). Although there were important fluctuations, support in both parties rose during the Carlin administration and fell during the Hayden administration; and positions on capital punishment became increasingly polarized along political party lines.

The *outcome* of this protracted legislative debate was symbolic legislation. When Kansas finally passed a death penalty statute, it applied to only a handful of potential murder cases. Even the most vocal proponents of the death penalty were hard-

TABLE 2

Mean Proportional Support for Death Penalty Legislation Given by Kansas Republican and Democratic Lawmakers, 1975–1994

Administration	Mean Proportional Support for Death Penalty Bills*	
	Republicans	Democrats
Republican Robert Bennett [1975–1979]	.630 (N=8 votes)	.339
Democrat John Carlin [1979–1987]	.735 (N=13 votes)	.412
Republican Mike Hayden [1987–1991]	.708 (N=4 votes)	.190
Democrat Joan Finney [1991–1994]	.810 (N=4 votes)	.148

Note:
*Number of legislative votes of death penalty bills only (see Table 1 for specific bills and years).

pressed to argue that the new law would have any measurable effect on criminal violence in the state; Republican Senator Mark Parkinson, chief Senate sponsor of the
1994 capital punishment legislation asserted: "I'm willing to admit it [the death
penalty] might not usually deter these terrible crimes. . . . But if it *ever* deters, it
will be worth the effort" (TCJ 1994c, emphasis added). This is the same solution
eventually reached in New York State after years of death penalty debate; the New
York Legislature enacted a capital punishment law that will apply to almost no one
(Zimring 1996).

A restricted death bill represents a symbolic victory for proponents and opponents
alike in that it serves to demarcate the "community (normative) boundaries" for both
sides of the debate. Erikson wrote that each community:

> has a specific territory in the world as a whole, not only in the sense that it occupies a
> defined geographic space but also in the sense that it takes over a particular niche in
> what might be called cultural space and develops its own 'ethos' or 'way' within that
> compass. Both of these dimensions of group space, the geographical and the cultural,
> set the community apart as a special place and provide an important point of reference
> for its members. (1966:9–10)

The reinstatement of the death penalty can be seen as an attempt to fill out an ever-
shifting, ambivalent "cultural space" for Kansans. Proponents could point to the
enacted death bill as a collective representation of both the affirmation for human life
and the dramatization of evil. Moreover, the importance of the death penalty may not
be in its actual use, but rather in the symbolism of having it on the books:

> this may be seen as just another weapon, if not the supreme weapon, that can be brought
> out occasionally and used against persons who murder. It is a way of symbolically dis-
> playing to actual murderers and would-be murderers that the state can be just as deadly
> as those who would take another person's life. (Bedau 1982:69; cf. Marquart et al.
> 1994).

Weisberg, commenting on the death penalty in California, expresses a similar view:

> We could say that California has conceived a fiendishly clever way of satisfying the
> competing demands on the death penalty: We sentence vast numbers of murderers to
> death, but execute virtually none of them. Simply having many death sentences can sat-
> isfy many proponents of the death penalty who demand capital punishment, because in
> a vague way they want the law to make a statement of social authority and control.
> (1996:287)

At least some Kansas death penalty opponents also were willing, albeit reluctantly, to accept the new law because it would apply to few cases. Although prefer-
ring no capital punishment law at all, they also considered the Kansas statute much
better than those found in states, such as Florida, Texas, Georgia, Louisiana, and Virginia, that accounted for most post-*Furman* executions (NAACP 1996). For other
legislators who were moderates on the death penalty, the Kansas statute represented
a compromise between "the extreme groups who want either no executions or as

many as possible" (Weisberg 1996:286), as well as a welcome end to a long, contentious, partisan debate. As in New York: "[The state] has purged itself of a certain angry and destructive and distracting populism by getting the law on the books. And it has made the death penalty a non-issue" (Weisberg 1996:287).

The argument for the symbolic nature of this legislation is reflected in the actual application of the law. In the 30 months following the effective date of the death penalty bill (July 1, 1994), there were an estimated 397 homicides in Kansas,[4] but only 15 defendants (3.8%) charged with capital murder. Of these, no one has yet been sentenced to death.[5]

Claims about symbolic legislation notwithstanding, both anti-trust law (Edelman 1964) and alcohol prohibition (Gusfield 1955, 1963, 1967) had instrumental qualities as well. The same dual nature of law is found in the Kansas death penalty legislation. Proponents of capital punishment bills routinely argued that they would support reinstatement even if there was only the chance of saving one innocent life, but, death penalty statutes have instrumental qualities beyond actual executions. For instance, prosecuting attorneys undoubtedly find it easier to secure guilty pleas in exchange for a prison sentence in cases that have the potential of the death penalty.

The current situation in Kansas is consistent with its early history of death penalty politics. Kansas' tradition resembles an abolitionist state more than a death penalty retentionist state, in that it infrequently used the death penalty even when available. Given this tradition and current death penalty law, it is unlikely that Kansas will become another death-belt state where hundreds of inmates are condemned to death rows and scores receive a final sanitized needle. The Kansas legislative debate between 1973 and 1994, and the ultimate resolution, reflected a normative ambivalence toward the death penalty that is part of the state's cultural tradition.

REFERENCES

Acton, Richard
  1991   "The magic of undiscouraged effort: The death penalty in early Iowa, 1838–1878."
          Annals of Iowa 50:721–750.
Bedau, Hugo A.
  1974   "Challenging the death penalty." Harvard Civil Rights–Civil Liberties Law Review
          9(May):624–643.
  1982   The Death Penalty in America, third edition. Chicago: Aldine.
Bohm, Robert M.
  1991   "American death penalty opinion, 1936–1986: A critical examination of the
          Gallup polls." In The Death Penalty in America: Current Research, Robert M.
          Bohm, (ed.), 113–145. Cincinnati, Ohio: Anderson.

---

[4]Complete data on the number of Kansas homicides for this 30 month period are not yet available from the Kansas Bureau of Investigation. Based on available information provided by that agency (Howerton 1997), the estimated figure of 397 is based on one-half of the 1994 homicides (170), as well as known first-quarter figures for both 1995 (37) and 1996 (41).

[5]Data on capital murder cases were provided by the Kansas Attorney General's office (Debenham 1997).

Bowers, William J.

1974   Executions in America. Lexington, MA: Lexington Books.

1984   Legal Homicide: Death as Punishment in America, 1864–1982. Boston: North-eastern University Press.

1993   "Capital punishment and contemporary values: People's misgivings and the court's misperceptions." Law & Society Review 27:157–175.

Bowers, William J., and Patricia H. Dugan

1994   "Kansans want an alternative to the death penalty." Unpublished Manuscript.

Capote, Truman

1965   In Cold Blood. New York: Random House.

Castellano, Thomas C., and Edmund F. McGarrell

1991   "The politics of law and order: Case study evidence for a conflict model of the criminal law formation process." Journal of Research in Crime and Delinquency 28:304–329.

Conley, Patrick T.

1986   "Death knell for the death penalty: The Gordon murder trial and Rhode Island's abolition of capital punishment." Rhode Island Bar Journal 34:11–15.

Debenham, David

1997   Personal communication with James M. Galliher (January 16).

Durkheim, Emile

1984   The Division of Labor in Society. Translated by W.D. Halls. New York: Free Press.

Edelman, Murray

1964   The Symbolic Uses of Politics. Urbana: University of Illinois Press.

Erikson, Kai T.

1966   Wayward Puritans. New York: John Wiley & Sons.

Fox, James Alan, Michael L. Radelet, and Julie L. Bonsteel

1990–   "Death penalty opinion in the post-Furman years." New York University Review of
1991   Law & Social Change 18:499–528.

Galliher, John F. and Linda Basilick

1979   "Utah's liberal drug laws: Structural foundations and triggering events." Social Problems 26:284–297.

Galliher, John F., Gregory Ray, and Brent Cook

1992   "Abolition and reinstatement of capital punishment during the progressive era and early twentieth century." Journal of Criminal Law and Criminology 83:538–576.

Gusfield, Joseph R.

1955   "Social structure and moral reform: A study of the Woman's Christian Temperance Union." American Journal of Sociology 61:221–232.

1963   Symbolic Crusade: Status Politics and the American Temperance Movement. Urbana, IL: University of Illinois Press.

1967   "Moral passage: The symbolic process in public designations of deviance." Social Problems 15:175–188.

Haines, Herbert H.

1996   Against Capital Punishment: The Anti-Death Penalty Movement in America, 1972–1994. New York: Oxford University Press.

Howerton, Mary
    1997   Personal communication with James M. Galliher (January 24).
Hutchinson News (HN)
    1979   "New legislators and violent crime may boost death bill." (January 11).
    1994a   "Carlin defends his death penalty stand." (March 12).
    1994b   "Holcomb murders haunt death penalty debate." (March 14).
    1994c   "Proposal was drafted by Rock." (April 9).
    1994d   "Death penalty 4 days away." (April 18).
Johnson County Sun (JCS)
    1993   "Will death penalty become law in '94?" (August 25).
Kansas City Kansan (KCK)
    1994   "Death penalty: Kansas couple mounting own campaign for reinstatement." (January 1).
Kansas City Star
    1979   "Death penalty debate age-old." (April 29).
    1994a   "Death penalty gets an initial OK in Kansas." (February 11).
    1994b   "Schmidts push for death penalty." (February 18).
    1994c   "Kansas senate approves death penalty." (March 2).
Kansas City Times
    1986   "Hayden wants death penalty by July." (December 13).
    1990   "40-year prison term becomes law." (February 24).
    1994   "Kansans pass death penalty." (April 9).
Koch, Larry W., and John F. Galliher
    1993   "Michigan's continuing abolition of the death penalty and the conceptual components of symbolic legislation." Social and Legal Studies 2:323–346.
Marquart, James W., Sheldon Ekland-Olson, and Jonathan R. Sorensen
    1994   The Rope, the Chair, and the Needle: Capital Punishment in Texas, 1923–1990. Austin: University of Texas Press.
McGarrell, Edmund F., and Thomas C. Castellano
    1991   "An integrative conflict model of the criminal law formation process." Journal of Research in Crime and Delinquency 28:174–196.
    1993   "Social structure, crime and politics: A conflict model of the criminal law formation process." In Making Law: The State, the Law, and Structural Contradictions, William J. Chambliss and Marjorie S. Satz, (eds.), 347–378. Bloomington, Indiana: Indiana University Press.
McGarrell, Edmund F., and Marla Sandys
    1996   "The misperception of public opinion toward capital punishment." American Behavioral Scientist 39(February):500–513.
NAACP
    1996   Death Row, U.S.A. (Winter). New York: NAACP.
Olathe Daily News
    1993   "Finney opens door to death penalty." (August 24).

Pierce, Glenn L., and Michael L. Radelet

1990–91   "The role and consequences of the death penalty in American politics." New York University Review of Law and Social Change 18:711–728.

Schriver, Edward

1990   "The reluctant hangman: The state of Maine and capital punishment, 1820–1887." The New England Quarterly 63:271–287.

Topeka Capital-Journal

1993a   "Death penalty: Seen as dead issue at capitol." (January 7).

1993b   "Death walks among us." (July 30).

1994a   "Death penalty supported." (February 18).

1994b   "Finney testifies against death penalty." (February 19).

1994c   "Senate oks death bill." (March 2).

1994d   " 'I held the power of life and death'." (March 12).

U.S. Department of Justice, Federal Bureau of Investigation

1994   Crime in the United States, 1993. Washington, DC: U.S. Government Printing Office.

U.S. Bureau of the Census

1995   Statistical Abstract of the United States, 115th edition. Washington, D.C.: U.S. Government Printing Office.

Warr, Mark

1995   "Public opinion on crime and punishment." Public Opinion Quarterly 59(Summer):296–310.

Weed, Frank J.

1995   Certainty of Justice: Reform in the Crime Victim Movement. New York: Aldine De Gruyter.

Weisberg, Robert

1996   "The New York statute as cultural document: Seeking the morally optimal death penalty." Buffalo Law Review 44(Spring):283–302.

Wichita Eagle-Beacon

1976   "Foes of death penalty need 4 more votes." (March 12).

1977   "Kansas executions: Legislature will decide on return to gallows." (February 6).

1994a   "Inevitable? Death penalty picks up speed in Topeka." (January 16).

1994b   "A father tells why he wants death penalty." (January 26).

1994c   "House backs death penalty." (February 11).

1994d   "Panel oks death penalty compromise." (February 25).

1994e   "Death penalty in house today." (March 18).

1994f   "No consensus is reached on death penalty." (March 19).

1994g   "House members offered broader death penalty." (March 25).

1994h   "Schmidt crusade getting results." (March 27).

1994i   "House gives final push to death bill." (April 4).

1994j   "Schmidt crusade getting results." (April 9).

1994k   "Finney won't pick up pen, stop penalty." (April 22).

1994l   "Finney sticks to promise to permit death penalty." (April 23).

180   GALLIHER AND GALLIHER

Zimring, Franklin E.
  1996   "The wages of ambivalence: On the context and prospects of New York's death penalty." Buffalo Law Review 44(Spring):303–323.
Zimring, Franklin E., and Gordon Hawkins
  1986   Capital Punishment and the American Agenda. Cambridge: Cambridge University Press.

Legal Citations

Furman v. Georgia, 408 U.S. 238, 92, 2726 (U.S. Sup. Ct. 1972).
Gregg v. Georgia, 428 U.S. 153, 96, 2909 (U.S. Sup. Ct. 1976).
Kansas Statutes Annotated, 21-3439 (L. 1994, ch. 252).

A "COMMONSENSE" THEORY OF DETERRENCE AND THE "IDEOLOGY" OF SCIENCE: THE NEW YORK STATE DEATH PENALTY DEBATE

JAMES M. GALLIHER*

and

JOHN F. GALLIHER***+

Capital punishment is one of the most contentious public policy debates in the United States. While surviving since colonial times,[1] the debate has become especially heated since the U.S. Supreme Court decision in *Furman v. Georgia* in 1972.[2] In that decision, the Supreme Court outlawed executions as then practiced due to the arbitrary and capricious manner in which they had been administered.[3] Most states rushed to reinstate capital punishment statutes they hoped would pass constitutional review. In the equally historic decision of *Gregg v. Georgia* in 1976,[4] the Supreme Court cleared the way for the resumption of legal executions by approving death penalty statutes containing "guided discretion" provisions. Actual executions began again on January 17, 1977 after a ten-year hiatus with the execution of Gary Gilmore in Utah.[5]

The states that led the movement to restore capital punishment typically had long traditions of executions, especially those states of the former Confederacy.[6] Zimring and Hawkins argued that:

> [A] history of frequent executions . . . serves as a kind of precedent, reassuring political actors that their own participation is neither inhumane nor immoral . . . on the grounds that, historically, executions do not violate local community morality.[7]

---

*American Academy of Family Physicians, Department of Sociology, University of Missouri-Kansas City.

**Department of Sociology, University of Missouri-Columbia.

+Thanks are due to Hugo Adam Bedau, Alan Strathman, Lucille Salerno, Russell Geen, Fr. Fred Thayer, Gideon Sjoberg, Michael Radelet, Mary Jo Neitz, Herbert Haines, David Keys, Susanne Carter and James Acker for assistance with an earlier version of this paper. The authors are also indebted to Elaine Clark and other staff of the New York State Library for their assistance. An earlier version of this research was presented at the annual meetings of the American Society of Criminology in San Diego (CA), November 22, 1997.

[1] Herbert H. Haines, Against Capital Punishment: The Anti-Death Penalty Movement in America, 1972–1994 (1996); Herbert H. Haines, *Flawed Executions, the Anti-Death Penalty Movement, and the Politics of Capital Punishment*, 39 Soc. Problems 125–138 (1992).

[2] Furman v. Georgia, 408 U.S. 238 (1972).

[3] Charles L. Black, Jr., Capital Punishment: The Inevitability of Caprice and Mistake 19-20 (1974).

[4] Gregg v. Georgia 428 U.S. 153 (1976).

[5] *Gilmore is Executed After Stay is Upset; "Lets Do It!" He Said,* New York Times, Jan. 18, 1977, at 1.

[6] James W. Marquart, Sheldon Ekland-Olson, & Jonathan R. Sorensen, The Rope, The Chair, and the Needle: Capital Punishment in Texas, 1923–1990 x (1994).

[7] Franklin E. Zimring & Gordon Hawkins, Capital Punishment and the American Agenda 144 (1986).

Reprinted by special permission of Northwestern University School of Law, *The Journal of Criminal Law and Criminology.*

And, based on local experience, it wasn't only southern states that rushed to enact new death penalty laws. New York is a case in point. According to the Espy file on executions,[8] New York ranked second among American states in the number of legal executions prior to *Furman* with 1,130 executed between 1630 and 1963. Correspondingly, polls of New York state legislators in the 1980s and 1990s indicated that a majority supported capital punishment.[9] We will demonstrate in this Article that the New York State Senate and Assembly debated death penalty bills for nineteen consecutive years beginning in 1977.

Kansas is another American state having had a protracted death penalty debate. In the Kansas State Legislature, the death penalty was annually debated between 1975 and 1993. Capital punishment bills typically only passed both houses of the legislature when a death penalty opponent was governor who promised to veto all death penalty bills.[10] Some legislators apparently felt they could support death penalty initiatives only when sure of a gubernatorial veto.[11] In 1994 the legislature passed a death penalty bill during the term of a capital punishment opponent who, contrary to precedent, allowed the bill to become law without her signature.[12]

In New York from 1977 to 1995, we will show that during each of these nineteen legislative sessions, the New York Assembly and Senate debated death penalty bills and passed them, by large margins, only to have the bills vetoed by Democratic governors (Hugh Carey, 1975–1983 and Mario Cuomo, 1983–1994). During some sessions, the Senate was successful in overriding the governor's veto while the assembly's efforts always fell short by only a few votes. George Pataki, elected Governor in 1994, fulfilled a campaign promise when he signed a death penalty bill into law on March 7, 1995,[13] making New York the thirty-eighth and most recent state to do so.

I. STATEMENT OF THE PROBLEM

This research will consider the principal claims and counterclaims made by death penalty supporters and opponents, as well as document the manner in which these claims were advanced or refuted. The nineteen-year debate provides a natural laboratory that can assist our understanding of why the United States is the only Western industrialized democracy to retain capital punishment. As Zimring has observed: "The ongoing debate in New York was the most visible and sustained at any level of

[8]M.W. Espy & J.O. Smykla, Executions in the United States, 1608–1987 (1987), computer file.
[9]Timothy J. Flanagan, Pauline Gasdow Brennan, & Debra Cohen, Attitudes of New York Legislators Toward Crime and Criminal Justice: A report of the State Survey—1991 1 (1991); Timothy J. Flanagan & Edmund F. McGarrell, Attitudes of New York Legislators Toward Crime and Criminal Justice: A Report of the State Legislator Survey—1985, Working Paper 26 1 (1986).
[10]James M. Galliher & John F. Galliher, *"Déjà Vu All Over Again": The Recurring Life and Death of Capital Punishment Legislation in Kansas*, 44 Soc. Prob. 369, 373 (1997).
[11]*Id.*
[12]*Id.* at 379.
[13]New York State Assembly and Senate Records of Proceedings, 1977–1995, New York State Library, Albany.

government in the United States since 1980."[14] With a population of approximately eighteen million, New York is among the most populous of American states and its cities have the problems of urban decay, poverty, and crime found in other states.[15] Thus, there is no basis for suggesting that the underlying reasoning found in New York on capital punishment would not appear elsewhere in the United States.

II. COGNITIVE DISSONANCE THEORY AND THE "IDEOLOGY" OF SCIENCE

Just as social scientists construct theories to explain criminal behavior and conformity, such as cultural conflict, anomie, and social learning, so too do non-scientists. Hartjen presents the argument that human beings should be viewed as theorizers or "constructors of a commonsense reality."[16] He contends:

> [C]ommonsense actors are as fully engaged in reality construction as the scientist . . . That is, to study the apprehended realities of everyday actors—the results of *their* constructs—it is advantageous to treat these constructs as instances of theories, albeit commonsense ones.[17]

Swidler argues that while " 'ideology' is a highly articulated, self-conscious belief and ritual system, *aspiring* to offer a unified answer to problems of social action, . . . '[c]ommonsense' [refers to] the set of assumptions so unselfconscious as to seem a natural, transparent, undeniable part of the structure of the world."[18]

This paper will describe the underlying "commonsense" theory used by death penalty proponents. Lindblom and Cohen refer to commonsense thinking as "ordinary knowledge" which can be "highly fallible"[19] since it does not have its origins in social science research, but rather in speculation and casual observation, and is error prone due to "inferences based on small amounts of data."[20] The lay observer also believes that "punishment decreases [targeted behaviors since] people seek to maximize pleasure and minimize pain."[21]

Cognitive dissonance theory argues that people attempt to avoid inconsistency among their cognitions by selective perception.[22] Others have concluded: "It is unsurprising, therefore, that important social issues and policies generally prompt

---

[14]Franklin E. Zimring, *The Wages of Ambivalence: On the Context and Prospects of New York's Death Penalty*, 44 Buff. L. Rev. 303, 316 (1996).

[15]Bureau of the Census, U.S. Dep't of Commerce, Statistical Abstract of the United States (1990); Federal Bureau of Investigation, Crime in the United States, 1995 (1996).

[16]Clayton A. Hartjen, *Crime as Commonsense Theory*, 18 Criminology 435 (1981).

[17]*Id.* at 437.

[18]Ann Swidler, *Culture in Action: Symbols and Strategies*, 51 Amer. Soc. Rev. 271, 279 (1986) (emphasis added).

[19]Charles E. Lindblom & David K. Cohen, Usable Knowledge: Social Science and Social Problem Solving 12 (1979).

[20]Richard Nisbett & Lee Ross, Human Inference: Strategies and Shortcomings of Social Judgment 181 (1980).

[21]*Id.* at 30.

[22]Susan T. Fiske & Shelley E. Taylor, Social Cognition 360 (1984).

sharp disagreements, even among highly concerned and intelligent citizens, and thus disagreements often survive strenuous attempts at resolution through discussion and persuasion" because "people tend to interpret subsequent evidence so as to maintain their initial beliefs."[23] For example, research has found that subjects' attitudes toward the death penalty determine how evidence on the effectiveness of the death penalty as a deterrent is interpreted.[24] Still, it is true that "[p]eople place a premium on being rational."[25]

To make sense of these apparent contradictions between bias and rationality, research by Lord, Ross and Lepper used both those opposed to, and those in favor of, capital punishment.[26] Subjects were presented with information from studies demonstrating a deterrent effect on the death penalty and other studies showing the opposite. Subjects only remembered the limitations and critiques of research that contradicted their original beliefs, and thus the attitudes of the two groups became more polarized. The authors concluded that "social scientists cannot expect rationality, enlightenment, and consensus about policy to emerge from their attempts to 'furnish' objective data."[27]

We will show how protracted legislative debate in New York survived "strenuous attempts at resolution" in spite of the presentation of "objective data" from a host of scientific studies. Social science has arrived at different conclusions than lay opinion and thus is cast into the role of "ideology," irrespective of its scholarly merit. This Article will address the commonsense "ordinary knowledge" of the deterrent effect of capital punishment on homicides advanced by New York legislators, by far the most frequent justification for reinstatement of capital punishment in these legislative debates (Table 1). Other arguments included whether capital punishment is racist in application, and error prone yet impossible to rectify, each accounting for less than half of the debates about deterrence. Public opinion on capital punishment, financial costs of executions, and the role of retribution were mentioned only infrequently and debate on these issues was never really joined. We will see that at times speakers discussing deterrence appeared to refer to incapacitation of those executed (specific deterrence), sometimes to the prevention of crime among other potential offenders (general deterrence) and sometimes to both incapacitation and deterrence.

The statements of legislators we will study are undoubtedly a combination of their personal beliefs and what they feel they must say to represent the views of their constituents. In any case, their utterances give some cross-section of views of capital punishment in New York. For their part, social scientists have also expressed considerable interest in deterrence theory. After a slow start in the 1950s and early to mid-1960s deterrence research began a period of popularity in the late 1960s and

---

[23]Charles G. Lord, Lee Ross & Mark R. Lepper, *Biased Assimilation and Attitude Polarization: The Effects of Prior Theories on Subsequently Considered Evidence,* 37 J. Personality & Soc. Psych. 2098–109 (1979).
[24]*See* Nisbett & Ross, *supra* note 17.
[25]Thomas Gilovich, How We Know What Isn't So: The Fallibility of Human Reason in Everyday Life 53 (1991).
[26]*See* Lord, Ross & Lepper, *supra* note 20, at 2098–109.
[27]*Id.* at 2108.

TABLE 1

Number of Times Issues Appear in the New York Legislative Debate on Capital Punishment, 1977–1995*

Year	Deterrence	Racism	Innocence
1977	79	23	16
1978	107	37	32
1979	55	14	10
1980	70	14	10
1981	7	7	12
1982	21	8	10
1983	12	3	2
1984	7	0	5
1985	25	17	10
1986	5	7	4
1987	22	6	6
1988	8	7	6
1989	51	9	8
1990	19	11	10
1991	27	17	3
1992	21	19	7
1993	15	6	9
1994	17	27	22
1995	22	33	22
	590	265	204

*Figures reflect each time an issue was raised, not length of debate.

throughout the 1970s.[28] Between 1968 and 1979 there was an average of eight studies published per year in criminology, law, and sociology journals, compared to a total of only seven articles during the previous seventeen years.[29] Although most of the studies found no evidence of deterrence (especially in the case of capital punishment), the spate of articles demonstrated that scholars recognized this as a legitimate and important area of study. The most frequently cited studies in this body of research included an article by Ehrlich, often mentioned by death penalty proponents in the New York state legislature, emphasizing his conclusion that "an additional execution per year . . . may have resulted, on average, in 7 or 8 fewer murders."[30]

III. METHODS AND DATA

The research in this Article makes use of the verbatim text recorded in the New York assembly and senate. New York is one of the few states that transcribes all debates on the floors of both houses. While Kansas also experienced a long legislative

---

[28]Albert DiChiara & John F. Galliher, *Thirty Years of Deterrence Research: Characteristics, Causes and Consequences*, 8 Contemp. Crises 247 (1984).
[29]*Id.*
[30]Isaac Ehrlich, *The Deterrent Effect of Capital Punishment: A Question of Life and Death*, 65 Am. Econ. Rev. 397, 414 (1975).

debate on the death penalty,[31] it did not record the debate. There the record debate was available only from secondary sources, primarily the local newspapers, such as the Topeka Capital-Journal and the Wichita Eagle-Beacon. The New York legislative debate in the assembly and the senate analyzed here includes nineteen consecutive years (1977–1995). Each chamber's annual death penalty debate varied from several hours to over two days, followed by a vote. The process of abstracting and analyzing these archival materials for the purposes of this Article consisted of four steps. First, each year's debate was read for assertions related to the death penalty as a deterrent. Each specific passage where deterrence was mentioned was highlighted in the text. Second, the task of identifying and highlighting such texts was repeated so that relevant text would not be overlooked. Third, a computer file was created in which the identified deterrence text was copied verbatim, including the speaker's name, the date, and page number in the record.

Once a computer file was created, containing hundreds of deterrence quotes, each quote was classified into categories which appeared to exhaust the content of the deterrence arguments. The questions addressed in the text included: (1) What was said or implied about deterrence by supporters and by opponents of the death penalty? (2) What was the nature of the evidence used to support these claims? (3) How were these claims and evidence presented?; And, (4) How was this evidence interpreted and evaluated by supporters and opponents? (A similar procedure was followed for the issues of racism and innocence in death penalty administration.)

IV. BACKGROUND TO POST-*FURMAN* DEATH PENALTY DEBATE

Executions increased dramatically in New York after introduction of the electric chair in 1890, with 674 persons electrocuted between 1900 and 1963.[32] These executions peaked in the 1930s, with a drastic reduction after the 1940s.[33] The reduced use of the death penalty was accompanied by legislative efforts to abolish it altogether.[34] Between 1950 and 1963, there was at least one abolition bill introduced in the Legislature in every session. On July 1, 1963, New York became the last state in the country to abolish mandatory death for murder, although it remained mandatory for treason.[35] In 1965, the Temporary Commission on Revision of the Penal Law and Criminal Code (the Bartlett Commission) recommended that the death penalty be abolished in the state.[36] The legislature enacted a new statute, effective June 1, 1965, which "so narrowed the class of capital offenses that *de facto* abolition of capital punishment had almost been accomplished."[37] The sanction remained a possible pun-

---

[31]*See* Galliher & Galliher, *supra* note 10, at 369–85.

[32]William J. Bowers, Legal Homicide: Death as Punishment in America, 1864–1982, 117 (1984); Michael Lumer and Nancy Tenney, *The Death Penalty in New York: An Historical Perspective,* 4 J. L. & Pol. 81, 98 (1995).

[33]*Id.*

[34]James R. Acker, *New York's Proposed Death Penalty Legislation: Constitutional and Policy Perspectives,* 54 Alb. L. Rev. 522. (1990).

[35]*Id.* 522–523.

[36]*Id.* 524.

[37]*Id.* 525.

ishment for "deliberate and premeditated" murder of an on-duty police officer or a murder committed by the offender when either serving a life prison sentence or when in the process of escape from serving a life prison sentence.[38]

In spite of the narrow coverage of New York's death penalty statute, the New York Court of Appeals ruled in the 1973 *People v. Fitzpatrick* case that the state's death penalty statute allowed too much jury discretion.[39] In response, the New York Legislature enacted a mandatory death penalty statute in 1974 for the intentional killing of a police officer, a correctional officer, or a killing committed by a life-term inmate, a statute very similar to the state's 1965 discretionary death penalty law.[40] In 1976, the U.S. Supreme Court rejected mandatory death penalty statutes for murder and approved the "guided discretion" capital punishment statutes of Georgia, Texas, and Florida.[41] Such was the legal situation when the state legislature met in January, 1977 to consider once again a bill to reinstate the death penalty.

By the mid-1970s, when the New York Legislature began to debate reinstatement of a death penalty, the number and rate of homicides had risen dramatically (Table 2). In 1965, there were 833 cases reported and an increase to a rate of 4.6 (per 100,000 state inhabitants). At its peak, the number increased over 210% to 2605 in 1990. In 1991, homicides began to decrease in New York and throughout the United States. By 1995, when reinstatement occurred, New York homicides had declined 40% compared to their 1990 level, but were still 86% higher than in 1965.

V. PRESENTING THE DETERRENCE ARGUMENT IN SUPPORT OF CAPITAL PUNISHMENT

From the opening of the 1977 legislative session to enactment of a capital punishment law in 1995, deterrence was the principal issue driving the death penalty debate. Early on, Assemblyman Mega argued: "Deterrence, we spoke about whether or not capital punishment is a deterrent and the Supreme Court mentioned that the question of deterrence is something that each individual state should consider when they consider a capital punishment bill."[42] Similarly, the bill's annual senate sponsor, Senator Volker cautioned: "We are going to get into all sorts of arguments. . . . We are debating several issues. One is certainly the issue of the death penalty itself, and the issue of it as a deterrent."[43] Assemblyman Hevesi insisted: "The deterrent effect. That is the main argument for the advocates of the death penalty and if it is not, ladies and gentlemen, say so on this floor."[44] Senator Bernstein also asserted: "I've been through [the debate] like everybody else for years and years. We hear the same things, the

---

[38]*Id.* 525.

[39]People v. Fitzpatrick, 346 N.Y.S.2d 793 (N.Y. 1973).

[40]Acker, *supra* note 34 at 531.

[41]Jurek v. Texas 428 U.S. 262 (1976); Profitt v. Florida, 428 U.S. 242 (1976); Gregg v. Georgia 428 U.S. 153 (1976).

[42]Assemblyman Mega, New York State Assembly Debate, AB8815, 1977, 7632.

[43]Senator Volker, New York State Senate Debate, SB 7250, 1978, 1562.

[44]Assemblyman Hevesi, New York State Assembly Debate, AB 1070, 1989, 76.

TABLE 2

*Number and Rate of Homicides in New York
and the United States, 1965–1995**

Year	New York Number	New York Rate[+]	U.S. Rate[+]	Year	New York Number	New York Rate[+]	U.S. Rate[+]
1965	833	4.6	5.1	1981	2166	12.3	9.8
1966	879	4.8	5.6	1982	2013	11.4	9.1
1967	993	5.4	6.1	1983	1958	1.1	8.3
1968	1180	6.5	6.8	1984	1786	0.1	7.9
1969	1320	7.2	7.2	1985	1683	9.5	7.9
1970	1493	7.9	7.8	1986	1907	10.7	8.6
1971	1817	9.9	8.5	1987	2016	11.3	8.3
1972	2020	11.0	8.9	1988	2244	12.5	8.4
1973	2034	11.1	9.3	1989	2246	12.5	8.7
1974	1913	10.6	9.7	1990	2605	14.5	9.4
1975	1996	11.0	9.6	1991	2571	14.2	9.8
1976	1969	10.9	8.8	1992	2397	13.2	9.3
1977	1919	10.7	8.8	1993	2420	13.3	9.5
1978	1820	10.3	9.0	1994	2016	11.1	9.0
1979	2092	11.9	9.7	1995	1550	8.5	8.2
1980	2228	12.7	10.2				

*Source: F.B.I. Uniform Crime Reports 1965–1995.
+Rate per 100,000 inhabitants

same arguments. What is the purpose of the proposed death penalty if not as a deterrent?"[45] Assemblyman Ortloff summarized the situation: "It has been said here, as it is every year, that the issue in this matter is whether capital punishment deters."[46] Even toward the end of the debates, the question remained: "Is this [death penalty] a deterrent? You know that's the great question of our day."[47]

A. *Deterrence Works: Dead Men Don't Commit Crimes*

Death penalty proponents buttressed their deterrence arguments by including the incapacitation of convicted offenders. According to Assemblyman Gromack: "[T]oo often we have seen convicted murderers get out for good behavior only to kill and murder again."[48] Estimates were provided by Assemblyman Robach: "I think that number [of recidivist murderers] is at least 200 a year across this state, if not higher,"[49] and also by Assemblyman Kauffman: "Do you know that 850 people last year who were convicted of murder and got out of jail committed murder again? . . . But, I tell you, if you had the death penalty, 850 people would not have

---

[45]Senator Bernstein, New York State Senate Debate, SB 600, 1989, 424.
[46]Assemblyman Ortloff, New York State Assembly Debate, AB 8960, 1990, 105.
[47]Assemblyman Singer, New York State Assembly Debate, AB 360, 1993, 139.
[48]Assemblyman Gromack, New York State Assembly Debate, AB 305, 1991, 95.
[49]Assemblyman Robach, New York State Assembly Debate, AB 9028, 1994, 37.

been out to kill again."[50] When asking what the punishment other than capital punishment should be given to deter incarcerated murders from killing again, Assemblyman Saland answered: "What are we going to do when he kills the next time? Take away his conjugal visits? That is really good. Maybe we can take away his library privileges, or you know what, tell him he cannot pump iron two hours a day."[51]

While the imposition of the death penalty would result in no future crimes being committed by the person executed, this represents the incapacitative effect rather than the deterrent effect of capital punishment.[52] Assemblyman Vitaliano referred to this as the "incapacitative deterrent" effect.[53] Assemblyman Skidman claimed: "[A]ll I know is that if that murderer is given the death penalty, he will murder never again, and that is deterrent enough for me."[54] Senator Farley agreed that "there's [deterrence] studies on both sides, but . . . it would be a deterrent to that person that has killed several times. He won't kill again."[55] And Assemblyman Tedisco summarized the argument:

> I suggest to you that it is irrefutably a deterrent. . . . And for all those individuals who have been given the death penalty and are no longer in existence, you cannot stand up and tell me they will murder again. They will not only never murder again, they will never steal your car or rape your wife or your daughter.[56]

Yet Bedau has noted that it is impossible to measure incapacitation since most people convicted of homicide do not kill again, thus making it impossible to know which convicted murders will become recidivists.[57] Whatever the empirical merits of death penalty proponents' position, the confluence of incapacitation and deterrence appears to have made their commitment to deterrence much stronger.

B. Increased Homicides and Perceived Need for Capital Punishment

An undisputed fact that death penalty proponents seized on throughout the debate was that homicides in the state had increased dramatically since the mid-1960s—at about the same time when executions ceased in New York. In opening the 1977 debate, the bill's lower house sponsor, Assemblyman Graber argued: "I am not saying the only reason for this increase [in homicides] was because the death penalty has declined . . . [but it is true that] homicides have increased at the same time that capital punishment has declined."[58] Senator Knorr was more explicit:

[50]Assemblyman Kauffman, New York State Assembly Debate, AB 4843, 1995, 158.
[51]Assemblyman Saland, New York State Assembly Debate, AB 1070, 1989, 137.
[52]Jack P. Gibbs, Crime, Punishment, and Deterrence 22 (1975).
[53]Assemblyman Vitaliano, New York State Assembly Debate, AB 4843, 1995, 77.
[54]Assemblyman Skidman, New York State Assembly Debate, AB 9028, 1994, 94–95.
[55]Senator Farley, New York State Senate Debate, SB 6600, 1990, 522.
[56]Assemblyman Tedisco, New York State Assembly Debate, AB 9028, 1994, 77.
[57]Hugo Adam Bedau, The Controversy over Deterrence and Incapacitation, in The Death Penalty in America: Current Controversies 127–34 (Hugo Adam Bedau ed., 1997).
[58]Assemblyman Graber, New York State Assembly Debate, AB 8815, 1977, 7586.

We all know in 1965 they abolished capital punishment. Prior to the abolishment . . . there [were] . . . approximately 400 innocent victims of murder. But as soon as the capital punishment was abolished within a period of three years the numbers of innocent victims of murder arose to around 1500 per year.[59]

Senator Volker calculated that "since 1965, 41,667 people have been murdered as opposed to the previous 23 years, when only 11,513 were murdered. And last year we set a record."[60] Later, he said, "more people have been murdered on the streets of New York than were killed in the entire Vietnam War."[61] Assemblyman George Pataki voiced this same concern: "I believe the cause and effect is clear: the absence of a death penalty has led to a massive increase in the instances of rational murder."[62] And, the chief sponsor of death penalty legislation in the assembly asserted: "I would not be proposing this [death penalty] bill, incidentally, if our murder rate was as low as it was in [other] nations."[63] These arguments clearly demonstrate that existing biases dictate how co-variation is interpreted.

C. Predicted Effectiveness of a Reinstated Death Penalty

If the premise was true that the absence of a death penalty resulted in increased homicides, according to Senator Volker, it was reasonable to conclude that reinstatement of the death penalty would result in decreased homicides: "If we had the death penalty in this state, we would not have as much murder."[64] Senator Knorr argued: "I am voting here today to save the lives of several hundred innocent victims annually in the near future."[65] Assemblyman Friedman asserted: "[C]apital punishment would deter a significant part of them and the percentages would be greater than simply saving 10 percent, it would be a very large percentage of the intentional killings."[66] And Assemblyman Hickey echoed this sentiment: "I agree that the restitution of the death penalty will significantly drive down the murder rate in this state."[67] Assemblyman Seminerio even referred to reducing all criminal activity: "I am begging you to vote for the death penalty if you want to stop crime."[68] All of these comments reflect the overconfidence Nisbett and Ross say is typical of the lay observer.[69] All the quotes in this subsection could be construed as referring to the incapacitative powers of capital punishment, as well as deterrence.

While supporters of capital punishment would often refer to the deterrence argument in relationship to previous and future homicides, there was little mention

---

[59]Senator Knorr, New York State Senate Debate, SB 7250, 1978, 4258.
[60]Senator Volker, New York State Senate Debate, SB 6600, 1990, 462.
[61]Id. at 1183.
[62]Assemblyman Pataki, New York State Assembly Debate, AB 8657, 1988, 193.
[63]Assemblyman Graber, New York State Assembly Debate, AB 1070, 1989, 62.
[64]Senator Volker, New York State Senate Debate, SB 4144, 1979, 3731–32.
[65]Senator Knorr, New York State Senate Debate, SB 7250, 1978, 4260.
[66]Assemblyman Friedman, New York State Assembly Debate, AB 8657, 1988, 83.
[67]Assemblyman Hickey, New York State Assembly Debate, AB 9028, 1994, 111.
[68]Assemblyman Seminerio, New York State Assembly Debate, AB 8431, 1980, 133.
[69]See Nisbett & Ross, supra note 17.

of research supporting the death penalty as a deterrent. The notable exception was periodic reference to Ehrlich's work:[70] "[Professor Ehrlich] offered his evidence that the death penalty has a . . . remarkable deterrent effect. I have since encountered no valid study to rebut his position."[71] This limited reliance on scientific literature was not an oversight by death penalty supporters; there simply was very little published research to support the death penalty as a deterrent. Clearly, these attitudes toward capital punishment influence how evidence of the deterrent effect of capital punishment is interpreted.

VI. THE OPPOSITION'S CHALLENGE TO THE DETERRENCE ARGUMENT

Opponents could not deny that homicides in the state had increased since *de facto* abolition of the death penalty in 1965. Nonetheless, they did not accept this fact as evidence of the deterrent effect of capital punishment. For example, Senator Bernstein argued: "You have not established in your argument that the abolition of the death penalty in 1965 is the *causal factor* for the increase in homicides. . . . The increase is national, and . . . caused not by the abolition of the death penalty [in New York]."[72] Instead, the opponents argued that the burden of proof in proving the deterrent value of capital punishment is "on those who are for it."[73] The opponents insisted on scientific research evidence. Senator Goodman asked: "Who says that the death penalty deters? Where is the evidence? Produce it forthwith. Now is the time we need it to evaluate this measure."[74] And, Senator Leichter lamented: "I don't think that the absence of proof can be overcome by parroting over and over again the phrase 'The death penalty will be a deterrence.' . . . All we have is the claim, we don't have the proof."[75]

If death penalty supporters seldom relied on scientific studies, the opposition devoted most of its attention to the results of social science research to argue that the death penalty in New York would not be a deterrent to homicide. Early in the annual debates, Assemblyman McCabe claimed: "[A]s some people have already said, the death penalty is a deterrent to the crime of murder, I have searched all the literature I could find, and I can find no evidence that proves that such is the case. . . . [T]he deterrent argument appears to be without merit."[76] Believing that death penalty opponents had met their responsibility in presenting research evidence against deterrence, Assemblyman Stringer asked rhetorically: "So, how many studies and statistics do you need. . . . to figure out that as far as deterrence goes, the death penalty is an

---

[70]*See generally* Ehrlich, *supra* note 26, at 397–417 (where each legal execution was alleged to reduce homicides several-fold); Isaac Ehrlich, *Capital Punishment and Deterrence: Some Further Thoughts and Additional Evidence*, 85 J. Pol. Econ. 741, 741–88 (1977).

[71]Assemblyman Walsh, New York State Assembly Debate, AB 8431, 1980, 146.

[72]Senator Bernstein, New York State Senate Debate, SB 6600, 1990, 512 (emphasis added).

[73]Assemblyman Ryan, New York State Assembly Debate, AB 8815, 1977, 8920.

[74]Senator Goodman, New York State Senate Debate, SB 7250, 1978, 1600.

[75]Senator Leichter, New York State Senate Debate, SB 7250, 1978, 4068.

[76]Assemblyman McCabe, New York State Assembly Debate, AB 8815, 1977, 8804.

abysmal failure?"[77] And, Assemblyman Hevesi concluded: "So, you have evidence, you have citations, you have academic studies and you have numbers."[78]

Some death penalty opponents argued that the penalty actually had a "brutalizing" effect resulting in increased homicides. Such claims were supported by the research of Bowers and Pierce which found that in New York, from 1907–1963, approximately two additional homicides occurred the year after an execution.[79] Possibly drawing on this study, Senator Nolan explained: "Executions spread violence by signaling that it is acceptable to kill."[80]

In addition to this criticism, in 1994 Senator Leichter noted a change in local crime rates: "In fact, in New York State in the last two years, the homicide rate has gone down. So, so much for that argument."[81] A year later, Senator Gold observed the same trend: "[I]n the *New York Post* today . . . [it was reported] here that from last year to this year, the murder rate . . . is down 36 percent."[82] By this time, however, the state had a new pro-death penalty governor (George Pataki) and these patterns didn't matter. Caught up in the continuing and strident debate, death penalty opponents argued that no evidence existed to support capital punishment as a possible deterrent. It would have been more precise for them to have said that there is little scientific evidence that capital punishment is a more effective deterrent than long-term imprisonment.

VII. DEFENDING THE DETERRENCE ARGUMENT AGAINST CHALLENGES

Given the evidence presented against the deterrent effect of the death penalty, proponents reacted by challenging the research literature. Their response was three-fold: (1) they questioned the objectivity and honesty of deterrence researchers and, thus, the validity and relevance of the deterrence literature; (2) they presented other non-scientific evidence of deterrence; and (3) they argued that the burden of proof rested with the opposition to disprove deterrence.

A. The Reported Research Evidence Is Flawed

From the beginning, death-penalty supporters questioned the validity and relevance of published research challenging the deterrence argument. Not only did the research fly in the face of their "commonsense" theories of crime and punishment, but death penalty proponents also questioned the motives and qualifications of social science researchers. Senator Volker argued: "Almost all of the deterrence studies that have found that the death penalty has no deterrence [value were] done by people who started out opposing the death penalty and wanted to find out how in effect they could

---

[77]Assemblyman Stringer, New York State Assembly Debate, AB 4843, 1995, 282.
[78]Assemblyman Hevesi, New York State Assembly Debate, AB 1070, 1989, 84.
[79]William J. Bowers & Glenn L. Pierce, *Deterrence or Brutalization: What Is the Effect of Executions?* 26 Crime & Delinq. 453, 473 (1980).
[80]Senator Nolan, New York State Senate Debate, SB 6600, 1990, 473.
[81]Senator Leichter, New York State Senate Debate, SB 6350, 1994, 1021.
[82]Senator Gold, New York State Senate Debate, SB 2850, 1995, 1961.

find out how to oppose it through the deterrence argument."[83] Senator Ruiz agreed: "[A]ll the so-called studies that have been done by the so-called liberal experts [claim] that there is really no deterrence if there's a death penalty."[84] Assemblyman Saland remarked: "I heard a lot of talk of studies. . . . These studies basically are the work of criminologists, of social scientists; and why they are called scientists, I don't know."[85] This same Assemblyman later observed: "None of your social scientists, and I use the word rather loosely, none of them have the ability to measure this type of conduct."[86] In referring to this academic research, Senator Volker concluded: "We have looked at all the so-called deterrence studies, and what we determined is they are all phonies."[87]

Assemblyman Graber also asserted: "I would surmise that . . . we are going to hear about statistical studies that seem to show capital punishment is not a deterrent. . . . I would like to indicate I am not impressed by [the] Sellin [study]."[88] The debate also was punctuated with frequent negative characterizations of deterrence research and empirical studies. Assemblyman Nicolosi claimed: "[W]e can play the statistics game . . . the statistics are unclear, sure they are. Because figures don't lie, but liars figure."[89] And Assemblyman Frisa observed: "We have heard a lot of arguments in opposition to this measure. Most of them have tended to rely on statistics and studies and logic that is not very logical and sense that is not very common."[90] Senator Volker sarcastically added:

> [S]o the anti-death penalty people that did those wonderful studies back in the '60s, after they decided that they were opposed to the death penalty, they did studies to prove why they were right . . . it's unbelievable. . . . [Father] Hessburgh . . . now president of Notre Dame, the celebrated anti-death penalty opponent, did a study which I think a third grader could probably tear apart on the issue of deterrence.[91]

The next year, he continued, saying that: "[T]here are some people in this country who are so opposed to things that they will manufacture facts. . . ." Then, referring to the legislative committee testimony of Professors Hugo Bedau and Michael Radelet, Volker added, "they manufactured facts and, if they did it here, I'm sure they did it in other places across this country."[92]

As to a possible brutalization effect documented in the research literature, this was even harder for death penalty proponents to consider seriously. Assemblyman Van-Varnick remarked: "I reject that possibility [that one more person would be murdered

---

[83]Senator Volker, New York State Senate Debate, SB 7250, 1978, 4040.

[84]Senator Ruiz, New York State Senate Debate, SB 7600, 1982, 2470.

[85]Assemblyman Saland, New York State Assembly Debate, AB 9379, 1982, 7019.

[86]*Id.*, SB 7040, 1986, 59.

[87]Senator Volker, New York State Senate Debate, SB 4414, 1979, 3698.

[88]Assemblyman Graber, New York State Assembly Debate, AB 12, 1979, 174–75; Thorsten Sellin, The Death Penalty 135 (1959).

[89]Assemblyman Nicolosi, New York State Assembly Debate, AB 8815, 1977, 8762–8763.

[90]Assemblyman Frisa, New York State Assembly Debate, AB 8657, 1988, 181.

[91]Senator Volker, New York State Senate Debate, SB 6600, 1990, 457–458.

[92]*Id.*, SB 200, 1991, 1290.

due to the death penalty and its brutalization effect]."[93] And Assemblyman Proskin claimed that the deterrent effect was not inconsistent with increasing murder rates: "The figures shown to us that . . . where there is a[n] execution, that the rate of killings may rise. That doesn't say that the death penalty is not a deterrent."[94] Assemblyman Friedman explained: "[P]erhaps the murder rate in those states [with the death penalty] would be twice what it is today if they didn't have capital punishment."[95]

Thus, the reported research and empirical evidence presented by death penalty opponents showing either no measurable deterrent effect of capital punishment or a "brutalization effect" were simply dismissed. Assemblyman Friedman stated: "[C]apital punishment is a deterrent, there is no question about it, and the findings of any studies notwithstanding."[96] A similar view was presented by Assemblyman Kremer: "I don't work with charts . . . I am in the real world. . . ."[97] This was reiterated by Assemblyman Healey: "Don't give me statistics . . . what we are living [with] in New York State is a condition that is out of control."[98]

Others suggested sardonically that if severe punishments did not deter, then the criminal sanctions needed revision—to make them *less* severe. Assemblyman Friedman argued: "[A] compilation of statistics and charts that are aimed at proving that a more severe penalty does not result in less crime. . . . I [suppose] what he is really saying is that the less severe the penalty the less crime we will have."[99] And Assemblyman Tedisco then concluded:

> The logical conclusion tells me that when those states go to a death penalty, they seem to increase the amount of murders. . . . So, the logic to that is we take them [the murderers] to dinner, buy them a drink, we treat them nice and say, "Don't do it anymore," and that will solve all the problems.[100]

This sarcasm reflects both a strong belief in punishment and an inability to alter opinions based on disconfirming evidence. Politicizing the research of social scientists makes this intransigence possible.

In the end, there would be little agreement on any of these issues by the contending parties—one's position on deterrence and the death penalty were typically one and the same. As Senator Eckert remarked to a death penalty foe: "[Y]ou are not opposed to capital punishment because you don't think it's a deterrent. You don't think it's a deterrent because you're opposed to it."[101] The same could be said of those in favor of the sanction. This theme was repeated by Senator Ohrenstein: "I

[93]Assemblyman VanVarnick, New York State Assembly Debate, AB 9031, 1992, 162.
[94]Assemblyman Proskin, New York State Assembly Debate, AB 1039, 1987, 150.
[95]Assemblyman Friedman, New York State Assembly Debate, AB 9031, 1992, 142.
[96]*Id.*, AB 12, 1979, 205.
[97]Assemblyman Kremer, New York State Assembly Debate, AB 8657, 1988, 111.
[98]Assemblyman Healey, New York State Assembly Debate, AB 8657, 1988, 124.
[99]Assemblyman Friedman, New York State Assembly Debate, AB 8657, 1988, 72–73.
[100]Assemblyman Tedisco, New York State Assembly Debate, AB 8657, 1988, 132.
[101]Senator Eckert, New York State Senate Debate, SB 7100, 1980, 87–88.

think . . . that nobody is going to convince anyone on either side as to whether capital punishment deters or doesn't deter."[102]

B. Other Evidence in Support of Deterrence

While proponents could advance little scientific research in support of their assertions of a deterrent effect of capital punishment, they did rely on other more personal and direct forms of evidence. Assemblyman Greenberg injected this:

> It is true I haven't any statistics . . . in fact, I doubt if anything I say can be documented, but I offer you the benefit of the instinct and knowledge I have acquired while dealing with the criminal element. . . . Instinct and experience tells me the threat of execution is a deterrent to murder.[103]

This position was also presented by Assemblyman Kisor: "I would like to speak in favor of this bill, and I don't speak from some academic study. . . . I speak from 25 years of experience with the New York State police."[104] Senator Ruiz referred to his constituents:

> I think it [the death penalty] truly is a deterrent and it's not because I've made this determination by myself. It's because I've walked my district, I've talked to hundreds of . . . people in my district and they tell me, 99 percent of them, that if there is a death penalty they would . . . think twice before they killed anyone. . . .[105]

Assemblyman Smoler mentioned other evidence: "I want to cite, finally, the experts. The experts are killers who are under a death sentence and being marched before the firing squad, and they say, 'There is only one way to stop added killings, and that is to have capital punishment.' "[106] In a similar fashion, Davis has concluded that since death is generally the most feared punishment, commonsense tells us that it must be the most effective deterrent.[107] The comments in this Section reflect the lay person's reliance on a small number of cases, a belief in punishment, reliance on myth, and considerable overconfidence.

C. Burden of Proof: Show that Sanctions Don't Deter

Death penalty proponents argued that the deterrence provided by the death penalty was no different from deterrence provided by other legal sanctions. Senator Eckert claimed early in the debate: "[T]he argument that we cannot conclusively prove that capital punishment deters begs the question. All of our law is based on the presumption that there is a relationship between the penalty imposed and the likelihood of the

---

[102]Senator Ohrenstein, New York State Senate Debate, SB 7100, 1980, 157.
[103]Assemblyman Greenberg, New York State Assembly Debate, AB 8815, 1977, 8800–8801.
[104]Assemblyman Kisor, New York State Assembly Debate, AB 12, 1979, 261.
[105]Senator Ruiz, New York State Senate Debate, SB 4414, 1979, 3755.
[106]Assemblyman Smoler, New York State Assembly Debate, AB 8431, 1980, 150.
[107]Michael Davis, *Justice in the Shadow of Death: Rethinking Capital and Lesser Punishments* 13–14 (1996).

occurrence of crime."[108] And given this underlying principle upon which American corrections is based, Assemblyman Vitaliano asserted:

> I submit the burden is on the opponents to establish the exception, not on us to prove the rule . . . [I]t is on the opponents to establish the deviation from the norm, the deviation from the bedrock principles which undergird our criminal justice system and the common sense understanding of the desire to avoid death.[109]

Capital punishment opponents have left themselves vulnerable to such criticism because these "abolitionists look like fools if they insist (as they often do) that 'the death penalty is no deterrent to murder' since this flies in the face of what passes for common sense."[110]

Assemblyman Mega testified: "My belief is [that] nothing is feared more than death, and I believe it is a deterrent. . . ."[111] Assemblyman Fremming concurred: "It simply defies all common sense and my knowledge of human nature to argue that a penalty of death does not act as a deterrent."[112] Senator Maltese concluded that: "[C]ommon sense and the fact that just about every responsible law enforcement group has come out in favor of the death penalty indicates that it is a deterrent."[113] Assemblyman Solomon shared this conviction: "There is no question in your minds, and there is no question in mine that this is a deterrent."[114] Senator Bloom concluded: "[T]here is no more effective deterrent than the condemning to death for taking the life of another fellow citizen."[115] And finally, Assemblyman Wemple stated his belief in the deterrent effect of a capital-punishment law even if never used, because of the message it sends to potential offenders: "I think the death penalty is a deterrent. Whether it's ever used or not, it's a deterrent because it will be on the books of the State of New York."[116] Only in this last instance is it clear that the speaker was referring to deterrence as opposed to incapacitation. Once again, we see an inability for lay observers to change their minds when confronted with disconfirming information.

VIII. CONCLUSION: LEGISLATIVE DEBATE ON DEATH PENALTY AND DETERRENCE

At the end of the debates, very few minds had been changed regarding the deterrent effect of capital punishment. Assemblyman Behan lamented: "I feel like I've been here 2,000 years debating this bill . . . you're not going to change my mind at

---

[108]Senator Eckert, New York State Senate Debate, SB 7100, 1980, 2734.

[109]Assemblyman Vitaliano, New York State Assembly Debate, AB 4843, 1995, 76–78.

[110]Bedau, *supra* note 57, at 129.

[111]Assemblyman Mega, New York State Assembly Debate, AB 9421, 1978, 2076.

[112]Assemblyman Fremming, New York State Assembly Debate, AB 9421, 1978, 2109.

[113]Senator Maltese, New York State Senate Debate, SB 200, 1991, 1199.

[114]Assemblyman Solomon, New York State Assembly Debate, AB 9421, 1978, 2242.

[115]Senator Bloom, New York State Senate Debate, SB 7250, 1978, 4051.

[116]Assemblyman Wemple, New York State Assembly Debate, AB 12, 1979, 225.

all. I haven't even changed my socks since Christmas. I'm certainly not going to change my vote on this bill from sixteen years ago."[117]

We have demonstrated that a commonsense theory of capital punishment is strongly and widely held, just as Nisbett and Ross claimed, even though it is based on small amounts of empirical observation, as well as unreliable and idiosyncratic sources, leading to capricious inferences about the control of human behavior.[118] We have also shown that "[m]istrust of the criminal justice process is inherent in public advocacy for punitiveness. It is reflected in a cultural common sense that holds that courts do not punish severely or effectively enough, that prisons release incarcerated offenders 'far too soon.'"[119]

Even though the preponderance of published research did not support the deterrence argument, it was often assumed to have been conducted by liberal social scientists opposed to capital punishment, and thus the published evidence could be dismissed as invalid, inconclusive, or ideological. Some proponents of capital punishment shared a disdain or even contempt for social scientists and criminologists, much like that displayed by a conservative newspaper columnist:

> Unlike the victimized, our Advanced Thinkers argue that the problem isn't crime, but the jail [or punishment]. The trouble . . . isn't the criminals, but that too many are being locked up. To borrow a line from George Orwell, you have to be an intellectual to believe that sort of thing; ordinary folks have too much sense.[120]

The same skepticism was found regarding evidence of the brutalization effect of the death penalty; it was contrary to the claims advanced by proponents of deterrence, counterintuitive, and based on suspect evidence. In its place, other published research[121] or non-statistical evidence in the form of "expert" testimony from selected law-enforcement officials, potential-perpetrators, or convicted murderers was introduced, along with legislators' own claims of the deterrent effect, supported by instinct, or "ordinary knowledge" based on personal experience with crime and criminals. When faced with contradictory evidence, cognitive dissonance is thus reduced by focusing on critiques of research and researchers opposing capital punishment as a deterrent. The annual votes in favor of capital punishment bills and surveys of legislators' attitudes confirmed widespread support for the death penalty, while patterns found in this legislative debate show some of the reasons how and why these lawmakers came to this position. The fundamental issue of the morality of capital punishment was only infrequently debated, perhaps because unlike the empirical issue of deterrence the basic moral principles of legislators do not lend themselves to floor debate. Unlike these legislators' opinions that seemed invariable for

---

[117]Assemblyman Behan, New York State Assembly Debate, AB 9028, 1994, 129–130.
[118]*See* Nisbett & Ross, *supra* note 17.
[119]Benjamin D. Steiner, William J. Bowers, & Austin Sarat, *Folk Knowledge as Legal Action: Death Penalty Judgments and the Tenet of Early Release in a Culture of Mistrust and Punitiveness*, 33 L. & Soc'y Rev. 461, 465 (1999).
[120]Paul Greenberg, *Liberals Need to Face Reality about Crime*, Kansas City Star, April 30, 1998, at C7.
[121]*See* Ehrlich, *supra* note 26, at 397–417.

nearly two decades, Ellsworth and Gross found increasing support of capital punishment as retribution among the general public since the 1970s.[122] And perhaps one
reason for the relative stability of legislators' justifications for support of capital
punishment is that, unlike those surveyed in polls, many legislators had gone on public record with their positions early in the debates.

By comparison with New York, Kansas has experienced an equally extended
period of legislative death penalty debate.[123] Unlike New York, however, Kansas previously had a long tradition of abolition.[124] Thus, it is not surprising that the Kansas
legislature passed a largely symbolic law that would apply the death penalty to
almost no one, making it an option only in selected types of murders, including those
also involving kidnapping and rape.[125] On the other hand, based on the evidence presented here, it seems clear that majorities in both houses of the New York state legislature wanted a capital punishment law that would be broadly applicable.

This analysis suggests that proponents held three central arguments favoring the
deterrence proposition that could not be contested readily and, when taken together,
constituted a commonsense theory of punishment and crime. First, some legislators
relied on the "dead-men-don't-commit-crimes" conception of deterrence, referred to
by one legislator as "incapacitative deterrence."[126] While criminologists might argue
that this term makes no theoretical sense (because those who have been executed cannot refrain from committing new crimes due to fear of legal punishment), the commonsense logic of this notion was to combine incapacitation and specific deterrence
and make the deterrence (as crime prevention) argument much stronger. Moreover, to
the extent that proponents claimed that first-time killers were responsible for vast
numbers of subsequent homicides (either in prison or after release) the argument
became even more compelling. Indeed, a series of studies suggest that incapacitation
may be more important in people's thinking than previously imagined.[127]

Second, without a death penalty as the ultimate punishment, homicides would
increase. Homicide rates had increased dramatically since the 1960s, the time when
executions stopped and death penalty laws had been abolished. These rates were promoted as evidence in favor of deterrence, along with the logically consistent prediction that a reinstated death penalty would result in fewer homicides. Had these rates
remained fairly constant after the moratorium of the death penalty in 1965, chances
of reinstating a death penalty might have been greatly reduced. Part of the basis for
these increases was implied to have been the subsequent killings by convicted murderers. Death penalty opponents' evidence that homicides had in fact increased in
Florida and Texas after those states reinstated the death penalty and began executing

---

[122]Phoebe C. Ellsworth & Samuel R. Gross, *Hardening of the Attitudes: Americans' View on the Death Penalty, in* The Death Penalty in America, *supra* note 47, at 90–115.
[123]Galliher & Galliher, *supra* note 10.
[124]*Id.*
[125]*See* Galliher & Galliher, *supra* note 10, at 369–85.
[126]Vitaliano, *supra* note 53.
[127]*See generally* Ellsworth & Gross, *supra* note 122, at 90–115 for the argument that life in prison without parole is increasingly seen as a satisfactory alternative to execution.

inmates was countered by the untestable proposition that these states' homicide rates might possibly be even higher without the death penalty.

The third position was the proponents' argument that the death penalty was similar to other penalties in at least one respect; it was imposed by the state with the legislative intent of deterrence. Harsher penalties had received widespread support in New York's recent past for offenses ranging from the sale of illicit drugs and drunk driving to spousal abuse.[128] Proponents further argued that deterrence underlies American jurisprudence and corrections, and to require proof of the law's effectiveness would impose an unnecessary burden on legislators. Such proof had not been demanded of other sanctions, so why was it now being required for capital punishment? Moreover, this might be setting a precedent, requiring uncontested evidence in the form of published research about the deterrent effect of other legal sanctions. Thus, to argue against deterrence supplied by the death penalty and, by implication, legal penalties in general, was to argue against the philosophical foundations of American jurisprudence: (1) legal penalties of some sort are necessary to deter potential offenders; (2) harsher penalties deter more effectively than less severe penalties; and (3) the death penalty is the ultimate, or most severe, of all sanctions.

This commonsense theory of crime and punishment allowed legislators to support the deterrence proposition regardless of empirical evidence to the contrary. Research showing no deterrence was routinely criticized as biased and untruthful. The commonsense theory made sense to its proponents: its assertions were logically consistent; others tended to agree with it; it was parsimonious; it had a wide scope of applicability; and it had clear public-policy implications. Given this theory, even the most rigorous and value-neutral research can be dismissed by proponents holding little confidence in social science and statistics as a way of obtaining knowledge. When the published research is faulted on methodological grounds, whether deserved or not, and its authors' political motives and scientific status are questioned, then the purported evidence can be easily dismissed. The scientific evidence then takes on the epistemological status of opinion, the personal views of those attempting to undermine the legal system and institutionalized world view upon which it is based. Ideology thus becomes authoritative and science becomes ideological.

Not surprisingly, after two decades of debate in which the preponderance of scientific evidence presented did not support the deterrence argument, the 1995 New York death penalty bill concluded that: "The enactment of the death penalty will . . . send a strong deterrent message to persons who might be inclined to commit such crimes."[129] We found no evidence of changes in arguments over time, in spite of reductions in New York homicide rates during the 1990s immediately prior to reinstatement. The widespread "ordinary knowledge" or commonsense theory of crime and punishment uncovered in this debate make it all the more remarkable that capital punishment is still abolished in twelve American states.

---

[128]See for example: "The Nation's Toughest Drug Law: Evaluating the New York Experience." National Institute of Law Enforcement and Criminal Justice. Washington, D.C. (March 1978).

[129]Laws of the State of New York, Ch. 1 at 1 (1995). New York State Library, Albany, N.Y.

DEATH PENALTY POLITICS AND SYMBOLIC LAW IN HONG KONG

MARK S. GAYLORD
City Polytechnic of Hong Kong

and

JOHN F. GALLIHER
University of Missouri-Columbia

Under Hong Kong law those persons convicted of murder, treason, and piracy with violence are sentenced to death. But ever since Great Britain itself abolished capital punishment in 1965, Hong Kong's colonial governors have been forced to commute such sentences to life imprisonment under edict of the home government. News reports and victimization surveys indicate that residents of Hong Kong chafe at this denial of the public will while recognizing that, in 1997 when the People's Republic of China regains sovereignty, there will be no official compunction whatsoever when it comes to enforcement of the death penalty. For now, however, the death penalty is neither enforced nor abolished.

Social scientists have long confronted the paradox posed by certain laws that, while passed and defended as social controls, nevertheless go unenforced (Gusfield 1963; Edelman 1964). Such law is often called symbolic legislation as opposed to routinely enforced instrumental legislation actually meant to alter human behaviour. In discussing America's national prohibition of alcohol, Gusfield (1963) cited the Eighteenth Amendment to the U.S. Constitution as a classic example of a symbolic law. Coincident with the lack of its enforcement, symbolic legislation typically runs counter to public opinion. For example, in retrospect it is clear that, for the vast majority of Americans, the prohibition of alcohol was anathema. Yet not all unenforced legislation is symbolic legislation. Some laws remain unenforced solely due to overworked, corrupt or inadequately funded police, others due to ambiguity in the law itself.

In this paper we describe the course of death penalty politics in Hong Kong over nearly two decades. It is our contention that the colony's unenforced death penalty can be understood as symbolic legislation. Further, we will show that, to understand the legislative process and the consequences of law once passed, it is necessary to identify the various audiences addressed by it. Such distinctions are of vital importance. The impact of any communication depends not merely on the intentions of those who issue it, but more importantly on the perceptions of those who receive it. In the case of death penalty abolition in Hong Kong, the relevant audiences include the British electorate, the Hong Kong Chinese, other nations and the British government itself. Our analysis should allow some conclusions about the relative significance of these audiences.

The authors are grateful to Robert Kidder, Michael Radelet, Larry Koch and Harold Traver for their comments and suggestions. An earlier version of this paper was read at the Joint Meeting of the Law and Society Association and the Research Committee on the Sociology of Law, Amsterdam, June 1991.

Reprinted from *International Journal of Sociology of Law* 22 (1994), by permission of Elsevier Science.

Interviews were conducted with local and foreign journalists, academics, and members of the Royal Hong Kong Police Force, the Attorney General's Chambers, the Judiciary, and the Correctional Services Department. Other data sources included: official crime statistics; police and correctional services reports; and feature articles, news reports, and editorials published in Hong Kong's English language dailies. Data from surveys on Hong Kong public opinion on various issues related to capital punishment were also reviewed.

INTRODUCTION

At the end of the 19th century, Emile Durkheim developed one of the most influential theories of law creation. Durkheim postulated that the criminal law embodies the most deeply felt morality of a people. This morality is a reflection of the religious and customary values "found in all healthy consciences" (Durkheim 1933: 73). Yet it would be naïve to assume that in all societies the criminal law reflects a widely shared moral consensus. Hong Kong is a case in point. The origin of law in Hong Kong is quite different from that suggested by Durkheim. Throughout the 19th century, British colonialism exported Western concepts of crime and criminal justice to much of its empire without regard for structural or cultural differences between motherland and colony (Vagg & Traver 1991; Merry 1991). The historical record in Hong Kong offers many examples of how the law was used to protect, first and foremost, the lives and property of European residents rather than the Chinese (Crisswell & Watson 1982). Little thought was given to how well Western legal concepts and procedures would be received by Hong Kong's indigenous population. Nor has little changed today. Nevertheless, it remains to be seen if this Western transplant will be rejected by its host after 1997, when China resumes sovereignty over Hong Kong, or if the Hong Kong Special Administrative Region government will work to develop a hybrid criminal justice system comprising elements both of Chinese and Western values (Gaylord & Traver n.d.).

The terms 'legal liberalism' and 'benign transfer' have been used to describe the suppression by colonial governments of traditional forms of social control and conflict resolution and their replacement by Western legal systems (Cohen 1982). Colonial powers typically justify this behaviour by asserting that Western law is a major instrument in furthering the goals of development, such as equality, well-being, rationality, individual freedom and citizen participation. In late 19th-century British thinking, advanced peoples had an obligation to help those less advanced, to provide guidance and instruction and even to rule them (Darby 1987). Many British colonizers acted with a sense of the moral superiority of Christianity, belief in progress and civilization, commitment to an idea of white racial supremacy, and faith in the rule of law and individual rights (Merry 1991). Cohen (1982: 89), however, argues that the seemingly humanistic intentions behind legal liberalism are merely a mask that "succeeds in passing off repression as being fair, natural or even just."

Given the intense culture conflict inherent in colonialism, with protagonists perceiving their adversaries as either evil or benighted, symbolic law would seem appropriate for mitigating legal struggles between mother country and colony. One method of minimizing conflict in such situations is to insure that all parties to the dispute receive some mollifying reward or incentive from the law (Becker 1963). For example, when prohibition was used in the U.S. to assert the superior way of life of rural Protestants, the masses of Irish and German immigrants were undoubtedly at least somewhat placated by being allowed easy access to illegal alcohol. Similarly, Norway's housemaid's law (Aubert 1966) and U.S. antitrust legislation in the early 20th century (Edelman 1964) are illustrative of other legal measures designed intentionally to appease audiences with widely divergent interests.

While much has been written about the origins of criminal law in the West, relatively less attention has been devoted to the study of colonial governments' imposition of criminal law on their subjects. One such instance, involving capital punishment, is described by Seidman (1965) in which colonial governments refused to allow Africans to impose the death penalty on witches even though such was the traditional punishment for witchcraft throughout sub-Saharan Africa. "The colonial governments, having but recently abolished equally barbaric measures against witches in the metropole, abolished them in the colonies as well" (Seidman 1965: 47). Similarly, for nearly three decades the British government, in apparent disregard for Hong Kong public opinion, has prevented one of its colonies from imposing the death penalty on convicted murderers.

According to Foucault (1977: 9), executions are risky for the state because they may "invert the shame inflicted on the victim into pity or glory . . . [and convert] the legal violence of the executioner into shame." In 18th-century England, for example, many new capital offences were created while the number of *actual* executions declined. By snatching convicts from the gallows, Hay (1975) argues, the British government hoped to symbolize its exercise of mercy and justice while simultaneously emphasizing the law's majesty. Hay (1975: 47) concludes that "pardons were part of the basic tissue of paternalism, expressed in the most personal terms." If such a practice was found to be useful as a means for British authorities to control their own citizens, it is equally successful, we contend, as a means to control colonial subjects.

THE DEATH PENALTY IN HONG KONG

Even though Hong Kong's population doubled to 5.8 million between 1967 and 1993, thus creating one of the highest population densities in the world, the homicide rate has remained consistently low, roughly comparable to that found in the Nordic countries (Table 1).

Moreover, most homicides in Hong Kong are not street crimes. Table 2 demonstrates that "gang attack" and "robbery" represent a combined total of only 22 per cent of all homicides, 1976–92. In cases for which a cause was determinable, "family disputes," "other disputes," and "love affairs" predominated, suggesting the threat to the general public was minimal and the effectiveness of deterrence questionable.

A letter from the Hong Kong Correctional Services Department (1993) indicates 106 executions and 32 commutations of convicted murderers between 1946 and 1966, while the period 1967–92 shows no executions and 261 commutations (Table 3). In 1973, in a significant departure from the pattern of routine commutation, the

TABLE 1

Murder and manslaughter rate per 100,000,
Royal Hong Kong Police, 1976–92

Year	Number of homicides	Homicide rate
1976	82	1.8
1977	57	1.3
1978	63	1.4
1979	68	1.4
1980	86	1.7
1981	105	2.1
1982	93	1.8
1983	84	1.6
1984	84	1.6
1985	89	1.7
1986	67	1.2
1987	72	1.3
1988	71	1.3
1989	102	1.8
1990	137	2.4
1991	92	1.6
1992	108	1.9

Governor of Hong Kong, Sir Murray Mac-Lehose, refused to commute the death penalty of Tsoi Kwok-cheung, a convicted murderer. While British law allowed Tsoi to appeal his conviction to the Privy Council in London on a *point of law*, it did not permit an appeal against the death sentence *itself* (*South China Morning Post* [*SCMP*] 1974c; Pannick 1982).

Sir Murray's decision may well have been influenced by the fact that there had been a steady build-up of public pressure on the government to carry out Tsoi's sentence, based on the prevalent view that Chinese rather than Western concepts of

TABLE 2

Analysis of homicide by motive,
Royal Hong Kong Police Force Statistics, 1976–92

Motive	Number	Percent
Gang attack	73	5
Robbery	248	17
Family disputes	117	8
Other disputes	277	19
Revenge	88	6
Mental illness	58	4
Love affairs	58	4
Others	190	13
Unknown	351	24
	1460	100

TABLE 3

Commutations and executions, Hong Kong Correctional Services Department, 1946–92

Year	Execution	Commutations
1946/47	10	5
1947/48	11	2
1948/49	6	0
1949/50	3	3
1950/51	12	1
1951/52	9	0
1952/53	8	2
1953/54	5	2
1954/55	4	0
1955/56	6	0
1956/57	4	1
1957/58	4	1
1958/59	5	0
1959/60	9	2
1960/61	2	1
1961/62	3	2
1962/63	4	2
1963/64	0	2
1964/65	0	1
1965/66	0	4
1966/67	2	2
1967		4
1968		5
1969		3
1970		0
1971		5
1972		6
1973		12
1974		13
1975		15
1976		19
1977		10
1978		7
1979		16
1980		3
1981		12
1982		16
1983		13
1984		9
1985		22
1986		5
1987		20
1988		16
1989		6
1990		6
1991		5
1992		13

punishment should be observed in dealing with criminals in Hong Kong (*SCMP* 1973*d*). Thus Tsoi's last hope appeared to rest with an appeal to the Privy Council even though the local authorities seemed to think success was unlikely (*SCMP* 1973*e*). Hong Kong's Chief Justice and Attorney General were dispatched to London by the Governor with a brief to stress the Hong Kong government's desire to see Tsoi's death sentence carried out. Confident of the futility of Tsoi's appeal, Hong Kong officials stressed that Tsoi's petition to the Queen simply asked for mercy and was not an appeal to the Privy Council (*SCMP* 1973*f*).

Shortly after Tsoi's appeal was received in London, the Foreign Secretary wrote to a Labour M.P. to say that, in his opinion, intervention at this point would be "unusual" (*China Mail* 1973*b*). However, given the fact that Parliament had recently voted overwhelmingly against restoring the death penalty in England, Scotland and Wales, and would soon thereafter abolish the death penalty in Northern Ireland as well, the usual rules no longer seemed inviolable. Former Labour Prime Minister, Harold Wilson, who was then the Opposition leader, even threatened a Parliamentary fight over the issue unless Tsoi was granted a reprieve (*China Mail* 1973*b*).

It was widely reported in the British and Hong Kong press that if the Queen would not commute Tsoi's death sentence a combination of Labour and anti-hanging Conservative M.P.'s would unite to vote against the government (*SCMP* 1973*g*). One journalist judged that "this would . . . [place] the Prime Minister, Mr. Edward Heath, in a position which would probably . . . [force] the resignation of his government" (*SCMP* 1973*g*). However, even today there is considerable debate about this interpretation, for although Miners (1986: 232) agrees that a vote of censure would have been highly embarrassing for the Conservatives, a negative vote, in his opinion, was not likely to have forced the government to resign. Overshadowing the merits of this debate, however, is the simple fact that Tsoi was indeed granted a reprieve by the Queen.

Almost immediately, a judge in Hong Kong complained that "[t]he interference from London was really quite intolerable" (quoted in Miners 1986: 232). The Governor also complained in a speech to the Hong Kong Legislative Council in October 1973 that "the reprieve, on the advice of Her Majesty's Government, of a convicted murderer [goes] against the express advice of the Governor-in-Council and the *wishes of the overwhelming majority of the population*" (Hong Kong Hansard 1973/ 1974: 3; quoted in Miners 1986: 232, emphasis added).

Sir Murray's attempts to influence the British government could not have occurred at a worse time, for following his decision to refuse Tsoi a reprieve, the House of Commons voted against the death penalty in quick succession on two more occasions. On 11 April 1974 it voted 320 to 178 against reintroduction of capital punishment in Great Britain, and on 14 May 1974 it extended abolition, by a vote of 253 to 94, to Northern Ireland. Moreover, the Opposition had already threatened to raise a motion of censure against the Conservative government for "countenancing lower standards of justice in Hong Kong than in the U.K., if a reprieve were not granted" to Tsoi (Miners 1986: 232). The question of "lower standards" for a colony is, of course, an especially sensitive issue for any British government in the late 20th century since most European nations have abandoned their remaining colonies. The day after the May 14th vote, the Secretary of State granted Tsoi's petition for mercy.

It was reported in Hong Kong that, henceforth, convicted murderers would *not* be executed (*China Mail* 1973*d*). Soon thereafter, three visiting M.P.s heard protests about these developments from leading members of the Chinese community (*China Mail* 1973*e*). The next year, after the Governor had visited the U.K. to press for imposition of the death penalty in Hong Kong, the British government again rejected Hong Kong government pleas to restore capital punishment in the colony (*SCMP* 1975*a*). There were renewed demands for executions in the debate on the Governor's address at the beginning of the 1975–76 session of the Hong Kong Legislative Council. The Colonial Secretary, in reply to a question on the issue of capital punishment, made the following conciliatory comment: "In [the] future, whenever he commutes a death penalty, the Governor will impose the alternative punishment of life imprisonment, unless, in exceptional circumstances, he feels able to accept advice from Executive Council that a lesser sentence should be imposed" (Hong Kong Hansard 1975/ 1976: 222–225; quoted in Miners 1981: 90). The dilemma now stood as follows: What was the point of having a death penalty if it were never used? Answers to this question in Hong Kong ranged from calls for abolition of the death penalty to equally outright calls that convicted murderers be hanged.

Yet nearly a decade later, in the early 1980s, the issue remained unresolved. It was reported that government officials refused to comment on the Chief Justice's declaration that "judges would rather not go through the 'pantomime' of passing the death sentence on capital offenders when they know the sentences will be automatically commuted to life imprisonment" (*SCMP* 1982). The Chief Justice was further quoted as stating that passing the death sentence on a convict with the knowledge that it would be commuted "doesn't add to the dignity of the proceedings." The next year the Hong Kong Attorney General explained the dilemma to the Legislative Council:

> Capital punishment is popular [here] and the recent British Parliamentary vote was a disappointment to the people of Hong Kong. So let's keep capital punishment. On the other hand it makes a mockery of our system to retain the procedures of capital punishment given the present realities. So let's get rid of capital punishment . . . *But given the feelings of the ordinary people of Hong Kong and of the Parliament in Westminster, I see no immediate prospect of action here in Hong Kong to satisfy either of [these] demands* (Thomas 1983; emphasis added).

A later editorial in a Hong Kong newspaper concluded:

> There seems no good reason why capital punishment should be retained on the books, when in fact it is never carried out . . . What this means is that the Hong Kong Government has no position on the issue. It neither respects public opinion nor is opposed to the death penalty on principle. It does not carry out the death penalty not because it respects public opinion but merely because it is a colonial government, and Britain won't allow it (*SCMP* 1989*c*).

While the Attorney General made quite clear that he personally was an abolitionist, the government decision to leave the law unchanged was "both political and practical" (*SCMP* 1983):

> [O]ne cannot imagine the Governor precipitating a constitutional crisis by deciding to represent his constituents and decline to commute a death sentence. . . . An appeal would then be made to the Queen and her Secretary of State for Foreign and Commonwealth Relations would then be bound to overrule him (*SCMP* 1986c).

Given the intensity of the opposition, it was explained to the members of the Hong Kong Legislative Council that in giving advice to the Queen, the Secretary of State, responsible to the Parliament, *must* take into account the likely reaction of that body (Colonial Secretary 1975).

ATTITUDES AND REACTIONS IN THE UNITED KINGDOM

The opinions of Members of Parliament, and not of the British public, are important in death penalty decisions in the U.K. It has been demonstrated that since its inception in 1965 there has been little public support for Britain's abolition of capital punishment. Zimring & Hawkins (1986) note that the percentage favouring the death penalty increased from 70 per cent immediately *prior* to suspension of the death penalty to 76 per cent the year *following* suspension. Most M.P.s, however, disagree with British public opinion (Gallup Poll 1983).

Accordingly, the Conservative Prime Minister, Edward Heath, wrote in a letter that the government had no proposal for re-opening the issue of capital punishment in Hong Kong (*SCMP* 1973d). After yet another death penalty bill was easily defeated, 320–178, in 1973, a Hong Kong newspaper editorial argued: "If the British Parliament can reject [capital punishment] by a two-to-one majority the same considerations must compel . . . [the Secretary of State of the Foreign and Commonwealth Office] to urge the Queen to follow a similar course" in Hong Kong (*China Mail* 1973c). And while Parliament has the unquestioned right to decide what is best for Britons, it can be argued that the people of Hong Kong should be left to decide for themselves what is best. Yet, in a colony "(p)ublic opinion of course has no way of expressing itself . . . except through the press and Government-created information channels" (*China Mail* 1973c).

Another bill, in 1975, attempting to reinstate the death penalty, had no greater success. After a highly emotional debate, Parliament rejected the call to resume death by hanging for terrorist murders, 364–232, notwithstanding the fact that 88 per cent of Britons were in favour of such action, according to a poll published in the *Daily Express* (*SCMP* 1975c).

By 1983, the U.K., in the person of Margaret Thatcher, had a Conservative Prime Minister who staunchly supported the death penalty. However, Thatcher had always allowed a "free vote" on capital punishment—indicating her recognition of the intensity of feeling among those who opposed it—and thus legislative results in the 1980s have been no more successful than during the previous decade. In April 1987, the death penalty was once again debated by Parliament and defeated by 342 to 230.

Later in the year a general election was held returning the Conservative Party to power with a somewhat decreased majority. This led, in 1988, to yet one more death penalty bill debate in Parliament. Again reinstatement of capital punishment was defeated. Labour, Liberal and Social Democrat M.P.s were overwhelmingly opposed (*SCMP* 1988*a*). The vote marked the 18th attempt to reinstate capital punishment in the 23 years since it was first abolished on a trial basis (*SCMP* 1988*b*). Throughout all these years it has been clear that the Conservative party was not about to run the risk of letting Hong Kong public opinion embarrass the government.

ATTITUDES AND REACTIONS IN HONG KONG

According to the 1990 victimization survey conducted by the Fight Crime Committee and the Census and Statistics Department, on the question of whether the death sentence should be abolished, about 30 per cent said that it should be abolished, 50 per cent said it should not, and the rest had no opinion. The greatest support for abolition came from people aged 18–29 (Victimization Survey 1991). Public opinion regarding capital punishment in Hong Kong is also reflected, at least to some degree, in the press. Such opinion, obviously, is of limited value as a data source; it places heavy emphasis on the views of those with easy access to the mass media, such as political leaders and other influential citizens. In any case, if British public opinion on the death penalty is of little or no importance to Parliament, such is also the case with Hong Kong public opinion.

While it may come as no surprise to learn that prison officials in Hong Kong are predisposed to the return of capital punishment ("either abolish it or use it"), it may be quite enlightening to discover that a survey of 1000 former *convicts* indicates a majority in favour of the reintroduction of the death penalty (*Hongkong Standard* 1985). Traditional neighbourhood leaders (*Kaifong* chiefs) support a return of capital punishment "to deter potential criminals" (*SCMP* 1973*a*). The leader of the Buddhist Sanghs Association is reported to have indicated approval of the death penalty as a "basic remedy to crime" (*SCMP* 1974*c*). The President of the Chinese Manufacturers Association believes murderers should be hanged and armed robbers killed "on the spot" (*SCMP* 1974*b*). A Hong Kong legislative councillor argued that Hong Kong, rather than the Queen, should have the final say on the death penalty. The legislator received support from the Chairman of the Home Affairs Committee of the Hong Kong General Chamber of Commerce (*SCMP* 1975*a*). Hong Kong newspaper editorials joined in the chorus denouncing the unenforced law. "To pay lip service to a law that cannot be enforced is to make a mockery of all law. And once the rule of law is mocked, all society is threatened" (*China Mail* 1973*g*). And another editorial:

> It is wrong in principle that the British Prime Minister should in this way have the power to override a decision by the Hong Kong courts [and] our own view . . . is that if Britain is determined not to allow the death penalty in Hong Kong it would be preferable to do away with it all together and prescribe alternative punishments which would demonstrate the community's repugnance for the kind of wanton killing that has become such a feature of present-day society (*SCMP* 1974*a*).

Table 3 shows that prior to Great Britain's abolition of capital punishment, less than 25 per cent of such sentences resulted in commutation. The rise in commuted sentences since 1967 shows to what extent the demands by Hong Kong residents for retribution have been frustrated.

In recent years numerous Hong Kong Chinese leaders have expressed support for the death penalty. As a case in point, an outspoken legislative councillor called emphatically for its reinstatement as applicable for drug traffickers and leaders of gang violence: "I am a Chinese at heart. The law of the gods says they that kill should die" (*SCMP* 1986*b*). Miners (1986: 89) has observed that the death penalty is not likely to be repealed since Hong Kong Chinese community leaders are so staunchly opposed to abolition.

Sixty-eight per cent of 1312 people polled in a *South China Morning Post* survey supported capital punishment for convicted murderers while 12 per cent were opposed and the others unsure (1986*d*). In response to this and similarly strong endorsements, the Attorney General has assured the public that the death penalty will remain on the statute books despite the pleas of local officials to abolish the law since it is not enforced (*SCMP* 1983). Alternatively it could be argued that Hong Kong Chinese chafe under the moratorium on executions not so much from a desire to see the penalties fully exacted but simply because it has been imposed upon them from without. On the other hand, in Hong Kong there is no evidence of general opposition to the laws imposed by the British.

Some editorial writers look forward to Britain's handover of Hong Kong in 1997 to a Chinese government not as squeamish as the U.K.'s in administering the death penalty:

> [China] has again shown in no uncertain terms how it punishes violence and lawlessness on its streets. Death. Execution at pistol point. That was the sentence carried out there on a Hong Kong man last weekend. Guilty. Sentence carried out, corpse disposed of, case closed. . . . Hong Kong needs tougher penalties for violent crime. These people should not be allowed to get away with light sentences for outrages against individuals and society (*SCMP* 1986*a*).

All the apparent enthusiasm for capital punishment notwithstanding, there remains growing concern over China's increasing appetite for executions. By the early 1990s, with the spectre of Hong Kong's return to China looming nearer, new concerns have arisen. For instance, the post-1997 fate of convicted murderers now in Hong Kong's jails, whose sentences have been commuted to life imprisonment by the Governor, is uncertain. Hong Kong's Chief Justice has tried to allay these concerns and has stated that prisoners with commuted sentences have nothing to fear after 1997 unless China changes the law, which is precisely what some predict will happen (*SCMP* 1986*d*).

Recently, a legislative councillor suggested removing capital punishment from local statutes for treason due to his concerns over China's definition of treason. "'[A]fter 1997, freedom of speech now enjoyed by local people will be affected,' he declared. Under Article Three of the Chinese regulations on punishment of counter-revolutionaries, persons colluding with imperialists and betraying their mother-land shall be sentenced to death" (*SCMP* 1989*a*). Thus, in the absence of rigorous public opinion data, and in light of the United Kingdom's fast approaching handover of Hong Kong to China, it may be more accurate to say that Hong Kong's rhetorical support for capital punishment is more based on quicksand than on solid ground.

THE DEATH PENALTY IN CHINA

Whereas we might expect to find symbolic legislation aimed at mediating con-flicting views in a democratic state, the presence of such legislation in an authoritar-ian regime would be surprising. Since 1981 China has doubled the number of criminal offences that can result in death upon conviction. The list now includes theft, bribery, embezzlement, organizing a secret society, molesting women, gang fighting, drug trafficking, pimping, passing on methods of committing crimes (Amnesty International 1984; Scobell 1990) and "speculation and the illegal export of valuable cultural relics" (1984: 57).

On 30 August 1983, 30 people were executed at a mass rally of 100,000 in Beijing: 19 for murder, 10 for rape and 1 for theft (Amnesty International 1984: 59). It has been estimated that between July 1983 and February 1984 there were more than 6000 executions in China for a wide variety of nonviolent crimes (Bonavia 1984). And in 1989 nearly 100 people were executed during the first 20 days of the year in China's southern province of Guangdong (*SCMP* 1989*b*). China's paramount leader, Deng Xiaoping, voices the Chinese government's position regarding capital punishment's putative deterrent value: "by killing one, we save a hundred . . . [or] killing a chicken to frighten the monkeys" (*Washington Post* 1987).

An even more direct threat to Hong Kong was made recently by the Chinese leadership:

> China's top law enforcer warned yesterday that decadent bourgeois ideology and crim-inals from Hong Kong and Macau threatened the country's social order. . . . In 1983, senior leader Deng Xiaoping launched a major campaign against crime, and an esti-mated 10,000 people were executed over the next three years. . . . 'Activities of interna-tional criminal gangs from Hong Kong and Macau, and the corrosive influence of decadent bourgeois idealogy in culture and lifestyles are external factors tempting people to commit offences' [he said] (*SCMP* 1988*c*).

If actions speak louder than words, the violent response of Chinese leaders to the 1989 student-led democracy movement leaves little doubt about China's willingness to use violence. Amnesty International estimated at least 1000 people were killed in Tiananmen Square and elsewhere in Beijing when the People's Liberation Army attacked the student demonstrators, and an additional 300 more were killed in south-ern China. Following the official crackdown were numerous executions. Soon after, a Hong Kong editorial concluded: "Many in the territory, having seen how the death penalty is so widely used on the mainland, now feel it is dangerous to allow it to remain as part of Hong Kong law after 1997. . . . Keeping capital punishment on the statute books guarantees that the death penalty will actually be carried out after 1997, when China resumes sovereignty" (*SCMP* 1989c).

Most recently the Chinese leadership has left few doubts about its plans for future terror. In January 1990, China's highest judicial official, the president of the Supreme People's Court, was quoted as saying "It is a mistake to think that, because there is the law, justice can be executed without the guidance of the policies of the [Communist] party" (*SCMP* 1990). In other words, the Chinese government will not be bound by written law in apprehending and punishing wrongdoers.

DISCUSSION

Just as alcohol prohibition was imposed on Americans against their wishes, the abolition of capital punishment, both in Hong Kong and the U.K., has apparently been imposed on deeply divided publics. Colonial governments have typically justified Western-style policies on the basis of uplifting their subjects to higher standards of civility. Although most colonizers were motivated by desires for power and wealth, some were humanitarians endeavouring to bring God, progress, and civilization to unappreciative peoples they thought of as fundamentally different from themselves (Merry 1991). According to Lethbridge (1984), Hong Kong is made up of two rather distinct communities: one European, the other Chinese. Each is relatively autonomous, with its own symbols, rituals, rules, and gradations of status. It is a society in which members of the two communities come together principally in the market-place. Otherwise, there is little value consensus. Hong Kong's *de facto* death penalty abolition has involved intense passions regarding what its supporters, who are disproportionately drawn from the European community, see as a sacred mission to uphold the value of human life. Death penalty commutations are justified by Westminster on the humanitarian grounds of saving Hong Kong's subjects from their own misguided conception of justice.

Moreover, the struggle in the U.K. over capital punishment is primarily a status conflict, with abolitionists present in all three major political parties. In turn, British politicians, through the Foreign and Commonwealth Office, dictate "appropriate" policy to Hong Kong, including wealthy Chinese business leaders. Thus the struggle in Hong Kong is clearly not one of traditional class conflict, but rather between the leading segments of Britain's political élite and Hong Kong's Chinese élite.

Negative reference groups have a significant influence on symbolic legislation. Thus Parliament could be expected to be especially sensitive to death penalty legislation since capital punishment is a penalty that now clearly distinguishes the European democracies from the former East European communist regimes. When the U.K. acted in the 1960s finally to abolish capital punishment, it was mainly following the precedents of other Western European nations by whose examples the Members of Parliament became strongly influenced. Indeed, had the British not done so, they would have found themselves sole reactionaries among the European Community and embarrassingly in the company of such despotic regimes as Iran, Iraq, and the People's Republic of China (Amnesty International 1989). The common standards of the E.C. thus carried more weight in official decision-making, as regards the imposition of the death penalty, than did general public opinion, whether in Hong Kong or the home country.

As regards Hong Kong today, a genuine interest is lacking among British lawmakers in the instrumental use of capital punishment. Parliament shows but doubtful scorn for its deterrent effect: the death penalty is simply seen as morally repugnant. And even in Hong Kong, the deterrent effect is not always of paramount concern. As early as 1973, Hong Kong's Crown Prosecutors warned that attempts to execute convicted killers would serve only to make murder convictions more difficult to win (*China Mail* 1973*a*). It was said that many jurors would refuse to vote for conviction if they believed that an execution would eventually follow. Recall, too, that Table 3 indicates executions virtually disappeared from Hong Kong even before the abolition of capital punishment in the United Kingdom. Moreover, a failure to secure sufficient signatures to a referendum that would reinstate death by hanging in the colony may be interpreted as the public's recognition of the positive role served by an unenforced death penalty law (*China Mail* 1973*f*).

The legacy of colonialism for a Western democracy places the U.K. in a dilemma that is resolved only by inaction. The law is neither changed nor enforced. The U.K. can continue to respond symbolically to homicide in Hong Kong because the homicide rate has been consistently low in the past decade (Table 1). When governments hold that a criminal activity poses no real threat to society at large, they may attempt simply to mollify the public with symbolic legislation. Parliament and the people of Hong Kong appear to have such divergent opinions on the issue of capital punishment that only a symbolic death penalty law achieves a satisfactory resolution. Unenforced capital punishment exists in Hong Kong to appease, in part, the local Chinese population, and to satisfy the majority in Parliament. Perhaps these efforts at appeasement are facilitated by the fact that the two audiences for these divergent symbols are separated by vast geographical and cultural distances.

POSTSCRIPT

On 7 October 1992, Christopher Patten, the colony's new governor, expressed the government's position during the Governor's Annual Address to the Legislative Council:

> Any society based on the rule of law must ensure that its laws reflect the realities of contemporary life and thought. *I think it is wrong in principle to leave laws on the Statute Books which are out of date, which we do not use and which we have no intention of using.* I am referring here to the law on capital punishment. On 26 June last year [1991], the Council voted for a motion in favour of the repeal of capital punishment. [Legislative councillors voted 24–12 in favour of abolition.] In the debate, many Members recognized that laws which are not used or are out of date should be repealed. We have therefore prepared draft legislation to replace the penalty of capital punishment with life imprisonment. This amending legislation will be presented to the Council during this new session (Hong Kong Government 1992, emphasis added).

On 21 April 1993, after 27 years as a legal fiction, the death penalty was struck from Hong Kong's statute books. The Crimes (Amendment) (No. 3) Bill, which sought the abolition of the penalty, was passed by a vote of 40–9, with two abstentions. Shortly thereafter, the 41 convicted murderers held in Stanley Prison's Condemned Block were removed and their sentences commuted to life imprisonment.

Following the Legislative Council's vote, the editor of the *South China Morning Post* (1993*b*) declared that "only the need to pander to local sensibilities and, perhaps, to those of the crustier members of the establishment kept the death penalty on the statute books for so long after it fell into disuse." This position was seconded by Andrew Wong Wang-fat, the chairman of the bills committee studying the legislative amendment, who declared that the abrogation of the death penalty was "long overdue" (*SCMP* 1993*a*).

But the question remains, why now? Why should the Hong Kong government choose this moment in history to abolish capital punishment? There seem to be two reasons: the colony's recently enacted Bill of Rights, and the imminence of China's resumption of sovereignty over Hong Kong.

The Hong Kong Bill of Rights Ordinance was proposed by the Hong Kong government as part of a series of measures aimed at alleviating the local crisis of confidence after the suppression of the pro-democracy student movement in mainland China in June 1989 (Chen 1991). Enacted into law in 1991, it must be considered a step forward in the consolidation of Hong Kong's existing system for the protection of human rights in general and of its relatively liberal safeguards for criminal defendants' rights in particular. As the Hong Kong Bill of Rights largely reproduces the wording of the International Covenant on Civil and Political Rights, one of the most significant implications of the Bill is that it facilitates the introduction of standards in international human rights law into the domestic law of Hong Kong (Schabas 1993). The enactment of the Bill of Rights, when complemented by appropriate amendments of Hong Kong's present constitutional instrument (the Letters Patent), enables Hong Kong courts to strike down laws, such as the death penalty, that fall foul of such human rights standards. After the enactment of the Bill of Rights, it became even more unlikely that Hong Kong would bring back the rope for as long as the colony remained under British control.

The second factor, discussed earlier, that has produced the change has been the approach of 1997. The fear that the future Special Administrative Region government might be less inclined to leave the death penalty in abeyance left no room for complacency on the part of the colonial government.

Ultimately, however, Hong Kong's constitutional provisions, including the Bill of Rights, are merely pieces of paper. Whether the protections they embody will be translated into reality depends on how much deference is paid to them, or to what extent they are taken seriously, by the leaders of the Chinese Communist Party and the Chinese government, the officials, politicians, judges and lawyers in the Hong Kong Special Administrative Region, and not least, by the ordinary men and women who will make Hong Kong their home after 1997 (Chen 1991; Jackson n.d.). Abolitionists must not relax their guard. Executions are routine in China. As the American example shows, liberal laws can be reversed. Unless the public accepts that capital punishment has no place in a civilized society, that it cannot undo the harm the criminal has done, it would be only too easy for a future Hong Kong administration to reintroduce the death penalty.

REFERENCES

Amnesty International (1984) *China: Violations of Human Rights*. London: Amnesty International Publications.

Amnesty International (1989) *When the State Kills . . . The Death Penalty: A Human Rights Issue*. New York: Amnesty International Publications.

Aubert, V. (1966) Some functions of legislation. *Acta Sociologica,* **10,** 99–100.

Becker, H. S. (1963) *Outsiders: Studies in the Sociology of Deviance*. New York: The Free Press.

Bonavia, D. (1984) Repent or die. *Far Eastern Economic Review* (16 February).

Chen, A. H. Y. (1991) Justice after 1997. In *Crime and Justice in Hong Kong* (Traver, H. & Vagg, J., Eds). Hong Kong: Oxford University Press.

China Mail

    1973*a* Hanging: sentence may change (3 April).

    1973*b* Wilson cracks the whip (12 April).

    1973*c* The case against hanging (22 April).

    1973*d* Spared (30 May).

    1973*e* M.P.s hear protests (30 May).

    1973*f* Bring back rope drive failing (9 August).

    1973*g* Changing the laws (17 October).

Cohen, S. (1982) Western Crime Control Models in the Third World: Benign or Malignant? In *Research in Law, Deviance, and Social Control* (Spitzer, S. & Simon, R. J., Eds), Greenwich, CT: JAI Press.

Colonial Secretary (1975) Speech by the Hon., the Colonial Secretary, in Legislative Council, 11 November.

Correctional Services Department (1993) Letter from J. Ashworth, Assistant Commissioner for Operations, Hong Kong Correctional Services Department (14 January).

Crisswell, C. & Watson, M. (1982) *The Royal Hong Kong Police (1841–1945)*. Hong Kong: Macmillan.

Darby, P. (1987) *The Three Faces of Imperialism*. New Haven, CT: Yale University Press.

Durkheim, E. (1933) *The Division of Labour in Society*. New York: The Free Press.

Edelman, M. (1964) *The Symbolic Uses of Politics*. Urbana: University of Illinois Press.

Foucault, M. (1977) *Discipline and Punish: The Birth of the Prison*. New York: Vintage Books.

Gallup Poll (1983) *Social Surveys Limited*. United Kingdom (July).

Gaylord, M. S. & Traver, H. (n.d.) The Hong Kong Criminal Justice System. In *Introduction to the Hong Kong Criminal Justice System* (Gaylord, M. S. & Traver, H., Eds). Hong Kong: Hong Kong University Press, in press.

Gusfield, J. R. (1963) *Symbolic Crusade: Status Politics and the American Temperance Movement*. Urbana: University of Illinois Press.

Hay, D. (1975) Property, Authority and the Criminal Law. In *Albion's Fatal Tree: Crime and Society in Eighteenth Century England* (Linebaugh, P., Rude, J. G., Thompson, E. P. & Winslow, C., Eds). New York: Pantheon.

Hong Kong Government (1992) *Our Next Five Years: The Agenda for Hong Kong.* Hong Kong: Government Printer.

Hong Kong Hansard (1973) *Reports of the Sittings of the Legislative Council of Hong Kong.* Hong Kong: Government Printer.

Hong Kong Hansard (1975) *Reports of the Sittings of the Legislative Council of Hong Kong.* Hong Kong: Government Printer.

Hongkong Standard (1985) "Former convicts favour return of death penalty" (30 August).

Jackson, M. (n.d.) Criminal Law. In *Introduction to the Hong Kong Criminal Justice System* (Gaylord, M. S. & Traver, H., Eds). Hong Kong: Hong Kong University Press, in press.

Lethbridge, H. J. (1984) The Social Structure: Some Observations. In *The Business Environment in Hong Kong* (Lethbridge, D. G., Ed). Hong Kong: Oxford University Press.

Merry, S. E. (1991) Law and colonialism. *Law & Society Review,* **25,** 889–922.

Miners, N. (1981) *The Government and Politics of Hong Kong.* 3rd edn. Hong Kong: Oxford University Press.

Miners, N. (1986) *The Government and Politics of Hong Kong.* 4th edn. Hong Kong: Oxford University Press.

Pannick, D. (1982) *Judicial Review of the Death Penalty.* London: Gerald Duckworth and Company.

Schabas, W. A. (1993) *The Abolition of the Death Penalty in International Law.* Minefeld, Denmark: Gratius.

Scobell, A. (1990) The death penalty in post-Mao China. *The China Quarterly* **123,** 503–520.

Seidman, R. B. (1965) Witch murder and mens rea: a problem of society under radical social change. *The Modern Law Review* **28,** 46–61.

South China Morning Post

1973*a* Revive death penalty, urge kaifong chiefs (1 February).

1973*b* Heath "no" on hanging issue plea (3 April).

1973*c* Killer living in shadow of the gallows (11 April).

1973*d* Alternatives of capital punishment (11 April).

1973*e* Tsoi's last hope (12 April).

1973*f* Plea to Queen by murderer (19 April).

1973*g* A hanging could have toppled Heath govt (30 May).

1974*a* Hongkong and the death penalty (12 June).

1974*b* Support for death penalty (20 June).

1974*c* Death penalty supported (4 September).

1975*a* It's still "no" to hanging (15 April).

1975*b* Support for Mrs. Symons (23 October).

1975*c* Britons want death penalty returned (2 December).

1975*d* U.K. "no" to hanging again (13 December).

1982 Sir Denys draws no response (4 September).

1983 Threatened death penalty is reprieved (11 November).

1986*a* Making our streets safe (1 June).

GAYLORD AND GALLIHER

1986*b* Hangman who waits for call (8 November).
1986*c* Death penalty doubts after China takes over (8 November).
1986*d* Executions gain new support (16 December).
1986*e* Nothing to fear on death row (9 December).
1988*a* Defeat likely on vote for hanging (6 June).
1988*b* M.P.s likely to reject hanging in new vote (8 June).
1988*c* HK's decadent influence and criminals threatening China (31 August).
1989*a* Lee to seek abolition of death penalty (17 March).
1989*b* Executions hit 100 mark as crime worsens (28 January).
1989*c* Death penalty must go (17 November).
1990 China puts communist party above rule of law (6 January).
1993*a* Death penalty abolished (22 April).
1993*b* Law matches reality (23 April).

Thomas, M. (1983) Speech by the Hon. Michael Thomas, Q.C., the Attorney General, in Legislative Council, 10 November.

Vagg, J. & Traver, H. (1991) Introduction: Crime and Punishment in Hong Kong. In *Crime and Justice in Hong Kong* (Traver, H. & Vaff, J., Eds). Hong Kong: Oxford University Press.

Victimization Survey (1991) *Crime and Its Victims in Hong Kong 1990.* Hong Kong: Government Printer.

Washington Post (1987) "More executed as part of morals crackdown" (16 September).

Zimring, F. E. & Hawkins, G. (1986) *Capital Punishment and the American Agenda.* Cambridge: Cambridge University Press.

DEATH PENALTY POLITICS AND SYMBOLIC LAW IN RUSSIA

OLGA B. SEMUKHINA* and JOHN F. GALLIHER**

ABSTRACT

In contemporary Russia there is widespread support for the death penalty. Recent Russian presidents have endorsed the nation's entry into the European Community (EC). The dilemma is that the price of membership into the EC is total abolition of capital punishment. The Russian Duma is much less popular than the president, even though it sides with public opinion in supporting capital punishment. Since 1997, these conflicting political positions have been temporarily neutralized by leaving capital punishment legislation in place but allowing the Russian president to offer clemency to all sentenced to death. In 1999, the Constitutional Court of Russia placed a moratorium on all death sentences until jury trials are re-introduced throughout the nation.

1. INTRODUCTION

In 1996, the Russian Federation introduced a *de facto* moratorium on the death penalty in an effort to gain membership in the Council of Europe (CE) and to gain full integration into the European community after the breakdown of the USSR. Yet, 13 years later, Russia is the only member of the CE that signed, but refused to ratify, Protocol No. 6 to the European Convention of Human Rights (ECHR). Protocol No. 6 is a major legal instrument intended to create a death penalty-free European community. The *de facto* moratorium in Russia consists of numerous legal documents such as the Criminal Code (CC) of Russia, the Criminal Execution Code (CEC) of Russia, the Russian Constitution, various Presidential Decrees, and the Ruling of the Constitutional Court of Russia. Different political actors and institutions with contradictory agendas are involved. They include supporters of the death penalty, such as the State Duma, as well as the majority of the Russian population and opponents of capital punishment that comprise the Russian President and the Parliament Assembly of the Council of Europe (PACE), with the Constitutional Court of Russia[1] holding the middle ground.

*Marquette University, Department of Social and Cultural Sciences, P.O. Box 1881, Milwaukee, WI 53201-1881, United States
**University of Missouri, Department of Sociology, 335 Middlebush Hall, University of Missouri, Columbia, MO 65211-6100, United States
[1]The Constitutional Court of Russia is the highest judicial institution, created for the sole purpose of enforcing the principles of the Russian Constitution. The Constitutional Court does not try any criminal or civil cases, but only reviews the situations when the existing laws are in possible violation of the Constitution.

Reprinted from *International Journal of Law, Crime and Justice* 37 (2009), Elsevier Ltd.

The application of symbolic law theory to death penalty politics can provide insight into legislative acts that were previously considered "irrational" or chaotic and can better explain the dynamics of political actors (Edelman, 1971; Gaylord and Galliher, 1994; Gusfield, 1963). Symbolic law can have its impact by merely being on the statute books without actually being enforced. Pioneering research on symbolic law theory by Gusfield (1963) describes American alcohol prohibition as a means of satisfying protestant forces, epitomized by the Woman's Christian Temperance Union (WCTU), who felt threatened by Roman Catholic immigrant groups and their rapidly increasing numbers. These immigrant groups consumed alcohol and they seemed to be usurping Protestant political dominance. The solution to the problem was the passage of a national alcohol prohibition, which proclaimed that the Protestant way of life was superior. However, the prohibition was unenforced, allowing Catholic drinkers to continue their customary consumption. Similarly, Edelman (1971) found unenforced symbolic law to be a means of achieving agreement between parties with contradictory economic interests. Edelman draws on the example of the anti-trust legislation of early 20th century America. While the American public demanded control over the monopolistic practices of corporations, the powerful corporations wanted to be left alone to pursue maximum profits. Accordingly, anti-trust legislation was enacted, appeasing the masses, but was not enforced, thus satisfying corporate leaders. More to the point of the death penalty, Gaylord and Galliher (1994) found that unenforced death penalty legislation stretching over several decades in Hong Kong was a means of attempting to mollify both the local Chinese population, which demanded this severe punishment, and the British government, which had ultimate legal authority that eschewed capital punishment. Local Hong Kong courts continued to sentence convicted murderers to death only to have the executions blocked by British authorities. In the light of the above examples, we seek here to explain unenforced death penalty legislation in contemporary Russia by using the symbolic theory of law.

2. BRIEF HISTORY OF THE DEATH PENALTY IN RUSSIA

The use of the death penalty in Russian politics has a long history. According to existing historic accounts, the death penalty in ancient Russia originated as a tribal vengeance for the crime of murder in the early 5th century (Malinovskyi, 1908). In the 11th century tribal vengeance was prohibited by the Grand Prince in an effort to weaken the tribes. Instead, the death penalty became a prerogative of the state and was repeatedly used for political oppression during the 11th to 12th centuries (Budzinskyi, 1870; Tagantsev, 1912; Zagoskin, 1892).[2] Between the 14th and 16th centuries, the death penalty was introduced as an official punishment for crimes against the Grand Prince, crimes against the church and the state, for crimes of murder, and for some

---

[2]For example, mass executions were ordered for the crimes of treason and abstraction of religion in 1069, 1071 and 1157 (Budzinskyi, 1870; Tagantsev, 1912; Zagoskin, 1892).

property offences (Adams, 1970; Kistyakovskyi, 1967; Mikhlin, 1997; Ponomarev and Mikhlin, 1995).[3]

In the 17th and 18th centuries the death penalty became instrumental for the politics of expansionist Russian monarchs. Executions were used by Ivan the Terrible and then by Peter the Great to strengthen and centralize their power and to defeat their political opponents (Moutchnik, 2006; Zagoskin, 1892).[4] During these periods, the number of capital offences increased and especially barbaric execution styles were often selected by the Tsar to produce the highest levels of fear among his subjects (Adams, 1970). Whereas the Court Code (Sudebnoe Ulozhenie) of 1649 introduced by Tsar Alexei Mikhailovich listed 63 crimes punishable by over 12 types of methods, the Military Articles (Voinskie Artikuly) of 1715 created by Peter the Great had already listed 123 capital offences and over 20 execution styles (Sergeevskyi, 1887). Under Chapters 1–3, 21, 22 and 25 of the Court Code of 1649, capital punishment was prescribed for all crimes against the state and the Tsar, crimes against church, and the crimes of murder, rape, and selling tobacco (Shargorodskyi, 1957). The Military Articles of 1715 added new crimes punishable by death including 13 new types of treason, interference with the administration of justice and the delivery of state mail, cutting down trees in the parks belonging to the Tsar, dueling, sodomy, and robbery (Kistyakovskyi, 1896). Nevertheless, only 50 years later, the Instructions of Catherine the Great (Feldshtein, 1909) not only declared disapproval for the death penalty in general, but they also stated that the death penalty does not serve the purposes of deterrence and rehabilitation[5] (Feldshtein, 1909). Historians agree that the Instructions did not have any practical meaning and that they were mostly just considered a declaration of royal intentions and a sign of the royal family's adherence to the standards of the enlightenment (Shargorodskyi, 1957).

It was only in the second half of the 19th century that Russia took practical steps in limiting the use of the death penalty. In 1864, for the first time in Russia the Regulations of the Criminal Proceedings (Ustav Ugolovnogo Sudoproizvodstva) offered provisions for the appeal and pardon of death sentences (Rozin, 1913). In 1903, the new Criminal Code (Ugolovnoe Uloz-henie) eliminated the use of the death penalty for juveniles, the elderly, and female offenders (Sergeevskyi, 1910). The list of military laws of the 1870s–1880s that allowed the death penalty for non-capital crimes when committed during a declared state of emergency was also seriously truncated

---

[3]The death penalty was originally mentioned for the crimes of triple theft in Dvin's Charter (Dvinskaya Gramota) adopted in 1398; the Pskov Court Charter (Pskovskaya Sudnaya Gramota) issued in 1457 allowed the death penalty for four new crimes, including a treason, arson, theft from a church, and a theft of a horse; the Moscow Sudebniki of 1497 and 1550 introduced the death penalty for all crimes against the Grand Prince and the state.

[4]According to some historians, one of the most massive death penalty executions was conducted by Peter the Great in 1698 for the treason of 2000 men who participated in the Streltsy Uprising (Moutchnik, 2006). The historians also estimate that Ivan the Terrible executed over 4000 people during his reign and tsar Alexei Mikhailovitch executed over 7000 people (Shargorodskyi, 1957).

[5]Articles 209 and 210 of the Nakaz, cited from Feldshtein (1909).

during 1902–1903 (Gordon et al., 1911; Rawson, 1984). In 1906, the first Russian parliament (Gosudarstvennaya Duma) attempted to abolish the death penalty for all crimes, including military and state offences. The draft of this law was unanimously approved by the lower chamber of the Duma on June 19 of 1906, but failed at the State Council, the upper chamber of the parliament (Mikhlin, 1997). The second Russian Duma drafted a proposal on death penalty abolition in 1907 but was dismissed before it was able to adopt the proposal (Nethercott, 2007). The third Duma sent the proposal to the legislative commission for further discussion, but decided against it in the end (Gernet, 1913).[6] In all three Dumas the proposals to abolish the death penalty were drafted by a coalition of the socialist, constitutional-democratic, and labor parties, which suggests that both left and centrist political forces in the early 20th century were united in the effort against the death penalty. However, on all three occasions, the conservative right, the executive government, and the royal family successfully blocked such attempts, justifying the need for the death penalty by pointing to spreading political crimes and instabilities (Adams, 1970). In his 1913 book, Gernet noticed that such a political situation around the death penalty issue was not unique to Russia. Reactionary political forces in power tended to advocate for the death penalty, even when the general population did not always support such views (Spasovich, 1863). Leading criminologists in late imperial Russia, who predominantly supported the abolition of the death penalty, suggested that the death penalty was used in the Russian Empire by conservatives as an instrument of "regime protection" when other means of securing its legitimacy were failing (Tagantsev, 1913; Viktorskii, 1912).

During the five years following the February revolution of 1917, the legislation on the death penalty in Russia was constantly changing. It was repeatedly abolished and then reinstated by both the Provisional[7] and Bolshevik governments. Just a month after the February revolution of 1917, the Provisional government abolished capital punishment for all criminal offences (Browder and Kerensky, 1961). The new Provisional government declared that the death penalty was an ineffective reactionary measure previously used by the conservative Tsar government and therefore should be abolished in the light of a new doctrine of revolutionary Russia (Browder and Kerensky, 1961). However, four months later, on July 12th of 1917, the death penalty was restored for all military crimes, murder, rape, and offences against the state committed during war time (Browder and Kerensky, 1961). This measure was adopted by the Provisional government as a result of the deteriorating political and economic situation in Russia due to its unsuccessful participation in WWI and associated civil disturbances (Naumov, 2002). Yet, in September of 1917, the Provisional government declared a moratorium on the use of the death penalty (Adams, 1970). Thus the

---

[6]The first two Dumas were predominantly comprised of the representatives of the socialist, liberal and centrist parties. The third Duma had a much larger proportion of right-wing and conservative representatives.
[7]In February of 1917, Russia experienced a democratic liberal revolution that was led by the middle-class intellectuals (named "intellegentsiya"). The Provisional government was formed after the revolution of February 1917 and was replaced by the Bolshevik government in October of 1917.

struggle of the Provisional government with the issue of the death penalty was common. The Provisional government was torn apart by the contradictions between an ideological and populist need to abolish the death penalty and the fear of growing political opposition that was attempting to take over the country.

After the Bolshevik's *coup d'etat*, also known as the Red October Revolution of 1917, the death penalty was again abolished in October of 1917[8] as "a bourgeois measure contradicting the revolutionary consciousness of the socialist proletariat" (Belyaev and Shargorodskyi, 1970, p. 23). Yet four months later, on February 21 of 1918, it was reinstated by the Decree-declaration titled "Socialist Motherland is in Danger!" (Estrin, 1935). The Decree was adopted in response to the exigencies of a civil war and foreign intervention experienced by Russia during 1917–1919. The Decree authorized the extrajudicial "Emergency Commissions" to sentence the offenders who committed counter-revolutionary crimes, such as sabotage and treason, without trial or appeal (Estrin, 1935). A new Decree adopted on June 16 of 1918 also instructed the Revolutionary People's Courts[9] to use the death penalty as the only punishment for counter-revolutionary offences (Mikhlin, 1997). Finally, in September of 1918, the Decree called "About Red Terror"[10] directed that "all persons having links with White Guard organizations,[11] or involved in conspiracies and revolts" were subject to immediate shooting based on decisions adopted by the Emergency Commissions, which allowed extrajudicial and immediate application of the death penalty (Feldbrugge, 1964). Based on these documents, the Bolshevik government launched an unprecedented campaign of violence resulting in both judicial and extrajudicial applications of the death penalty in Russia to more than 12,000 people during 1917–1920 (Naumov, 2002). Even the official Soviet statistics admit that at least 766 people were executed on the basis of judicial decisions of the Revolutionary tribunals between 1918 and 1920 (Juviler, 1976). This is almost twice as many people who were sentenced to the death penalty by the Tsarist government between 1876 and 1905 (Gernet, 1906).[12] Soviet historians justified the massive use of the death penalty by Bolsheviks during 1917–1919 in accordance with the tenets of Marxism-Leninism ideology. They pointed out that it was the only available means to "reduce, localize and simplify the blood-thirsty agony of the old society and the bloody birth of the new society" (Shargorodskyi, 1958, p. 64).

---

[8]Sobranie uzakonenii i rasporyazhenii rabochego i krestyanskogo pravitel'stva RSFSR [The collection of statutes and regulations issued by the Factory and Peasant Government of the Russian Soviet Federative Republic] (henceforth cited as SU RSFSR), # 1, article 10.
[9]The Revolutionary People's Courts were the first trial criminal courts, organized by the Bolshevik government. Unlike the "Emergency Commissions", the People's Courts were considered a judicial agency and were instructed to follow the provisions of the criminal proceedings.
[10]SU RSFSR, # 65, article 710.
[11]The name "White Guard" refers to the imperial troops in Russia that did not accept the Bolshevik revolution and were fighting to restore the tsarist regime during the civil war of 1917e1919. The term "white" is contrasted with the term "red" that was often used by the Bolshevik military organization (e.g. Red Army).
[12]According to Tagantsev (1912), between 1866 and 1890, 134 people were sentenced to the death penalty and 44 of them were executed.

On January 17, 1920,[13] the death penalty was abolished again since "the enemies of the Red Revolution were defeated in most territories of Soviet Russia" (Piontkovskyi et al., 1970, p. 18). However, the Decree of 1920 allowed the use of the death penalty by the military tribunals and also provided a justification for the possible use of the death penalty in the future. The Decree stated that "only renewed attempts. . . to disturb the steady position of Soviet power by armed interventions or material support of. . . Tsarist generals can force the Soviet Government to revert again to terrorist methods" (Kucherov, 1970, p. 67). In the mid-1920s Soviet Russia entered a period called the New Economic Policy (NEP),[14] and adopted two new Criminal Codes (CC) in 1922 and in 1926. The first CC of 1922 was an initial attempt to codify existing Soviet laws since 1917. Debates preceding the adoption of this document were focused, among other things, on whether the death penalty should be used in the new "classless" society. The drafts of the CC prepared by the Peoples Commissariat for Justice (Narkomyust) and the Institute of Soviet Law argued for the removal of the death penalty from the measures of criminal punishment since the enemies of the Red Revolution were no longer threatening the existence of the Soviet state (Gerzenzon et al., 1948).[15] However, these views were thought to be erroneous and dangerous and the abolition of the death penalty was rejected by the "special commission" of the Small Council of People's Commissars (Malyi Sovnarkom) (Kuznetsov, 2002; Timasheff, 1953). As a compromise, the death penalty in the CC of 1922 was listed as a temporary and exceptional measure, a tradition that was later followed by all Soviet codes. The CC of 1922 allowed the death penalty in the form of shooting for 19 separate crimes, most of which were offences against the state (Zakhartsev, 2004).[16] However, in 13 out 19 capital crimes, according to the CC of 1922, the judges had full discretion to replace the death sentence with only five years of imprisonment (Kuznetsov, 2002). The focus of the CC of 1922 was mostly rehabilitative, which diminished the use of the death penalty by the courts (Solomon, 1980).

The Constitution of the USSR, enacted in 1924, transferred the general principles of criminal law from the constituent Republics to the Union (Timasheff, 1953). This fact, together with the numerous imperfections of the CC of 1922, became an impetus for the development of new all-Soviet criminal codes, including the Fundamental Principles of Criminal Law of USSR of 1924 and the new CC of Russian Soviet Federative Socialist Republic (RSFSR)[17] of 1926 (Zakhartsev, 2004). The new Code

---

[13]The Decree "About abolishing the highest measure of punishment (shooting)" was adopted by the All-Russian Central Executive Committee and Council of People's Commissars (SU RSFSR, # 4–5, article 22).
[14]The New Economic Policy, also known as NEP, was a temporal liberalization of the state control policy over the market that was conducted in order to improve the overall economic situation in Russia after WWI and the civil war of 1917–1919.
[15]The two drafts did not have identical opinions on the death penalty. The draft by the Narkomyust allowed the use of the death penalty in territories where the state of emergency was declared. The Institute of Soviet Law advocated full abolition of the death penalty by the Soviet state.
[16]The crimes of murder and rape were not considered capital offences. The emphasis on the state interest is another legal tradition that was started by the CC of 1922 and continued through the entire Soviet period.
[17]Russian Socialist Federative Soviet Republic was used as an official title for Russia during the time when it was a part of the Soviet Union (1923e1991).

was adopted in 1926 and it retained capital punishment for all political crimes, but reduced the number of other capital offences (Krylenko 1934).[18] Both The Principles of 1924 and the CC of 1926 continued to declare that capital punishment was an exceptional measure temporarily restored only for the protection of the state and the people, and that it should be used only until its abolition by the All-Russian Central Executive Committee (Butler, 1999).[19] Despite this declaration, capital punishment was not abolished in the USSR. The end of the NEP period in the late 1920s marked a new era of political repression.

In the late 1920s the Politburo of the Communist party inserted itself in the judicial process to exercise significant political control over penal policy and proceedings resulting in the death penalty. The Special Commission for Political Cases was created in 1928 by the Politburo to oversee indictments of political importance where death penalty sentences were possible (Khlevniuk, 1997). Between 1929 and 1940, the CC of RSFSR of 1926 was supplemented by a number of new capital political offences. In 1929, amendments to the CC of RSFSR of 1926[20] provided that officials who defect or take bribes while in office should be treated equally with the perpetrators of crimes against the state and sentenced to death (Berman, 1972). In 1932, the Decree on "Socialistic property"[21] directed the People's Courts that a theft of goods transported by rail or water as well as a theft from collective farms or cooperative property should be considered counter-revolutionary crimes and could be punished by the death penalty (Berman, 1972). In 1934, the crimes against the state were supplemented by a notoriously known capital offence named the "betrayal of the Motherland"[22] (Ponomarev and Mikhlin, 1995). The principle of analogy[23] was allowed when applying these provisions, which made it possible to include all conceivable activities against the state and regular crimes under the umbrella of the "betrayal of the Motherland" offence (Feldbrugge, 1973). During World War II (WWII), the principle of analogy was also responsible for the criminal prosecution of numerous acts, which previously seemed harmless or of minor danger, without requiring amendment of the Criminal Code (Hazard, 1948). According to the official statistics between 1921 and 1953, 790 thousand people were executed for the counter revolutionary offences by both judicial and extrajudicial agencies (Kuznetsov, 2002). However, many historians believe that the actual number of those executed is much higher

---

[18]According to Krylenko (1934), 7.6% of all crimes in the Criminal Code of RSFSR of 1922 were punishable by death penalty. In the Criminal Code of RSFSR of 1926 only 3.4% of all crimes were considered capital offences.

[19]Article 21 of the Criminal Code of 1926, cited from Belyaev and Shargorodskyi (1970).

[20]Sobranie zakonodatel'stva [The code of laws] (henceforth cited SZ), (1929), # 76, article 732.

[21]SZ, (1932) # 62, article 350.

[22]Included in the CC of RSFSR of 1926 by the Statute on Crimes against the State (SZ, 33, article 255).

[23]The principle of analogy, which allows the courts to use criminal law on their own discretion in situations that are similar to the situation described in the code, was originally introduced by the CC of 1922. It sparked a lot of debates and contradiction, but was not widely employed until the penal repressions of the late 1920s and 1930s. The use of the principle of analogy significantly diminished after the Stalin's death and was banned by the CC of 1960.

and that Stalin's political repressions were responsible for the execution of millions of innocent people (Ponomarev and Mikhlin, 1995).

A new attempt to abolish the death penalty in respect to crimes committed during peacetime was undertaken in 1947. The abolition was intended to mark the "victorious conclusion of WWII by the glorious people of Soviet Union" and was introduced by Stalin without the consent of Soviet jurists or the leading criminal law scholars (Solomon, 1978).[24] The death penalty was substituted, according to this Decree by 25 years in prison (Piontkovskyi et al., 1970). In 1950, the death penalty was restored again for offences against the state, including treason, "betrayal of the Motherland," and espionage (Belyaev and Shargorodskyi, 1970). The new CC of RSFSR was adopted in 1960 as a result of "the Kruschev thaw".[25] This code banned the principle of analogy and eliminated the notorious "betrayal of the Motherland" crime. At the same time, the new criminal code contributed significantly to the expansion of the death penalty in Russia by adding new crimes to the list of capital offences (Kistyakovskyi, 1967). The CC of RSFSR (1960) included the death penalty for all state crimes, a murder committed under aggravated circumstances, felonies committed during war time, and selected property crimes such as money counterfeiting, unauthorized dealing of foreign currency, and aggravated robbery by an organized group (Belyaev and Shargorodskyi, 1970; Solomon, 1978). There were more than 30 capital offences in the CC of RSFSR of 1960 despite the fact that the death penalty was still declared an exceptional measure of punishment by the general part of the CC of RSFSR.

Starting from the mid-1980s, many capital offences were gradually excluded from the CC of RSFSR, leaving only a few crimes against the state and crimes against persons. By the end of the 1980s, the number of crimes punishable by the death penalty according to the CC of RSFSR decreased to 24 (Naumov, 2002). In 1991, only 16 capital offences were listed in the CC of RSFSR, 5 of which were related to crimes against persons (Kudryavtsev and Naumov, 1997). Based on the available data, the number of defendants executed in the Soviet Union for crimes against the state gradually decreased since the mid-1970s. In 1962–1963, Berg estimated that about 2200 people were annually executed in the Soviet Union for first-degree murder (Berg, 1985). At the same time, Mikhlin asserted that only 116 people were executed by the Russian Federation in 1998 (2000). In the late 1980s, Soviet scholars and jurists were actively discussing the new direction of long needed criminal law reform. Accordingly, the Model Fundamental Principles of Criminal Legislation and the Model Penal Code were drafted in 1985 and 1986 in an effort to reform the existing criminal law. These documents were never enacted, but they created a meaningful discussion on the major points

---

[24]Vedomosti Verhovnogo Soveta SSSR [The bulletin of the Supreme Counsel of USSR], (hence force cited as VVS SSSR), 1947, # 17.
[25]"Krushcev thaw" is a period of temporal political liberalization that occurred while Nikita Khrushchev was appointed the Head of the Communist Party and the state. The Khrushchev campaign was intended to debunk the cult of personality developed by Stalin and provides some restrictions over the political oppressions.

of criminal law reform including the abolition of the death penalty in the late Soviet Union. Some authors of these drafts, such as Karelina and Sakarov were adamant opponents of capital punishment. However, faced with overwhelming public and scholarly support for the death penalty, they did not include the idea of abolition in either the Principles or the Criminal Code (Solomon, 1992). Instead, both documents supported an idea of limited death penalty application, available only for crimes against the state and the most heinous crimes against persons. The deep scholarly divide on the matter of the death penalty continued until the adoption of the new CC of Russia in 1996, with a large group of scholars arguing for the death penalty.[26] This historic overview illustrates that both the adoption and abolition of death penalty through the Russian history was not a question of mere instrumental necessity. Instead, it can be argued that death penalty law was used by both Tsars and Soviet leaders to communicate various messages to existing political agents. The processes of strengthening the government's authority were usually related in Russia to the adoption or expansion of death penalty laws, whereas the historic moments of liberalization and enlightenment can be connected to the attempts of death penalty abolition.

Available data on death penalty sentences and executions in Russia is scarce and contradictory. It is unclear how many people were executed in Soviet Russia and the Soviet Union between the 1920s and the mid-1950s. Pristavkin, the adviser to the President of Russia and the head of the Clemency Commission[27] (Pristavkin, 2004), asserted that approximately 20,000 were executed in the Soviet Union for criminal activities each year between 1920 and 1954.[28] Data provided by Berg give some indication of death penalty executions in the Soviet Union during 1960s, but are also incomplete and based on a regional data set only (1985). His estimations suggest that at least 2200 people were executed annually during the early 1960s in the Soviet Union (Berg, 1985).

The most comprehensive data about death sentences and executions in Russia for the last 37 years was provided by Mikhlin (2000). He used official statistics on executions provided by the Russian Ministry of Corrections and revealed that for the last four decades the number of executions performed in the Soviet Union was reduced from 2159 people in 1962 to 116 people in 1998. Data provided by Barry and Williams (1997) corroborates tendencies reported by Mikhlin, but offers a different number for executions conducted between 1985 and 1990. Barry and Williams suggest that 770 individuals were executed in the Soviet Union in 1985, and by the year

---

[26]Some Soviet and Russian jurists supported the death penalty from traditional standpoints: they argued that the death penalty reduces homicide crime rates, restores social fairness in the society, and is the most effective measure of general deterrence (Galiakbarov, 1997; Mikhlin, 1997). Other jurists had more practical arguments including the fact that poor prison conditions in Russia would make the life sentence "more inhumane" than the death penalty itself (Boikov, 1999). At the same time, several leading legal scholar advocated the abolition of the death penalty, suggesting that this was a legal trend within all democratic societies that Russia should also follow (Petrukhin, 1999). For details on the important legislative acts adopted in relation to the death penalty during 1917–1991, please refer to Appendix 1.
[27]See Supra note # 35.
[28]He made his estimation based on the fact that 640,000 people were executed in the Soviet Union between 1921 and 1954.

of 1990, the number of executions dropped to 195. Since 1999, official statistics from the Russian Ministry of Justice show that no person was executed or sentenced to death. Nevertheless, the use of official statistics to estimate the scope of executions in the Soviet Union and Russia is problematic. The official Soviet and Russian statistics are known to have fundamental flaws, since they are manipulated for the purpose of plausible reports (Skomor-okhov and Shikhanov, 2006). In the absence of other available data, researchers have to use the official statistics for death penalty executions in Russia but should exercise caution over their reliability (Terrill, 1997).

3. LOOKING WEST: THE DEATH PENALTY UNDER
THE CURRENT CRIMINAL LAW IN RUSSIA[29]

Since the dissolution of the Soviet Union in 1991, the attitudes of ruling political elites towards the death penalty in Russia have undergone significant change. Many of the "new democrats"[30] considered capital punishment an atrocity of the totalitarian past and were ready to abolish it. Thus, in the early 1990s the death penalty was often viewed as a temporary measure that would be discontinued in the very near future (Ignatov and Krasikov, 1999). This vision was reflected in the Constitution of the Russian Federation adopted in 1993.

The Parliamentary Assembly of the Council of Europe (PACE) is one of the most prominent opponents of the death penalty in Europe. In 1980, this organization appealed to the members of the Council of Europe (CE) with a declaration to abolish the death penalty in the entire territory of Europe. In 1983, Protocol No. 6 to the European Court of Human Rights (ECHR) was created to eliminate the death penalty in Western Europe; it was signed by the 21 members of the CE. With time, the ratification of Protocol No. 6 to the ECHR became a necessary condition for membership in the CE (Barry and Williams 1997). In the effort to integrate into the European community, in 1992 Russia applied for membership in the Council of Europe. On January 25, 1996, membership was granted pending ratification of Protocol No. 6 by Russia within the next three years.[31] In Opinion # 193, the PACE declared that it was

---

[29]The information for this section was acquired from several sources. The texts of historic legal documents were taken primarily from the official sources on Soviet legislation, which include the Collection of Statutes and Regulations issued by the Factory and Peasant Government of the Russian Soviet Federative Republic, the Collection of Statues of the USSR, and the Bulletin of the Supreme Soviet of the USSR. The current Russian legislative documents and court decisions were provided by the official online depositary of all Russian legislation run by a private company, "Consultant".

[30]"New democrats" is a label used for political groups and parties organized in the early 1990s as a result of the democratic changes and transformations occurring in the Soviet Union. The new democrats were ideologically juxtaposed to the conservative communist party. Later, the new democrats split into different political groups and branches including the current ruling centrist party.

[31]Such a conclusion can be drawn based on the language of Opinion # 193 by the PACE adopted on 01.25.1996. This document states in Article 10 that "The Russian Federation shares fully its understanding and interpretation of commitments entered into as spelt out in paragraph 7, and intends:. to sign within one year and ratify within three years from the time of accession Protocol No. 6 to the European Convention on Human Rights on the abolition of the death penalty in time of peace, and to put into place a moratorium on executions with effect from the day of accession". Cited from http://assembly.coe.int.

an understanding of the European community that Russia, as a member of the CE, would accept the international obligation to ratify Protocol No. 6.

In accordance with this international obligation, the President of Russia issued Decree # 724 "On the gradual decrease of the application of the death penalty in connection with accession to the CE".[32] President Yeltsin instructed the government of Russia to prepare and introduce a bill to the State Duma, which allowed Russia to sign and ratify Protocol No. 6. The appropriate draft was prepared by the government by the end of 1996, but was never passed by the State Duma.[33]

But also in 1996, the State Duma adopted a new Criminal Code of Russia (CC of Russia), which recognized the death penalty as one of the possible criminal punishments. Article 58 of the CC of Russia allowed the death sentence for five capital offences, all of which pertained to crimes against life (Butler, 1999).[34] What is more important, the CC of Russia of 1996 provided an opportunity to replace the death penalty by life imprisonment or imprisonment for a term of 25 years if clemency is granted.[35] According to the Constitution of Russia (1993), the only person who can grant clemency in such cases is the President of Russia.[36] The President created the Commission on Pardon and Amnesty to process the clemency requests.[37] In order to bring the current penal law in accordance with the new CC of Russia, the new Criminal Executive Code of Russia (CEC of Russia) was adopted in 1997. Provisions in articles 184–186 of the CEC of Russia allowed the execution of the death sentence only after the President of Russia denied the defendant's application for clemency.[38] The combined provisions of these three documents—the Constitution of Russia, the CC of Russia of 1996, and the CEC of Russia of 1997—dcreated a situation where the death penalty was at least partially *de facto* abolished, as long as the President of Russia granted clemency to all defendants sentenced to death.[39] In the absence of a binding directive to the Commission on Pardon and Amnesty, this situation still allowed the courts, at least theoretically, to carry out existing death penalty sentences, which made this *de facto* abolition incomplete.

---

[32]Retrieved from www.consultant.ru on 04.23.08.

[33]According to the recollections by Pristavkin (2004), one out of seven representatives in the Duma voted for the moratorium, but the Communist party strongly opposed such a decision.

[34]According to the CC of Russia of 1996, the following crimes are considered capital offices: murder with aggravating circumstances, attempted assassination against the state or a public figure, attempt on the life of a person administering justice or preliminary investigations, attempt on the life of a law-enforcement officer, and genocide (Articles 105 (2), 277, 295, 317, and 357 of the CC of Russia).

[35]Par. 3 Article 58 of the CC of Russia of 1996. English translation is cited from Barry and Williams (1997).

[36]See Article 89, par. C of the Constitution of Russia of 1993. Retrieved from www.consultant.ru on 04.23.08.

[37]Clemency Commission is an advisory body to the President of Russian Federation. It was created in 1991 in order to assist the President with the decisions of pardon for criminal defendants. The Clemency Commission was dismissed after 1999, when the Constitutional Court of Russia temporary banned the death penalty executions. For more information on the functioning of the Clemency Commission please see Mikhlin (2000).

[38]Par. 4 Article 184 of the CEC of Russia of 1997. The text of the CEC of Russia was retrieved from www.consultant. ru on 04.23.08.

[39]This abolition is sometimes called "partial" since under the law of 1997 the possibility of the execution still exists for the defendants who choose not to apply for the Presidential clemency.

The *de facto* partial abolition did not preclude Russia from executing convicted individuals after 1996. According to Report # 7746, presented on January 28, 1997, PACE received a confirmation "that in the first half of 1996, at least 53 executions were carried out in Russia, in flagrant violation of the commitment entered into by the country upon accession to the Council of Europe to put into place a moratorium on executions immediately".[40] Based on this report, on January 29, 1997, the PACE adopted Resolution # 1111, which condemned Russia's actions and "warn[ed] the Russian authorities that it [would] take all necessary steps to ensure compliance with commitments entered into ... The Assembly may consider the non-ratification of the credentials of the Russian parliamentary delegation at its next session".[41]

In response to this criticism, on February 27, 1997 the President of Russia issued an order instructing the Ministry of Foreign Affairs to sign Protocol No. 6. In compliance with this Order, Protocol No. 6 was signed by Russia on April 16, 1997 in Strasburg. At the same time, a group of pro-presidential representatives introduced a bill in the State Duma to declare a three-year moratorium on executions.[42] In the explanatory note to the bill the representatives argued that due to a high number of judicial errors and miscarriages of justice in Russia, and under international obligations of Protocol No. 6, it was the duty of the State Duma to declare a legislative moratorium on the executions.[43] The bill was defeated by the State Duma with only 75 out of 257 representatives voting for it. Both communist and centrist political parties opposed the bill as "a document that does not reflect on the current Russian reality, where the crime rates are drastically increasing every year" (Pozdnov, 2003, p. 50). No word was made of PACE obligations during this defeat.

Soon after that, on January 8, 1998, new amendments were introduced to the provisions of articles 184–185 of the CEC of Russia.[44] These amendments allowed the President of Russia to pardon defendants sentenced to death, even if these defendants did not apply for clemency. This situation is sometimes described as a complete *de facto* abolition of the death penalty (Pozdnov, 2003). In 1999, the President of Russia made another attempt to abolish the death penalty. On August 6, 1999, he introduced a draft of a bill that entirely abolished the death penalty in

---

[40]Cited from Report # 7746 "Honouring of the commitment entered into by Russia upon accession to the Council of Europe to put into place a moratorium on executions of the death penalty" adopted by PACE on 01.28.97. Retrieved from http://assembly.coe.int on 4.23.08.

[41]Cited from Resolution # 1111 "Honouring of the commitment entered into by Russia upon accession to the Council of Europe to put into place a moratorium on executions of the death penalty" adopted by PACE on 01.29.97. Retrieved from http://assembly.coe.int on 4.23.08.

[42]The Draft of the Bill # 97803716-2 was introduced to the Duma on December 20, 1997. Retrieved from www. consultant.ru on 04.23.08.

[43]The explanatory note to the draft of the bill # 97803716-2. Retrieved from www.consultant.ru on 04.23.08.

[44]Amendments were introduced by Statute # 11-FZ on 01.08.98. Retrieved from www.consultant.ru on 04.23.08.

Russia.[45] The bill was again defeated by the State Duma. The Duma made it impossible for Russia to ratify Protocol No. 6, which had been signed in 1997.

That same year, a third player was introduced into the conflict between the Russian parliament and the President of Russia. The Constitutional Court of Russia[46] decided to contribute to the death penalty debate by issuing a ruling on February 2, 1999.[47] In its ruling the Constitutional Court asserted that article 20 of the Russian Constitution guarantees a jury trial for every defendant who could face a death sentence. Since by 1999, the jury option in most of the regions was not available, the Constitutional Court ruled that the use of the death penalty in Russia is currently unconstitutional. The Constitutional Court also stated that the death penalty could not be applied even in the nine regions of Russia where the jury trials existed by 1999 because this would violate the principle of equal protection (Barry, 2002). The possibility of jury trials in all Russian regions was introduced by the new Criminal Procedural Code (CPC) adopted in December 2001.[48] However, due to both organizational and financial difficulties, it was decided that jury trials would not be established simultaneously through the entire territory of Russia. In 2002, Russia had few judges who had any experience working with jury trials. Moreover, most of the courts had no funding and no experience dealing with the process of jury selection including the creation of venire and *voir dire*. The Statute "On the effect of CPC of Russia of 2001"[49] provided that jury trials would resume in 9 regions of Russian starting July 2002; in 62 regions starting January 2003; in 13 regions starting July 2003; in 4 regions starting January 2004; and in 1 region, Chechen Republic, starting January 2007. In 2006, the State Duma extended the deadline to introduce jury trials in Chechen Republic until January 2010.[50] As of now, jury trials exist in all regions of Russia except the Chechen Republic. Beginning in 2010, the Russian courts can again sentence defendants to death. However, existing provisions of Articles 184–185 of the CEC of Russia (1997) still allow the President to pardon every defendant sentenced to death. Since Russia is a Presidential Republic, the Presidential pardon will take over the court's prerogative. Thus the Russian Federation remains the only country out of 46 CE members who signed, but has not ratified the Protocol No. 6. Since 1997, 14 former Soviet-bloc countries have signed and ratified this Protocol.

---

[45]The draft # 99077736-2 was introduced to the State Duma on 08.06.1999. Retrieved from www.consultant.ru on 04.23.08.

[46]See Supra Note # 1.

[47]The Constitutional Court Ruling # 3-P About the review of the constitutionality of articles 41 and 42 of the CPC of RSFRS, and provisions 1 and 2 of the Decree of Supreme Council" adopted on 07.16.93 "About coming into the effect for the "Statute on court system", the CPC of RSFSR, the CC of RSFSR and the AC of RSFSR according with complaints of the citizens and by the inquiry of the Moscow city courts", adopted on 02.02.1999. Retrieved from www. consultant.ru on 04.23.08.

[48]Article 30 of the CPC of Russia of 2001. Retrieved from www.consultant.ru on 04.23.08.

[49]Article 8, par 2 of Statute # 177-FZ "On the effect of the CPC of Russia of 2001" adopted on 12.18.2001. Retrieved from www.consultant.ru on 04.23.08.

[50]The amendment # 241-FZ to the Statute "On the effect of the CPC of Russia of 2001" was adopted on 12.27.2006. Retrieved from www.consultant.ru on 04.23.08.

4. ATTITUDES AND REACTIONS TO THE DEATH PENALTY IN RUSSIA: PEOPLE, THE STATE DUMA, AND THE PRESIDENT

4.1. The public[51]

According to the available data, most Russians express overwhelming support for the death penalty.[52] Since the late 1980s, when Glasnost[53] was declared the principle of new post-Soviet Russia, a number of research companies have been allowed to measure public opinion on the death penalty. The first known study was conducted by the All-Russian Center of Public Opinion Research (VCIOM) in 1989. It revealed that 62% of all Russians believed that the application of the death penalty should be continued and even extended beyond the existing capital offences (the Foundation of Public Opinion, (FOM, 1997a)). Five years later, 65% of respondents in a representative sample of Russia agreed that the death penalty should be used and only 5% of Russians thought that capital punishment should be immediately abolished (VCIOM, 1994).

In 1997, according to a study by FOM, 70% of all Russians continued to think that the capital punishment should be used (FOM, 1997c). The study also discovered that 55% of all Russians thought that the moratorium declared on the death penalty in 1996 was a mistake, and 63% of all Russians argued for immediate restoration of capital punishment (FOM, 1997b).

In 2000, public support for the death penalty in Russia increased according to the study by VCIOM. Based on VCIOM data, 73% of all respondents favored capital

---

[51]The secondary data onpublic opinion about death penaltyinRussia was available online from polling research companies such as VCIOM, FOM and ROMIR. VCIOM is agovernment research center created inthe late 1980s. The data was retrieved from www.wciom.ru. FOM is an abbreviation for the Foundation of Public Opinion, an independent non-profit research organization. The data was retrieved from www.fom.ru. ROMIR is an abbreviation for the Russian Public Opinion Research Group. It is an independent for-profit research organization. The data was retrieved from www.romir.ru. Levada is the last name of the director of the Levada Center. Henceforward, Levada Center research will be referred to in this paper as Levada. All companies use similar sampling methodology. A representative sample of the Russian population is drawn by the multistage random cluster sampling technique. The sampling process is usually conducted in five stages. (1) A list of regions within federal circuits is commonly used as a sampling frame for the first stage. Regions are weighted using population demographics consisting of: gender, age, professional occupation, average income, and proportion of rural to urban population. According to the Russian Constitution, the 86 regions are geographically grouped into the larger fractions called "federal circuits". There are currently seven federal circuits in Russia. (2) In the second stage of sampling, the cities, towns, and villages are selected fromthe clustered regions. (3)Inthe third stageof sampling, the election districts are usually selected from the list of cities, towns, and villages. (4) Inthe fourth stage ofsampling, households registered with each election district are selected. (5) In the fifth stage of sampling, individual respondents are selected within the households. In each of the three survey companies, the sampling selection varies by the number and type of stratification and selection methods used during each stage. However, for all data used for this paper, the sampling error does not exceed 5%, which allows us to assert that the public opinion data are representative of the entire Russian Federation.

[52]This conclusion is also supported by the content analysis of the Russian mass media. For example, according to a study conducted by Moscow Academy of MVD (Borovikova, 2002), 28.5% of all publications in the Russian newspapers are devoted to the death penalty. Within these publications, over 80% reflect support for the death penalty as the best method to deter offenders from committing heinous crimes.

[53]Glasnost is one of the principles of democratic change declared in the late 1980s by Gorbachev. It refers to the ideas of free press and information, in contrast to the control of information by the state used during the USSR period.

punishment (VCIOM, 2000). The proportions of death penalty supporters were highest among respondents over 45 and those with less than a college degree (VCIOM, 2000). In 2001, VCIOM reported another increase in public support of capital punishment in Russia. According to their study, in 2001, 79% of all Russians believed that some heinous crimes in Russia should be punishable by death (VCIOM, 2001). The study by FOM, also conducted in 2001, corroborates these findings, showing that 63% believed that the moratorium on the death penalty should be revoked (FOM, 2001a).

Conducted in 2002, a study by VCIOM showed further growth in public support for the death penalty in Russia. According to this study, 82% of all respondents agreed that the death penalty should be restored (VCIOM, 2002). In a study by the Russian Public Opinion Research Group (ROMIR), 57.9% of all respondents were in favor of lifting the moratorium on the death penalty in Russia (ROMIR, 2005a). The most recent studies by leading research centers show that public support for the death penalty in Russia remains strong. Data by FOM (2006) indicates that 74% of all respondents consider the death penalty an appropriate measure of social control and punishment. Finally, a study by Levada in 2007 shows that only 17% of all Russians believe that the death penalty is morally unacceptable (Levada, 2007). This number is much higher (36%) for users of the Internet, who tend to be younger and more educated than the general population (RuNet, 2008).

Differences observed over the years by the different polling companies can be, to a certain degree, attributed to differences in the questionnaire methodology used in each study. For a better understanding of the questionnaires used to assess public attitudes on the death penalty in Russia, we provide a summary in English translation of the questions used by the various surveyors. None of the surveys provided respondents with questions on life imprisonment as an alternative to capital punishment. Please see Appendix 2 for details. Notwithstanding the observed differences, the public polls suggest that, despite the major changes in both political and economic systems of the former Soviet Union, public approval of the death penalty remains strong and stable.

4.2. Russian Duma

The opinion of the State Duma, the lower chamber of the Russian parliament, concurs with public opinion on the death penalty (Zveyagin, 1997). Since 1996, the Duma made every effort to avoid the *de jure* abolition of the death penalty in Russia despite continuous and strong pressure from the Russian President. The Duma defeated both bills to abolish the death penalty in 1997 and the legislative moratorium on the death penalty in 1999. On February 15, 2002, the Duma adopted a declaration addressed to the President of Russia expressing serious concerns over a possible abolition of the death penalty in Russia in a situation of rising crime rates. It stated that the abolition would contradict the repeatedly expressed popular will and would make Russian people feel insecure and abandoned.[54]

---

[54]See State Duma Decree # 2483-III-GD issued on 02.15.2002. Retrieved from www.consultant.ru on 04.23.08.

Only minority liberal parties that had never dominated the Russian legislative body favored abolition and attempted to ratify Protocol No. 6 (Pristavkin, 2004). Some researchers believe that the Duma's reluctance to abolish the death penalty in Russia is due to fear of adopting an unpopular law (Mikhlin, 2000). The Duma's approval ratings over the last 10 years has remained very low (VCIOM, 2008). According to most polls, the Duma is one of the least popular and least trusted political institutions in Russia (FOM, 2000).[55] Some other researchers speculate that the Duma's actions represent the personal views of the Duma members along with the instrumental views of their parties (Mitroshenkov, 2004).[56] With the overwhelming public support for the pro-presidential "United Russia" party[57] and its victory in the last Duma's election, it is unclear whether the current Duma is still concerned with aligning its position on the death penalty with general public opinion (Gadjiev, 2008). It is possible to suggest that the current Duma may change their opinion on the death penalty abolition to align their views with Prime Minister Putin, who plays a critical role in the party's public success.

4.3. The President

Unlike the public and the State Duma, both presidents Yeltsin and Putin of Russia[58] can be considered supporters of the abolition of the death penalty. President Yeltsin championed the idea of death penalty abolition by applying to the Council of Europe in 1992 in an effort to integrate Russia into the European community (Ritter, 2000). President Putin continued this line of foreign policy by creating the conditions for the *de facto* abolition of the death penalty in Russia.[59] Putin urged the State Duma to confirm international obligations taken on by Russia as a result of signing Protocol No. 6 in 1997.

Paradoxically, survey results confirm that the popular image of the Russian Presidents did not suffer from their unpopular views on abolition. In the study by FOM (2001b), 55% of respondents reported that they were aware of the presidential idea

---

[55]For example, according to the study by FOM (2000), the State Duma was among top three least trustworthy institutions in Russia in 2000.

[56]According to Mitroshenkov (2004), 70% of all public servants, including the representatives of the State Duma, believed that capital punishment in Russia should be restored.

[57]United Russia is a pro-presidential centrist party that was created in 2000. At the Duma's election of 2007, United Russia received an overwhelming majority of the seats in the Duma. For the last two years, according to the VCIOM (2008) data, United Russia's approval rating has ranged from 45% to 62%. This is compared to approval ratings of less than 10% for all the other political parties. Liberal parties like Yabloko, who supports the abolition of death penalty, consistently received 1% of popular approval for the last two years. The literature on the current public situation in Russia suggests that the high ratings for the "United Russia" are directly resulting from the public approval for Prime Minister Putin. Surprisingly, the high approval ratings for the majority party in Duma, do not translate into the increase of public support for the Duma itself (Gadjiev, 2008).

[58]Here we are referring to presidents Yeltsin and Putin. As of now, the elected president Medvedev has not had a chance to express his opinion on the issue of death penalty abolition. However, his adherence to the public policy of president Putin allows us to suggest that Medvedev will remain a supporter of death penalty abolition, as did the presidents before him.

[59]Here were are referring to the adoption of the new CC of Russia in 1996, the new CEC of Russia in 1997 and the amendment to the new CEC of Russia in 1998.

to abolish the death penalty, and 60% of respondents said they disapproved. At the same time, the study conducted by ROMIR (2005b) suggests that the President remains the most trusted political figure in Russia.[60] A possible explanation for this paradox was reflected in interviews conducted by FOM in 2001. According to FOM's data, people in Russia believe that the official position of the Russian President is just a tribute to the European community, and that he is forced to hold these views under the pressure of current foreign policy (FOM, 2001b). Interviews conducted by FOM in conjunction with the survey showed that people believe that the abolition of the death penalty is an alien Western idea that was imposed on Russia due to its weak political and economic position in the world. For that reason, they "forgive" the President and believe that once Russia becomes politically stronger, the head of state will no longer seek to abolish the death penalty (FOM, 2001b).

5. SUMMARY AND CONCLUSIONS: THE WAY AHEAD

When speculating over the potential number of death penalty executions that could take place in Russia if the death penalty were restored, one should probably rely on current statistics on murder convictions. The CC of Russia adopted in 1996 lists only two major categories of capital offence – crimes against the state and aggravated murder. Studies on the death penalty in the last two decades of Soviet Union's history show that over 90% of all people executed were offenders convicted on the charge of aggravated murder (Mikhlin, 2000). The number of people who were executed for crimes against the state diminished by the mid-1980s and remained insignificant (Duyunov, 2000; Turetskyi, 1985). Currently, such offenders receive life imprisonment terms as the only constitutionally allowable substitution for the death penalty (Kuznetsov, 2002). Official statistics from the Ministry of Justice and the Judicial Department of the Supreme Court show that, for the last five years, the number of people annually sentenced to life imprisonment in Russia for aggravated murder range from 45 to 96.[61]Assuming that the number of crimes against the state will not increase dramatically, it is safe to suggest that if Russia were to resume death penalty executions, they might apply to dozens of offenders annually.

The promise of the eventual abolition of capital punishment in Russia has kept Russia in the hunt for eventual membership in the European Community. Whatever happens after 2010, public opinion will not likely be the determining factor. Throughout Europe and the U.S., abolition has not been grounded in public opposition to capital punishment. If Russia resumes executions, even at a low level, CE membership will be forfeited. Even if *de facto* abolition is maintained, membership is unlikely. Finally, should Russia resume wholesale executions it will find a kindred soul in the Peoples' Republic of China (the PRC), its large and influential neighbor in the East.

---

[60]In this study, 34% of respondents said that they trust the President, compared to only 8% who said they trust the government, and 4% who said they trust the State Duma.
[61]The data is retrieved from http://www.sopcourt.ru on 12.10.08.

   The Soviet Union and Russia have a long tradition of frequent executions. Yet for over 100 years there has existed a slender reed of Russian abolitionist thought. As in other settings, symbolic, unenforced law in Russia serves the age-old goal of attempting to bridge the gap between incompatible parties. Frequent executions would incite an adamant official response from the EC and make membership impossible while outright abolition would antagonize Russian citizens since. We have demonstrated conclusively that Russian opinion polls show solid support for the death penalty. On the other hand it must be said that this public opinion is not totally unlike that found in Western Europe, which has no capital punishment laws.

   Yet public opinion is where the similarities between Russian and Western Europe end. In the past the Russian Duma seemed to be afraid to contradict public opinion and thus overwhelmingly supported the death penalty. However, in the recent election the pro-presidential party of United Russia took over the Duma, which suggests that current Duma may reverse their opinion regarding support of the death penalty and align with the presidential position. The Duma remains very unpopular with the Russian electorate, even though the United Russia party has a strong public support. Recent Russian presidents Yeltsin and Putin seem totally committed to improving the external relations of Russia with the West and hope for eventual integration into the EC. Such membership would facilitate trade relations and likely ease international tensions. The President alone has the legal authority to offer clemency to all who are sentenced to death and has pushed for the abolition of the death penalty. The President remains a very popular institution even with this support for abolition. The Russian public can have it both ways; they support the death penalty but also support a President who does not. Complicating matters further the Constitutional Court of Russia has ruled that no capital trials can occur without juries and yet juries will not be established throughout all regions of Russia until 2010. How long this stalemate will last, no one can predict. In Hong Kong local courts for several decades continued to sentence convicted murderers to death and complained bitterly about British interference with executions (Gaylord and Galliher 1994). This situation changed once unification with the PRC neared. Now Hong Kong politicians determined that formal abolition was superior to the threat of wholesale executions at the hands of the PRC. It may be that the Russian Duma will behave similarly after 2010 when Russian executions will again become a legal reality.

APPENDIX 1. CHRONOLOGICAL LIST OF IMPORTANT LEGISLATIVE ACTS RELATED TO THE DEATH PENALTY IN POST-TSARIST AND SOVIET RUSSIA, 1917–1991

Agency and act	Date	Significance
Provisional Government. The decree of the Provisional Government	3.12.1917	Death penalty was completely abolished.
Provisional Government. The decree of the Provisional Government	7.12.1917	Death penalty was restored for heinous crimes committed during war time.
Provisional Government. The decree of the Provisional Government	9.28.1917	The use of the death penalty was postponed until a "special order of Provisional Government".
Second Congress of Soviets. The decree of the Second Congress of Soviets. "Reinstated by Kerensky death penalty at the battle fields is abolished"	11.7.1917	Death penalty was completely abolished.
Council of People's Commissars. The Decree-declaration titled "Socialist Motherland is in Danger!"	2.21.1918	Death penalty was allowed for selected counter-revolutionary crimes.
Peoples Commissariat for Justice. The Decree	6.16.1918	The Emergency Commissions were allowed to use the death penalty based on their "revolutionary consciences".
Council of People's Commissars. The Decree "About Red Terror"	9.05.1918	Death penalty was allowed for all counter-revolutionary crimes without the right to appeal. Sentenced defenders are subject to immediate execution.
Council of People's Commissars. The Decree to introduce "Leading Principles of criminal law"	12.12.1919	Death penalty was included in the system of criminal punishments according to Soviet criminal law. It was considered a temporary measure to be used until the full abolition by the government.
All-Russian Central Executive Committee and Council of People's Commissars. The Decree "About abolishing of the highest measure of punishment (shooting)"	1.17.1920	Death penalty was abolished, but the conditions for resuming it in future were stated.

(continued)

Agency and act	Date	Significance
All-Russian Central Executive Committee and Council of People's Commissars. The Decree "About Announcing Emergency Situation for Some Provinces"	5.11.1920	Military tribunals were allowed to sentence defendants to death in provinces under the emergency situation.
Third Congress of All-Russian Central Executive Committee (10th convocation). Criminal Code of Russian Soviet Federative Socialist Republic	7.01.1922	Death penalty was included in the system of criminal punishments as a temporary and exceptional measure.
Second Congress of All-Russian Central Executive Committee (11th convocation). "Fundamental principles of criminal legislation of USSR and Union Republics'	10.31.1924	Death penalty was not included in the major system of criminal punishments. It was listed separately as an exceptional measure. Principles also noted that the death penalty should be regulated by the Criminal Codes of the Union republics.
Second Congress of All-Russian Central Executive Committee (12th convocation). Criminal Code of Russian Soviet Federative Socialist Republic (RSFSR)	11.22.1926	Death penalty was declared an exceptional and temporal measure for protection of workers and law and order. It remained in the system of criminal punishments.
All-Russian Central Executive Committee and Council of People's Commissars. The Decree on the "Socialistic property"	8.07.1932	A theft of goods transported by the rail or water as well as a theft of collective farms or cooperative property were considered counter-revolutionary crimes and were punishable by the death penalty.
All-Russian Central Executive Committee. The Decree "About introduction of Amendments to the CC of RSFSR"	6.8.1934	Introduced new article 58 to the CC of RSFSR, "Betrayal of Motherland", punishable by death. This led to mass executions during 1930s.
Presidium of Supreme Soviet of USSR. The Decree "About Measures of Punishment for the German Fascists."	4.19.1943	Introduced death penalty for the crimes committed by Nazi's invaders during the German occupation of USSR.
Presidium of Supreme Soviet of USSR. The Decree "About Abolition of Death Penalty"	5.26.1947	Abolished death penalty for all crimes and supplemented it with 25 years of camp labor.

Presidium of Supreme Soviet of USSR. The Decree "About Application of Death Penalty to the Traitors of the Motherland, Spies, Diverters"	1.12.1950	The death penalty was reinstated for certain types of crime against the state.
Presidium of Supreme Soviet of USSR. "Fundamental principles of criminal legislation of USSR and Union Republics"	12.25.1958	Included death penalty as exceptional and temporal measure of criminal punishment. Crimes against the state and murder under aggravated circumstances were considered capital offences.
Third Congress of Supreme Soviet of RSFSR (5th convocation). Criminal Code of RSFSR	10.27.1960	Criminal Code included death penalty as an exceptional measure of criminal punishment and listed over 20 capital offences.
Presidium of Supreme Soviet of USSR. The Decree "About Strengthening the Struggle with very serious crimes against Socialist Property"	5.5.1961	Theft of socialist property was included in the list of capital offences.
Presidium of Supreme Soviet of USSR. The Decree. "About Strengthening Struggle against violations of Foreign Currency Transactions"	7.01.1961	Unauthorized foreign currency transactions were included in the list of capital offences.
Presidium of Supreme Soviet of USSR. The Decree. "About Strengthening Criminal Liability for Rape, Murder and other Heinous Crimes"	2.15.1962	Rape under aggravated circumstances and murder of a law-enforcement officer were included in the list of capital offences.
Presidium of Supreme Soviet of RSFSR. The Decree. "About Strengthening Criminal Liability for Crimes Committed at the Air Transport"	4.17.1973	Hijacking of a plane included in the list of capital offences.

**APPENDIX 2. SUMMARY OF QUESTIONNAIRES ON
DEATH PENALTY CITED IN THIS STUDY**

Study by FOM (1997a). The majority of Russians are Still Against the Death Penalty Abolition

Exact Russian wording
Как вы считаете, смертную казнь следует отменить или расширить ее применение?
Следует отменить (или постепенно идти к ее отмене)
Следует оставить (или даже расширить применение смертной казни)

Author's English translation
Do you think that the death penalty should be abolished or should be expanded?
Should be abolished (or gradually abolished)
Should remain (or gradually increase) the use of the death penalty

Study by FOM (1997c). The Russians and the Jail

Exact Russian wording
Как вы думаете, следует ли в России отменить смертную казнь?
Да/нет

Author's English translation
Do you think that Russia should abolish the death penalty?
Yes/no

Study by FOM (1997b). About Death Penalty

Exact Russian wording
В 1996 призидент Росии принял решение о введение моратория на сметрную казнь в Росии. Как вы относитесь к этому решению – одобряете еГо или нет?
Одобряю/ Не одобряю/Затрудняюсь ответить

Author's English translation
In 1996, the President of Russia made a decision to place a moratorium on death penalty in Russia. How do you feel about this decision?
Approve/Disapprove/Do not know

Study by VCIOM (2000). All-Russian survey. Item # 57_K

Exact Russian wording
В какой мере Вы соГласны или не соГласны что смертная казнь должна быть отменена?
соврешенно соГласен/ скорее соГласен/ скорее не соГласен/ совршенно не соГласен

Author's English translation
To what degree to do you agree or disagree that the death penalty should be abolished? Completely agree/somewhat agree/somewhat disagree/completely disagree

Study by FOM (2001a). About the Moratorium on the Death Penalty

Exact Russian wording

Уже около пяти лет Россия соблюдает мораторий на исполнение смертных приГ оворов. Судя по нашим данным, осведомлены об этом 68% россиян. Как же следует поступать в дальнейшем?

привести в псполнение смертные приГоворы

не приводить вынесенные смертные приГоворы в исполнение (соблюдать мораторий)

вообще отменить смертную казнь

Author's English translation

For about five years now, Russia has been complying with the moratorium on death penalty executions. According to our data, 68% of all Russians know about it. What should we do next?

Execute offenders that are sentenced to death

Do not execute offenders that are sentenced to death according to moratorium (comply with the moratorium)

Abolish the death penalty completely

Study by VCIOM (2001). All-Russian Survey. Item # 36

Exact Russian wording

Как Вы думаете должна ли существовать в России смертная казнь за тяжкие уГоловные преступления?

Author's English translation

What do you think, should Russia have the death penalty for heinous (serious) crimes?

Yes/no

Study by VCIOM (2002). All-Russian Survey. Item # 47

Exact Russian wording

Как Вы думаете должна ли в нашей стране существовать смертная казнь?

Да/нет

Author's English translation

What do you think, should our country have death penalty?

Yes/no

Study by ROMIR (2005a). The Attitude Towards the Death Penalty

Exact Russian wording

Как Вы относитесь к смертной казни?

Мораторий на смертную казнь надо отменить

Смертная казнь недопустима

Затрудняюсь ответить

Author's English translation
How do you feel about death penalty?
Moratorium should be lifted
Death penalty is unacceptable
Do not know

Study by FOM (2006). About Death Penalty

Exact Russian wording
по вашему мнению, в принципе допустимо или недопустимо приговаривать преступников к смертной казни?
допустимо/ не допустимо/ не знаю

Author's English translation
In your opinion, as a matter of principle, is it acceptable or not to sentence offenders to death?
Acceptable/unacceptable/do not know

Study by Levada (2007). The Moral Acceptability of Different Behavior and Study by RuNet (2008). The Survey of Russian Internet

Exact Russian wording
пожалуйста, скажите, вы считаете морально приемлемым или морально неприемлемым смертную казнь?
морально приемлимо/ морально неприемлимо

Author's English translation
Do you think that death penalty is morally acceptable, or not?
Morally acceptable/morally unacceptable

REFERENCES

Adams, W., 1970. Capital punishment in imperial and soviet criminal law. The American Journal of Comparative Law 18 (3), 575–594.

Barry, D.D., 2002. Capital punishment in Russia: the post-soviet phase. In: Feldbrugge, F.J.M., Simons, W.B. (Eds.), Human Rights in Russia and Eastern Europe. Martinus Nijhoff Publishers, The Hague, London and New York, pp. 3–14.

Barry, D.D., Williams, E.J., 1997. Russia's death penalty dilemmas. Criminal Law Forum 8 (2), 231–258.

Belyaev, M.A., Shargorodskyi, M.D., 1970. Kurs sovetskogo ugolovnogo prava. Chast' obschaya (The Course of Soviet Criminal Law), vol. 2. Leningrad State University Press, Leningrad.

Berg, G.P.v.d., 1985. The Soviet System of Justice: Figures and Policy. Martinus Nijhoff Publishers, Dordrecht, Boston and Lancaster.

Berman, H.J., 1972. Soviet Criminal Law and Procedure. Introduction. Harvard University Press, Cambridge, MA.

Boikov, A., 1999. Smertnaya kazn' -problema otmeny (Death penalty - the problem of abolition). Zakonnost' 8, 32–43.

Borovikova, V.V., 2002. Problemy osvesheniya prestupnosti v sredstvah massovoi informatsii i profilakticheskaya deyatel'nost' vnutrennih del (The problems of covering the crime rates in the media and the preventive function of the Ministry of Interior Affairs). Moscow Academy of MVD, Moscow.

Browder, R.P., Kerensky, A.F., 1961. The Russian Provisional Government: 1917. Documents. Stanford University Press, Stanford, CA.

Budzinskyi, S., 1870. Nachalo ugolovnogo prava (Beginning of Criminal Law). Glavnyi sklad v knizhnykh magazinakh Kozhanchikova v St. Peterburge, Varshave i Kazani, Warsaw.

Butler, W.E., 1999. Russian Law. Oxford University Press, Oxford, UK.

Duyunov, V.K., 2000. Problemy ugolovnogo nakazaniya v teorii, zakonodatel'stve i sudebnoi praktike (Problems of criminal punishment in theory, legislation and court practice). Press of Regional Open Social Institute, Kursk.

Edelman, M., 1971. Politics as Symbolic Action. Markun Pub. Co., Chicago.

Estrin, A.Y., 1935. Osnovy i istoriya sovetskogo ugolovnogo prava. Chast' obshchaya. Uchebnik. Vyp. 1 (The Basics and History of Soviet criminal law. General Part. Textbook. Volume 1). Soviet Publisher, Moscow.

Feldbrugge, F.J.M., 1964. Soviet Criminal Law. General Part. A.A. Sythoff, Leiden.

Feldbrugge, F.J.M., 1973. Encyclopedia of Soviet Law. Oceana Publications, Leiden.

Feldshtein, G.S., 1909. Glavnye techeniya v istorii nauki ogolovnogo prava Rossii (The Major Tendencies in the History of Criminal Law Science in Russia). Tipografiya Gubernskogo Pravleniya, Yaroslavl'.

FOM, 1997a. Bol'shinstvo rossiyan po prezhnemu protiv otmeny smertnoi kazni (The Majority of Russians are Still Against the Death Penalty Abolition) Retrieved 05.05.2008, from <www.fom.ru>.

FOM, 1997b. O smertnoj kazni (About Death Penalty). Retrieved 05.05.2008, from <www.fom.ru>.

FOM, 1997c. Rossiyane i tur'ma (The Russians and the Jail). Retrieved 05.05.2008, from <www.fom.ru>.

FOM, 2000. A komu iz etih organov vlasti, organizatsii, sotsial'nyh institutov Vy ne doveryaete (Whom From the Following Agencies, Organizations and Societal Institutions You Do Not Trust?). Retrieved 05.50.2008, from <www.fom.ru>.

FOM, 2001a. O moratorii na smertnuyu kazn' (About the Moratorium on the Death Penalty). Retrieved 05.05.2008, from <www.fom.ru>.

FOM, 2001b. Smertnaya kazn': za i protiv (Death Penalty: For and Against). Retrieved 05.05.2008, from <www.fom.ru>.

FOM, 2006. O smertnoi kazni (About Death Penalty). Retrieved 05.01.2008, from <www.fom.ru>.

Gadjiev, K.S., 2008. Politologiya. Osnovnoi kurs (Political science. The bases). Yurait, Moscow.

Galiakbarov, R.R., 1997. Ugolovnoe pravo Rossikoi Federatsii. Obschaya chast' (Criminal law of Russian Federation. General part). Saratovskaya Vysshaya Shkola MVD, Saratov.

Gaylord, M., Galliher, J., 1994. Death penalty politics and symbolic law in Hong Kong. International Journal of the Sociology of Law 22, 19–37.

Gernet, M.N., 1906. Obschestvennyaya prichiny prestupnosti: sotsialisticheskoe napravlenie v nauke ugolovnogo prava (Social Reasons for Crimes: Sociological Studies in the Criminal Law). Izdanie S. Skirmunta, Moscow.

Gernet, M.N., 1913. Smertnaya kazn' (Death Penalty). Tipographiya A. Dankin i Ya. Khomutov, Moscow.

Gerzenzon, A.A., Gringauz, S.D., Durmanov, N.D., Isaev, M.M., Utevskyi, B.S., 1948. Istoriya Sovetskogo ugolovnogo prava. (History of Soviet Criminal Law). Yuridicheskoe izdatel'stvo MYu SSSR, Moscow.

Gordon, V.M., Kisilev, A.D., Palienko, N.P., Popov, B.V., Raevskiy, A.A., Temnikovskyi, E.N., et al., 1911. Ugolovnoe pravo iz kursa pravovedeniya po Narodno entsiklopedii. Tom 1. Obschestvenno-yuridicheskie nauki (Criminal Law According to the Jurisprudence Course from the People's Encyclopedia. Volume 1. Social-legal Sciences). Tipographiya tovarischestva I.D. Sytina, Moscow.

Gusfield, J.R., 1963. Symbolic Crusade. University of Illinois Press, Urbana, and Chicago, IL.

Hazard, J.N., 1948. Drafting new soviet codes of law. American Slavic and East European Review 7 (1), 32–44.

Ignatov, A.N., Krasikov, Y.A., 1999. Ugolovnoe pravo Rossii (Criminal law of Russia). Norma-Infra, Moscow.

Juviler, P.H., 1976. Revolutionary Law and Order. The Free Press & Collier Macmillan Publishers, New York and London.

Khlevniuk, O.V., 1997. The Politburo penal policy and legal reforms in 1930s. In: Solomon Jr., P.H. (Ed.), Reforming Justice in Russia, 1864–1996. M.E. Sharpe, New York and London, pp. 190–206.

Kistyakovskyi, A., 1896. Issledovanie o smertnoi kazni (Research About Death Penalty). Izdanie L.F. Panteleeva, St. Petersburg.

Kistyakovskyi, A., 1967. Issledovanie o smernoi kazni (Research About Death Penalty). Nauchna dumka, Kiev.

Krylenko, N.V., 1934. Sovetskaya ugolovnaya repressiya (Soviet Criminal Repression). Soviet Legislation, Moscow.

Kucherov, S., 1970. The Organs of Soviet Administration of Justice: Their History and Operation. E.J. Brill, Leiden. Kudryavtsev, V.N., Naumov, A.V., 1997. Rossiiskoe ugolovnoe pravo. Obschaya chast'. Uchebnik (Russian Criminal Law. General Part. Textbook). Spark, Moscow.

Kuznetsov, N.F., 2002. Kurs urolovnogo prava. Tom 1 (Course of the Criminal Law. Volume 1). Zertsalo, Moscow.

Levada, 2007. Moral'naya priemlimost' razlichnyh postupkov (The Moral Acceptability of Different Behavior) 05.05.2008, from. <www.levada.ru>.

Malinovskyi, I.A., 1908. Krovavaya mest' i smertnyya kazni, Vyp 1 (Tribal Vengeance and Death Penalty Issue 1). Tomsk Imperial University, Tomsk.

Mikhlin, A., 1997. Smertnaya kazn'. Vchera, segodnya, zavtra (Death Penalty. Yesterday, Today, Tomorrow). Legal Literature, Moscow.

Mikhlin, A., 2000. Vysshaya mera nakazaniya: istoria, sovremennost', budushee. (The highest measure of punishment: history, present and future) Delo, Moscow.

Mitroshenkov, O.I., 2004. Otnoshenie naseleniya i gossluzhaschiih k suschestvuyushemu pravoporyadku (The attitudes of people and the public servants towards the law and order). Sociological Research 5, 113–120.

Moutchnik, A., 2006. Der Strelitzen-Aufstand von 1698. In: Löwe, H.v.H.D. (Ed.), Volksaufstände in Rußland Von der Zeit der Wirren bis zur "Grünen Revolution" gegen die Sowjetherrschaft. Harrassowitz Verlag, Wiesbaden, pp. 197–222.

Naumov, A.V., 2002. Rossiiskoe ugolovnoe pravo. Obshcaya chast'. Uchebnik. (Russian Criminal Law. General Part. Textbook). Bek, Moscow.

Nethercott, F., 2007. Russian Legal Culture Before and After Communism. Routledge, London and New York.

Petrukhin, I.L., 1999. Pravo na zhizn' i smertnaya kazn' (The right of life and the death penalty). Zakonnost' 5, 80–90.

Piontkovskyi, A., Romashkin, P.S., Chkhikvadze, V.M., 1970. Kurs ugolovnogo prava. Nakazanie. T.3. (The Course of Criminal Law. Punishment), vol. 3. Nauka, Moscow.

Ponomarev, P., Mikhlin, A., 1995. Primenenie smertnoi kazni v istorii rossiiskogo gosudarstva (The Application of Death Penalty in the History of Russian State). Delo, Moscow.

Pozdnov, M.S., 2003. Ponyatie i suschnost' smertnoi kazni (The understanding and the nature of death penalty). New legal thought 1, 45–53.

Pristavkin, A., 2004. The Russian Federation and the Death Penalty. In: Hood, R., Badinter, R. (Eds.), The Death Penalty Beyond abolition. Council of Europe Press, Haag, pp. 199–204.

Rawson, D., 1984. The death penalty in late tsarist Russia: an investigation of judicial procedures. Russian history 11 (1), 29–52.

Ritter, K.L., 2000. The Russian death penalty dilemma: square pegs and round holes. Case Western Reserve Journal of International Law 32 (129), 1–33.

ROMIR, 2005a. Otnoshenie k smertnoi kazni (The Attitude Towards the Death Penalty). Retrieved 05.05.2008, from <www.romir.ru>.

ROMIR, 2005b. Tsifry i facty (Numbers and Facts). Retrieved 05.05.2008, from <www.romir.ru>.

Rozin, N.N., 1913. Ugolovnoe sudoproizvodstvo: posobie po lektsiyam. (Criminal Procedure: Study Guide for Lectures). Tipografiya Tomskago Imperskogo Universiteta, Tomsk.

RuNet, 2008. Opros RuNet. Fevral', 2008. (The Survey of Russian Internet. February, 2008) Retrieved 05.05.2008, from <www.runet.ru>.

Sergeevskyi, N.D., 1887. Nakazanie v Russkom prave XVII veka (Punishment According to Russian Law 17 Century). Izdanie knizhnago magazina A.F. Zinzerlinga, St. Petersburg.

Sergeevskyi, N.D., 1910. Russkoe ugolovnoe pravo. Chast' obschaya (Russian Criminal Law. General Part). Tipografiya M.M. Stasyulevitcha, St. Petersburg.

Shargorodskyi, M.D., 1957. Nakazanie po ugolovnomu pravu (Nakazanie po ugolovnomu pravu ekspluatatorskogo obschestva). (Punishment According to the Criminal Law (Punishment Under the Law of Exploiter Society)). Gosyurizdat, Moscow.

Shargorodskyi, M.D., 1958. Nakazanie po ugolovnomu pravu (Nakazanie po sovetskomu ugolovnomu pravu). (Punishment According to the Criminal Law (Punishment Under the Soviet Criminal Law)). Gosyurizdat, Moscow.

Skomorokhov, R.V., Shikhanov, V.N., 2006. Ugolovnaya statistika i problema sotsial'noi deformtasii organov vnu-tennikh del. (Criminal statistics and the problem of professional deformation of the agencies of interior affairs). State and Law 3, 62–70.

Solomon Jr., P.H., 1978. Soviet Criminologists and Criminal Policy. Columbia University Press, New York.

Solomon Jr., P.H., 1980. Soviet penal policy, 1917–1934: a reinterpretation. Slavic Review 39 (2), 195–217.

Solomon Jr., P.H., 1992. Reforming criminal law under Gorbachev: crime, punishment and the rights of the accused. In: Barry, D.D. (Ed.), Toward the "Rule of Law" in Russia? M.E. Sharpe, London and New York, pp. 235–256.

Spasovich, V., 1863. Uchebnik ugolovnogo prava. Tom 1. Vyp 1 (Textbook of Criminal Law. Volume 1. Issue 1). Tipografiya Iosafata Ogrizko, St. Petersburg.

Tagantsev, N.S., 1912. Russkoe ugolovnoe pravo. Lektsii. Chast' obschaya. T.2. (Russian Criminal Law. Lections. General Part, Volume 2). Nauka, Moscow.

Tagantsev, N.S., 1913. Smerntaya kazn'. Sbornik statei (Death penalty. The collection of articles). Gosudarstvennaya tipografiia, St. Petersburg.

Terrill, R.J., 1997. World Criminal Justice Systems: A Survey. Anderson Publishing Company, Cincinnati, Ohio.

Timasheff, N.S., 1953. The impact of the penal law of imperial Russia on Soviet penal law. American Slavic and East European Review 12 (4), 441–462.

Turetskyi, M.V., 1985. Osobo opasnye gosudartsvennye prestupleniya (Very dangerous state crimes). Izdatel'stvo Moskovskogo Universiteta, Moscow.

VCIOM, 1994. Chelovek sovetskiy - pyat' let spustya (The Soviet Person – Five Years Later) Retrieved 05.05.2008, from <www.wciom.ru>.

VCIOM, 2000. Vserossiskaya vyborka. Vopors 57_K (All-Russian Survey. Item # 57_K) Retrieved 05.05.2008, from <www.wciom.ru>.

VCIOM, 2001. Vserossiskaya vyborka. Vopors 36 (All-Russian Survey. Item # 36) Retrieved 05.05.2008, from <www. wciom.ru>.

VCIOM, 2002. Vserossiskaya vyborka. Vopors 47 (All-Russian Survey. Item # 47) Retrieved 05.05.2008, from <www. wciom.ru>.

VCIOM, 2008. Reiting obschestvennyh institutov (Rating of Societal Institutions) Retrieved 05.05.2008, from <www. wciom.ru>.

Viktorskii, S.N., 1912. Istoriia smertnoi kazni v Rossii i sovremennoe eia sostoyanie (History of Death Penalty in Russia and its Modern State). Tipografiia Imperskago Moskovskago Universiteta, Moscow.

Zagoskin, N.P., 1892. Ocherk istorii smertnoi kazni v Rossii. Rech chitannaya na godichno-makte Imperatorskogo Kazanskogo Universiteta. (The historic essay of the death penalty in Russia. Speech presented during the annual meeting of the Imperial Kazan' University) [Electronic Version]. Izvestiya i uchennye zapiski kazanskogo universiteta. (Bulletin and the Study Papers of the Kazan' University) 1 Retrieved 12.06.08, from <http://www.allpravo.ru/library/doc101p0/instrum2363/>.

Zakhartsev, S.N., 2004. Sovetskoe pravo v gody NEPa (1921–1929) (Soviet Law During the NEP (1921–1929)). Press of Tambov State Technical University, Tambov.

Zveyagin, Y., 1997. Moratorii na smertnuy kazn' i positsiya deputatov (Moratorium of the death penalty and position of representatives). The Journal of Russian Law 7, 156–158.

Olga B. Semukhina is an assistant professor of criminology and law studies at Marquette University. She received her MS in criminal justice from University of Central Florida (UCF) in 2001 and PhD in Public Affairs from UCF in 2007. She also holds LLB and LLM degrees from Law Institute of Tomsk State University in Russia. Her research interests include comparative criminal procedure, criminal procedure of international institutions, transnational crimes, comparative policing, and international standards of due process.

John F. Galliher is Professor of Sociology and Director of Peace Studies at Missouri University. He is interested in the history of drug laws as well as capital punishment and the biographies of progressive scholars. He also has studied how the U.S. government has abused its legal authority in administering drug laws and how some American states have done the same in executions. His overarching concern involves an increased understanding of human rights.

EDWIN SUTHERLAND'S RESEARCH ON THE ORIGINS OF SEXUAL PSYCHOPATH LAWS: AN EARLY CASE STUDY OF THE MEDICALIZATION OF DEVIANCE*

JOHN F. GALLIHER

and

CHERYL TYREE

University of Missouri-Columbia

Sutherland claimed that sexual psychopath laws were largely a result of the manipulation of public opinion by the press and the influence of psychiatrists on the legislative process. However, there are obvious gaps in his documentation of these laws and in his evidence on news stories about sex crimes. We analyze major newspapers in each state that passed a sexual psychopath law and find far greater diversity in the coverage of sex crimes than Sutherland claimed. Based on material in Sutherland's research files, interviews with his former students and colleagues, and a review of his other published works, we argue that Sutherland's interest in studying sexual psychopath laws was to debunk psychiatry. His strong opposition to psychiatric "interest groups" may account for his lack of careful attention to evidence and for his premature dismissal of alternative, structural explanations of the origins of this legislation.

Edwin Sutherland's (1950b) study of the diffusion of sexual psychopath laws in the U.S. is one of the earliest and best-known sociological investigations into the origins of a specific type of criminal law. Also, this is perhaps the first case study of the medicalization of deviance—a broad transformation of social control that has received considerable attention in recent years (e.g., Conrad and Schneider, 1980), Sutherland argued that sexual psychopath laws exemplified "a trend toward psychiatric policies [which are premised] on the assumption that the criminal is a socially sick person" (1950b:147). He was especially concerned about the potential erosion of legal rights by this movement toward "treatment of offenders as patients" (1950b:147).

This ground-breaking study influenced later analyses of the rule-making process (e.g., Becker, 1963; Schur, 1971) and continues to be cited frequently.[1] However, a close examination of Sutherland's research reveals some curious lapses and inconsistencies in the evidence he marshalled in support of his conclusions. For instance, he indicated that 12 states and the District of Columbia passed sexual psychopath

---

*We received generous advice from Donald Cressey, Malcolm Spector, Karl Schuessler, Alfred Lindesmith, Albert Cohen, William Chambliss, Richard Quinney, Sarah Boggs, and Mark Gaylord in the collection and analysis of the data. James McCartney and Neal Shover helped in organizing the ideas in earlier versions of the manuscript. Correspondence to: Galliher, Department of Sociology, University of Missouri, Columbia, MO 65211.

[1]We counted a total of 25 entries for this article in the *Social Sciences Citation Index* (1966–1981).

laws, yet he did not cite any of these statutes. Moreover, when we reviewed states' sessions laws for the period in Sutherland's analysis, we found that he overlooked a state (Missouri) that passed a sexual psychopath law and included another state (New Jersey) that did not enact such a bill.[2]

In this paper, we focus on these and other indications of a surprising lack of thoroughness in this eminent scholar's work on sexual psychopath laws. Drawing on historical evidence that Sutherland overlooked, we re-examine his claims about the influences of newspaper accounts and psychiatric opinion on the legislative process and reconsider alternative explanations he summarily dismissed. We also use material from Sutherland's research files and published works, and from interviews with his students and colleagues to shed light on professional concerns that shaped his views of "psychiatric policies."

THE SUBSTANCE OF SUTHERLAND'S CLAIMS

Sutherland argued that the concept of sexual psychopathy as defined in state statutes was so vague that the constitutionality and fairness of these laws had to be questioned. Typically, these laws provided for indeterminate confinement—by a probate rather than a criminal court—of individuals who were not proven mentally ill. Sutherland asserted that "these dangerous and futile laws are being diffused with considerable rapidity" and that "they continue to spread, with no indication of abatement" (1950b:142–3). Consequently, he asked: "What is the explanation of this diffusion of laws which have little or no merit?" (1950b:143). In an effort to answer this question, he developed a set of observations about events that generally precede passage of these laws:

> First these laws are customarily enacted after a state of fear has been aroused in a community by a few serious sex crimes committed in quick succession (1950b:143).

> A protracted man-hunt following a sex attack arouses additional fear. The newspapers report daily on the progress of the chase, and every real or imagined sex attack, from near and far, is given prominence (1950b:143).

Thus, Sutherland emphasized four crucial elements in press coverage of sex crimes: (1) a few serious crimes; (2) which are committed in quick succession; (3) reported in a protracted manner; and (4) given prominence by the press. He added that "sex murders of children are most effective in producing hysteria" (1950b:143).

Since Sutherland asserted that fear was heightened and spread by popular literature—especially newspaper coverage of crimes and subsequent man-hunts—it is

---

[2]The statutes of all the states listed by Sutherland make explicit reference to the psychic qualities of "sexual psychopaths," "sex perverts," or "degenerates," except the New Jersey (1949) law, which merely provided for mental hospitalization of those convicted of sex offenses if they were mentally ill. Therefore, New Jersey should not have been included as a state with sexual psychopath legislation. The following sexual psychopath laws are referenced at the end of this article: Michigan (1937, 1939); Illinois (1938); California (1939); Minnesota (1939); Vermont (1943); Ohio (1945); Washington (1947); Massachusetts (1947); Wisconsin (1947); District of Columbia (1948); Indiana (1949); New Hampshire (1949); Missouri (1949).

surprising that he made little reference to newspaper accounts in his work. He did not present a systematic examination of newspapers for any of the 12 states or the District of Columbia. In fact, the only newspaper account he cited was an article dealing with a brutal sex murder and mutilation in Los Angeles. Sutherland's summary of this case appears to support his claims about the nature of news coverage of sexual attacks and its impact on the "state of fear" in the community. However, it is important to note that this case occurred in 1949—a decade *after* the passage of the 1939 sexual psychopath law in California. Therefore, neither this case nor any other material in Sutherland's study provides direct evidence for his assertions about the influence of news accounts *prior* to the enactment of sexual psychopath laws. Later, we address this curious gap in Sutherland's research by analyzing news coverage of sex-related crimes in the year preceding the passage of such legislation in 12 states and the District of Columbia.

Another major theme in Sutherland's analysis is the crucial role played by psychiatrists in the development of sexual psychopath laws. He observed that a typical response to public agitation over notorious sex crimes is "the appointment of a committee, which in some cases has been guided by psychiatrists" (1950b:147). Sutherland went on to describe how this committee sets the agenda for the legislation of psychiatric policy:

> [It] organizes existing information regarding sex crimes and the precedents for their control and . . . presents a sexual psychopath law to the legislature and to the public as the most scientific and enlightened method of protecting society against dangerous sex criminals (1950b:147).

Through their participation on these committees and in other phases of the legislative process, "psychiatrists, more than any others, have been the interest group [in] back of the laws" (1950b:145). As Sutherland noted, psychiatrists had a material stake in promoting this kind of legislation:

> . . . since the sexual psychopath laws usually specify that the diagnosis for the court shall be made by psychiatrists, they have an economic interest in the extension of this procedure (1950b:146).

However, Sutherland also argued that these laws were based more fundamentally on a broad cultural "trend toward treatment and away from punishment" (1950b:147). He was apparently the first social scientist to recognize that a social movement to redefine crime as disease "has been gaining . . . ground" (1950b:147). He claimed that the medicalization movement was strongly implicated in the sexual psychopath laws:

> The most significant reason for the specific content of the proposals of these committees—treatment of the sex criminal as a patient—is that it is consistent with a general social movement (1950b:147).

In attempting to explain the regional patterning of this legislation, Sutherland suggested that the development of treatment policy was more prominent in certain areas of the country than in others:

These laws, in fact, have been enacted in a solid block of North Central states: Ohio, Indiana, Illinois, Michigan, Wisconsin, and Minnesota. On the other hand, no state in the southern, South Central, or Mountain regions has a sexual psychopath law. These regions also are less committed to treatment policies than are the regions which have sexual psychopath laws (1950b:148).

Yet, he acknowledged that this was an incomplete explanation since New York had an extensive commitment to treatment policies but had no psychopath law (1950b:148). He concluded his article with a cursory listing of other "statistical variables" which failed to distinguish states that passed these laws from those that did not:

... they are not differentiated by the rate of rape, by the racial composition of the population, by the proportion of immigrants in the population, by the sex ratio in the population, or by the extent of industrialization or urbanization (1950b:148).

Clearly, there are serious weaknesses in Sutherland's evidence. Neither his own interpretation of the passage of sexual psychopath laws nor his ready dismissal of other factors is adequately documented by case materials or statistical data. We now turn to our efforts to overcome and understand the limitations of his sociological analysis of this "psychiatric policy."

DATA AND SOURCES

We began by reviewing sessions laws for all states for the years 1937 to 1949 to confirm Sutherland's claims about the provisions of the sexual psychopath laws and the number of states with such statutes. We contacted the appropriate government offices in those states that had passed sexual psychopath legislation.[3] Only four states—Massachusetts, Minnesota, New Hampshire, and Wisconsin—could locate any evidence of a commission having been appointed to investigate sex crimes. None of the states contacted could provide records of public hearings or legislative floor debate on proposed laws. The sexual psychopath law for the District of Columbia was noted in the *Congressional Record* (U.S. Congress, 1948), but, even here, there was no debate on the legislation.

We also reviewed daily newspapers in each state that passed a sexual psychopath law during the 1937–1949 period (see Table 1). We selected the major daily newspaper with the largest circulation in each appropriate state.[4] Every page of every daily issue was reviewed for one year prior to the law's passage in a search for stories of sex crimes, sex offenders, community reaction to such crimes and people, or any other stories that might provide insight into the passage of these laws. Included in the sample were stories of unspecified attacks on women and on children of either sex, and in which there was any indication of sexual motives of the attacker, such as the description of a victim's partially or completely disrobed body. This sample included

---

[3]The specific office responsible for these records varied from state to state—e.g., the Secretary of State, the Clerk of the House or Senate, or the State Historical Society.
[4]The Minnesota newspaper with the largest circulation during the relevant time period is now defunct and microfilm copies are not available. Therefore, we used the paper with the second largest circulation.

attempts at rape or other attacks with apparent sexual motives, whether the attacks were successful or not. For comparison purposes the *New York Times Index* was consulted for the years 1930–1949 to assess the number of sex-crime articles in a state which did not enact sexual psychopath legislation.

To help understand the sources of Sutherland's ideas, we attempted to locate the materials that he used in his research, such as notes and documents. The file Sutherland used for the sexual psychopath research was in the custody of Donald Cressey, a former Sutherland student. Professor Cressey provided what he believed to be the complete folder of materials for Sutherland's research. We also checked the collection of Sutherland papers at the Indiana University library, without success, for any other relevant documents. Former graduate students and colleagues of Sutherland were interviewed to piece together the origins of Sutherland's interest in and information about sexual psychopath laws. The first four editions of his criminology textbook, published before his death, also were consulted to reconstruct the development of his thinking on this and related issues. Finally, state arrest rates for rape, and census figures by state on the sex ratio, the percent black, and percent urban were reviewed to check Sutherland's conclusions about these "statistical variables."

NEWSPAPER ACCOUNTS OF SEX CRIMES

Contrary to Sutherland's claims about consistent patterns in press reporting of sex-related crimes, we found contradictory results in different newspapers. As shown in Table 1, newspaper coverage in some states reflected little visible interest in rape or other sex crimes in the year prior to the passage of the sexual psychopath law. The *Cleveland Plain Dealer*, for example, published only 13 sex-crime stories during the year before the Ohio legislation passed in 1945. Vermont passed a sexual psychopath law in 1943, but in the prior year only 17 sex-crime stories were printed in the *Burlington Free Press*.

In other locales, the press coverage of such events was more intense. This is especially apparent in Massachusetts, where the *Boston Globe* published a total of 228 stories in the year before the passage of the state's sexual psychopath law in 1947. More specifically, there was a highly publicized case in Massachusetts involving a black male who was accused of sexually assaulting and killing a young woman. Sixty-six stories appeared on this single case. By comparison, all other sex-crime stories in other newspapers were relatively minor media events. Generally, Table 1 reveals little evidence of press coverage designed to create a crisis atmosphere by overreporting particular sex crime cases. The average number of articles per case is slightly fewer than two. Aside from the unusual coverage in Massachusetts, only the papers in Vermont and New Hampshire average over three articles per case.

The data in Table 2 indicate sex murders of children did not receive especially prominent coverage in states that passed sexual psychopath laws, with the exception of Missouri. Contrary to Sutherland's claim that "sex murders of children are most effective in producing hysteria" (1950b:143), the most highly sensationalized cases in Boston, Detroit, and Chicago involved adult victims. A highly publicized case in Milwaukee involved the rape of a child, not murder. While three of the five cases

TABLE 1

Number of Sex-Crime Articles and Cases in Local Newspapers
During the Year Prior to Passage of a State's Sexual Psychopath Law

State	Newspaper	Time Period Covered	Number of Sex-Crime Articles	Number of Sex-Crime Cases	Average Number of Articles per Case	Number of Articles on Most Frequently Cited Case
Michigan	Detroit News	July 1936–July 1937	209	103	2.03	21
Illinois	Chicago Daily Tribune	July 1937—July 1938	219	126	1.74	15
Minnesota	Minneapolis Journal	April 1938–April 1939	69	46	1.50	9
California	Los Angeles Times	June 1938–June 1939	75	65	1.15	4
Vermont	Burlington Free Press	March 1942–March 1943	17	4	4.25	13
Ohio	Cleveland Plain Dealer	July 1944–July 1945	13	13	1.00	1
Washington	Seattle Daily Times	March 1946–March 1947	59	54	1.09	3
Massachusetts	Boston Globe	July 1946–June 1947	228	75	3.04	66
Wisconsin	Milwaukee Journal	July 1946–July 1947	171	98	1.74	22
Washington, DC	Washington Post	June 1947–June 1948	132	76	1.74	7
Indiana	Indianapolis Star	March 1948–March 1949	174	105	1.66	9
New Hampshire	Manchester Union Leader	July 1948–July 1949	74	23	3.22	34
Missouri	St. Louis Globe Democrat	August 1948–July 1949	41	27	1.52	5
Total			1,481	815	na	na
$\bar{X}$			113.92	62.69	1.97	16

TABLE 2

*Proportion of Sex-Crime Articles Dealing with Out-of-State Cases,
with Black Attackers, and with Child Victims During the Year
Prior to Passage of a State's Sexual Psychopath Law*

State	Percent of Articles on Out-of-State Cases	Percent of Articles On Black Attackers	Percent of Articles on Child Victims (13 Years or less)
Michigan	33	11	23
Illinois	22	21	26
Minnesota	17	6	13
California	27	17	17
Vermont	94	0	0
Ohio	0	8	15
Washington	32	24	19
Massachusetts	17	32	9
Wisconsin	29	15	25
District of Columbia	21	11	27
Indiana	21	1	23
New Hampshire	12	47	7
Missouri	12	2	59
X̄ Percent	26	15	20

receiving the highest coverage involved black defendants, the percentages of articles on black attackers in Table 2 show no consistent pattern across states. Only an average of 15 percent of the articles in the newspapers sampled deal with black attackers. Neither is there evidence that newspapers routinely covered out-of-state stories of sex crimes. Vermont stands out in Table 2 as the only state with a large proportion of such articles (94 percent). In short, press coverage of sex crimes prior to the passage of sexual psychopath laws was more diverse than Sutherland implied.

To assess Sutherland's claims that (1) a few serious sex crimes, (2) committed in quick succession, (3) are given prominence in the mass media, (4) in protracted accounts of man-hunts, we devised a measure of each of these descriptors. For our purposes, serious sex crimes included only sexual assaults which also involved the murder of the victim. Crimes judged to have been committed in quick succession must have occurred within two weeks of one another. Stories given prominence must have appeared in the first five pages of the paper, and protracted coverage of a single case required two or more articles. Table 3 shows that, using these measures, we found 153 reports of serious sex crimes. In press reporting on these crimes, only 78 articles were given prominence, only 29 of these articles involved cases which occurred in quick succession, with only 17 of these cases being the focus of protracted reporting.[5] Thus, only 11 percent of the serious sex-crime reports reflects all the elements of the process described by Sutherland. We should also note that only

---

[5]We calculated prominence in reporting before quick succession to avoid rapid reduction in cases, since so few crimes occurred within two weeks of one another.

TABLE 3

News Reports of Serious Sex Crimes During the Year
Prior to the Passage of a State's Sexual Psychopath Law

Newspaper	Sex Slayings	Given Prominence	Occurring in Quick Succession	Protracted Coverage
Detroit News	24	12	8	6
Chicago Daily Tribune	26	12	4	1
Indianapolis Star	18	11	4	4
Boston Globe	11	8	5	4
Milwaukee Journal	17	8	4	2
Seattle Times	14	3	2	0
Los Angeles Times	8	5	2	0
Minneapolis Journal	9	5	0	0
Manchester Union Leader	7	5	0	0
Washington Post	11	3	0	0
St. Louis Post Dispatch	4	4	0	0
Burlington Free Press	2	2	0	0
Cleveland Plain Dealer	2	0	0	0
Total	153	78	29	17

four newspapers—the *Detroit News,* the *Minneapolis Journal,* the *Milwaukee Journal,* and the *Indianapolis Star*—made any editorial demands for government action to stop sex crimes.

Further doubt is cast on the relationship between media manipulation and sexual psychopath legislation by our examination of sex-crime reporting in the *New York Times* from 1930 to 1949. Following seven years (1930–1936) in which a sum total of three such articles appeared, the *Times* published 244 sex-crime stories in 1937. This is more than the number reported in any other newspaper, yet New York did not enact a sexual psychopath law. Sutherland (1950b:145) mentioned this New York City crisis of 1937 and allowed that, contrary to the typical pattern, the appointment of an investigative committee actually served to prevent legislative action.

SUTHERLAND'S SEXUAL PSYCHOPATH RESEARCH FILES

Material on Press Coverage

Since it appears that there is insufficient evidence in the public record to support all of Sutherland's conclusions about the influence of press coverage, we attempted to determine if anything in his private files could explain his reasoning. In addition to bibliographies, abstracts, and copies of professional publications on sex offenses,[6] his files contain a number of items from magazines and newspapers.

---

[6]There are seven bibliographies with the following titles: Sex, Sex Variants, Sex Offenses, Homosexuals, Exhibitionism, Sexual Psychopaths, and Sexual Psychopath Laws. The files also contain 15 articles and abstracts of professional books or articles.

The nine magazine articles in Sutherland's files are generally sensation-filled and lurid in detail. These include three articles from *True Detective Magazine* and an *American Magazine* article by J. Edgar Hoover, threateningly titled, "How Safe is Your Daughter?" A *Saturday Evening Post* article, "What Can We Do About Sex Crimes?," is illustrated with photographs of girls murdered in sex attacks and of individuals convicted of sex crimes. However, Sutherland's thinking about the importance of sex-crime panics may have been influenced especially by an article from *Time* (1947), which he cited in his study (1950b:143). It presents a vivid account of a climate of fear in Indianapolis, a city in Sutherland's own state:

> The terror started in October with the kidnapping of a young girl. She told police that half a dozen Negroes had raped her at knifepoint. About three weeks later, 68-year-old Mrs. Mabel Merrifield, clubwoman and wife of a former assistant attorney general of Indiana, was murdered in her suburban home. Her throat had been ripped open with a butcher knife. Her killing is still unsolved. Next, a cab driver was beaten to death. Five Negroes, who claimed he took 15 cents too much from them, will be tried for the murder. . . . Last week the jittery community suffered a further shock. In Meridian Hills, wealthy food broker Herschel Burney came home one night, found his 39-year-old wife, Mary Lois, dead on a bed, her face half blown away by a shotgun blast. Her murderer got away. In the Meridian Hills Country Club, a few nights later, 250 frightened, angry people met [and] drafted an open letter to Governor Ralph Gates. "Law enforcement and administration of justice in the city and county are a travesty," it said. They asked for a gubernatorial investigation. Even as they met, three women and a twelve-year-old girl were molested [and] three men were beaten and robbed.

There are 11 newspaper articles in Sutherland's file, most of which are from the *Indianapolis Star.* The link between public fear and legislative action that he developed in his study is reflected in articles like the following: "City Stiffens Penalty as Curb on Molestings"; "Candidate Pledges War on Sex Crimes." Sutherland also noted that the December 8, 1949 edition of the *Star* listed 11 states as having passed or considered sexual psychopath laws. He checked off seven that were not on his own list—including Missouri—but he unfortunately neglected to pursue the lead on that state's 1949 sexual psychopath legislation.

Material on State Legislation

Based on the material in his files, Sutherland appears to have been less than systematic in gathering and interpreting evidence on the legislative process in various states. Although it must be emphasized that these files may be incomplete, we were surprised to find copies of only two statutes, one from Ohio and another from New Jersey. There is detailed information from only three legislative committee reports (Minnesota, Illinois, and New York City).

Judging from the sheer volume of correspondence in these files, we believe that Sutherland relied most heavily on key informants for observations about sexual psychopath committees and legislation. We found 25 letters, mostly from sociologists and lawyers responding to his requests for information about psychopath laws in various states. Correspondence from prosecuting attorneys and physicians provided details on the actual operation of the laws in their states.

The New Jersey statute was enclosed with a letter dated October 17, 1949 from Paul Tappan, a sociologist-lawyer who was Secretary of the New Jersey commission to study sex offenders. Tappan apparently included the statute to support his statement in this letter that, "unlike those of the other jurisdictions, [the New Jersey law] is not cast in terms of the sex psychopath." Sutherland ignored this statement, perhaps because Tappan had mentioned psychopath laws in the District of Columbia and in 12 states—mistakenly including New Jersey—in an earlier letter of October 5, 1949. This same list appeared in Sutherland's article.

Other correspondence in Sutherland's files came from the editors of the *Journal of Criminal Law and Criminology,* Robert Gault and Fred Inbau. Writing on December 13, 1949 about a paper on the unfairness and ineffectiveness of sexual psychopath laws that Sutherland (1950a) was preparing for publication in that journal, Inbau said: "I do not believe that the number of states with sexual psychopath laws, in the sense in which you dealt with the subject, is as large as twelve. For instance, the statute in New Jersey." On November 29, 1949 Gault asked for specific "references to the laws so I can insert an appropriate footnote." Yet Sutherland still erroneously included New Jersey and he provided no citations to statutes in his later paper on the origins of sexual psychopath laws.[7]

Sutherland's subsequent claims about the heavy influence of psychiatrists on sexual psychopath legislation also seems to run against the advice of some of his informants. Sociologist George Vold, who chaired the Minnesota commission appointed to study sex offenders, wrote on August 22, 1949 to describe the legislative process in that state:

[The Governor] appointed a committee to study the problem and report to the legislature. The committee was composed of about 18–20 members, all psychiatrists except the chairman [Vold]. . . . The answer to whether psychiatrists were especially active in pressure for the law should probably be a qualified "no"! They were strongly opposed to criminal proceedings but had little faith that hospital commitment would accomplish what the newspapers had in mind, namely "cure" the psychopaths. . . . The present form of the law is the result of the drive by some attorneys for more power under which to prosecute.

Similarly, George Waite of the University of Michigan Law School conveyed the following secondhand information to Sutherland about the Michigan sexual psychopath law in a letter dated November 22, 1949:

I had occasion to ask a man who might know about it and he tells me that . . . he himself does not remember that any committee was appointed to deal with the matter; nor

---

[7]However, apparently in response to Gault's request, Sutherland did include citations to six sexual psychopath laws in the article in the *Journal of Criminal Law and Criminology* (1950a).

do I. . . . I am quite sure that the law was not written by psychiatrists and I doubt whether they were particularly active.

On the other hand, sociologist Marshall Clinard claimed in a letter dated August 3, 1949 that "the psychiatrists played a very prominent part in getting the law enacted" in Wisconsin. Nonetheless, in light of the negative evidence provided by Vold and Waite, the emphasis Sutherland placed on psychiatric "interest groups" hardly seems warranted.

SUTHERLAND'S STUDENTS AND COLLEAGUES

We interviewed former graduate students and colleagues of Sutherland in an attempt to piece together any details they could remember about his study of psychopath laws, including his motives for pursuing this type of research. Presumably, understanding his motives could help explain any gaps or flaws in this research. Presumably, understanding his motives could help explain any gaps or flaws in this research. Included in the interviews were former graduate students at Indiana University: Lois Greenwood Howard; Mary Beth Cameron; Karl Schuessler; Albert Cohen; and Donald Cressey. Two graduate students who studied with him during his years at the University of Chicago also were contacted: Alfred Lindesmith, with whom he also taught at Indiana University; and Marshall Clinard. All shared with Sutherland an interest in crime and could be expected to be especially well informed about his research. Cohen, Lindesmith, and Schuessler demonstrated a special interest in Sutherland's work through the editing of a collection of his writings, *The Sutherland Papers* (1956).

Schuessler remembered that Sutherland was motivated by an antipathy for personality or psychiatric explanations of behavior. Cressey agreed that Sutherland's anti-psychiatric orientation was behind his interest in critically examining sexual psychopath laws. He recalled sending Sutherland some newspaper clippings in the late 1940s on a widely publicized sex-crime case in Los Angeles—the case Sutherland summarized in his article. Both Cohen and Lindesmith remembered that some of Sutherland's initial thinking on such issues is found in the early edition of his criminology textbook, published before the appearance of his sexual psychopath articles in 1950. Clinard agreed that Sutherland's thinking is clearly reflected in the various editions of his textbook:

> The first edition of his textbook in 1924 was a multiple-factor approach which gave the same weight to psychological factors as to others. But if you trace his ideas through the different editions you will see that he became more anti-psychological, and psychopathy is the most extreme form of individualistic explanation. When the various states began to pass these laws in the 1930s and the 1940s this was just too much for him to take. Few papers by Sutherland were as activist-oriented and as critical as those on psychopath laws.

Sutherland's "activist orientation" toward this issue might explain why his conclusions are not completely supported by the data. Such inconsistencies were uncharacteristic of his research, for he had a well-deserved reputation for attention to detail. As Lois Greenwood Howard recalled, "Sutherland was a very careful scholar." Schuessler (1973:xxxv) also praises Sutherland's customary attention to detail:

> Sutherland's competence in method consisted of more than skepticism about calculations remote from the data. Most social scientists share that skepticism. Rather, it consisted in two habits of work: (1) his method of collecting, recording, and maintaining data, and (2) his requirement of a good fit between conclusions and data. Sutherland had no special method for collecting data, except his working rule that all elements in the data be open to inspection and that the process of data collection be reproducible. Thus, from Sutherland's files on white-collar crime, it is possible to examine the raw data in every detail and to reconstruct the operations by which those data were produced.

By comparison, Sutherland's sexual psychopath file makes examination of the "raw data" and research "operations" often difficult and sometimes impossible. And, as demonstrated here, the "fit between conclusions and data" about the passage of sexual psychopath laws leaves something to be desired.

SUTHERLAND'S CRIMINOLOGY TEXTBOOK

Armed with leads from the interviews, we examined the first editions of Sutherland's criminology textbook to help determine why his psychopath research was so uncharacteristic of his typical attention to detail. Prior to his publication of the sexual psychopath articles in 1950, there were four editions of his text. The first edition was published in 1924, the second in 1934, the third in 1939, and the fourth in 1947. As Clinard observed, the 1924 edition of *Criminology* includes a review of numerous factors as causes of crime. However, it is clear that Sutherland already had serious reservations about most individualistic, as opposed to cultural, causes of crime. He challenged the popular idea that immigrants commit more crimes than the native born (Sutherland, 1924:99). He also contended that criminals as a group were not more mentally defective than others (Sutherland, 1924:109). Indeed, he noted in his 1937 book, *The Professional Thief,* that those who committed such crimes were generally very intelligent. In the 1934 edition of his renamed *Principles of Criminology,* Sutherland more directly challenged individualistic theories of crime. For example, he claimed that the overrepresentation of ethnic and racial minorities was due to discrimination rather than constitutional traits (Sutherland, 1934:110–18). Sutherland first presented his differential association theory of the social learning of criminal behavior in the 1939 edition of *Principles of Criminology* (1939:4–9). The theory provided both a reflection of, and intellectual grounding for, his disenchantment with individualistic theories of crime causation.

Even in the first edition of his textbook, Sutherland (1924:123) described the circularity in the usual proof of psychopathy: "Some persons have used criminality as a test of psychopathy, and then used the psychopathy as the explanation of the criminality." Thus, as early as 1924, and continuing through later editions of his textbook, we find evidence of a strong anti-psychiatric ideology.

ALTERNATIVE EXPLANATIONS OF STATE LAWS

Available records indicate that Sutherland was correct in claiming that there is no consistent relationship between the rate of rape in a state and the presence of psychopath legislation. In 1933 the FBI (U.S. Department of Justice:1933–1949) first reported annual rates of rape by state. These rates were repeated until 1936, and again in 1944 through 1949—the last year relevant to this study. None of these 10 annual reports provided racial comparisons by state. In nine of these 10 years, exactly half of the 12 states with psychopath laws were among the top half of all states in the rate of rape. Among states with psychopath laws, only California, Michigan and Missouri were among the states with the highest rates of rape during all 10 years. Clearly there is no consistent relationship between the rate of rape and the passage of psychopath laws.

Unlike the model of elite-manipulated community arousal used by Sutherland, some research demonstrates the profound importance of the demographic, political, and economic environment in which specific laws are passed (Chambliss, 1964; Hall, 1935; Musto, 1973). Rather than focusing only on the motivations and tactics of specific interest groups, it is important to consider the structural context of the legal process as a source of potential or actual social conflict. For example, earlier research found that the most repressive drug laws were created to control the alleged effects of a specific substance on some threatening minority group (Helmer and Vietorisz, 1974; Musto, 1973). More specifically, legal prohibition of cocaine has been linked to white fears of black rapists throughout the United States (Helmer, 1975). Cocaine was alleged to cause madness and wild sexual attacks in black males. Such concerns were baseless, but resulted in lynchings in southern states.

Sutherland recognized the possibility that the sex ratio and degree of urbanization of states—as well as the percentage of blacks—might have an impact on the sexual psychopath laws. However, there is no evidence in his file or his writings that he actually investigated such data. Since women are presumably a major target of sex deviants, the percentage of females in a population might be a relevant consideration. Yet, there was too little variation across states in the sex ratio for it to hold much promise as an explanation of psychopath laws. Thus Sutherland seems correct in having discounted this factor. In examining the percentage of a state's population that lived in urban areas, we found from the 1940 census (U.S. Department of Commerce, 1975) that, except for Vermont, all of the states which passed psychopath laws were among the 23 most urbanized states. On the other hand, the states with the highest percentage of blacks in the population were southern or border states, and none passed psychopath laws. However, census figures on the *migration* of blacks within the nation from 1930 to 1950 show that, of the states passing psychopath laws, only New Hampshire and Vermont were not among the 22 states with the greatest numerical gains in their black population (U.S. Department of Commerce, 1975:95). The massive migration of blacks from the South to the urban North during this period was overlooked by Sutherland.

As suggested by earlier research linking anti-drug legislation and minority oppression, the percentage increase in a minority population may be of equal or greater importance than its sheer size in legal repression by dominant groups (Helmer and Vietorisz, 1974; Musto, 1973). For instance, dramatic increases in the Mexican population in the Southwest preceded the first state marihuana laws in that region and the subsequent federal Marihuana Tax Act of 1937. By the same token, rapid black in-migration to urbanized northern states may have created structurally conducive conditions (Smelser, 1962) for the passage of repressive sexual psychopath legislation. Just as there was no evidence of widespread reports of "marihuana-crazed Mexicans" in southwestern newspapers prior to state marihuana legislation (Galliher and Walker, 1977), we found no evidence here of extensive coverage of crimes by blacks in most states that passed sexual psychopath laws. In both cases, the more diffuse threat of a growing minority presence—rather than highly publicized minority crime waves—seems to have set the stage for repressive legislation.

Although New Hampshire and Vermont did not experience a heavy influx of blacks during this period, these two states were also characterized by exceptionally intense coverage of sex crimes in their major newspapers (see Table 1). Therefore, media manipulation of public opinion may have contributed to legislative action in these particular areas—much as Sutherland claimed was true of all states. Our point is not that urbanization, changes in racial composition, and other structural factors account completely for the regional patterning of sexual psychopath legislation, but that Sutherland was premature in dismissing these and other alternatives in favor of his narrowly focused model of interest group strategies.

CONCLUSION

It seems likely, given the absence of citations to statutes in Sutherland's work, that he did not actually review all the laws to which he referred. We may not have retrieved all the documents Sutherland used, but it is revealing that only two statutes were in his research file. Also, newspaper coverage was more diverse than Sutherland claimed. Not all the papers reflect a crisis atmosphere, and very few of the cases contain all of the elements in his model of media-induced crime panics.

A search of his research file suggests: (1) that he did not systematically review the newspapers from the states he discussed; (2) that his conclusions about the press were based on a very selective sample of sensationalistic pieces, especially lurid magazine articles; and (3) that in some instances he ignored or misinterpreted the suggestions of influential colleagues, while at other times he relied too heavily on their ideas. He ignored Tappan's advice and evidence about the New Jersey law, and Waite's and Vold's observations about the limited influence and ambivalence of psychiatrists. He also ignored the prodding of Inbau and Gault regarding the accuracy of his claims about the specific states having psychopath laws. At the same time, he placed undue emphasis on material from other colleagues, such as the news stories about the 1949 California sex crime that Cressey brought to his attention.

Both interviews with Sutherland's associates and our review of his textbook illustrate his anti-psychiatric views. Snodgrass (1973) found another illustration of Sutherland's antipathy toward psychiatric explanations of criminal behavior in *The Professional Thief,* where Sutherland did not mention his informant's drug addiction.

To do so, Snodgrass reasons, would have contradicted Sutherland's claims about the essential rationality and normality of criminal behavior because of the presumed relationship between drug addiction and maladjustment. Furthermore, an "activist orientation" similar to that mentioned by Clinard is evident in Sutherland's pioneering exposé of law violation in the business community, *White Collar Crime* (1949). Here, Sutherland attacked the press for its failure to report honestly on white collar crime. He said this subterfuge occurs "because these agencies of communication are owned or controlled by businessmen and because these agencies are themselves involved in the violations of many of these laws" (1949:50). Sutherland also dismissed the utility of psychiatric explanations in the genesis of the crimes of corporate leaders.

One plausible explanation for Sutherland's increasingly critical view of psychiatry is that he was lobbying for professional advantage for sociological criminologists. In the early editions of his criminology textbook, it is clear that Sutherland was attempting to carve out a new sociological identity for academic criminology. However, this sense of territory is especially apparent in the essay he published in the *Journal of Criminal Law and Criminology* (1950a:554):

> Certain psychiatrists have stated that they are interested in the sexual psychopath laws principally as a precedent; they believe that all or practically all criminals are psychopathic, that all should be treated as patients, and that psychiatrists should have a monopoly on professional advice to the courts. These laws are dangerous precisely from this point of view; they could be passed over in silence otherwise, as a product of hysteria. The question is whether psychiatrists have a monopoly of knowledge of human personality and human behavior which warrants their nomination as "the experts" in the field of diagnosis and treatment of criminals. Other disciplines, such as psychology, social work, and sociology, have as much training as does psychiatry, and have points of view, hypotheses, and techniques which should be used, together with psychiatry, in the diagnosis and treatment of sex offenders and other offenders. At many points the theories of one of these disciplines are in conflict with the theories of the other disciplines and one has as much scientific validity as the other.... There is no more reason for turning over to the psychiatrist the complete supervision of a criminal who is found to be psychopathic than for turning over to the dentist the complete supervision of a criminal who is found to have dental cavities. If the official agencies of the state are to use professional advice, the advisors should represent all the branches of knowledge and should be on an equal footing.

Thus, Sutherland staked out a professional turf covering much the same ground as that claimed by psychiatrists.[8] This sense of professional competition, together with his worries about the abrogation of civil rights, may have sealed his opposition to

---

[8]Another prime example of Sutherland acting as a disciplinary watchdog is his debate with the sociologist-lawyer, Paul Tappan, on the question, "Is 'White-Collar Crime' Crime?" (Sutherland, 1945; Tappan, 1947). Sutherland insisted that behaviors which violated written law were suitable objects of study for criminology, even if the actors were never convicted of crimes. That is, he insisted on a behavioral rather than a legalistic definition of crime.

these laws. We believe his skepticism of psychiatry predisposed him to blame psychiatrists as the "interest group" that manipulated the legislative process leading to potentially repressive laws. Such skepticism about psychiatric explanations is understandable from a scholar who developed a social psychological theory of criminal behavior which asserts that crime is not a perversion, but rather is learned in a normal manner like any other behavior. If criminal actors are seen as essentially rational and fully human, then they of necessity are imbued with specific human rights. Sutherland defended the rights of immigrants in 1924, professional thieves in 1937, and finally those accused of sex offenses in 1950. Over the years Sutherland was increasingly bold in his defense of the cause of less and less attractive minorities. This concern for the human rights of accused criminals has become a central theme in modern criminological discussions of the race and class-based injustice of American police, courts, and prisons.

Sutherland's work also anticipated later sociological investigations into the medicalization of deviance. He was no doubt correct in alleging that these laws were a part of a general social movement to medicalize crime. Even so, Sutherland placed too much emphasis on the direct intervention of psychiatrists in this particular case. His focus on individual interest groups draws attention away from social structural variables that are presumably the province of sociologists. As a result, he did not sufficiently explore the structural environment in which psychopath laws were passed. Neither media manipulation nor the activities of psychiatric interest groups adequately explain the spread of these laws, and it is time for students of the origins of law to reconsider their use of Sutherland's article as an authoritative source. While his work does provide an early warning of the dangers of the medicalization of deviance, it is a warning that stems from Sutherland's own life-long interest in protecting the professional turf of sociology.

REFERENCES

Becker, Howard S.
    1963   Outsiders. New York: The Free Press.
Chambliss, William J.
    1964   "A sociological analysis of the law of vagrancy." Social Problems 12:67–77.
Cohen, Albert, Alfred Lindesmith, and Karl Schuessler
    1956   The Sutherland Papers. Bloomington, IN: Indiana University Press.
Conrad, Peter and Joseph W. Schneider
    1980   Deviance and Medicalization: From Badness to Sickness. St. Louis: C.V. Mosby Company.
Galliher, John F. and Allynn Walker
    1977   "The puzzle of the social origins of the Marihuana Tax Act of 1937." Social Problems 24:367–76.
Hall, Jerome
    1935   Theft, Law and Society. Indianapolis: Bobbs-Merrill.
Helmer, John
    1975   Drugs and Minority Oppression. New York: Seabury Press.

Helmer, John and Thomas Vietorisz
    1974   Drug Use, the Labor Market, and Class Conflict. Washington, DC: Drug Abuse Council.

Musto, David F.
    1973   The American Disease: Origins of Narcotic Control. New Haven, CT: Yale University Press.

New York Times Index
1930–1949   New York: New York Times Press.

Schuessler, Karl (ed.)
    1973   Edwin H. Sutherland: On Analyzing Crime. Chicago: University of Chicago Press.

Schur, Edwin M.
    1971   Labeling Deviant Behavior: Its Sociological Implications. New York: Harper & Row.

Smelser, Neal J.
    1962   Theory of Collective Behavior. New York: The Free Press.

Snodgrass, Jon
    1973   "The criminologist and his criminal: the case of Edwin H. Sutherland and Broadway Jones." Issues in Criminology 8:1–17.

Social Sciences Citation Index
1966–1981   Philadelphia: Institute for Scientific Information.

Sutherland, Edwin H.
    1924   Criminology. Philadelphia: J.B. Lippincott.
    1934   Principles of Criminology (2nd edition). Philadelphia: J.B.Lippincott.
    1937   The Professional Thief. Chicago: University of Chicago Press.
    1939   Principles of Criminology (3rd edition). Philadelphia: J.B. Lippincott.
    1945   "Is 'white-collar crime' crime?" American Sociological Review 10:132–39.
    1949   White Collar Crime. New York: Dryden Press.
    1950a   "The sexual psychopath laws." Journal of Criminal Law and Criminology 40:543–54.
    1950b   "The diffusion of sexual psychopath laws," American Journal of Sociology 56:142–48.

Tappan, Paul W.
    1947   "Who is the criminal?" American Sociological Review 12:96–102.

Time
    1947   "Indianapolis: frightened city." (November 24):29–30.

United States Congress, House of Representatives
    1948   "Treatment of sexual psychopaths in the District of Columbia." 94:4885–87.

United States Department of Commerce
    1975   Historical Statistics of the United States: Colonial Times to 1970, Part 1. Washington, DC:U.S. Government Printing Office.

United States Department of Justice
1933–1949   Uniform Crime Reports. Washington, DC: Federal Bureau of Investigation.

Statutes Cited

California
    1939   Statutes of California, Ch. 447, "Sexual psychopaths." (June 6):1783–87.
District of Columbia
    1948   Public Laws, Ch. 428, "An act to provide for the treatment of sexual psychopaths
            in the District of Columbia, and other purposes." (June 9):346–50.
Illinois
    1938   Laws of Illinois, H.B. No. 36. (July 6):28–30.
Indiana
    1949   Acts of Indiana, Ch. 124 [H.2.]. (March 7):328–32.
Massachusetts
    1947   Acts and Resolves of Massachusetts, Ch. 123 A, "Care, treatment and rehabilita-
            tion of sexual psychopaths." (July 1):745–47.
Michigan
    1937   Michigan Public Acts, No. 196. (July 14):305–09.
    1939   Michigan Public Acts, No. 165. (June 6):323–24.
Minnesota
    1939   Laws of Minnesota, Ch. 369, No. 1584. (April 21):712–13.
Missouri
    1949   Laws of Missouri, "Crimes and punishments." (August 1):253–55.
New Hampshire
    1949   New Hampshire Laws, Ch. 314, "An act relating to the care, treatment and rehabil-
            itation of sexual psychopaths." (July 28):422–29.
New Jersey
    1949   Laws of New Jersey, Ch. 20 (April 11):65–67.
Ohio
    1945   Laws of Ohio, S.B. No. 87. (July 10):443–47.
Vermont
    1943   Vermont Acts and Resolves, No. 100. (March 23):120–21.
Washington
    1947   Laws of Washington, Ch. 273, S.B. 179, "Sexual psychopathic persons." (March 21):
            1161–67.
Wisconsin
    1947   Laws of Wisconsin, Ch. 459, No. 486 S. (July 30):814–17.

THE STUDY OF THE SOCIAL ORIGINS OF CRIMINAL LAW: AN INVENTORY OF RESEARCH FINDINGS

JOHN F. GALLIHER

INTRODUCTION

Social scientists interested in the study of crime have from time to time emphasized that a knowledge of the social origins of criminal law is central to a complete understanding of crime. The assumption is that before one can fully understand the patterns of crime in a society, one must first understand the origins of the criminal laws which are the guideposts indicating what behavior is to be defined as crime. As early as the 1920s, the eminent criminologist, Edwin Sutherland (1924:11), offers this analysis:

> An understanding of the nature of law is necessary in order to secure an understanding of the nature of crime. A complete explanation of the origin and enforcement of laws would be, also, an explanation of the violation of laws.

And C. Ray Jeffery (1956a:670–671) asserts:

> The question "what is crime?" is prior logically and historically to the study of the criminal. It is prior historically for a norm has to exist before it can be violated; it is prior logically for before an individual can be studied as a criminal he must first be classified as one.

The well-known legal scholar, Jerome Hall (1945:353–354), claims:

> The differentiation of normative facts from non-normative ones, of legal norms from other social norms, of penal law from other legal rules provides the distinctive structure of criminology, that which denotes specific social data and establishes their significance for criminology . . . hence Criminology, in this view, is synonymous with Sociology of Criminal Law.

Regarding legal norms, Hall (1945:355–356) says:

> The determination of this major theoretical issue suggests the general boundaries of criminology. It must be concerned, firstly, with the meanings of the rules of criminal law—and this requires investigation of their origins, the legislative history, the relevant preceding and accompanying social problems with emphasis on the opinions and attitudes of various groups, marked out from the more or less passive "majority," and, of course, the authoritative interpretations of the courts. . . .

More recently, Akers (1968:460–461) argues that:

> We will have to scrutinize more carefully the process by which the criminal law is formed and enforced in a search for those variables which determine what of the total

Reprinted from *Research in Law and Sociology* 33, no. 2 (1980), by permission of the author.

range of behavior becomes prohibited and which of the total range of norms become a part of the law.

Even more recently, the proponents of the new critical or radical criminology have also issued a call for research on the social origins of criminal law. Taylor et al., (1975:56) claim:

Materialist criminology must set about the task of seeking to explain the continuance, the innovation or the abolition of legal and social norms in terms of the interests they support, the functions they serve to particular material arrangements or production in propertied societies, realizing that the legal norms in question are inextricably connected with the developing contradictions in such societies.

Schumann (1976:288) also contends that a radical or critical criminology must ask: "why are some conflicts regulated by criminal law while many others are not?"

Although the call for research on the social origins of law has been repeatedly made, some feel studies of this kind have been produced only on selected types of laws. For example, Alix (1978:xxv) states:

Two things characterize the types of law-creation studies that have been conducted by sociologists: first, the creation of only a relatively few types of criminal law has been studied; and second, few of the laws studied focused on what commonly are considered to be the more serious crimes.

Also Carson (1974:71) observes:

The recent tendency to concentrate upon relatively marginal and frequently controversial areas of criminality has possibly fostered neglect of the consensus which may still prevail in more central regions of the criminal law. Added to the accumulating evidence of crime's prevalence and of its pervasiveness throughout the social structure, this tendency has encouraged us in viewing the law as bereft of any very substantial foundation in social agreement.

Perhaps researchers feel that laws concerning more serious criminal offenses will not have interesting and unexpected origins because they take for granted that all societies need them.

Moreover, not all of those scholars who have acknowledged the importance of this type of study have actually conducted such research. And of those who have done this type of research, most have conducted only one study of this type (Becker, 1963; Chambliss, 1964; Jeffery, 1957; Sutherland, 1950; Hagan and Leon, 1977; McCaghy and Denisoff, 1973). Perhaps the lack of researcher commitment to this type of study, together with the fact that existing studies span several academic fields including law, history, political science, and sociology, may help explain why no systematic, integrated research tradition has developed. This lack of integration seems to be a major limiting factor in theoretical and methodological advances in this body of literature. Indeed, at present there does not seem to be even rudimentary consensus on the meaning and use of methodological techniques or theoretical constructs

(Galliher and Walker, 1978). Collective confusion in the interpretation of data in such studies (Galliher and Walker, 1977) is thus quite common. Therefore, rather than making progress and developing new insights, this type of research has resulted in the continuous fighting of old battles.

It is evident in the work of some researchers that they are primarily concerned with defending a specific ideological position; i.e., that the laws are either the result of class domination (Platt, 1977; Chambliss, 1974) or pluralistic democratic process (Hagan and Leon, 1977). As Alix (1978:xxvi) has observed, "some writers have been concerned with championing, on ideological grounds, various models of law creation as characterizing criminal law in general." In the literature on the social origins of criminal law, there are two main traditions. One body of research emphasizes the moral foundations for criminal law (Becker, 1963; Hagan and Leon, 1977; Sinclair, 1962; Haskins, 1960), while another body of social science literature claims that while some laws ostensibly have moral origins, these moral origins in turn have their source in the political economy of the society (Platt, 1977; Gusfield, 1963; Musto, 1973; Mohr, 1978). Perhaps the intensity of this debate is fueled by the theoretical and methodological confusion found in research on this topic.

One way of developing greater theoretical direction is to generate more precise conceptual distinctions. Some distinction between the structural foundations of a law and the triggering events associated with a law (Galliher and Basilick, 1979) is crucial in this respect. Here, *structural foundations* refers to the economic, racial, or religious heterogeneity of a society and the consequent potential or actual social conflict. Such potential or real conflict can involve, of course, various social classes, blacks and whites, or Protestants and Catholics, to mention just a few possibilities. Of course, in any given social setting, social conflicts can involve some combination of all of these.

Triggering events on the other hand involve the tactics, power and motivations of legislative interest groups who sponsor or oppose the legislation. Such groups are myriad and include organizations like the American Medical Association, the Women's Christian Temperance Union, the Federal Bureau of Narcotics, the American Pharmaceutical Association, or the National Association for the Advancement of Colored People.

The lack of conceptual precision accounts for a general theoretical confusion, which in turn explains the lack of agreement regarding what type of data can address questions about the social origins of law. These disagreements are to be expected since there has been no specification as to exactly what type of research problem such questions about the social origins of law involve. Gibbs and Erickson (1975:38) claim such research, "must end with potentially falsifiable assertions about (a) the distinguishing characteristics of *individuals* who control the enactments of criminal law, [and] (b) the process by which laws are enacted . . ." (emphasis added). In this formulation, "(a)" includes information on *individual* legislative sponsors' motivations and assumes that they know their motivations and will report them, and "(b)" contains data on legislative sponsors' tactics. So Gibbs and Erickson are clearly calling for information on triggering events. Yet Jeffery (1956b:426) claims that such a mechanical "A causes B" orientation is essentially ahistorical and will ultimately shed little light on the origins of criminal laws, since it oversimplifies the world in which criminal laws are passed. As Hall (1952:14) observes, information about structural features, such as "existing legal, social, political and economic institutions," is often reflected in the "common and recurring" events found over a relatively broad historical period while "changes *within a short period of time* suggest the operation of individual, unique influences. . . ." The structural or institutional features of society provide the milieu within which these individual influences develop. Jeffery and Hall seem to be calling for more information on laws' structural foundations.

Indeed, each type of data has its own strengths and limitations. Data on triggering events does give convincing and often detailed information on exactly how the law was passed; i.e., the legislative process. However, because of its narrow focus, it tells little about *why* a law was passed. To understand why a law is passed requires a broader range of information on the structural foundations of the law. This type of information usually provides data on historical epochs and how they are in turn associated in time with specific legislation.

Often, the same law or laws are studied by researchers who emphasize either moral consensus or political and economic domination; and these various researchers predictably have come to vastly different conclusions because of the use of different data types. This lack of consensus is found even in what is generally regarded as the highest quality and best-known research on this topic and includes the work of Erikson (1966), Chambliss (1974), Platt (1977), Hagan and Leon (1977), Becker (1963), and Musto (1973); it cannot, therefore, easily be explained away as unusually shoddy scholarship. By using this distinction between triggering events and structural foundations, we can see that many researchers dealing with the origins of criminal law do not seem to be arguing about the same issue. Rather, they find different origins of the law because they are analyzing a different order or type of data: some studying triggering events, some structural foundations, and some both. Erikson (1966) has argued that the criminal punishment of witchcraft and other religious deviation in the Bay Colony in Massachusetts had its origins in a collective search for meaning among the citizens in an increasingly heterogeneous society. Punishing this behavior, the society established moral boundaries and new meaning for the group by demonstrating that this was the type of behavior that they would not tolerate in their society. However, Chambliss (1974) argues that the punishment was triggered by colony leaders who feared the loss of their high positions during periods when they were being challenged. Predictably, those who initiated the challenge were frequently singled out for punishment. Erikson seems to deal more with the structural foundations of the law by focusing on the religious heterogeneity of the society while Chambliss deals with the motivations of legislative sponsors or the triggering events.

Platt (1969) argues that juvenile codes and juvenile courts in the United States, which are a part of civil law, have their origins in the changing ethnic and religious composition of American society around the beginning of the twentieth century. Native born Protestants looked with fear on the increasing numbers of immigrants from southern and eastern Europe who shared neither their religious nor ethnic heritage. These Protestants felt some legislation was required to control the deviance among children in these immigrant groups. Platt rests his argument essentially on the changing religious and ethnic composition of America in the early 1900s; i.e., structural characteristics are emphasized. And Platt (1977:xi) criticizes an earlier (1969) edition of his own book, *The Child Savers*. He claims his earlier error was his "own scholarly and political immaturity" which he feels blinded him to the true structural foundations of the child-saving movement. These foundations, he claims, are the new forms of social control required by 20th-century capitalism. Yet Hagan and Leon (1977) convincingly demonstrate that the motivation of sponsors of delinquency legislation was humane and not coercive or punitive. Focusing on triggering events, they find a much different origin of delinquency laws which they maintain destroys the credibility of Platt's claims. Hagan and Leon fail to recognize, however, that they are dealing with a different order of events.

Becker (1963) demonstrates that the federal Marihuana Tax Act of 1937 was triggered by the lobbying of the director of the Federal Bureau of Narcotics, Harry Anslinger. Yet Musto (1973) ignores this type of evidence in a later study of the same law and claims that the legislation was a creation of racial and economic conflicts between Anglos and Mexicans in the Southwestern states—such was the law's structural foundations. Indeed, the disputes between various scholars studying the social origins of the Marihuana Tax Act of 1937 (Galliher and Walker, 1977) may be due to the concentration of most of these studies on minuscle triggering events such as the true motives of Federal Bureau of Narcotics Director, Harry Anslinger. What did Anslinger really have in mind when he supported this legislation? Did he do it because he truly believed in the evils of marihuana as Becker (1963) contends, or because he wanted to extend the purview of his organization as Dickson (1968) claims?

Even within a single study focusing solely on triggering events, such conflicts in interpretation on the origin of a law are apparent (Galliher et al., 1974). Nebraska was one of the first states to reduce the penalty for marihuana possession. The motivations of legislative supporters were very diverse. Some wanted more certain punishment of college student drug users, since few were being prosecuted under the felony marihuana law. Others more sympathetic to college student marihuana smokers wanted reduced penalties that would not jeopardize students' lives. While the motivations of this law's supporters were diametrically opposed, they agreed on penalty reductions. This case of deep divisions of opinion among sponsors of the same legislation demonstrates that the singular structural foundations of a law are not obvious from the motivations of legislative supporters.

Also, without greater conceptual precision, it is difficult to anticipate and interpret recent changes in American drug laws. The very morally conservative states of Nebraska and Utah were among the leaders in 1969 in reducing the penalties for first-offense marihuana possession. The comparatively liberal state of New York in the early 1970s increased the penalties for sale and possession of most types of drugs. Drawing on this distinction between structural foundations and triggering events, we see that in Nebraska early marihuana penalty reduction, and in Utah reduction of the penalty for possession of a variety of drugs, were passed into law because no local threatening minority existed in either state that could be associated with drug use. Clearly, many large and often threatening minorities (some associated with drug use) live in New York State. The notion of structural foundations draws attention to such political, racial, and economic disputes relevant in a given historical epoch, while the idea of triggering events sensitizes one to moral sentiments which are used to justify support of particular legislation.

During the past ten years, there has developed an increasing momentum in the development of a recognizable body of research dealing with the social origins of criminal law (see Tables 1–3). But this literature has accumulated largely through isolated case histories which have often ignored previous studies in this area. Therefore, these case studies have accumulated with little attempt to isolate research problems by locating existing gaps in the literature or to generalize findings to a larger body of knowledge. This being the case, it seems especially timely to determine the composite picture derived from this patchwork of literature to demonstrate any substantive and theoretical gaps in the extant research. Twenty-seven representative publications were reviewed in an attempt to understand the hodge-podge of isolated case studies. No claim is made that the following represent all the research on this topic; but this sampling does include the most widely cited studies, and it does reflect the major types of extant research. The survey includes only studies of substantive criminal law (as opposed to procedural law) and excludes studies of the origins of civil law or studies solely of the functions, use, or administration of the criminal law.

THE CASE STUDIES

Some of the earliest and best known of these studies deal with the control of behavior directly involved in economic change or conflict and analyze only structural foundations (see Table 1). Jeffery (1957) traces the development of criminal law in England during the Middle Ages and how this law, growing out of tribal law and feudal law, was influenced by the economic changes of the time. Jerome Hall (1952) analyzes the emergence of embezzlement laws in 15th- to 18th-century England which protected the interests of the increasingly powerful merchant groups. Chambliss (1964) focuses on the creation of vagrancy laws during the 13th to 15th century in England—laws which were ultimately designed to protect the economic interests of merchant groups from the economic threat presented by the poor. Currie (1968) traces the development of laws to combat witchcraft in 15th-century continental Europe and how such laws had an important economic basis: the confiscation of convicted witches' property. And finally, Nelson (1967) demonstrates a major change in focus in American criminal laws, arguing that increases in punishments for property offenses were a consequence of an economic recession in the early 19th century.

A relatively large number of studies (N = 12) have focused on some type of substantive criminal law, usually drug laws, and have emphasized the tactics, power, and motivations of legislative sponsors (see Table 2). Some studies mention the empire building of government bureaucrats (Becker, 1963; Dickson, 1968; Reasons, 1974; Lindesmith, 1965) or physicians (Pfohl, 1977). Others mention the influence of

TABLE 1

Characteristics of Studies of the Origins of Criminal Law Emphasizing Structural Foundations.

Author	Locale	Publica-tion Date	Topic	Discipline	Structural Foundation	Triggering Event or Agency	Associated Institutional Change	Time Period	Data Type
Hall	England and U.S.	1952	Theft	Law	Economic change including increased power of merchants	—	Yes	1450–1950 (500)	Secondary
Jeffery	England	1957	Total criminal code	Sociology	Economic change	—	Yes	400–1200 (800)	Secondary
Chambliss	England	1964	Vagrancy	Sociology	Economic change	—	Yes	1349–1743 (349)	Secondary
Nelson	U.S.	1967	Total Criminal code	Law and history	Economic depression	—	Yes	1760–1810 (50)	Secondary
Currie	England and Continental Europe	1968	Witchcraft	Sociology	Confiscation of property	—	Yes	1484–1736 (252)	Secondary

TABLE 2

Characteristics of Studies of the Origins of Criminal Law Emphasizing Triggering Events.

Author	Locale	Publication Date	Topic	Discipline	Structural Foundation	Triggering Event or Agency	Associated Institutional Change	Time Period	Data Type
Becker	U.S.	1963	Marihuana laws	Sociology	—	FBN lobby	No	1931–1937 (6)	Secondary
Lindesmith	U.S.	1965	Drug laws	Sociology	—	FBN lobby	No	1914–1963 (49)	Secondary
Dickson	U.S.	1968	Marihuana laws	Political Science	—	FBN lobby	No	1912–1944 (32)	Secondary
Roby	U.S.	1969	New York prostitution laws	Sociology	—	Police and social welfare lobbies	No	1909–1967 (58)	Primary and Secondary
Graham	U.S.	1972	Drug laws	Law	—	Pharmaceutical lobby	No	Sept. 1969– Nov. 1970 (1)	Secondary
Reasons	U.S.	1974	Drug laws	Sociology	—	FBN lobby	No	1932–1967 (35)	Secondary
Galliher et al.	U.S.	1974	Nebraska marihuana law	Sociology	—	Arrest of DA's son	No	Aug. 1968– Mar. 1969 (8 months)	Primary and Secondary
Bruun et al.	International	1975	Drug laws	Law	—	Government officials	No	1906–1972 (66)	Secondary
Berk et al.	U.S.	1977	California criminal code	Sociology	—	Police and civil liberties lobby	No	1955–1971 (16)	Secondary
Pfohl	U.S.	1977	Child abuse laws	Sociology	—	Medical specialists	No	1950–1972 (22)	Secondary
Goff and Reasons	Canada	1978	Anti-trust laws	Sociology	—	Government officials	No	1879–1977 (98)	Secondary
Alix	U.S.	1978	Kidnapping laws	Sociology	—	Public reaction and lobbyists	No	1874–1974 (100)	Secondary

social welfare groups (Hagan and Leon, 1977), including the American Civil Liberties Union (Roby, 1969), and several demonstrate the influence of a variety of interest groups (Berk et al., 1977; Alix, 1978), including parents of college students and "law and order" conservatives (Galliher et al., 1974). Relatively few studies demonstrate how economic interest groups lobby for specific legislation (Goff and Reasons, 1978; Graham, 1972). For example, Graham (1972) demonstrates the heavy hand of the American Pharmaceutical Association on the drafting of federal drug controls. Compared to studies emphasizing the structural foundations of law, these confine themselves to a very narrow time framework, usually just long enough to follow the sponsors' lobbying. Also, unlike those studies emphasizing structural sources of new legislation, these all deal with a recent time frame, in the 20th century.

A final group of studies (N = 10) attempts to marshall evidence of structural change, associate this change with the behavior, power, and motivations of legislative sponsors, and link both the structural and sponsors' characteristics to the eventual legal change (see Table 3). A number of these studies begin by focusing on such structural issues as economic change (Musto, 1973; Helmer, 1975; Haskins, 1960; McCaghy and Denisoff, 1973). For example, Musto shows how the Great Depression of the 1930s increased Anglo hostility toward Mexicans who were competing with them for fewer jobs, and how this hostility led to pressure on the head of the Federal Bureau of Narcotics to sponsor legal prohibition of the traditional Mexican marihuana use. Yet some studies are concerned not with economic or class issues as much as issues involving status concerns or threats to those of high social standing and respectability (Erikson, 1966; Gusfield, 1963). Gusfield demonstrates that Anglo-Saxon Protestants in the United States felt that they were losing status as a group during the early 20th century and attempted to combat this loss through enacting their moral values into national alcohol prohibition. And some research mentions that legal change results from what seems to be both economic and status-related issues, including racial-ethnic conflict and/or conflicts among professions (Bonnie and Whitebread, 1974; Mohr, 1978; Sutherland, 1950; Sinclair, 1962). Mohr (1978) shows that the American Medical Association lobbied for abortion legislation essentially to put competitive medical practitioners out of business and that the AMA gained some support for its drive from Protestant groups concerned that Roman Catholics were outproducing Protestant women. Other examples of the specific interest groups involved in triggering such legislation include business owners (McCaghy and Denisoff, 1973), physicians (Mohr, 1978; Sutherland, 1950; Sinclair, 1962), government officials (Musto, 1978; Bonnie and Whitebread, 1974; Helmer, 1975), or specific religious leaders or groups (Erikson, 1966; Gusfield, 1963; Haskins, 1960; Sinclair, 1962).

In the total research pool, we find an overriding concern with securing information on triggering events. Only five of these 27 studies reviewed have no information on such triggering events. By concentrating on triggering events, it apparently becomes difficult for social scientists to study economic changes which would involve analysis of the wealthy and politically powerful as triggering agents. The only way economic issues have been studied is at a distance: viewing broad historical trends instead of

TABLE 3

Characteristics of Studies of the Origins of Criminal Law Emphasizing Structural Foundations and Triggering Events.

Author	Locale	Publication Date	Topic	Discipline	Structural Foundation	Triggering Event or Agency	Associated Institutional Change	Time Period	Data Type
Sutherland	U.S.	1950	Sexual psychopath laws	Sociology	Treatment movement	Psychiatrists lobby	No	1937–1949 (12)	Secondary
Haskins	U.S. (Mass.)	1960	Total criminal code	History	Religious beliefs	Religious and political leaders	No	1630–1650 (20)	Secondary
Sinclair	U.S.	1962	Alcohol prohibition	History	Mobilization for war	Anti-saloon lobby	No	1840–1933 (93)	Secondary
Gusfield	U.S.	1963	Alcohol prohibition	Sociology	Status changes	Protestants	No	1826–1962 (136)	Secondary
Erikson	U.S. (Mass. Bay Colony)	1966	Several Bay Colony laws	Sociology	Social changes	Protestant church leaders	Yes	1630–1692 (62)	Secondary
Musto	U.S.	1973	Drug laws	Psychiatry and History	Economic changes	Politicians and FBN lobby	No	1906–1972 (66)	Primary and Secondary
McCaghy and Denisoff	U.S.	1973	Record-pirating controls	Sociology	Economic changes	Record industry lobby	No	1906–1971 (65)	Secondary
Bonnie and Whitebread	U.S.	1974	Marihuana laws	Law	Ethnic conflict	FBN lobby	No	1900–1973 (73)	Secondary
Helmer	U.S.	1975	Drug laws	Education	Economic changes	FBN lobby	No	1850–1973 (123)	Secondary
Mohr	U.S.	1978	Abortion laws	History	Changes in birth rate	AMA and Protestant groups	Yes	1800–1974 (173)	Secondary

focusing on specific groups or individuals. Indeed, social scientists know almost nothing about such wealthy and powerful people and groups (Green, 1971). And given this concentration on triggering events, what methodology and specific types of data are used? With rare exceptions, the search for specific details on triggering events involves a focus of attention on case studies of single pieces of legislation or a single type of legislation such as drug laws (Musto, 1973; Alix, 1978; Helmer, 1975). Only two of these studies of triggering events involve the development of a total criminal code (Haskins, 1960; Berk et al., 1977). Analysis of a wider range of laws seems more typical of studies using only structural foundations. Surprisingly, in the study of triggering events of recent legislation there is also a heavy reliance on secondary data such as congressional hearings and newspaper stories (Becker, 1963; Dickson, 1968; Sutherland, 1950; Graham, 1972; Lindesmith, 1965). There is, by contrast, little primary data (e.g., interviews) collected (Roby, 1969; Musto, 1973; Galliher et al., 1974). Perhaps many studies of the origins of contemporary law have neglected primary data or interviews because the earliest studies of the origins of law in the 1950s did not use interview data (Jeffery, 1957; Sutherland, 1950; Hall, 1952). These early studies did not use interview data even when the research involved contemporary legislation where interviews were a possibility (Sutherland, 1950; Hall, 1952). As a consequence of the practices in these early studies, the research die seems to have been cast for most later investigators.

It seems strange that so little emphasis is given to primary data; especially when focusing on triggering events can demonstrate the linkage of specific people and events. Primary data seem ideally suited to address such questions. In fact, its value becomes even clearer when we consider the problems with evidence that is "once removed." An excellent example in this regard is the evidence presented in congressional hearings, and used in many studies of the origins of law. As Moore (1974:75) suggests, "What has rarely been appreciated is that congressional committees were better dramatists than investigators, . . . investigating committees do little real investigating, but rather, they dramatize a particular perspective on a problem. . . ." One need only recall the Watergate saga to weigh the type and degree of information that developed from the committee hearings as opposed to *interviews* with key informants, especially "Deep Throat," who supplied information to *Washington Post* reporters. Without the interviews, the committee hearings alone would have provided little understanding of the complete episode. Also, in the studies of American organized crime, actual interviews with those involved (Chambliss, 1978) supply a totally different and more convincing picture of the problem than a mere review of government documents (Cressey, 1969).

Indeed, it has been demonstrated in two studies of the social origins of law that the use of such key informants, to discuss their own or others' behavior, can be very informative. Galliher et al., (1974) interviewed a Nebraska University Law School professor who indicated that the state senator who introduced a law reducing the maximum penalties for marihuana possession was motivated by a desire to protect a state prosecutor's son who had been arrested. In fact, the bill was retroactive to the day before the young man's arrest. The legislative record indicates that the senator was asked to specify this effective date by the defendant's attorney during the public hearings on the bill. And in Utah, Galliher and Basilick (1979) found that Mormon legislators attributed their state's low drug penalties to Mormon tolerance of the weakness of other religious groups. But non-Mormons in state government and the legislative record indicate that low drug penalties were passed explicitly to protect Mormon youth from possible prison terms.

CONCLUSION

As found earlier (Galliher and Pepinsky, 1978), we again see that few of the studies dealing with recent legislation cover laws dealing with economic matters. The present review also demonstrates Alix's point that few studies deal with laws to control serious offenses that are supported by wide consensus. Indeed consensus-based law usually involves economic issues or personal assault (Rossi et al., 1974). Perhaps this omission exists because consensus-based, economic laws have not been changing and therefore their origins are lost in the common law of the Middle Ages. Recent legal changes appear to be concentrated in public morals legislation (Galliher and Pepinsky, 1978). Perhaps the omission of economically based laws is also due to the political bias of researchers who study only morals legislation, or because of the special problems encountered in studying the former, or because economically based laws are taken for granted. In fact, the very consensus character of consensus-based laws probably serves to make them nonproblematic for researchers.

Of the studies reviewed, 12 analyze triggering events alone, ten deal with both triggering events and structural foundations, and relatively few (five) consider only structural foundations. Without this conceptual distinction, an earlier effort by the author to code such studies met with failure (Galliher and Pepinsky, 1978:28):

> For each of many of the cases of legislation, it appeared equally plausible that individuals, monolithic groups, and pluralistic forces had moved the legislators to act.

> In retrospect, the ambiguities are not very surprising. As one examines the process by which any piece of legislation is promulgated—especially major legislation—one is bound to find many *people* who favored the legislation and were involved in various stages of the process.

> [And] For each of the *actors,* there is no way of choosing between two causal propositions: that such legislation (1) would not have occurred if s/he had been absent or (2) would have occurred notwithstanding the absence of the others (emphasis added).

These quotes clearly demonstrate that *individual* actors and *individual* triggering events were the focus of concern. And, by their very nature, triggering events are many and diverse, while structural foundations provide less bias toward confusing pluralistic interpretations of legal origins. Indeed, the widespread confusion and debate in this area of study seem produced by researchers drawing on triggering events, or structural foundations, or both, apparently without recognizing that they were at times analyzing different types of data.

It is definitely not in style to study only structural foundations; immediate causes or triggering events dominate the thinking of many researchers. Considering those studies drawing only on structural foundations, it becomes clear that these are studies of laws passed centuries ago and perhaps the minutiae of triggering events simply cannot be retrieved. Four of these five studies deal with early English law, showing indirectly concern with the origins of American law. Among those studies of more recent laws that only rely solely on triggering events, the availability of these events suggests that some researchers believe that minute detail can replace consideration of structural foundations.

The majority of the studies drawing on triggering events, as well as those that also draw on structural foundations, are ethnocentric in both place and time: dealing with United States laws and focused on the 19th and mainly 20th century. It seems that the major research strategy and content of all this research is dictated by the need for information on triggering events. Researchers typically see the *current law* as a social problem. Accordingly, their goal is often to show how the current (despicable) state of affairs came about. Many of these exposés are studies of public morals legislation; and rather than studying the history that unfolds over a number of centuries—a strategy which would reveal through common patterning of events the institutional or structural features such as traditional social conflicts and racial composition of society—these studies generally involve at most an analysis of the specific triggering events for particular legislation, such as the arguments of a legislative sponsor (Galliher and Walker, 1978; Balbus, 1977:571–573).

To the extent that studies rely on triggering events, of course they emphasize individual or at most small-group action and often emphasize short-term history—usually just long enough to show the tactics of a legislative sponsor. This type of data on specific triggering events and people is, when used alone, social history only in the journalistic sense for it ignores the structural or institutional foundations of law. But even its status as quality journalism is suspect to the extent that it ignores or fails to develop interview data. Studies emphasizing triggering events also typically deal with the tightening of legal controls, and the writers generally see these laws as unfortunate and representative of coercion. By contrast, there has been little interest in the loosening of existing controls. (For exceptions, see Galliher et al., 1974; Galliher and Basilick, 1979.)

These studies of the triggering events for public morals legislation deal with legal alterations that often fall short of creating institutional changes; i.e., new conceptual categories or ways of defining behavior. From Hall (1952) and Chambliss (1964), for example, we learn that there was no common law, nor common sense, prohibition against embezzlement and vagrancy respectively. In those instances, new opinions about these behaviors eventually developed, either coincident with, or after, the passage of new legislation. Similarly, Currie (1968) traces the development of new fears and beliefs in witchcraft and relevant laws; Nelson (1967) shows how a belief developed in the need for punitive legislation to protect propertied classes' interests from the poor after a severe economic depression; and Jeffery demonstrates how the state and criminal laws emerged from tribal law in early England. But public morals legislation is noteworthy for its alleged failure to generate any new consensus, leading to wide-spread evasion of these laws (Gusfield, 1963; Williams, 1960; Bonnie and Whitebread, 1974; Galliher et al., 1974; Gardiner and Olson, 1967). In fact, the complaint of many of these researchers is that a new legal code attempts to force a new morality on an unwilling public. Often, these laws deal not with protection of property or persons, but with matters of personal taste such as the use of drugs and alcohol, or the purchase of sexual services. Such studies of personal taste also demonstrate a political pluralism where each interest group has some input and where status conflict is more apparent than conflict among economic classes. Not unexpectedly, pluralism is more apparent in matters of personal taste and consumption than in disputes more central to the economic foundations of society.

Most of this research on public morals legislation claims that the laws have their origins not in class conflict (as is true of the economically related laws of embezzle-ment and vagrancy), but in the conflict between various noneconomic status groups. Many studies focus on the conflict of certain Protestants with other religious groups (Gusfield, 1963; Mohr, 1978; Sinclair, 1962; Becker, 1963; Erikson, 1966). Other studies emphasize conflict between whites and other racial groups (Musto, 1973; Helmer, 1975). An additional focus is on conflict created by still other specialized status groups like the American Medical Association (Mohr, 1978), American Psy-chiatric Association (Sutherland, 1950), and other medical specialties (Pfohl, 1977). Still another group of studies of public morals legislation focuses on the conflict generated by government agencies, especially the Federal Bureau of Narcotics, in the creation of federal drug laws (Becker, 1963; Dickson, 1968; Lindesmith, 1965). The clear implication of much of this literature is that these organized special interest groups lobby energetically to mold the opinion of legislators and the public. The myth of liberal democracy is therefore maintained that United States's laws cannot be changed without a corresponding change in the majority opinion (Galliher and Walker, 1978), which is in turn generated by the efforts of diverse legislative interest groups. The development of a theory of legislative origins is clearly premature, hav-ing as we do information almost solely on morals legislation in the United States and England during the 20th century. Clearly Alix (1978:xxv) and Carson (1974:71) are correct in claiming that the study of the origins of law has had a misleading and nar-row focus on laws without widespread popular support.

ACKNOWLEDGMENTS
Prepared for presentation at the meetings of the Law and Society Association, May 10–12, 1979, San Francisco, California.

The author is grateful to Lynn Taylor for helpful criticism of several phases of this research.

REFERENCES
Akers, Ronald L., "Problems in the Sociology of Deviance: Social Definitions and Behavior." *Social Forces* 46 (1968):455–465.

Alix, Ernest Kahler, *Ransom Kidnapping in America, 1874–1974: The Creation of a Capital Crime.* Carbondale: Southern Illinois University Press, 1978.

Balbus, Isaac, D., "Commodity Form and Legal Form: An Essay on the 'Relative Autonomy' of the Law." *Law and Society Review* 11 (1977):571–588.

Becker, Howard S., *Outsiders: Studies in the Sociology of Deviance.* New York: The Free Press of Glencoe, 1963.

Berk, Richard A., Harold Brackman and Selma Lesser, *A Measure of Justice: An Empirical Study of Changes in the California Penal Code, 1955–1971.* New York: Academic Press, Inc., 1977.

Bonnie, Richard J. and Charles H. Whitebread II, *The Marihuana Conviction: A History of Marihuana Prohibition in the United States.* Charlottesville: University Press of Virginia, 1974.

Bruun, Kettil, Lynn Pan and Ingemar Rexed, *The Gentlemen's Club: International Control of Drugs and Alcohol.* Chicago: University of Chicago Press, 1975.

Carson, W.G., "The Sociology of Crime and the Emergence of Criminal Laws." Pp. 67–90 in *Deviance and Social Control.* Paul Rock and Mary McIntosh (eds.). London: Tavistock Publications Limited, 1974.

Chambliss, William J., "A Sociological Analysis of the Law of Vagrancy." *Social Problems* 12 (1964):67–77.

———, "Functional and Conflict Theories of Crime." *MSS Modular Publications.* New York: Module 17, pp. 1–23, 1974.

———, *On the Take: From Petty Crooks to Presidents.* Bloomington: Indiana University Press, 1978.

Cressey, Donald R., *Theft of the Nation: The Structure and Operations of Organized Crime in America.* New York: Harper and Row Publishers, 1969.

Currie, Elliott P., "Crimes Without Criminals: Witchcraft and its Control in Renaissance Europe." *Law and Society Review* 3 (1968):7–32.

Dickson, Donald T., "Bureaucracy and Morality: An Organizational Perspective on a Moral Crusade." *Social Problems* 16 (1968):143–156.

Erikson, Kai T., *Wayward Puritans: A Study in the Sociology of Deviance.* New York: John Wiley and Sons, Inc., 1966.

Galliher, John F. and Allynn Walker, "The Politics of Systematic Research Error: The Case of the Federal Bureau of Narcotics as a Moral Entrepreneur." *Crime and Social Justice* 10(1978):29–33.

———, James L. McCartney and Barbara Baum, "Nebraska's Marihuana Law: A Case of Unexpected Legislative Innovation." *Law and Society Review* 8 (1974):441–455.

———, and Allynn Walker, "The Puzzle of the Social Origins of the Marihuana Tax Act of 1937." *Social Problems* 24 (1977):367–376.

———, and Harold E. Pepinsky, "A Meta-Study of Social Origins of Substantive Criminal Law." Pp. 11–38 in *Crime, Law and Sanctions: Theoretical Perspectives.* Marvin D. Krohn and Ronald L. Akers (eds.). Beverly Hills: Sage Publications, 1978.

———, and Linda Basilick, "Utah's Liberal Drug Laws: Structural Foundations and Triggering Events." *Social Problems* 26 (1979):284–297.

Gardiner, John A. and David J. Olson, "Wincanton: The Politics of Corruption." Appendix B. Pp. 61–79 in *Task Force Report: Organized Crime.* The President's Commission on Law Enforcement and Administration of Justice. Washington, D.C.: U.S. Government Printing Office, 1967.

Gibbs, Jack P. and Maynard L. Erickson, "Major Developments in the Sociological Study of Deviance." Pp. 21–42 in *Annual Review of Sociology,* Vol. 1. Alex Inkeles, James Coleman and Neil Smelser (eds.). Palo Alto, California: Annual Reviews Inc., 1975.

Goff, Colin H. and Charles E. Reasons, *Corporate Crime in Canada: A Critical Analysis of Anti-Combines Legislation.* Scarborough, Ontario: Prentice-Hall of Canada, Ltd., 1978.

Graham, James M., "Amphetamine Politics on Capital Hill." *Transaction* 9 (1972):14–22, 53.

Green, Philip, "The Obligations of American Social Scientists." *The Annals of the American Academy of Political and Social Science* 394 (1971):13–27.

Gusfield, Joseph R., *Symbolic Crusade: Status Politics and the American Temperance Movement.* Urbana: University of Illinois Press, 1963.

Hagan, John and Jeffery Leon, "Rediscovering Delinquency: Social History, Political Ideology and the Sociology of Law." *American Sociological Review* 42 (1977):587–598.

Hall, Jerome, "Criminology." Pp. 342–365 in *Twentieth Century Sociology.* Georges Gurvitch and Wilbert E. Moore (eds.). New York: Philosophical Library, 1945.

———, *Theft, Law and Society,* 2nd Edition. Indianapolis: The Bobbs-Merrill Company, Inc., 1952.

Haskins, George Lee, *Law and Authority in Early Massachusetts: A Study in Tradition and Design.* New York: Macmillan, 1960.

Helmer, John, *Drugs and Minority Oppression.* New York: Seabury Press, 1975.

Jeffery, Clarence Ray, "The Structure of American Criminological Thinking." *Journal of Criminal Law, Criminology and Police Science* 46 (1956a):658–672.

———, "Crime, Law and Social Structure, Part 1: Methodology," *Journal of Criminal Law, Criminology and Police Science* 47 (1956b):423–435.

———, "The Development of Crime in Early English Society." *Journal of Criminal Law, Criminology and Police Science* 47 (1957):647–666.

Lindesmith, Alfred R., *The Addict and the Law.* Bloomington: Indiana University Press, 1965.

McCaghy, Charles H. and R. Serge Denisoff, "Pirates and Politics: An Analysis of Interest Group Conflict." Pp. 297–309 in R.S. Denisoff and C.H. McCaghy (eds.). *Deviance, Conflict and Criminality.* New York: Rand McNally and Co., 1973.

Mohr, James C., *Abortion in America: The Origins and Evolution of National Policy, 1800–1900.* New York: Oxford University Press, 1978.

Moore, William Howard, *The Kefauver Committee and the Politics of Crime, 1950–52.* Columbia: University of Missouri Press, 1974.

Musto, David F., *The American Disease: Origins of Narcotic Control.* New Haven: Yale University Press, 1973.

Nelson, William E., "Emerging Notions of Modern Criminal Law in the Revolutionary Era." *New York University Law Review* 42 (1967):450–482.

Pfohl, Stephen J., "The 'Discovery' of Child Abuse." *Social Problems* 24 (1977):310–323.

Platt, Anthony M., *The Child Savers: The Invention of Delinquency.* Chicago: University of Chicago Press, 1969.

————, *The Child Savers: The Invention of Delinquency.* 2nd Edition, enlarged. Chicago: University of Chicago Press, 1977.

Reasons, Charles E., *The Criminologist: Crime and the Criminal.* Pacific Palisades, California: Goodyear Publishing Company, Inc., 1974.

Roby, Pamela A., "Politics and Criminal Law: Revision of the New York State Penal Law on Prostitution." *Social Problems* 17 (1969):83–109.

Rossi, Peter H., Christine E. Bose and Richard E. Berk, "The Seriousness of Crimes: Normative Structure and Individual Differences." *American Sociological Review* 39 (1974): 224–237.

Schumann, Karl F., "Theoretical Presuppositions for Criminology as a Critical Enterprise." *International Journal of Criminology and Penology* 4 (1976):285–294.

Sinclair, Andrew, *Prohibition: The Era of Excess.* Boston: Little Brown, 1962.

Sutherland, Edwin H., *Criminology.* Philadelphia: J.B. Lippincott, 1924.

————, "The Diffusion of Sexual Psychopath Laws." *American Journal of Sociology* 56 (1950):142–148.

Taylor, Ian, Paul Walton and Jock Young (eds.), *Critical Criminology.* London: Routledge and Kegan Paul, Ltd., 1975.

Williams, Robin M., Jr., *American Society: A Sociological Interpretation.* 2nd Edition, revised. New York: Alfred A. Knopf, 1960.